Brigita Sebald
sebaldb@yahoo.com

Folklore and Society

Series Editors
Roger Abrahams
Bruce Jackson
Marta Weigle

Music in American Life

A Publication of the American Folklore Society

New Series

General Editor, Patrick B. Mullen

*Lists of books in the series Folklore and Society
and the series Music in American Life
appear at the end of this volume.*

TRANSFORMING TRADITION

TRANSFORMING TRADITION

Folk Music Revivals Examined

Edited by
Neil V. Rosenberg
Foreword by Alan Jabbour

UNIVERSITY OF ILLINOIS PRESS
Urbana and Chicago

This book is printed on acid-free paper.

Library of Congress Cataloging-in-Publication Data

Transforming tradition : folk music revivals examined / edited by
Neil V. Rosenberg ; foreword by Alan Jabbour.
    p.   cm.—(Folklore and society) (Music in American life)
(A Publication of the American Folklore Society. New series)
    Discography: p.
    Includes bibliographical references and index.
    ISBN 0–252-01982-2 (cloth : acid-free paper)
    1. Folk music—United States—History and criticism.
I. Rosenberg, Neil V. II. Series. III. Series: Music in American
life. IV. Series: Publications of the American Folklore Society.
New series (Unnumbered)
ML3551.T72 1993
781.62′13—dc20   92–26727
                                                      CIP
                                                      MN

In memory of

Mitzi Smith Rosenberg
Jess N. Rosenberg
Teya Rosenberg Newkirk

Contents

Foreword

Alan Jabbour

Back in the 1960s I had the joy and satisfaction of participating in a string band, the Hollow Rock String Band, that helped ignite a revival of interest in old-time string band music from the Upper South. We played tunes learned from old-time fiddlers I had been visiting and recording in North Carolina, Virginia, and West Virginia, and we assembled around us in Durham and Chapel Hill, North Carolina, a circle of devotees of instrumental folk music who carried on our music after our own band had broken up. Later, as I crisscrossed the nation (and ventured occasionally abroad) in the 1970s and 1980s, it gave me no little pride to observe that our tunes had passed into a wider repertory, and that our records (though hard to come by) were cited as pioneering contributions to the budding new string-band movement. We were, everyone said, contributors to the folk revival in America.

Or were we? Though scholarly and popular criticism in North America often alludes to the folk music revival of the twentieth century ("The Revival," as we expansively call it), in truth we owe it much more serious reflection than it has received to date. There are histories, of course, but their accounts of its development tend to take it for granted as a cultural phenomenon, or to explain it by reference to the creative contributions of its most famous figures. Such accounts are helpful in sorting out the facts and the players, and in clarifying the ideas and passions that motivated movement leaders. However, when it comes to understanding the cultural significance of the revival, or the larger forces that generated it and impelled it into prominence, or its relationship to other cultural revival movements, our histories of the folk music revival are less helpful.

In fact, the histories fail even to give us the certitude that we are contemplating a single cultural movement. It remains an interesting question whether twentieth-century North America has had a single folksong revival, or a number of revivals. Are the folksong revival of the 1950s and 1960s and the instrumental folk music revival of the 1970s and 1980s really part of the same larger movement, or should we speak of them separately? Do all branches of the revival really stem from the same central impulse, or should we differentiate between movements in different regions or different urban centers? Is there a relationship between our folk music revival and the roughly parallel crafts revival, as has clearly been the case in revival movements like the Tanchaz Movement in Hungary over the past decade?

Other important musical movements occupied the same decades in North America: bluegrass, rhythm and blues, the polka movement, the American Indian powwow movement. Are these, too, cultural revival or revitalization movements? Is there a relationship between them and what is called the folksong revival? How does the folksong revival connect with rock and roll and other forms and genres of popular music? What are we to make of parallel trends in the United States and Canada? If indeed we can speak of this as a single revival movement, what has been its international impact? Its long-term impact?

The term "revival" and the similar word "revitalization" reveal our perception that the phenomenon in question does not represent a new cultural development. In the world of the arts, we speak of a play, a musical composition, or a group of an artist's paintings or photographs as being revived when the creative work in question already exists and has been displayed or disseminated but has also encountered a period of dormancy or suffered from inattention.

If things have not changed or faded or disappeared, clearly there is nothing to revive. Thus when we speak of revival, we imply that something happening in the present somehow simultaneously resurrects the past. At the level of a single work of art, or of an oeuvre, such a perception is exciting or intriguing; we get to take part in something that we took part in before, or that we missed the opportunity of taking part in before, or that our forebears took part in before us.

At the broader level of a cultural movement, a revival is more mysterious, for it is harder to say just what is being "revived." When I learned a fiddle tune like "Over the Waterfall" from Henry Reed, my elderly mentor from Glen Lyn, Virginia, and a host of fiddlers learned it from our Hollow Rock String Band performances, jam sessions, and recordings, it represented direct transmission from fiddler to fiddler, ear to ear, spirit to spirit. We have a weaker claim than Henry Reed himself to having "revived" the tune. He at least could have pointed out that he preserved its memory during the several decades when he was not playing the fiddle in public; whereas we played it continuously from the time we learned it from him.

Nor can the Hollow Rock String Band claim comfortably that it "revived" a string band style. It may have given impetus to a renewed interest in certain instrumental stylistic combinations, but the older musicians from whom we drew our inspiration regarded our band more as a continuing development than as a revival of the tunes and styles they shared with us. What we were doing is hard to classify as a revival, by most uses of the term, but easy to describe as a cultural transfer of a musical tradition from one segment of American society to another. Looking back at another juncture in American cultural history, I often wonder whether the white banjo players of the nineteenth century who were learning from black mentors felt a bit the way we felt over a century later.

The way we felt, on reflection, may provide the clue to why we and others kept calling it a revival. Our revival was not so much a revival of specific artistic artifacts, like the revival of a Broadway musical, as a revival of symbolic values, like a religious revival. The periodic and ongoing revivals within grass-roots American religion have evoked the past and the ideal in order to intensify the values of the present. Similarly, we in our revival sought out—and created—a music to express simultaneously our quest for cultural roots, our admiration of democratic ideas and values, our solidarity with the culturally neglected, and our compulsion to forge our own culture for ourselves. In both the music we embraced and the passion with which we embraced it, our movement was not unlike a religious revival, which consciously selects and intensifies certain cultural values while casting its present endeavors within the framework of the traditions of the past.

How my revivalist peers and I fit into the larger web of cultural history remains to be seen. But all these matters call for fresh scholarship and deeper reflection. It is a pleasure to see this volume of essays, ably gathered together by Neil Rosenberg, beginning the task of approaching our revival (and others) with a thoughtful and critical eye. As time provides us greater perspective, it becomes clear that the twentieth-century folksong revival (if indeed it is one movement) occupies a place of real importance in our cultural history. This volume begins the task of building a body of critical scholarship worthy of that prominence.

Acknowledgments

Neil V. Rosenberg

During the assembling and editing of this collection of essays I have had support and assistance from a number of people. I am grateful to the individual contributors for valuable ideas about the shape and emphases of the book. Their assistance confirmed my feeling that, in spite of our differences in interpretation, this work represents a community of interest. I have had fruitful discussions with a number of others who share our interest in the topic, and I want to thank here John Bealle, Norm Cohen, Dianne Dugaw, Joe Hickerson, Ailie Munro, Mayne Smith, and Stephanie Smith for their help along the way.

To Archie Green, who encouraged me to write about folk music revivals, I owe special thanks for useful suggestions when the Introduction was in danger of foundering. Martin Lovelace's careful reading of the final draft of the Introduction was most helpful. Millie Rahn contributed considerably to the Bibliography and shared ideas flowing from her research on Club 47. Likewise, the anonymous readers for the University of Illinois Press and the Publications of the American Folklore Society offered useful suggestions, many of which were incorporated into the final draft.

And finally, Memorial University of Newfoundland has generously supported my work through the contribution of materials and labor. I would particularly like to thank Sharon Cochrane of the Department of Folklore staff for her help in this regard.

Transforming Tradition

Introduction

Neil V. Rosenberg

This book is a collection of essays by folklorists, ethnomusicologists, and others interested in the phenomena typically called "folk revivals." My decision to assemble the collection came as the result of a panel on revivalism at an American Folklore Society meeting. Extensive interest in the topic was manifest at that session: the meeting room was crowded and there was considerable discussion during the question period. The essays here include three of those read at that panel and three published earlier; the rest were written for this book. I first saw the volume as one that would include topics in folk revivalism in general, then narrowed its scope to folk music revivalism, and finally decided to focus primarily upon North American folk music revivals.[1] It is impossible, and inadvisable, to separate these completely from revivals elsewhere. Several papers include sections on revivals outside North America, and one paper, from Japan, has been included as an instance of the diffusion of folk music revivals from North America.

These essays were written mainly by folk music specialists, but their thoughts about revivalism embrace intellectual domains ranging far beyond this special interest. For example, they address broad social and cultural issues through the application and development of perspectives articulated by social scientists. They advance their arguments through historical exposition, thereby offering fresh data to intellectual and cultural historians. Since the information presented—whether from past or present—deals with aspects of American and Canadian life, there is much of interest here for those involved in American and Canadian studies. Political history and theory are recurrent themes in these essays—from the significant role of the American communists in the 1930s and 1940s to contemporary debates about the place of revival musicians in public-sector folklore programming. In a more general way, the politics of culture are a central concern of all those writing in this volume. Recent thinking concerning ethnographic reporting stresses the role of the reporter in creating texts. This has led to a new interest in the "reflexive" use of autobiographical materials to convey a fuller sense of the intellectual context in which ethnographic texts have been created—an approach reflected in every essay in this volume. Another recent intellectual theme is the issue of invented traditions, which, like the question of how to define and apply concepts of authenticity, runs like a thread through the essays in the volume. Finally, in addition to its contributions to contemporary intellectual issues, this book offers the many people who have been involved in folk music revivals new ways of reviewing a familiar past.

Many of today's professional scholars in folklore, ethnomusicology, and related fields first became interested in these subjects not at school but through informal involvement with musics variously called "folk" or "traditional." For everyone who followed this path there are many more for whom the interest in such music led elsewhere. Perhaps it was a passing fancy, later abandoned. Or it may have developed into a performance career. For some it has become an avocation or hobby, while for still others it is but one of many tastes expressed in leisure consumption of concerts, recordings, broadcasts, and so forth. Today few people have been untouched by the folk music revivals of the past half century. The success of *A Vision Shared,* an album on which pop stars perform the songs of two of the revival's chief icons, Woody Guthrie and Huddie Ledbetter (Leadbelly), underscores the widely accepted idea that the best in pop music is an outgrowth of these folk roots.[2] The studies in this book show the extent to which ideas about such roots have been shaped at all levels of society by the processes of revival.[3]

The organization of these essays reflects my thoughts about this phenomenon. In spite of widespread usage of the term, there is no such thing as *"the* folksong revival." Rather, the musical cultural events described as folksong revivals—whether accurately or not is a contentious point confronted by all who study such events, an issue to which I return later in this essay—happen again and again. Nevertheless, a strong consensus holds that in the late 1950s and early 1960s there was, centered in North America, *a* or *the* revival. Unusual in its diversity and its extensive social and economic dimensions, in retrospect it can be seen to have been a broad cultural movement. I call it the "great boom," and this sonic wave is the focus of the first group of essays in the book. Other, smaller revivals went on before, during, and after it—some within it, some outside. These are the subject of the rest of the essays in the book.

Robert Cantwell opens the first section of the volume by following the trail of "Tom Dooley" with his wide-ranging look at class and culture in the great boom. Following this comes Archie Green's memoir of his service as faculty guru for one of the most vigorous of the many university folksong clubs during the sixties, the University of Illinois's Campus Folksong Club. In the next essay Bruce Jackson traces the ways in which the boom laid the foundation and provided a cadre for the current federal folklife establishment. His closing lament, that folklorists generally did not study this revival when it was at its height, can be seen as a call for revival ethnography—a call answered by several of the later essays in this book. He has added a new afterword to this much-quoted essay. Ellen Stekert's pioneering study of 1966 is an early effort to bridge the gap between revival and academia, one that articulates useful descriptive terminology. She has written a new introduction to the paper for this volume. The section ends with excerpts from my 1979 interview of Kenneth S. Goldstein, who during the 1950s and 1960s produced or edited over five hundred albums of folk music for such companies as Stinson, Riverside, Elektra, Tradition, Folkways, and Prestige. Goldstein discusses the ways in which the intellectual issues of the great boom shaped his record-business activities.

The second section contains three essays about the revival activity Stekert called *the new aesthetic,* an approach that synthesizes elements from a variety of traditional forms to create a separate music-culture described as "folk," "traditional," or, most recently, "roots."[4] Musical styles of the new aesthetic vary as the elements in the synthesis change, but underlying the variation is a consistent rationale for this involvement in musics that are alternatives to popular forms, a rationale that emphasizes the relevant social messages these musics convey. Treating these revivalists as a kind of folk group, the essays in this section utilize Canadian examples. In an article published in 1979 in a revival magazine, I. Sheldon Posen uses autobiography as ethnography to explain what happened to him when he moved from revival to academia. He argues that the revival in which he participated can be considered authentic in terms of its own context, a viewpoint he qualifies somewhat in a retrospective introduction written for this book. Following this are a pair of linked studies that explore the idea of revival ethnography by adding content analysis to contextual analysis. Both examine the history of the late Stan Rogers's song "Barrett's Privateers." The folklorist Pauline Greenhill uses techniques of close textual study to probe such facets of the song as composition, performance, transmission, and meaning. The ethnomusicologist Anne Lederman's companion piece looks closely at the musical dimensions of Rogers's song and also communicates Lederman's own perspective as a performing musician.

The third section includes seven essays about movements involving those whom Stekert called *imitators* (she now prefers *emulators*), movements that I call *named-system revivals*. In contrast to the "new aesthetic" revivals, these build upon and interact with extant music-cultures such as blues, old-time fiddling, and bluegrass. Burt Feintuch discusses transformation in such systems–how revivalists, in naming or identifying them as unique traditions, create their own canons of repertoire, style, and authenticity—using examples from his recent research into the Northumbrian smallpipes, and his earlier experience in the old-time string-band revival. My paper on another such transformation in bluegrass discusses the ambivalence felt by revivalists involved in this process—ambivalence that comes with the discovery that realizing a new canon destroys the supposed unselfconsciousness of tradition that makes it attractive to revivalists. Philip Nusbaum's study compares bluegrass and revival (what I would call new aesthetic) music-cultures, showing how each music is enacted in the context of expressive culture, which functions to "traditionalize" the recurrent features of music-culture. This ethnographic approach suggests the emergence of a new unselfconsciousness.

Reflecting upon the blues revival movement of the period 1959–70, Jeff Todd Titon looks at "the interpreters' hegemony over the artists," with particular attention to the influential blues historian Samuel Charters. Titon reminds us that it is not just revivalists who play roles but also researchers, and that ultimately "no one is free from constituting domains through interpretive acts." Peter Narváez's analysis of the journal *Living Blues* shows that revivalist control of this significant publication was reflected in unrealistic antiquarian canons that were in effect sexist and racist. Richard Blaustein's essay considers the old-time fiddling revival that began in the late fifties, treating it in terms of anthropological models of revitalization and contemporary European folkloristic theory. He reaches a conclusion similar to Nusbaum's, although he proceeds in quite a different fashion, holding that participants in such grass-roots movements, whether they are natives or outsiders, share the experience and work together toward the creation of a more satisfying music-culture. Finally, Toru Mitsui presents and analyzes the fascinating story of Japanese involvement in the music of southern white Americans—old-time and bluegrass—from a Japanese perspective. A bibliography, a discography, and an index conclude the book.

The Roots of Folksong Revival in Twentieth-Century America

Fascination with folk music is a pervasive legacy in North American culture. In the 1830s, folk tunes, songs, and dances were transported from the rural plantation to the urban stage. Transformations like this—blackface minstrelsy, an early folksong revival—have been viewed as secondary issues by historians of folk music research, whose primary focus has been upon the motives of those who collected and published folk music, and who have stressed the intellectual history into which such researchers and their products fitted. Folksong collections have been published by, among others, abolitionists, populists, nationalists, and communists; some collectors have had literary, sociological, historical, anthropological, or other theoretical axes to grind while others have just wanted to place into print old and rare things they valued.[5] These issues of politics, theory, and aesthetics are important for an understanding of revivals, and will be discussed in the next section. Here I discuss briefly the results of a century of feeding music from the margins into the center, a cultural process that led to the great boom.

Whatever their goals, folk music collectors shape their publications to make them accessible; preservation and promotion go hand in hand. For a century and a half North Americans have been able not only to read about folk music but also to learn folk songs and melodies from published collections. Folk music has been considered accessible, easy to learn; and learning and performance have been encouraged through ideological support: this is authentic democratic (or regional, or ethnic, or individual) expression in the shape of a natural, unpretentious art. Frequently it has been touted as an antidote against the alienating and meaningless modern popular music of the times.

While the majority of collections come from rural working-class people of relatively little education and limited means, the majority of those who read them—and, since the 1940s, listen to them on recordings—have been urban and suburban middle-class people with relatively greater education and more disposable income. Some of the latter found folk music moving and meaningful, and as is so often the case when people become involved in new musical forms, they not only learned to perform but became enthusiastic supporters of folk music. Similar intense feelings motivated those who worked to fit folk music into public school curriculums, children's camp song repertoires, and other didactic entertainment for the young.

By the end of the second decade of this century a considerable number of collections of folksongs and music had been made and published. They attested to the common belief that folksongs could be found among pioneers, loggers, sailors, African-Americans, French-Canadians, mountaineers, cowboys, and other symbolic minorities. Middle-class people with highbrow pretensions bought books about and attended concerts or lectures on this fascinating topic.

A substantial proportion of those who have collected and published folk music have themselves been performers—some in private settings only, others in public. This is still true, but now folk music researchers who give public presentations about their work generally use sound recordings. In the 1920s about the only way one could give an illustrated lecture was by illustrating it oneself. At that time many of those who collected and published folksongs, like Texas cowboy song expert John Lomax, French-Canadian and Indian specialist Marius Barbeau, Kentucky mountain composer John Jacob Niles, and proletarian poet Carl Sandburg, graced lecture podiums and concert stages presenting folksongs to educate and entertain. Typically they dramatized the danger and difficulty involved in gathering this rare and wild stuff. Often they portrayed themselves as popular scientists, working in remote places like botanists hunting rare specimens or biologists seeking new pieces in evolutionary puzzles, to illuminate a past rapidly being destroyed by the modern world. But the main focus was on the songs themselves, and as performers they were involved aesthetically in the music. Like their books, these lecturers inspired some in their audiences to sing.

A logical extension of this activity was the presentation of the actual folk in live concerts. The "folk festival" as it is popularly known today—a series of concerts at which folk performers are presented—began taking its present shape during the 1920s. Called festivals because they celebrated regional, ethnic, or national identity, these events also had a commercial public-relations dimension. The Canadian Pacific Railroad's head of publicity, John Murray Gibbon, organized over a dozen major folk festivals at the company's hotels between 1927 and 1930, bringing, for example, representatives of Quebec's folk culture in music, song, dance, and craft (with the collaboration of Marius Barbeau) to the Chateau Frontenac in Quebec for several such events. These, and the western Canadian festivals that stressed ethnic groups, were meant not only to illustrate the idea of the Canadian mosaic of cultures in which Gibbon believed passionately, but also to draw tourists to the company's hotels.[6] Similarly, in 1928 the city of Asheville, North Carolina, invited a local lawyer, Bascom Lamar Lunsford, by then well known as a recorded performer, popular lecturer, and published collector of North Carolina's folk music, to organize a folk song and dance festival as part of the city's annual Rhododendron Festival. It became an annual event that drew people from afar.[7] By 1934, when Sarah Gertrude Knott established the National Folk Festival, a network of festival performers and organizers was developing—one that persists to this day.[8] Like collections and public lectures, folk festivals are still intended to educate and to valorize folk traditions, but whatever the aims of their organizers, they draw an audience filled with many who come to learn new songs.[9]

In both Canada and the United States national recognition of the significance of folk music research led to its incorporation in government institutions. In Canada's National Museum, Marius Barbeau—a member of the Anthropological (later Human History, and then Ethnology) Division from 1911 until his retirement in 1948—was given free rein to document folk traditions.[10] In Washington, the Library of Congress found room for the Archive of American Folk Song, established in 1928 by Robert W. Gordon.[11] Like Barbeau, Gordon was a folksong polymath—university professor, author of a popular interactive folksong column in a national magazine, popularizer, lecturer, singer. Their collections became the basis for national archives, now treated as treasured public heritage and utilized by performers as resources.

This genteel and individualistic activity might have continued at a leisurely pace had not larger historical events intervened in the 1930s. With the deepening of the Great Depression new kinds of social consciousness emerged, particularly in the United States, where the Communist party, along with a variety of like-minded socialists and liberal populists, embraced folk music as the expression of the American masses who had been hit hard by economic depression. For these new political advocates, folksong was not so much antimodern symbol as contemporary proletarian protest about social conditions—trenchant political commentary. Young radicals swelled the ranks of those interested in folk music. One such recruit was Alan Lomax, son of the Texas folklorist John Lomax. These two began collecting together in the early 1930s, took over from Gordon at the Library of Congress in 1933, and published their first popular omnibus collection in 1934. Through their influence and that of the composer and musicologist Charles Seeger, a considerable amount of collecting and publicity involving folk music was done during the 1930s through national agencies, like the WPA, created by Roosevelt's New Deal. The cultural leftists in the New Deal who collected folksong believed in their innate goodness and saw them as oppositional in relation to a banal and escapist contemporary pop music. They also sang the material they and their colleagues collected—with each other at parties, and to their children.

Paralleling and feeding this activity was a growth of scholarly interest in studying American culture. In the 1930s, students and scholars at American universities were eager to learn more about their own past, to understand their own mythology. By 1939, when Harvard established its American Studies degree program, American intellectuals were reading and writing more about the national culture than ever before. In this climate books about America's folk had great appeal, and, as in Washington, young college students sang the newly discovered songs at parties.

The spirit of these times is engraved in my memory in this way: In 1961 I drove to a family reunion with an older cousin, a professor of English at a midwestern university. En route we passed the site of a bloody labor battle of the late thirties, and my cousin, the son of a Jewish immigrant who was a labor organizer, recalled how as a graduate student he had visited the site soon after the event and had been moved to write a ballad that he sent to the noted radical composer Earl Robinson in New York, who set it to music. During the fifties it was included (under Robinson's copyright) in John Greenway's *American Folksongs of Protest*,[12] a fact my cousin viewed with ironic amusement, since he thought himself a poet and not a folksinger. Not long after this I saw 78 rpm folksong albums dating from the later 1930s and early 1940s in a dusty bookcase in his spare bedroom.

Thus in the 1930s, interest in folksong surged as three streams converged: the older work of various collector/lecturer/author types active for some time, the then-new political left, and the Americanists. A middle-class popular-culture youth market for folk music emerged. Like most such markets, this began with what Richard Peterson has called a "vital fad," a social trend that both anticipated and precipitated commercial exploitation.[13] As with most American cultural trends of that era this fad resonated from the center of the entertainment industry, New York City. Until the late 1950s most of the trends in popular folksong moved from small, young, bohemian enclaves there into the mainstream.

For such people, folk music was "a passionate avocation"[14] that viewed this music in opposition to commercial musics. Consequently, those who emerged from the enclaves to become popular folksingers embraced and clung to a public image of themselves as nonprofessionals, or preindustrial artisans, or minstrels. Their dilemma: how to make a living selling this music commercially as a professional when it was supposedly a noncommercial, amateur expression? The folksong revival as it developed in the 1940s was a professionalized music with an ethos of nonprofessionalism.

Likewise, although the *idea* that such a thing as folksong existed was an intellectual construct—the recent history of that construction is the topic of the next section in this essay—an essential aspect of the construct was that folk music was unselfconscious behavior. Hence many among the existentially inclined young folk music enthusiasts were not comfortable spending time talking about the hows or whys of folk music. Where it was from and what it was about were enough; anything more was academic bullshit. In this sense the nascent revival was an intellectual music with an anti-intellectual ethos.

Histories of the interest in folksong that emerged in New York at this time make much of the leftist activities that brought authentic singers like Woody Guthrie and Aunt Molly Jackson to town and prompted middle-class youth to emulate them. New York–based groups like the Almanac Singers, featuring the charismatic young Pete Seeger as well as Guthrie, developed many of the patterns for performance and presentation that characterized the revival in its early years.[15] But the most successful performer to emerge from this New York scene was Burl Ives, who parlayed his folk youth and bohemian college years into a career as radio minstrel and, ultimately, movie star. As "The Wayfaring Stranger," jolly and bearded, he was a popular figure on radio and records from the early 1940s into the 1950s whose repertoire, style, and image was much copied by self-styled "folksingers."[16]

In the late 1940s the radical political side of this New York–based scene faced strong opposition as anti-Communist sentiments grew. The Weavers, pop-oriented successors to the Almanac Singers, had a string of hits in the early 1950s, but their career was cut short by anti-Communist blacklisters. Nevertheless the middle-class appetite for popular folk music was by then well established, particularly on college campuses, and with the advent of the LP the folk music catalogue grew steadily. By 1958, the year the Kingston Trio appeared on the scene to initiate the great boom, one could buy folk music recordings of many kinds—from Library of Congress albums of the Lomaxes' 1930s field recordings, to the Weavers, Burl Ives, and a host of young "folksingers," many of whom were living in Greenwich Village following the bohemian trail earlier trod by Ives. There were many new books, magazines, newsletters, and radio shows devoted to "folk music." And by this time similar urban bohemian folk scenes existed in other North American cities, including Boston, Montreal, Chicago, San Francisco, and Los Angeles.[17]

The great boom dissipated after 1965 as the merging of folk with rock shrank the popular folk music market. But many people remained involved with folk music, carrying on the kinds of activities initiated during the boom years through festivals, clubs, magazines, and record companies. Some continued to embrace a variety of forms of folk music, while others specialized in specific types. Today the idea of folk music and folksinging remains a vital aspect of North American culture.

During the 1960s the stereotype of the folksinger entered into the realm of popular culture. "Hootenanny," a prime-time television show, brought folksingers into millions of households; national magazines wrote about them. *Time* put Joan Baez on its cover, and Bob Dylan was profiled by the *New Yorker* and interviewed by *Playboy*.[18] Folksingers became celebrities—people who were well known for being well known. Al Capp introduced a new character into his widely syndicated comic strip "Little Abner" named "Joanie Phonie." Based on Baez, this figure embodied many of the stereotyped perceptions of the folksinger at this time: pretentious, naive, iconoclastic in appearance—the women with long "stringy" hair and the men sporting "long" (in pre-Beatles terms) hair and beards or mustaches. Clothing too was viewed as pretentious; these were wealthy middle-class urbanites in blue-collar outfits. The countercultural revolution of the late 1960s more or less coopted and ultimately muted the visual aspects of this stereotype. "Folknik," originally an in-group word, gained wide currency, and like today's popular "folkie" used a diminutive form to convey an image of immaturity and, as Capp felt, both social and intellectual phoniness. By 1968 such stereotyped thinking was being used metaphorically by folklorists, as when Henry Glassie, in comparing traditional American log construction to "the nonfolk 'rustic' construction of which hunting lodges and park structures are built," stated that "such construction is to traditional logwork as a Brooklyn folknik is to a traditional ballad singer from Newfoundland."[19]

A more positive side to the stereotype of the folksinger also developed in the 1960s. The social and intellectual iconoclasm of the great boom was a catalyst for social change, and from this came the belief that a folksinger is someone who performs serious, "meaningful" songs. Today this usually means that such persons compose songs of this kind. The popular image of the folksinger of today is that of a professional artist who trades broad commercial success for intellectual integrity, someone who deals directly with difficult social issues in the forum of popular culture.[20]

Like any stereotype this one is an oversimplification. This is particularly true with regard to the way in which scholars perceive folk music and define "folksinger." Yet the idea and the word came from the scholars, and over the years they too have redefined it as their perceptions have changed. Ultimately the present state of affairs is as much a result of academic trends as one of popular stereotyping.

The Shifting Sands of Folk Authenticity

In the years when the great boom flourished, folk music scholars—with a few exceptions—took the position that much of what was happening in the boom was outside the bounds of what could be considered authentic and therefore ought not to be included within the mainstream of academic study agendas. They did this through the use of descriptive terminology that reflected the shifting ways in which they perceived or constructed "authenticity."

The intellectual roots of folk music studies lie in the late eighteenth and early nineteenth centuries in Europe, when romantic nationalist movements began to argue that the best foundation for statehood was one that united people who shared the same language. The native land and the mother tongue were seen as part of an organic whole, a foundation of ancient heritage upon which a modern nation could grow. The resultant surge of interest in the vernacular sent writers and scholars for the first time to humble rural districts in search of pure folk expression that, it was believed, was manifested best in story and song. The result was a new body of literature and, as the nineteenth century came to a close, new academic disciplines engaged in its interpretation.

Ideas about authenticity in folk music at the end of the first two decades of this century were dominated by considerations of *text*. Many saw folk music as a vestige of an earlier stage of cultural evolution. It was believed that folksongs were the oral equivalents of arrowheads or potsherds, which could be dated scientifically in terms of their morphology. Collecting folk music was laborious, requiring the cooperation of performers who could repeat texts while collectors wrote what they heard. The resultant manuscripts—and others created by performers themselves or by interested friends, relatives, neighbors, or amateur collectors—were the primary documents of folk music scholarship. Following the powerful examples of scholars like Francis James Child, for verbal text, and Cecil Sharp, for musical text, researchers drew conclusions about authenticity on the basis of what could be seen on the written or printed page: meter, rhyme, mode, scale, theme.

There were, of course, other considerations. Folksongs had to be old, anonymous, and exist in variant forms; they had to emanate from unlettered rural folk of modest means. Many collectors, however, obtained songs they considered authentic from performers who did not fit the latter criteria but had themselves learned or collected them from acceptable, if obscure, sources. A typical example is Nancy Stikeleather of Asheville, North Carolina, a member of a local family with, in the words of folklore historian Debora Kodish, "pretensions to 'culture' and large repertoires of valued songs." Between 1924 and 1930 Stikeleather sang her version of "Georgie" for three different collectors, all of whom published it. This version of the ballad, which Child had classified as #209 and titled "Geordie," was valued because its text and tune closely resembled those of the versions of the song found in Scots oral tradition rather than those of the versions commonly found in North America emanating from commercially published British broadsides.[21] Oral tradition, then, was folk tradition; broadsides represented trashy urban commercial intrusions that debased folk tradition. Because of its form Stikeleather's song was "authentic."

An extension of the construction of folk music authenticity was inevitable with the advent of sound recordings, which offered the possibility of converting evanescent oral performances into permanent aural records—first on cylinder, later on disc, then wire, and finally tape. During the twenties and thirties, folksong collectors turned ever more frequently to the new technology, creating a valuable body of what we now call "field recordings" (this term does not seem to have come into use until the fifties) that documented folk music performances. One of the pioneers was John A. Lomax, whose recordings of cowboy songs in the first decades of the century foreshadowed the extensive recording trips he made with his son Alan for the Library of Congress's Archive of Folk Song in the 1930s and 1940s.

At the same time, folk music scholars began to recognize that a new kind of urban commercial intrusion existed—the twentieth-century equivalent of the broadside—in what were then called "hillbilly" and "race" records.[22]

By the forties ideas of authenticity were changing, in response to field recordings and these new broadsides, to include hitherto ephemeral aspects of text as well as previously unnoticed aspects of performance, usually described as "style." No individual embodied so many aspects of this change better than Alan Lomax. Ensconced at the Library of Congress, but also involved with a small circle of left-wing intellectuals in New York City who were folk music enthusiasts, he was at the leading edge of a new way of perceiving folk music in the forties.

Lomax recognized the power of this still-new medium. In 1940 he published, through the auspices of the Library of Congress, a "List of American Folk Songs on Commercial Records." Based on "three thousand odd commercial records of white and negro [*sic*] songs and tunes from the South," it listed 350 "representative titles." In a brief introduction Lomax explained his criteria: "Some of the records are interesting for their complete authenticity of performance; some for their melodies; some because they included texts of important or representative songs; some because they represented typical contemporary deviations from rural singing and playing styles of fifty years ago; some to make the list as nearly as possible typical of the material I examined." What was new about these criteria was that they added the textural elements of "performance" and "style" to the older textual criteria. Lomax was redefining authenticity to include aural dimensions. American folk music, he declared, was not in decline but was "growing new directions to compete with 'thick' commercial music." Today, he contended, it is, "in its most 'distorted' form[,] in a healthier condition, roving the radio stations and recording studios[,] than it has been or ever will be in the notebooks of collectors."[23]

The following year Lomax edited the *Friends of Music Album*, a modest set—two ten-inch 78 rpm records—of Archive of Folk Song field recordings comprising two ballads from southern whites, and a holler and a work song from black southern convicts. These were among the first field recordings of this type of music marketed in the United States. Folk music collectors had been using the sound recording as a convenient tool for generating transcriptions of texts that became primary documents in manuscripts, books, or articles. With this, the first of a long series of Library of Congress field recording albums, Lomax effectively replaced the written or printed text with the recorded aural performance as the primary document.

Alan Lomax's emphasis upon new criteria of authenticity based on aural means was linked in his thinking with another shift of perspective, one initiated by his father. This was what Gene Bluestein describes as "a forthright rejection of the ballad tradition in favor of the varied materials which he found to be characteristic of American folksong." Between 1934 and 1947 the Lomaxes published three omnibus collections of American folksong—the last, in 1947, included "Tom Dooley"—which, as Bluestein indicates, shaped a "new canon" of American folksong, a set of categories that evoked a populist and nationalistic portrait of American culture.[24] From this perspective, the *Friends of Music Album*'s two African-American work songs were equally important as the two white ballads—one of which was accompanied by the African-derived banjo.

Lomax's pioneering work did more than shift the grounds on which texts were evaluated, however; it also brought performers to the forefront. Lomax, quoting with approval Malinowski's statement that anthropologists "have the duty to speak as the native's advocate," held that "the folklorist has the duty to speak as the advocate of the common man."[25] Lomax's populist advocacy reflected a specific political context, that of the American Communist Party in the years just before World War II. Robbie Lieberman's history of this milieu, which she calls the "movement culture of the old left," identifies Alan Lomax as "even more influential" than Charles Seeger (father of Pete Seeger and, under the pseudonym of Carl Sands, a writer on the politics of music for the *Daily Worker*) "in shaping the outlook of the left-wing folk movement." Describing folk music as "a democratic American art," Lomax enlisted the sympathies not just of the far left but of the many who embraced the cultural agendas of the New Deal era.[26]

He believed folk music performers should have access to modern mass communications systems as spokespersons for voiceless groups, and with a matchless genius for recognizing musical talent in this domain, used his Washington connections to bring to the ears of the American public through records and radio such people as Josh White, Burl Ives, Woody

Guthrie, Huddie Ledbetter (Leadbelly), and Pete Seeger.[27] While Lomax considered himself an advocate, he was in his activities what we would today recognize, following the work of David Whisnant, as an intervenor.[28] He coached these performers to shape their repertoires and styles to fit the criteria of authenticity he valued.[29]

The perceptions and interpretations of advocates and intervenors have dominated the literature about folk music; little has been written about personal responses to this phenomenon by the people they study, for and about whom they speak. This is not surprising, given that the former have an active intellectual agenda while the latter are, at least in the first instance, passive. A few documents tell how some felt; for rodeo cowboy Glenn Ohrlin, the experience was a positive one: "... my involvement in the folk music scene since my first meeting with folklorists and aficionados in 1963 has been a great experience. Besides meeting a heck of a lot of swell people and having fun at it, the same folks have helped me gain a new appreciation for much that my cowboy buddies and country friends and I had taken for granted. Also, it has been enjoyable to find missing parts to half-remembered old songs as well as turn up stuff I'd never have known about."[30] As Stekert points out in her article, others, like Woody Guthrie and Sarah Ogan Gunning, were more ambivalent about the experience. More research is needed on this aspect of the revival process—how did the people "discovered" by the Lomaxes and their successors feel about being presented as symbols of authenticity?[31]

Questions of this sort were not debated in the left-wing-movement culture, particularly in New York City, that provided a ready audience for this ideologically acceptable and fashionably exotic music. By the late forties the movement culture, even though under siege by cold war anti-Communism, had laid the seeds of the great boom described in the first five articles in this book.

All of this did not go unnoticed by folk music specialists, but they were slow to respond to the new perspective to which Lomax contributed so much. In large measure this was because the shift was articulated in media the theoretical implications of which scholars during the forties were just beginning to comprehend—radio, and, most importantly, records.

Not until 1948–49 did the *Journal of American Folklore* publish its first record reviews. In the first piece Charles Seeger set forth new terminology for the description of authenticity, based on performance style. He spoke of a stylistic spectrum based on "alternate highways" (Anglo- and African-American) from "authentic folk" to "authentic fine-art or concert," with intermediate points at "hillbilly-citybilly" on one highway and "blues-swing-jazz" on the other. The eight 78 rpm albums he reviewed in 1948–49, almost all produced by Alan Lomax, included commercial reissues of some of the race and hillbilly records Lomax had listed in 1940, and performances by such singers as Burl Ives, Richard Dyer-Bennet, and the Almanac Singers. Initially Seeger evaluated the records with abbreviations based on his spectrum and suggested that there seemed to be a tendency for performers to move stepwise on the spectrum: f (folk) to hb (hillbilly) to cb (citybilly); or c (concert) to cb (citybilly) to hb (hillbilly).[32] One could interpret this early formulation of textural criteria to mean that stylistic authenticity was not immutable—that just as singers could learn authentic texts, so could they learn authentic performance styles. But Seeger ultimately denied this, hewing to old romantic orthodoxy when he concluded that "inheritance always shows, no matter how extreme the adaptation to the environment."[33]

Seeger's terms, most of which carried connotations of social context, were rarely used by other scholars in exactly the sense that he used them, but his one new coinage, "citybilly," did achieve wide currency and is still encountered today. It was the first succinct description of a new social group, later to be called "urban folksong revivalists," and suggested that citybillies were urban migrants acculturating to rural ways, just as hillbillies were rural migrants acculturating to urban ways.

In his 1949 review, Seeger did not use his terminology of the previous year but introduced another metaphor for the same process when he spoke of "the artful re-insemination of vast sections of the American people with a heritage of their own dominant majority," calling this—in words that today read like a restatement of the melting-pot theory—"the really complex processes of hybridization and acculturation we are all involved in."[34] He also pointed out that the same process had gone on in Europe in the nineteenth century and he speculated that it had been delayed in the New World by the impact of twentieth-century technology—"radio, sound-film and disc, which have kept nineteenth-century music romanticism artificially alive beyond its day," or by "the general lag in colonial culture."[35]

"Folknik" was the term Alan Lomax used when, in 1959, he returned to the New World from political self-exile in Europe to confront the great boom. One of his very first statements about authenticity came in the form of liner notes to citybilly Guy Carawan's album, reprinted in *Sing Out!* magazine.[36] Here he urged folkniks to learn authentic styles. Lomax would develop the idea of stylistic authenticity much further in the next decade, as he developed "cantometrics," an elaborate system of universal musical description and comparative analysis. At about the same time, Charles Seeger was working with the "melograph," a machine that transcribed music electronically. Like Lomax's system, this one sought to discover universal and comparable elements in the aural evidence provided by sound recordings.[37]

By this time—the early sixties—theories about folk music authenticity were moving in a somewhat different direction, one that can be characterized by one word: context. During the fifties a new generation of folklorists had begun to emerge. They were more likely to be full-time folklorists—Indiana University awarded its first doctorate in folklore in 1954. In a parallel movement during the mid-fifties, scholars like Charles Seeger who had identified themselves as comparative musicologists or students of folk, primitive, and Oriental art music recast their discipline under the rubric of ethnomusicology.

These new professionals were comfortable with sound recordings. The tape recorder was now a familiar tool of their trade and they accepted at the outset the idea of authentic performance style. No longer constrained by worries about how text and performance could be captured and preserved for study, they began to think more about the settings in which it took place. Conceiving of folkloristics as a synthesis of literary and anthropological concerns, and ethnomusicology as a synthesis of musicological and anthropological concerns, these scholars broadened their focus from text and performance style to include the relationship between these authenticities and the cultural context. Henry Glassie has written of the remarkable scholarly works that emerged in 1964 heralding the new shift eventually to be combined under the rubric of "performance."[38]

At this point it became convenient to describe the combined authenticities of text, performance style (or "texture"), and context with a single word—*tradition*.[39] Ellen Stekert's 1966 article, reprinted in this volume, reflects this shift; her classification system begins with "traditional singers," defining them as "singers who have learned their songs [text] and their style of presentation [texture] from oral tradition as they grew up [context]."[40] Under such criteria, the efforts of urban youth to heed Lomax's advice to learn authentic performance style counted for little. John Cohen, a member of one of the groups acclaimed for such authenticity, the New Lost City Ramblers, came from Stekert's own cultural context; she saw his music as "incongruous," not authentic.

During the decades since then, theories about tradition have been honed and developed with regard to cultural context, a term no longer used frequently. Glassie chose to describe the overall trend as "performance" because this—the realization of text and texture in some kind of context—is the nexus between the individual and society. It is no longer assumed by folklorists or ethnomusicologists that the individual performer speaks *for* the group. Contemporary thought holds that performance may express any or all of a variety of concerns endemic to the problems of individuals in complex social webs. A wide spectrum of theoretical approaches—structural, semiotic, rhetorical, to name but a few—have been adopted by folklorists and ethnomusicologists in working to understand and illuminate the meanings of performance. In the process awareness has grown of the importance of including the person who observes and reports—the ethnographer—in the description and analysis of performance. In a recent message to the members of the Society for Ethnomusicology, the president of the group, Charlotte Frisbie, expressed the concerns of the discipline: "Interests in critiquing our own history continue, as do others in gender, the practice and problems of representation, and the connections between music, political policy, power relations, and identity."[41] While the wording might be somewhat different, most contemporary folklorists would agree that they share these concerns.[42] And there is no doubt that the essays in this volume approach the questions surrounding folk revival with one or more of these concerns in mind.

What "Revival" Means

Why "revival"? During the early sixties this word was being used with reference to the great boom. Perhaps its immediate source was Charles Seeger, who used it in a 1953 article of his that *Sing Out!* reprinted in 1958; there he contrasted it with "survival."[43] But in England it had been current since 1907, when Cecil Sharp closed his *English Folk-Song: Some Conclusions* with an affirmation of his belief that the English folk song is "music of the very highest quality" and "that alone is sufficient justification for advocating its revival."[44] As might be expected, Sharp here is talking about the combination of words and music—text—rather than texture or context. Later, he spoke of his hope that English music would be "re-born."[45] The idea of national cultural rebirth was hardly novel; indeed it was at the very roots of folklore studies in their late eighteenth-century nascence. But the use of "revival" with regard to folk culture seems a twentieth-century phenomenon.

The word, however, has been used since the middle of the seventeenth century to refer metaphorically to aspects of culture and society, a usage that, according to the *Oxford English Dictionary* (2d edition) predates its more literal use with reference to human life by a century. Moreover, this latter meaning was also predated by fifty years by a third meaning, that of religious reawakening. It was a North American, Cotton Mather, who seems to have been the first to use the term in this way. By the end of the nineteenth century, revival had been used in its first sense to refer to drama (1664); to learning, letters, and literature—particularly the Renaissance (1785); and to architecture—specifically the Gothic revival (1850).[46] Three years before Sharp used the term in his seminal book, the United States Department of Commerce and Labor published Max West's *The*

Revival of Handicrafts in America. The handicrafts revival grew out of William Morris's arts and crafts movement, and, as Dillon Bustin has shown, the values of Sharp and those who followed him were significantly shaped by the thoughts and actions of Morris and his followers.[47]

Indeed, the connection between "movement" and "revival" seems crucial in this regard. In his book *The Irish Literary Revival,* W. P. Ryan spoke of a "literary movement,"[48] and it is in this sense that the term achieved currency among students of folk culture during the years after 1950, used both retrospectively, as in Albert Friedman's *The Ballad Revival* (1961), and to discuss the present, as in B. A. Botkin's "Little Magazines of the Folk Revival."

I hope some diligent researcher will look closely at the vast ephemeral literature by and about the folksong enthusiasts of this century to find when, where, and by whom "revival" was first used alongside "folksong" and "urban." It is not surprising that, when this question arose at a folksong revival conference in 1991, former *Sing Out!* editor Irwin Silber linked the first appearance of the term in the pages of that influential magazine with the writing of English revival ideologue Ewan MacColl. But what seems most important to note here is that it did not begin to achieve widespread currency until after the great boom was under way, and that for those already involved in folk music it took over the semantic niche previously occupied by "movement." One possible explanation for the word's new popularity among academics and enthusiasts was that it did not evoke the notion of political action in the way that "movement" did. This reflected the fact that at the height of the great boom, its roots in the culture of the old left movement seemed embarrassingly anachronistic to young citybillies. Indeed, many of those who were newly attracted to folk music during the boom, at a time when the cold war mentality permeated politics, shunned all musical-political connections. But even for those who were not shy about embracing such connections, "movement" was already being used to describe two new ongoing social actions, both precursors of the new left: the civil rights movement and the antinuclear movement.

The word "revivalist" and the phrase "urban folksong revival" became useful terms for folklorists at about the same time as "tradition" became useful—and for the same reason: both referred to cultural or social contexts, the most recent aspect of authenticity in the definition of folklore. But as the idea of authentic cultural or social contexts developed, many folklorists tended to follow the line of thinking most succinctly expressed in 1979 by Jan Brunvand in his *Folklore: A Study and Research Guide.* Brunvand held that the revival may produce "interesting manifestations of popular culture, but they are largely irrelevant to the study of folklore."[49] A good working definition of "popular culture" is given by Narváez and Laba in the in-

troduction to their *Media Sense: The Folklore-Popular Culture Continuum:*
"popular culture refers, in a restrictive interpretation, to cultural events
which are transmitted by technological media and communicated in mass
societal contexts."[50] A similarly restrictive definition of folk culture would
in contrast speak of folklore being transmitted orally and communicated
in small groups, face to face. But the essays in *Media Sense* argue in favor
of a continuum between these two kinds of cultural events rather than a
conception of folk and popular culture as antithetical modes. And it is
ironic that the judgment of irrelevance of popular culture to folklore should
come from Brunvand, the folklorist who has specialized in the study of
modern urban legends—the very acme of folklore in the mass media.[51]

The essays in this book are in agreement that folk music revivals are
relevant to the study of folklore and ethnomusicology. But they offer different reasons for this relevance. In sifting through the nuances of the
arguments presented, I find two basic emphases. One is an extension of
Lomax's idea of advocacy, filtered through B. A. Botkin's idea of "applied
folklore" and now most commonly expressed in terms of "public-sector
folklore." The proponents of this stance tend to view folk music revivals
as discrete cultural movements that stand apart from folk culture. As Archie
Green says in his essay, they do "not wish to surrender 'folksinger' to
revival grandchildren." Lomax's "common man" is, for them, not a part
of such movements. From this perspective, folk music revivals are relevant
to the concerns of folklorists and ethnomusicologists because they constitute an urban middle-class intellectual community that, in seeking al-
ternates to mass culture music, develops an interest in, appropriates, and
consumes the music produced by the people for whom informed scholars
act as advocates. This community produces the young people who choose
to become involved in the academic study of folk music. This view of
revival as social elite casts it in the role of interventionist and stresses the
ways in which revivalists, in transforming traditions, represent the established political and social agendas of the group from which they emerge
in contrast to the agendas represented by the nonrevival folk groups in
whose music they are interested.[52]

A second stance focuses upon the ways in which individuals, whatever
their backgrounds, interact when involved in revivals. Considering folk
music revivals susceptible to the same kinds of description and analysis of
individual-group interaction as other modern cultural phenomena—like legends, joke cycles, and rock music—that many folklorists and ethnomusicologists have come to see as being within their legitimate purview, it
seeks to describe and understand the "ethnographic reality" of revival
processes. This view of revival as social consensus, which owes much to
the thinking of Anthony F. C. Wallace on revitalization movements, sees

it not so much as a representation of existing political and social agendas as an effort to develop new agendas.[53]

In this connection one might think that the idea of the invention of tradition articulated by Eric Hobsbawm would have relevance to the study of folk revivals, and indeed several papers in this volume do allude to his work. But most do not. I think there are some good reasons for this. Hobsbawm's initial definition—"a set of practices, normally governed by overtly or tacitly accepted rules and of a ritual or symbolic nature, which seek to inculcate certain values and norms of behaviour by repetition, which automatically implies continuity with the past"[54]—might well be applied to musical systems. But there are several problems in applying it to folk music revivals. When he says that "insofar as there is such reference to a historic past, the peculiarity of 'invented' traditions is that the continuity with it is largely factitious," this seems to emphasize an extreme. Most of the revivals treated here are more akin to what Hobsbawm calls "custom." Situating it in "so-called 'traditional' societies," he contrasts it with "traditions" (invented or not) that, he says, have as their object and characteristic *invariance*. Conversely he depicts custom as having "the double function of motor and fly-wheel" so that innovation and change are intertwined with precedent from the past. Hobsbawm's concept of "custom" is consistent with major aspects of folklore definitions. But many folklorists would argue that Hobsbawm is mistaken in limiting such a concept to "so-called 'traditional' societies.' "[55]

When one follows the descriptions of "invented traditions" in the volume of essays that Hobsbawm and Ranger edited and to which they contributed, it can be seen that they focus upon the formal activities of governments, nations, and institutions. Many shades of meaning have been ascribed to "tradition" by students of folk culture, but almost always the emphasis is on those aspects of culture that are thought to be informal, non-elite, marginal, or interstitial—all of which are, again, more like what Hobsbawm calls "custom." Hence while there is certainly cultural invention in folk music revivals, Hobsbawm's formulations do not seem a particularly apt way of dealing with it.

There is considerable disagreement among those interested in folk music—scholars, performers, festival organizers, public-sector folklorists, and others—concerning the two positions, elite and consensus, that I have sketched. Some, stressing the social elite point of view, argue that revivals are commercial middle-class intrusions that fall outside the definition of folk music proper. Others, holding to the social consensus point of view, respond that folk music is not and has never been the pure stream that the social elitists' argument implies.

Each of the essays in this book takes a different position on these two stances. Some incorporate both, while others embrace one and reject or downplay the other. Many of them echo Philip Bohlman's point that revival is "an overt and explicit act of authentication" relying heavily "on new symbols masquerading as the old."[56] But what is the "old" being symbolized in the revivals described in this volume? Is the idea of social consensus another way of expressing the inevitability of assimilation, and the identification of social elite another reflection of the struggle to maintain cultural pluralism? These are particularly difficult questions in North America where the dominant majority and all but a few of the minorities trace their lineage to immigrants from other continents. In tackling these questions the writers confront and illuminate issues of identity: personal, social, class, gender, regional, ethnic, and more. I will not here rehearse all of the nuances of argument set forth in the essays that follow, for I think that these are best discovered by the reader.

In soliciting and editing these essays I was aware that most of the writers had been active in one or more revivals. In discussing this experience many of us agreed that behind the decision to embark upon a career including the study of folk music as professional scholar lay the feeling that much of what we had read about folk music—whether by scholars or by enthusiasts, for typically we sought out whatever we could find—was inadequate or inaccurate. Consequently I encouraged contributors to talk about their own revival involvement, believing that only by exposing and examining our own past can we understand why we embrace certain ways of viewing the present and arguing for the future. Many told me that in responding to this request and in a more general way just by writing about phenomena that are not exotic but rather part of one's own experiences, they found the essay took a long time to write, or was difficult to complete. I hope that readers will agree with me that the personal effort that the contributors to this volume have made was worthwhile in casting light into a corner of folkloristic and ethnomusicological research about which many have opinions but which few have examined closely.

Today the word "folk" is used sparingly in revival circles, while "roots" is frequently encountered in its place. "World music" is fashionable. These essays, looking as they do to the recent past, do not treat the latest trends in folk revivalism. But the issues they raise are, I think, relevant to our understanding of such trends. I am confident that future students of these music cultures will be better able to shape new perspectives about the politics of culture because of this work.

NOTES

1. A considerable amount of relevant history and scholarship has been published concerning revivals elsewhere—the British folk music revival in particular. Some examples from this literature are included in the bibliography at the end of this volume.

2. *Folkways: A Vision Shared* was issued in 1988—it won a Grammy—as a benefit to help pay for the costs incurred when the Smithsonian purchased Folkways Records. The first new album issued by Smithsonian Folkways was *Leadbelly and Woody Guthrie*, which offers the originals of many of the songs performed on *A Vision Shared*. Jim Brown's seventy-two-minute documentary video with the same title as the CBS album was also released by CBS. See Orr, "Motion Picture Reviews."

3. A similar process occurred in eighteenth-century Britain, according to Dugaw, "The Popular Marketing of 'Old Ballads.' "

4. Slobin and Titon, "The Music-Culture as a World of Music," describe a music-culture as having four major components: ideas about music, social organization of music, repertoires of music, and material culture of music.

5. Wilgus, *Anglo-American Folksong Scholarship*, although dated, remains the standard history. Anyone updating the book using collections published since 1959 would have little trouble fitting them into the categories Wilgus developed for the first half of the century.

6. McNaughton, "John Murray Gibbon."

7. Whisnant, "Finding the Way"; Jones, *Minstrel of the Appalachians*, p. 40ff.

8. A brief history of the National Folk Festival is given in Wilson and Udall, *Folk Festivals*, pp. 6–8. See also Knott, "The National Folk Festival."

9. Camp and Lloyd, "Six Reasons."

10. Preston, "C. Marius Barbeau." Barbeau's central role in Canadian folklore studies is discussed by Carpenter in *Many Voices*.

11. Kodish, *Good Friends and Bad Enemies*, pp. 152–203, details Gordon's role at the Library of Congress. The Archive of American Folk Song is now the Archive of Folk Culture, and is part of the American Folklife Center, established in 1976 at the Library of Congress.

12. Greenway, *American Folksongs of Protest*, pp. 232–33.

13. Peterson, "A Process Model."

14. The phrase is that of Jacques Barzun, quoted by Early in his "One Nation under a Groove," p. 36.

15. See, for example, Klein, *Woody Guthrie*.

16. See Burl Ives, *Wayfaring Stranger*.

17. For example, the Boston-Cambridge scene is described by von Schmidt and Rooney in *Baby, Let Me Follow You Down;* for the Montreal scene see Verrier, *The Songs of Wade Hemsworth*.

18. For the extensive coverage given Joan Baez in popular periodicals, see Caesar, "Joan Baez." Many of the pieces on Dylan were republished in McGregor, *Bob Dylan,* including the *New Yorker* piece (pp. 44–61) and the *Playboy* interview (pp. 124–45).

19. Glassie, "The Types of the Southern Mountain Cabin," p. 366, n. 29.

20. Norm Cohen, "Record Reviews: The Revival," stresses the differences between record industry and folklorists over the definition of folk music.

21. Kodish, *Good Friends and Bad Enemies,* p. 69.

22. This analogy was first articulated in Wilgus, "A Note on 'Songs from Rappahannock County,'" p. 320.

23. Alan Lomax, "List of American Folk Songs," p. 126.

24. Bluestein, *The Voice of the Folk,* p. 103. The Lomaxes were not alone in this vision; members of the nascent American Studies movement of the thirties were working to canonize American literature.

25. Alan Lomax, "Preface," p. x.

26. Lieberman, *"My Song Is My Weapon"* pp. xv, 37. For a discussion of Charles Seeger's role in the movement, see Reuss, "Folk Music and Social Conscience." See also Hirsch, "Cultural Pluralism and Applied Folklore."

27. For a critical discussion of this aspect of Lomax's theory, see Evans, "Record Reviews: American Folklore and Music," p. 620. Evans suggests "one might . . . make just as valid an argument for preserving folk traditions by protecting them from exposure to the media." For another critique of the approach advocated by Lomax see Camp and Lloyd, "Six Reasons."

28. For the definitive statement on "cultural intervention," see Whisnant, *All That Is Native & Fine,* pp. 13–14.

29. On 16 November 1978, Alan Lomax spoke on "Early Electronic Recording: The Lomax Era," at the conference titled "The Archive of Folk Song: 50th Anniversary Symposium," held at the Library of Congress. Among his comments was a description of how, after helping to get Leadbelly out of prison and prepared for a performing career in the North, he spent many hours coaching the black songster away from such songs as "That Silver-Haired Daddy of Mine" (then a national hillbilly hit for Gene Autry) to singing songs from his own heritage. Lomax's work to bring charismatic individual folksingers before the public was *not* typical of the times. Lawrence W. Levine points out that sociologists, WPA folklore collectors, and FSA photographers all tended to present their subjects "not as individuals but as representations"; see "The Historian and the Icon," pp. 25–26.

30. Ohrlin, *The Hell-Bound Train,* p. 237. Notice that while Ohrlin distinguishes between aficionados and folklorists, he groups them together as a community in contrast to his own.

31. Some suggestive information from performers can be found in Warner, Warner, and Proffitt, "Frank Noah Proffitt"; Ritchie, *Singing Family,* pp. 224–56; and Abrahams, *A Singer and Her Songs.*

32. Charles Seeger, "Reviews," 1948 and 1949. Alan Lomax's 1940 "List of American Folksongs" also utilized a system of stylistic terminology identified by abbreviations.

33. Charles Seeger, "Reviews," 1948, p. 216.

34. Charles Seeger, "Reviews," 1949, p. 68.

35. Ibid., p. 70. See also Seeger's "Professionalism and Amateurism."

36. Alan Lomax, "The 'Folkniks,'" originally published as liner notes to *Guy Carawan Sings, Volume 2,* Folkways FG 3548 (New York, 1959). Charles Seeger

mounted a similar argument in "Folk Music in the Schools": "Millions can now learn to sing, if we only insist upon it, from hearing the voices of authentic singers" (p. 29).

37. Lomax presents cantometrics in *Folk Song Style and Culture*. Charles Seeger's interest in questions involving the representation of style in musical transcription and analysis was more speculative and philosophical than applied. Two of his articles in particular, "Prescriptive and Descriptive Music Writing" and "Toward a Universal Music Sound-Writing," reflect his work with the melograph. See also Nettl, *The Study of Ethnomusicology*, pp. 76–77. Seeger saw the melograph as one facet of musical description and analysis, and called Lomax's total reliance on extrinsic rather than intrinsic data an "extreme viewpoint"; see Charles Seeger, "Singing Style," p. 6.

38. Glassie, *Passing the Time*, pp. xv, 723.

39. A similar shift took place in ethnomusicology; in 1964 one of the largest ethnomusicological archives, the Indiana University Archives of Folk and Primitive Music, changed its name to the Archives of Traditional Music.

40. This terminology is based on that introduced by Dundes in "Texture, Text and Context." Charles Seeger articulated a similar division in his 1958 article "Singing Style," p. 4, but included four rather than three categories—singing style, repertory, culture-community, and singer. It compares interestingly with the four categories of "music-culture" outlined by Slobin and Titon, "The Music-Culture as a World of Music."

41. Frisbie, "President's Report," p. 2.

42. For example see the work of Kirshenblatt-Gimblett, "Mistaken Dichotomies" and "Authoring Lives."

43. Charles Seeger, "Folk Music in the Schools." In the same year folktale scholar Stith Thompson, in an address delivered to the National Folk Festival Association, stated that while the "age-old custom of telling folktales is . . . dead," this is not so with folksong and folk dance: "The public eagerly participates in them and there is a continual revival." See his "Folklore and Folk Festivals," p. 11. Folk music scholar Samuel P. Bayard disagreed with Thompson: "The so-called folk-song revivals of today in America are not actually revivals: they are for the most part the renditions of folk-song items divorced from the tradition in which they were made, by performers who are complete aliens to the traditional art." See "Decline and 'Revival,' " p. 74. It would be interesting to know what Thompson, who died in 1976, would have to say about today's popular revival of folktale performance.

44. Sharp, *English Folk-Song*, p. 140.

45. Sharp, *Folk Songs*, p. xi.

46. *Oxford English Dictionary*, vol. 13, p. 834. Raymond Williams did *not* include "revival" in his vocabulary of culture and society, *Keywords*.

47. See Jane S. Becker, "Revealing Traditions," p. 27; and Bustin, " 'The Morrow's Uprising.' "

48. Ryan, *The Irish Literary Revival*, p. v.

49. Brunvand, *Folklore*, p. 22.

50. Narváez and Laba, *Media Sense*, p. 1.

51. Brunvand, *The Vanishing Hitchhiker, The Choking Doberman, The Mexican Pet,* and *Curses! Broiled Again!*

52. Whisnant, "Public Sector Folklore," p. 244. For a masterful portrait of one such social elite see von Schmidt and Rooney, *Baby, Let Me Follow You Down;* my review of it in *Ethnomusicology* discusses the issue of revival as social elite in some detail.

53. Wallace, "Revitalization Movements."

54. Hobsbawm, "Introduction: Inventing Traditions," in Hobsbawm and Ranger, *The Invention of Tradition,* p. 1.

55. Ibid., p. 2. Standard definitions have been articulated in Brunvand, *The Study of American Folklore,* pp. 7–11.

56. Bohlman, *The Study of Folk Music,* pp. 130–31.

PART 1

The Great Boom

Between fall 1958, when the Kingston Trio's "Tom Dooley" ascended the pop hit charts, and summer 1965, when Bob Dylan went electric at Newport, the American folk music revival competed with some success in the volatile popular music industry with jazz, rock and roll, and other established forms. This is what I call the "great boom." Like any popular musical phenomenon, it did not happen overnight. Its beginnings can be seen at least as far back as the early fifties in the success of the Weavers in the pop market. To date its end with Dylan's iconoclastic appearance at the premier folk festival backed by Paul Butterfield's electric blues band is similarly arbitrary—the Byrds had preceded him in this direction by many months.

In another way, the great boom never really ended, it just became part of the pop music scene. It led to the currency of the term "folksinger" in the North American English vocabulary, and moved folk music from the domain of academic inquiry into the world of commercial music. The five papers in this section examine the boom from different perspectives, looking at the cultural matrix from which it emerged, considering its intellectual implications, and pondering its continuing impact upon questions of national identity.

In "When We Were Good: Class and Culture in the Folk Culture," Robert Cantwell offers an overview of the great boom as a period in which folk music, involvement in which one sociologist had characterized in the early fifties as "deviant,"[1] became the dominant youth music of its time. Looking at this movement from two perspectives—as a former participant and as a critical observer of American cultural history—Cantwell shows how aspects of this musical movement broke with the past in ways consonant with the deeper structures of American cultural history. At the same time, he argues, certain parts of this new preoccupation with old music can be seen as a generation's response to the new society in which they were coming of age, with its postwar changes that the old structures did not anticipate.

Starting with the obscure North Carolina murder ballad that swung the Kingston Trio to stardom, Cantwell builds his narrative with illustrations from folklore, popular culture, and literature. This essay, written from an American studies perspective, illustrates vividly how frequently the cultural levels of art often labeled arbitrarily as folk, pop, and elite overlap and blend. In his examination of intersections and convergences, Cantwell offers a new, improved map of familiar territory.

While Cantwell provides an overview of the great boom, Archie Green offers in "The Campus Folksong Club: A Glimpse at the Past" his personal commentary on it in a microcosm. A Los Angeles native, Green graduated from the University of California in 1939 and spent the next two decades as a carpenter in San Francisco. During the 1950s a growing interest in folk music, stemming from his exposure to the same "movement culture" that Robbie Lieberman has chronicled, stimulated Green's curiosity about labor history and song's role in it. In 1961, after completing a degree in library science, he became the librarian for the Institute of Labor and Industrial Relations at the University of Illinois in Urbana. It was at this point that he became involved with the university's Campus Folksong Club (CFC). In 1965 he began work on a Ph.D. in Folklore and Folklife at the University of Pennsylvania. Green subsequently became the lobbyist for and principal moving force behind the effort to establish a national folklife center. The fruit of his labor was the passing of the Folklife Bill in 1976, which established the American Folklife Center in the Library of Congress. A substantial spin-off of his activity was the establishment of folklife-related offices in the Smithsonian and the National Endowment for the Arts.

Today Green is widely viewed as the founding father of the Public Sector Folklore movement in the United States. Through his work in establishing and writing for the John Edwards Memorial Foundation (JEMF) at UCLA, he also played an important role in advocating the study of hillbilly and other parallel commercial music systems based on folk music.[2] His continuing calls for folklorists to examine their own ideological underpinnings are only now receiving the attention they deserve.[3] His essay began as part of the liner notes for a Rounder Records album of the Blue Sky Boys, an influential hillbilly duet whom Green brought out of retirement in 1964 to perform for the University of Illinois Campus Folksong Club.[4] It has grown to a reflexive consideration of Green's central role during the period when he was the club's faculty adviser. It also sketches his earlier involvement in the nascent boom, with attention to the small San Francisco network of record collectors in which he began his intellectual quest.

Many college campuses had folksong clubs during this period, and the rules for officially sanctioned clubs typically required that they have a faculty adviser. Most such advisers were figureheads, avuncular types who, sharing the aesthetic involvement of the students, acted in the then widely accepted stance of faculty as *in loco parentis,* guarding against excesses. Not so with Archie Green. In an academic setting in which folk music studies were conspicuously absent, he presided over a movement as teacher and counselor. He describes life "in the eye of a cultural storm," working with a generation of folk music "partisans" to nurture a "far out" scene in a "straight" context. Seen from the perspective of the present, the CFC was a rehearsal for his later involvement in moving American folklorists into the public sector. Green was counseling intellectual activists to confront social issues long before most folklorists were talking about "applied folklore."[5]

Bruce Jackson's paper "The Folksong Revival," one of the most frequently cited recent publications on the topic, was first read at the conference "Culture, Tradition, Identity" at Indiana University in 1984, and published in *New York Folklore* in 1985. Like Cantwell and Green, Jackson describes the great boom, but he then moves to tie it to later developments within the folklore establishment. In introducing his topic he describes revivals as appealing "primarily to individuals who celebrated traditions not their own." He ends, however, by arguing for the revival as a community with its own kinds of learning and tradition. He links this process with the growth of public sector folklore work in the United States.

In doing so he argues against the interpretation of the revival as a kind of "folklorismus" or, in its anglicization, "folklorism." A succinct operating definition of "folklorism" was given at the same conference and panel by a Hungarian folklorist, Vilmos Voigt, who in his paper "The Concept of *Today's Folklore* as We See It from Budapest, Hungary, Europe" says that "the concept of *Folklorism* for us means the transmission of folklore into non-folklore."[6] In the discussion following Voigt's and Jackson's papers, Alan Dundes pointed out that the two papers represented contrasting worldviews. The European past-oriented worldview, said Dundes, leads to "difficulty in seeing modern materials as proper folklore" so that in Hungary folklorismus "really is a revival in the sense that you are going to revive something from the past and make it touristically or commercially viable."[7] By contrast, Dundes argues, in America "we have a future-oriented world view." Thus it is "perfectly normal" to have new folksongs. Jackson responded that the folksong revival boom heralded the start of a new way of thinking, a perspective in which things past have become more important than before—an argument echoed in Cantwell's article.[8]

Indeed one of Jackson's key points is that the boom, reflected in the Smithsonian festivals and the emergence of public-sector folklore, is an expression of this shift of perspective. He characterizes it as a new kind of urban renewal, in which wholesale destruction of the past has been superseded by a sense of the need for historic preservation: it is a setting in which respect for things old is greater than before. Dundes agreed but noted that even this still involved *renewal*—creating something new.[9] And so the argument goes.

Arguments about "folklorism" and "folklorismus" have to do with folklorists' judgments about criteria of classification. The two terms most frequently mentioned in connection with it are tourism and commercialization. Both reflect a process of decision making about the defining characteristics of folklore in the realm of process: "folklorism" is used to describe situations in which process renders product inauthentic as folklore. At the conference many different stances were taken on this subject. Linda Dégh, drawing on her comparative experiences in Hungary and America, concluded that "rigid academic distinctions between *folklore* ('pure,' 'original,' 'genuine'), *fakelore* ('spurious and synthetic [rewritings] from earlier literary and journalistic sources'), and *folklorism* (commercial exploitation of uprooted and displaced folk art) are not helpful terms for a definition of folklore in today's society."[10] We will return to the question of folklorism later, in Richard Blaustein's article. Jackson has added a postscript to his article for this volume.

Ellen Stekert's "Cents and Nonsense in the Urban Folksong Movement: 1930–66" first appeared in *Folklore and Society,* the 1966 festschrift for B. A. Botkin that Bruce Jackson edited. As Jackson notes, Botkin was one of a handful of folklorists of the forties and fifties who viewed the revival benignly. No doubt there was some connection between this stance and the relegation of Botkin to the margins of academic folklore in the fifties and sixties by Richard M. Dorson, who was prompted by Botkin's *Treasuries* to coin the term "fakelore."[11] While Jackson, writing in the eighties, stresses the connections between academic folklore and the great boom by showing how young revivalists of the fifties and sixties became part of the academic and public sector establishment of the seventies and eighties, Stekert, writing from a much closer perspective, stresses the distance between the revival and the academics during the fifties and sixties.

As a new folklore Ph.D. who had emerged from the revival—during the late fifties and early sixties she gave concerts and recorded for Stinson, Riverside, Folkways, and Elektra—Stekert undertook the difficult task of writing about something very close in time and personal experience. She saw the revival as "a new idiom of popular entertainment," and sought to make sense of the many threads of style and content within it by classifying the performers into four different groups: the traditional singers, the imitators, the utilizers, and those of the new aesthetic. It is a set of categories that remains useful, helping to shape the organization of this volume. But her essay conveys more than just this careful intellectual sifting of evidence by a young scholar; it also smolders with Stekert's authentic anger at what Cantwell calls Bob Dylan's "gallant fraudulence" and Guthrie's role as poetic poseur;[12] and her distress at the revival's "anti-intellectualism" and "profound distrust of academia." This paper reminds us that in spite of, or, perhaps more accurately, because of the many cultural and social connections between the academic folklorists and the folk enthusiasts, they are often at doctrinal loggerheads, like members of warring religious sects. Stekert has written a new introduction to this important article, placing it in the context of her present thinking.

This section closes with "A Future Folklorist in the Record Business," edited excerpts from my 2 January 1979 interview with Kenneth S. Goldstein. A native of New York City, Goldstein became a folksong enthusiast in the mid-forties and was a central figure in the early years of the boom, dividing his time between his occupation as a market analyst for Fairchild Publications and his avocation of folksong activism. Circumstances gradually drew him into the record business, and by the mid-fifties he had become one of the best known producers of folk music albums. He eventually worked on over five hundred such projects for such companies as Stinson, Riverside, Elektra, Tradition, Folkways, and Prestige. His liner notes were, for many revivalists, the first introduction to the intellectual dimensions of folk music. Goldstein also became involved in publishing—an early project involved the 1956 reprinting of Francis James Child's *The English and Scottish Popular Ballads*. Ultimately, an academic career developed. In 1958 he attended the Summer Folklore Institute at Indiana University and in the following year began working toward what would be the first Ph.D. in folklore and folklife at the University of Pennsylvania. He went on to become a distinguished folklorist.

In the interview I asked Goldstein to discuss the ways in which, in the context of the highly pragmatic popular music business, he dealt with the intellectual issues and ideas at the confluence of folk and popular music. During the late fifties and early sixties no record producer was mentioned more frequently—usually with approval—in folklore journal record reviews than Goldstein. Nevertheless, many of his productions were deemed not worthy of review because they were simply popular or were by revival singers rather than authentic folk. This interview sheds light on the ways in which he juggled scholarly agendas, popular mandates, and personal values.

This interview was not edited as one might edit an oral-history interview in order to convey oral style. Instead, I made excerpts that Goldstein then read and, where he thought it was appropriate for purposes of clarity, made editorial changes.[13] My interview questions are in italics. I have arranged portions of the interview into six sections.

Section one encompasses a discussion of the philosophical questions emerging from business considerations. The idea of mixing "commercial"—salable—products with less commercially viable but more authentic ones, in order to (1) use the former to bankroll the latter and (2) use the former as a bait to draw new consumers to the latter, was widespread in the boom years. This aspect of the boom business had important implications for amateur and professional musicians alike.

In section two, the focus shifts to the mechanics of record-album liner notes, with an exploration of earlier models, consideration of the development of writing style, and reflections on decisions about what to communicate and how.

Section three explores the important role of liner notes as a source of intellectual dialogue within the revival. Goldstein explains his practice of asking singers to write their own notes—an early recognition of the ethnographic value of such work.

In section four, motives for recording singers are considered, along with theme and "concept" albums. Goldstein tells how he worked from America to stimulate the contemporaneous British revival—a sort of left-wing artistic Marshall Plan. The connections between style and message and their implications for decisions about record production are touched upon here.

Section five turns to the political and philosophical issues underlying the mechanics of recording and editing. Embracing the concept of the record as a rhetorical platform, Goldstein speaks of the central role of intuition and subjectivity in his early writing, and the role played by his own catholic tastes in converting listeners, through "stars," to folk music.

Finally, in section six, comes a discussion of editing and the producer's responsibility. From a description of performer responses to test pressings Goldstein moves to issues of authentic context and to questions of how people wish to present themselves.

NOTES

1. Kaplan, "A Study of Folksinging."
2. Edwards was an Australian collector of American hillbilly records who died in 1960. His will stipulated that his collection should go to the United States for the

furtherance of scholarly studies in recorded folk music. Since 1983 the collection has been housed as part of the Southern Folklife Collection in the Wilson Library at the University of North Carolina; the JEMF record series is handled by Arhoolie Records of El Cerrito, California; and the *JEMF Quarterly*, after changing its name to the *John Edwards Memorial Forum*, has moved to the Center for Popular Music at Middle Tennessee State University, which now publishes it as *American Vernacular Music*.

3. E.g., Green, "Interpreting Folklore Ideologically."

4. *The Blue Sky Boys in Concert 1964.*

5. A significant exception is Botkin's "Applied Folklore."

6. Voigt, "The Concept of *Today's Folklore*," p. 167.

7. Dundes et al., "Commentary," p. 182.

8. Ibid., p. 184.

9. The debate is reflected in the title and contents of the 1988 exhibition mounted in honor of the one hundredth anniversary of the American Folklore Society by the Museum of Our National Heritage in Lexington, Massachusetts: *Folk Roots, New Roots: Folklore in American Life.*

10. Dégh, "Uses of Folklore," p. 188.

11. Dorson, "Fakelore," p. 59.

12. Stekert was not alone among folklorists in this evaluation of Guthrie; D. K. Wilgus wrote in 1967 that "anyone who sees [Guthrie] as a major literary figure needs to be bored for the simples." Wilgus, "From the Record Review Editor," p. 204.

13. The original interview, which is considerably longer and differs in some details, is on deposit in the Memorial University of Newfoundland Folklore and Language Archive (MUNFLA) under accession number 79–009.

When We Were Good: Class and Culture in the Folk Revival

Robert Cantwell

"I need a steamshovel mama, to keep away the dead!" Bob Dylan declared in 1965, having personally terminated the popular folksong revival, some thought, by picking up an electric guitar and sending his message around the world with it, "I need a dump truck mama, to unload my head. . . ."

Having shared and brought to light so much of the experience of his generation, perhaps Dylan was remembering an evening in the parlor back in Hibbing, Minnesota, in front of the new television set, where in films supplied by the Department of the Army a man with a surgical mask, operating a bulldozer, was moving a naked trash-heap of human corpses into an open pit. Or it may have been the sudden rising of a momentary sun over Bikini Atoll, disemboweling the sky in membranous sheets of dust and light and summoning out of the earth a pillar of smoke and steam in which the Pacific tried to leap out of itself. Or maybe he was remembering a dim Senate committee room where bespectacled men in front of microphones shouted at one another with anger and indignation, or, like automatons, gravely intoned a refusal to answer on the strange "grounds" that their answer might "tend to incriminate" them. No wonder he saw history, on that same record album, as the work of a fancy promoter, who, when asked whether he could produce "the next world war," says, "yes, I think it can be very *easily* done!"—"just put some bleachers out in the sun" and have it out on the old Mississippi delta highway, "Highway Sixty-one!"

It was between, roughly, 1958, when a collegiate West Coast trio, the Kingston Trio, recorded an Appalachian murder ballad, "Tom Dooley," which sold nearly four million discs, and 1964, when the Beatles and other

British groups began to dominate American popular music, that folksongs, and original songs conceived and performed as folksongs, sung by young folksong revivalists such as Bob Dylan, Joan Baez, Peter, Paul, and Mary, and literally hundreds of others enjoyed an unprecedented commercial popularity. They inspired thousands of young middle-class men and women to learn folksongs, to accompany themselves on folk instruments, particularly the guitar and banjo, to search out and lionize authentic folk musicians, and finally to dress, groom, speak, comport themselves, and even attempt to think in ways suggestive of the rural, ethnic, proletarian, and other marginal cultures to whom folksong was supposed to belong. In this process, many kinds of music that at other periods had been commercially performed and recorded, such as blues, old-time, and bluegrass music—music chiefly of southern or southeastern rural origin—came to be regarded as folk music and enjoyed a revival on that basis, to be followed in the next decade by Irish ceili, Klezmer, and other ethnic musics.

This was the postwar "folk revival." The commercial recording that set it in motion was, again, a traditional ballad that commemorated the murder of Laura Foster, of Wilkes County, North Carolina, by a Civil War veteran, Tom Dula, and his co-conspirator and lover Annie Melton, in 1866. Dula had a reputation as a desperado, apparently, and a ladies' man. Reporters from as far away as New York covered his trial, and at least one of the ballads about him or attributed to him may have been composed by a journalist named Thomas Land. Dula was hanged for the murder in 1868. His song entered tradition in Tennessee and North Carolina, where in 1938 an ingenious young mountaineer from Pick Britches Valley, Tennessee, Frank Proffitt, sang it for a folksinger-collector named Frank Warner; Warner was visiting Profitt's father-in-law, Nathan Hicks, a dulcimer maker from nearby Beech Mountain, North Carolina. Proffitt, whose grandparents had been personally acquainted both with the murderer and his victim, thought of Dula as a man who "didn't conform to rules."[1] Proffitt had first heard "Tom Dooley" from his father, who taught it to him on a homemade banjo. "My earliest recalection," he later wrote to Warner, "is of waking on a cold winter morning in a log cabin on old Beaver Dam and hearing the sad haunting tune of Tom Dooly picked by my father along with the frying of meat on the little stepstove and the noise of the coffeemill grinding the Arbuckle."[2]

Frank Warner was a dedicated singer of southern mountain ballads and, having used "Tom Dooley" in his own folksong concerts for twenty years, had recorded it himself in 1952 for a fledgling folksong record company called Elektra, which operated out of a Greenwich Village shop called the Record Loft.[3] Though not a mountaineer himself, Warner had grown up in Durham and had studied under the folklorists Frank C. Brown and

Newman Ivey White at Duke. With his wife, Anne, he had become a pioneer in the use of portable recording equipment in the collection of folksongs; indeed the vice-president of Philco Radio had created for them in 1940 a battery-powered portable recording machine specifically for that purpose.[4] In subsequent years Frank Warner distinguished himself as president of the New York Folklore Society, program director of the Pinewoods folk music camp, vice-president of the Country Dance and Song Society, and trustee of the National Folk Arts Council.[5]

Warner had gone to New York in 1931 to become program director for the Grand Central YMCA, having already established several HiY programs and directed a summer camp for that organization. It is probable that folksong had proved useful in Warner's recreational work. By the early 1940s, having moved to West Nineteenth Street, he had become an intimate of the folksong enthusiasts in Greenwich Village, among whom was the folklorist Alan Lomax; Lomax was preparing broadcasts of folksong for Armed Forces Radio, enlisting Warner among other performers such as Burl Ives, Sonny Terry, Woody Guthrie, and Huddie Ledbetter, or "Leadbelly," for his programs.[6] Lomax printed "Tom Dooley" without the third stanza in his book *Folk Song U.S.A.*, in 1947, attributing it to "that flavorsome North Carolina singer, Frank Warner."[7] Warner's version, as Lomax printed it, which lyrically and melodically Warner had worked out in his years of performing the song, somewhat simplified the detailed narratives in the available traditional texts in favor of an evocative lyricism reminiscent of folksongs sung in school; Ruth Seeger's sturdy musical arrangement, however, dispelled what to the school-trained ear are the melodic vagaries of the traditional Appalachian singing style.

Songs transmit themselves, for the most part, aurally; this is particularly true of folksongs, which after all have evolved in an aural milieu. Typically singers and musicians are struck by what they hear, more than by what they may find in books, though they often have recourse to a printed collection in order to build a repertoire, or to reconstruct their own performance of what they may have heard only once or twice. It is very likely then, that "Tom Dooley" entered oral circulation among folksong enthusiasts through the combined influences of Frank Warner's performances in New York and, after 1956, at Camp Woodlands, and through the Lomaxes' widely available collection. It was being sung on Washington Square, for example, in the late 1940s and by 1951 had been recorded on an esoteric Greenwich Village label, Stinson, by three Washington Square singers, Bob Carey, Erik Darling, and Roger Sprung, the Folksay Trio.[8]

By the mid-1950s the song was abroad on the West Coast, where on a Wednesday night in 1957 the aspiring young folk trio from Hawaii called the Kingston Trio heard it sung by a greying folksinger who, like them, was auditioning for a job at San Francisco's nightclub the Purple Onion. The melody haunted them, as it had Frank Proffitt—but for the words they went to another artifact of the folksong movement of the 1950s, Beth and Dick Best's *New Song Fest,* a paperbound campfire collection privately published in 1948 and again, commercially, in 1955, "in recognition of the present trend towards folksongs and ballads."[9] Like the other songs in the collection, the Bests' "Tom Dooley," printed without attribution, seemed simply to be in the public domain, a song that belonged, and would belong again, to everyone.

With its major tonality and foreshortened melodic range, "Tom Dooley" is a kind of sober, almost a pious duty, like planting a tree. With the simplicity of a bugle call, its tune climbs sadly in four nearly identical phrases from a grave fifth below the tonic to a weary second or third above it, where it pauses to rest, lingering in one of the two chords, tonic or dominant, that resignedly bear away the stanza. What is haunting about it, perhaps, is the strange, uneasy confederacy of its melody, which strikes an urbane, almost sophisticated note, with a harmony in which one can hear echoes, in a wild pentatonic mode, of some old fiddler's farewell. The economy of its statement, the authenticity of its voice, and the compatibility of its lyric and melody are finally unforgettable:

> Bout' this time tomorrow,
> Reckon where I'll be—
> Down in some lonesome valley
> Hangin' from a white oak tree.

David Guard, banjo player in the Kingston Trio, had first been inspired to undertake the instrument in 1957, when he was a student in Palo Alto. The occasion was a Weavers concert, with banjoist Pete Seeger, at Nourse Hall in San Francisco; a very young Joan Baez was also in attendance, with her parents. Guard learned banjo chords from Seeger's little book, *How To Play the 5-String Banjo,* which Seeger had first published, in mimeograph, in 1948, and a three-finger picking technique, a "backwards" variant of the bluegrass or "Scruggs" style, from Bay Area virtuoso Billy Faier.[10]

Guard took to the banjo readily, having already learned, as a Hawaiian, to play the guitar in the Hawaiian open G tuning, which is traditional for the banjo as well. His own interest in folk music, however, had begun during World War II, when the director of the Melbourne Symphony, Fritz Hart, detained in the islands on account of military restrictions, conducted choral singing of folksongs such as "Greensleeves" and "Shenandoah" for schoolchildren. "Everybody bought guitars," Guard recalls, when in 1950 the Weavers, of which Pete Seeger was of course a leading member, came out with their hit recording of "Goodnight, Irene."[11]

By the time he was a college student in California, Guard was a folksong performer as well as an enthusiast, and he formed with Bob Shane and Nick Reynolds a new band they called the Kingston Trio, in order to associate it with the calypso music recently popularized by a handsome young black actor called Harry Belafonte, who had recorded several albums of calypso songs. Bob Shane, the trio's lead singer, went further by imitating Belafonte's husky, after-hours singing voice. Belafonte had begun his career as a folksinger in 1948 at Town Hall,[12] where he played the role of the southern preacher in the cantata *The Lonesome Train*, a tribute to Abraham Lincoln composed by the Popular Front composer Earl Robinson and the Almanac Singer Millard Lampell in 1940.

From all this, the immediate background of the Kingston Trio's "Tom Dooley," one might vaguely surmise that the song had not sprung fullblown out of the imagination of a Capitol Records promoter in 1958: that it had a complex lineage of scholarly, entrepreneurial, musical, theatrical, and political activity of fairly long standing, and thoroughly authentic origins that were utterly effaced by its commercial success. Neither the Kingston Trio, in fact, nor Frank Warner, nor the Folksay Trio had been the first to record "Tom Dooley." G. B. Grayson, a blind fiddler of Mountain City, Tennessee, and a descendent of the "Grayson" who had arrested the murderer, had recorded the song for Victor in the 1920s—a time when record companies were discovering regional markets for traditional music—along with "Handsome Molly," "Little Maggie," and other songs that would become staples of the folk revival.[13]

One has only to scratch the surface of "Tom Dooley," then, as thousands of its young admirers did, to discover that the emergent commercial youth culture of the late 1950s had suddenly been intersected by a rich and energetic tradition of folksong scholarship, collection, and performance extending back at least into the regional festivals, folk dance societies, and outing clubs of the 1920s. In the larger historical perspective, however, that tradition belonged to a particular family of theatrical, literary, and musical representations of folksong and folk culture that had begun in America on the minstrel stage—in the 1830s, when T. D. Rice introduced the Negro stableman's tortuous jig he called "Jump Jim Crow."

In 1912, for example, outdoorsman Teddy Roosevelt endorsed John Lomax's *Cowboy Songs*, noting that in their "sympathy for the outlaw" the cowboy songs resembled the British ballads, particularly those celebrating another outdoorsman, Robin Hood. It was the president's inscription of the book that hastened its popularity and provided the foundation for Lomax's career as a folksong entrepreneur and collector. Lomax had studied under the ballad-scholar George Lyman Kittredge at Harvard; with his son Alan he produced in three decades a series of influential folksong books and conducted a sweeping tour of the Depression South creating the great collection of folksong field recordings now deposited at the Library of Congress. Among the Lomaxes' discoveries was of course the great black songster Huddie Ledbetter, or "Leadbelly," who in 1934 accompanied the Lomaxes to New York, where he was enthusiastically, if uncomprehendingly, embraced by the tiny left-wing folksong community that included a young Harvard dropout, New England blueblood, and fledging banjo-player called Pete Seeger.

In 1950, Seeger's folksong quartet, the Weavers, made Leadbelly's "Goodnight, Irene" the most popular song of the year. They made a hit of Leadbelly's "Kisses Sweeter Than Wine" as well, and of Woody Guthrie's dustbowl anthem "So Long, It's Been Good to Know Ya," along with the South African "Wimoweh" and the Appalachian "On Top of Old Smokey." But *Red Channels: Communist Influence on Radio and Television*, published that same year, which cited Pete Seeger thirteen times, soon terminated the Weavers' career, and show-business blacklisting drove folksinging underground for most of the decade. It was precisely this temporary obscurity, the effect of the association of folksong with the political left forged in the 1930s, that opened the immense aural and written resources of folksong and folksinging to the young and made it, by virtue of their independent recovery of it in the postwar period, their own. When folksong reemerged into the light of popular culture in 1958, its ideological as well as its cultural connections having been largely suppressed, abandoned, forgotten, or lost, it welled up with all the freshness and vitality of a renewed cultural symbol eager for a rearticulation of itself.

The immediate foreground of "Tom Dooley," too, may suggest what fertile cultural ground lay to be discovered in the folk tradition. The folksong enthusiast and musician Ralph Rinzler was inspired by a scholarly reissue LP anthology, released in 1953, of folksongs recorded commercially in the 1920s. This was the influential Folkways *Anthology of American Folk Music*, which recalled to him the Library of Congress field recordings he had heard in his youth. Rinzler journeyed to North Carolina in early 1961 to record the by then elderly banjoist and singer Tom Ashley, who had been an early associate of G. B. Grayson on the medicine show circuit.[14] Ashley's "Coo Coo Bird," a mountain song with medieval English roots, had become a folk revival standard after its reissue on the *Anthology*. Ashley introduced Rinzler to a blind rockabilly guitarist living nearby named Doc Watson, who, when he learned of Rinzler's interest in folksong, picked up a banjo and sang, at a lively mocking tempo, a version of "Tom Dooley" closely related but at the same time quite independent of the Kingston Trio's popular version, one that retained something of the ghastliness and moral squalor of a genuine murder:[15]

> You left her by the roadside
> Where you begged to be excused;
> Left her by the roadside
> Then you hid her clothes and shoes.

And again:

> You dug the grave four feet long
> And you dug it three feet deep;
> You rolled the cold clay over her
> And you tromped it with your feet.

This "new" version, it happened, and the whole story of the murder, had been in Watson's family for generations—his great-grandmother, Betsy Tripplett Watson, had been at the deathbed of Tom's accomplice, Annie Melton, to hear her confession. Yet Rinzler needn't have traveled far to find the version he knew from the Kingston Trio: Frank Proffitt lived a few minutes down the road.

Tom Ashley, Frank Proffitt, and other rediscovered mountain banjoists such as Hobart Smith and Roscoe Holcomb, alongside country bluesmen such as Mississippi John Hurt and Son House, many of them having become quite elderly, returned with the encouragement of enterprising revivalists like Rinzler to university concert halls, coffeehouse circuits, and seasonal festivals at Newport, Philadelphia, Chicago, and Monterey to play the songs and tunes they had recorded commercially thirty-five or forty years earlier. Doc Watson, an expert singer and instrumentalist intimately acquainted with traditional mountain music, became one of the titans of the folk revival, while Ralph Rinzler, after conducting fieldwork for the Newport Folk Foundation on Cape Breton and among the Cajuns of Louisiana, went on to become, in 1967, the director of the Smithsonian Institution's Festival of American Folklife on the National Mall. Rinzler's name, incidentally, had been suggested to James Morris, director of the Smithsonian's Division of Performing Arts, by Joe Hickerson, now director of the Archive of Folk Culture at the Library of Congress;[16] the occasion was a memorial gathering in Washington for the man who nearly thirty years earlier had given away his father's song—Frank Proffitt, who died in 1965, at the age of fifty-two. "The strange mysterious workings which has made Tom Dooly live is a lot to think about," he had written to the Warners two years earlier; "Other like affairs have been forgotten."[17]

For those who first heard it on the radio in 1958, however, "Tom Dooley" had its meaning not against the backdrop of folksong scholarship or left-wing politics but as an unexpected departure from, and at the same time an ingenious sublimation, almost a reinterpretation, of what was, at that point, one of the most remarkable entrepreneurial successes in the youth market, rock-and-roll music—remarkable because of its apparently obscure sociocultural origins and its violent overthrow of the class standards of popular music. Rock and roll grew out of the practice by white performers, begun sometime in the 1940s, of "covering" black rhythm-and-blues recordings normally distributed only within the black community. But when black "jump" blues was covered in Memphis, beginning in 1954, by young white working-class southerners, the best known of whom was of course Elvis Presley, rock and roll found a popular audience.

This music, disseminated by the portable radio and on 45 rpm discs, both of which made it readily available to the young and a constant accompaniment to their lives, was unquestionably a kind of folk music, with roots extending deeply into the black and white folk culture of the South. The inexpensive and virtually indestructible 45 rpm rockabilly disc was in the weeks of its currency a kind of cryptogram that could be deciphered—much to the dismay of parents—by constant repetition. If its message seemed an urgent one, one that established itself only by increments in young people's understanding, it was because at the moment of their sexual awakening an exotic sexual culture, the culture of the levee and the boondocks, where abandoned lovers take up lodgings at the end of Lonely Street, stand at their windows and moan, or sneak into one another's houses like dogs, was for the space of a few moments borne in upon them on the rhythms of the jukejoint and barrelhouse, but in trappings that disarmed their resistance to it: a straining vocality, sinewy with sexual tension, of young white men. The arm languidly pointing, the sneer, the sideburns, the sidelong grin, the sexual footwork: Presley's image—the image of poverty and young manhood in the postwar urban South—was the pattern for thousands of pubescent boys lip-synching before the bedroom mirror with their first cheap guitar. What did the twelve- or fourteen-year-old know of the idiom and manners of the frankly erotic, unsentimental, and passionate black underworld of New Orleans or Memphis? Nothing: but rockabilly music, like the thief who doffs his clothes to baffle the guard dog, had made it a part of his life.

It needn't be repeated that one of the great contributory streams of American music and culture, what Alan Lomax calls the "Old Tar River," has for nearly two hundred years, in minstrelsy, spiritual song, ragtime, jazz, blues, and rock, flowed from African-American life and culture into European and Anglo-American culture at every social level. Black performances, by singers such as Little Richard, Chuck Berry, and Fats Domino, and by the great rhythm-and-blues groups such as the Platters and the Orioles, continued to provide the touchstone of rock-and-roll music throughout the period. From the viewpoint of the folk revival, however, it is the rockabilly singer, who could convincingly reproduce, in the black style, a jump blues or a rhythm-and-blues song, who is principally of interest—for this was a young man who *through* the music seemed to have thrown off, like blackface minstrels and white jazzmen before him, the weight of polite society and its values. Even at the Newport Folk Festival, where southern black bluesmen such as Sleepy John Estes and Mississippi John Hurt, or mountain balladeers such as Sara Gunning or Almeda Riddle, were regarded with admiration, reverence, and even awe, it was nevertheless the young white revivalist such as Joan Baez or Bob Dylan who attracted the enormous crowds and inspired the most calculated musical and personal imitation.

The authentic rockabilly sound swiftly declined in the face of massive commercialization, marketing, and sex scandals, and, most of all, the disappearance of the authentic performers: Presley was drafted into the army; Carl Perkins seriously injured in an auto accident; Chuck Berry and Jerry Lee Lewis disgraced by liaisons with young women who had not attained their majority; Buddy Holly, Eddie Cochran, and Gene Vincent killed— so sweeping was the catastrophe that one can almost imagine some sinister quasi-official conspiracy behind it. Equally significant in its ultimate demise, however, were the social and cultural affinities of rockabilly; though its popularity was hardly confined to the working class, rockabilly was a southern working-class music already identified—an identification vigorously seconded by a hostile Tin Pan Alley—with what was then officiously called "juvenile delinquency"; racists of course saw something still more sinister in it, and political paranoiacs regarded it as yet another manifestation of the worldwide communist conspiracy.

The crass commercialization of this music only alienated its young middle-class listeners, now entering college, from those who permitted themselves to be led by each new commercial simulacrum of it; Fabian and Frankie Avalon, men whose backgrounds were European ethnic, not southern poor white, had been conceived with Frank Sinatra freshly in mind. A vacuum in popular music had opened, and a broad sector of the middle-class young turned, at that moment, with the blessing of a relieved commercial establishment, to a music that ingeniously subdued already awakened musical proclivities on behalf of a new and more fastidious social self-awareness. The genie, it seemed, had been put back in the bottle.

Like the rockabilly combos, the Kingston Trio and its many imitators such as the Cumberland Three, the Chad Mitchell Trio, or the Highwaymen were small string bands of three or four young white men singing in natural voices, accompanying themselves with open chords on at least one freely resonating acoustic guitar—a deposit from traditional country music. In fact, as Dave Guard recalls, the untrained, but far from amateur, vocal sound was the conscious product of professional coaching in phrasing, vowel sounds, and speech accent. Thus, though it did not have the homegrown character of rockabilly, the Kingston Trio's music, usually professionally arranged, nevertheless seemed essentially aural, amateur, and traditional—what would loosely be called "folk" music—and hence independently reproducible, theoretically, with a little application, by any untrained person.

This is the most important respect, perhaps, in which the new folk groups resembled the rockabilly bands. But the Kingston Trio's "Tom Dooley" had more strictly musical affinities with rockabilly as well. Like many other young men of his and other generations, Dave Guard had been a dedicated listener to black music: in Guard's case, to the rhythm-and-blues radio stations broadcasting from San Francisco and Oakland.[18] Consequently the trio's "Tom Dooley" had a rhythmic shuffle and a vocal countermelody strongly reminiscent of rhythm and blues, and a pronounced syncopation in the lyric; indeed the Kingston Trio's "Tom Dooley" could plausibly have been covered by the Coasters, with an irony even folk revivalists could have appreciated.

Most important, though, "Tom Dooley" told a story, not frankly sexual but darkly so, of murder and execution, furnished like a folktale with vivid concretions—the knife, the white oak tree, a man called Grayson—putatively sung in a cloaked, melancholy voice by a hapless mountaineer with an Irish name, and accompanied by a banjo that spoke obscurely of the frontier. It carried the listener's imagination away from high school corridors and sock hops, where exploitative commercial songwriters had largely confined their material, into another world, one that fully a century of popular literature and imagery, including the imagery and literature of the schoolroom, had stereotyped and legitimated.

At the same time, the Kingston Trio's music was delivered with an articulation and phrasing perceptibly polite and bookish, in musical settings wholesomely pianistic; with their colorful short-sleeve Ivy League shirts, close-cropped hair, their easy drollery and unambiguous enthusiasm, the group was manifestly collegiate, happily parodying in their presentations the on-stage pedantry of the previous generation of balladeers and folksong collector-performers. The Kingston Trio seemed to be on spring break somewhere, on the beach at Waikiki, perhaps, where one of their jacket photos pictured them; and, in fact, banjoist Dave Guard and guitarist Bob Shane had begun together in Hawaii as high school boys entertaining servicemen's teenage children, familiar with the Weavers, Burl Ives, and other popular folksingers, with take-offs on their songs.[19] Yet, in the music of this group, underneath the gleam of sporty arrangements and expensive harmonies, there was something solemnly beckoning, a horizon of possibilities; though unapologetically commercial and almost cunningly Ivy League they performed the principal office of music, what some of the great rock-and-roll tunes from Memphis such as Presley's "Heartbreak Hotel" or Carl Perkins's "Blue Suede Shoes" had done, which is to carry the spirit beyond itself into regions where the human story tells itself unabridged and unencumbered.

There are elements in the folk revival, then, with histories of their own: folklore and ballad scholarship, minstrelsy, left-wing politics, popular music and culture; but their particular conjunction in the folk revival has its meaning in the psychosocial and economic setting of postwar America. If you were born between, roughly, 1941, and, say, 1948 or 1950—born, that is, into the new postwar middle class—you grew up in a reality perplexingly divided by the intermingling of an emerging mass society and a decaying industrial culture: a society in which the automobile, the television, the research laboratory, and the transcontinental market would begin to displace the railroad, the radio, the factory, and the regional market, changes that in less than a generation would reshape patterns of settlement, the structure of the family, networks of communication, and the material environment itself, in a general way further atomizing an already atomized society. Obscurely taking shape around you, of a definite order and texture, was an environment of new neighborhoods, new schools, new businesses, new forms of recreation and entertainment, and new technologies that in the course of the 1950s would virtually abolish the world in which your parents had grown up.

At the same time, you had been born soon enough to take the lingering traces of an earlier way of life, in the form of its many palpable cultural deposits, into your own nature. You may have been reared, for example, in your infancy, much as your parents had, in a slightly more rigorous style than that shortly to be advocated by Dr. Benjamin Spock, author of a best-selling mass-market paperback book on childrearing. And you absorbed, as you grew to awareness, your parents' almost unlimited hopes for you—for to them, who had grown up in depression and war, the relatively prosperous and tranquil life of postwar America was the end of rainbow, a new dispensation in which the inevitability of success seemed assured; very likely you saw yourself growing up to be a doctor or lawyer, scientist or engineer, teacher, nurse, or mother—sexual discrimination being still quite marked—images held up to you at school and at home as pictures of your special destiny. You probably attended, too, an overcrowded public school, typically a building built shortly before World War I to which a new wing had recently been added to accommodate the burgeoning school-age population, may have had to share a desk with another student, and in addition to the normal fire and tornado drills had from time to time to climb under your desk in order to shelter yourself from the imagined explosion of an atomic bomb: "first there's a flash of light. . . ."

That such a thing might come, and soon, was one of the axioms of daily life; you had seen the atomic explosion on the television that had come into your parlor around 1952 or 1953, and all around you, but particularly on television, in the Saturday afternoon movie matinees, and in the immediate memory of parents and teachers was evidence of the major global catastrophe that had recently spent itself. There was, moreover, a dark colossus, the Soviet Union, and an insidious influence, the Communist Party, which in some obscure way were connected to one another, were foreign in a colorless, unsavory way, and were dedicated, you were taught, to conquering us from above, with a rain of bombs, or from within, through an unexplained but picturesque technique called "brainwashing." It is not inconceivable, in fact, that a neighbor was actually digging a fallout shelter in his backyard.

Your house in the suburbs, with its new television set, your two-car garage, the gleaming, garish cars parked therein, perhaps the college degree that your parents persistently evoked as the key to happiness: these were trophies of the enthusiastic consumerism of the postwar period, the uninhibited reaching after a dream long deferred by wartime deprivations. Consequently in this vision of consumer Valhalla there was a lingering note of caution, even of dread, so that although quite glamorous it had very little of the unconventional in it, and none of the revolutionary. Being widely shared and widely promulgated, and largely mass produced, the vision brought with it a certain uniformity on the social landscape. To grasp it probably required the principal wage-earner in your family, most likely your father, to give himself over to the tightly regimented, highly competitive, and bureaucratic organization of the newly efficient, even somewhat militarized, postwar American business establishment whose ethos penetrated the entire managerial and executive classes.

Bureaucratization, conformity, and consumerism did not perhaps touch you as immediately as they touched your parents; nevertheless they touched you. You tended, for example, to identify yourself with children your own age, who socially and culturally were more or less like yourself, and to think of the more or less uniform world of children in which your parents had made shift to place you, as the ultimate aim of their escape from the small town or the urban ghetto, as a norm. You were not, in other words, much acquainted in your immediate experience with other classes or cultures, and may have been inclined, or even taught, by means of ethnic or racial epithets, allegorical science fiction films, lingering wartime attitudes and expressions, propaganda and other encouragements, to look upon difference with suspicion. The nuclear family to which you belonged, moreover, bivouacked in the suburbs with other families more or less like itself, had effectively reduced the generational spectrum to a bipolar relation, that between parent and child, while the new consolidated public school you attended was strictly stratified by grade, and in some schools even more scrupulously, by less visible standards like "aptitude." In fact as you advanced in school you were subject to ever more elaborate forms of quantitative evaluation to distinguish you from your fellows—so difficult to distinguish in other ways—a process of IQ tests, achievement tests, aptitude tests, and the like whose crowning glory was the new Scholastic Aptitude Test with its inexorable power to define, delimit, and foreclose.

At the same time, though, you were granted intimations of a variegated and enigmatic world beyond the suburban street that occasionally disturbed the otherwise uniform surface of social reality. There were the desks in the old school building, for example, with their inkwells, and of course the elderly schoolmarms and schoolmasters, with their old-fashioned discipline. There were the old houses on Main Street, too, as well as Main Street itself, whose deterioration would not be complete until business had moved entirely out to the shopping mall—a process that required little more than a decade. Perhaps you had European-born grandparents, still in their stuffy East Side flat or on the farm; or knew a "colored man," born in Mississippi, who came to mow the lawn, and played the harmonica; or had a schoolmate with a southern accent, whose father had come from Kentucky to work at the foundry or the auto plant—and who, to your amazement, brought a giant flat-top guitar to the fifth-grade talent show, playing and singing in a piping voice "Your Cheatin' Heart."

Similarly disquieting, perhaps, and fascinating, was the gang of young toughs from the other side of town, slightly older perhaps—the "hoods" or "greasers" you called them—who wore, with their long hair and sideburns, the uniform of the motorcyclist: black leather jackets with many zippers and pockets, a garrison belt, faded blue jeans, and black engineer boots with silver buckles. One of them, who had perhaps sat behind you in Mechanical Drawing, may have failed out of school and been arrested for petty thievery. Indeed the fifth-grade country singer and the high school dropout may have been, after the passage of a few years, the same person, an unwitting victim of his own social and cultural dislocation.

If these figures in the remoter parts of the social landscape had attracted your attention, it was perhaps because of their certain strange resonance with realms of your cultural life more strictly imaginary, whose romantic texture and tensile strength made your own world seem chimerical by comparison. Wild Bill Hickock, the Lone Ranger, the Cisco Kid, Wyatt Earp, and a hundred other western heroes galloped across television and movie screens on Saturday mornings and afternoons; frontiersmen Mike Fink and Davy Crockett conquered the wilderness in weekly after-dinner episodes; Ichabod Crane, Johnny Appleseed, Pecos Bill, and other folk legends came to life again in Disney's animated cartoons. In music class you may have sung "Cindy," "She'll Be Comin' 'Round the Mountain," and other folksongs because folklorist and anthologist B. A. Botkin, then president of the American Folklore Society, had at the national convention of music teachers in 1944 called for the use of folksong in elementary music education;[20] and very likely in reading class you learned of frontier childhoods in Laura Ingalls Wilder's "Little House" books, republished in a new edition illustrated by Garth Williams in 1953. You may have sung folksongs at summer camp, too, where there was a college-age counselor with a banjo, or at Scout camp, where you practiced the arts of wilderness survival and learned Indian lore; or very likely you heard folksongs sung on the phonograph: the Children's Record Guild, Young People's Records, and other companies had designed special series of folksongs, accompanied by pictures and narratives of such scenes as the completion of the transcontinental railroad.[21]

In short you had been the beneficiary, in school and at home, of cultural traditions both learned and popular that had already enjoyed a long life in America. During the epoch of your childhood these were being hastily quarried out of literature and the arts to supply swelling public school enrollments, a swiftly expanding new commercial market, the youth market, and capacious new media such as television and microgroove record. In the various departments of domestic and public life in which it moved, the experience of your generation—what we may call for convenience, and only half in jest, the Pepsi generation—was chiefly of itself. But its awareness of itself *as* a generation was constituted principally in the marketplace by a series of entrepreneurial incursions that saturated the field of awareness with revelations of its own desire.

No one should be surprised that the imaginations of the folkniks—that is what Alan Lomax, by analogy to "beatniks," called the folk revivalists[22]— had been shaped by their many cultural advantages. Among these was of course education itself, the importance of which had been consistently emphasized at home, with the unforeseen consequence that certain young idealists, perhaps those whose parents had most impressed them with the importance of education, when introduced to the great philosophers, poets, and writers of Europe and America in the college classroom, inclined to take them seriously—though the effects upon attitudes and values tended to be disruptive, since postwar society showed little of the conscious influence of, say, Nietzsche. For once in college—and nearly half of the Pepsi generation would attend college—the folkniks encountered, in others like themselves, a new boldness, even a subtle nonconformity—a willingness, for example, to undertake academic majors in art, philosophy, or literature in place of more careerist programs in the social or natural sciences. Allied to the interest in folk music, moreover, was an intriguing new style of uncertain origin: young women with long, natural hair, peasant skirts, handcrafted sandals and barrettes, young men whose hair had been clipped by their girlfriends, not by the barber, with sideburns or beards, workshirts, handcrafted leather belts with brass buckles—all brought to the campus by children of urban, and likely eastern and upper-middle-class, background, perhaps from the galleries, street vendors, and import shops of bohemian enclaves such as Greenwich Village, or from summer watering spots and artists' colonies such as Woodstock, Provincetown, or Martha's Vineyard.

Slowly a conception formed, more taste than ideology, more style than discourse, more interpersonal than historical—the way for it having been opened by the assent of one's peers and the sanction of the college environment—that the world had been gravely mismanaged by the parent generation. For set cruelly against the high expectations for the future that parents had inculcated, and against the richness and color of the promised world, was the nagging fear that the future might at any moment be suddenly destroyed, or that failure to measure up to some arbitrary standard would close off access to it; through the glory with which the world had been invested ran a thick streak of the sinister. And, in case anyone had forgotten about the bomb, the Cuban missile crisis was there in 1962, on television, to refresh the national memory, and to fill the atmosphere with a mood of apocalypse that was anticipated by poets and musicians in Harlem, in North Beach, and in other bohemian communities and that morally and psychologically consolidated the folk revival as a quasi-political movement.

In such an atmosphere it seemed essential to take matters into one's own hands—after all, young people seemed to fill the field of vision; they had become a power. This was an urgent and intoxicating idea, but it differed from the revolutionary ideas of the Vietnam-era counterculture, which would shortly bury the folk revival, in one important respect: it tacitly sought, or tacitly believed in, until deep political and social polarizations betrayed that belief, the blessing of the parent generation. Its high purposes were precisely the return on the investment the parent generation had made in its children. By the late 1950s stirrings of activism, largely dormant since the 1930s, now underwritten by a cautious and watchful confidence in its fundamental compatibility with the ideals and values that class and education had inculcated, began to reappear on college campuses: politically in organizations such as the Student Peace Union, culturally in a new enthusiasm for folk music and everything associated with it. These two movements were united in the goal of bringing about the world implicitly promised by the parent culture—one by removing the most conspicuous impediment to it, the bomb, and the other by summoning up a visionary culture in which a war- and weapon-liberated people might live—a culture rooted in prewar America, one that could not be suburbanized out of existence.

Thus the folk revival was neither reactionary nor revolutionary, though it borrowed the signs of other such movements and subcultures to express its sense of difference from the parent culture; it was, instead, conservative, or, more precisely, restorative, a kind of cultural patriotism dedicated to picking up the threads of a common legacy that the parent generation had either denied or forgotten to reweave into history. In spite of appearances this was the dream of children fundamentally obedient—of good kids; underneath the "cultivated, ultimately clean-cut unkemptness" of the folk revivalist, wrote Paul Nelson, "there beat the heart not of a ramblin' gamblin' hobo (as he thought), but of a Boy Scout."[23]

For many of course the amateur singing of folksongs was simply a dormitory pastime that after graduation went the way that tarot cards and love beads would a few years later. But often, as Carl Sandburg wrote in his *American Songbag* of 1927, "a song is a role. The singer acts a part. . . . all good artists study a song and live with it before performing it. . . . There is something authentic about any person's way of giving a song which has been known, lived with and loved, for many years, by the singer."[24] To study a song, remarked Israel Young, proprietor of Greenwich Village's Folklore Center on MacDougal Street, "makes a student feel allied to it. It enables a girl who grew up surrounded by the best of everything to sing with some conviction the kinds of blues and spirituals that, theoretically, could be sung honestly only by a prisoner on a Southern chain gang."[25] To this an especially sensitive observer of the folk revival, Susan Montgomery, a fashion writer, added: "Why American college students should want to express the ideas and emotions of the downtrodden and the heartbroken, of garage mechanics and millworkers and miners and backwoods farmers, is in itself an interesting question. But there is certainly good reason for students today to find the world brutal and threatening, and one suspects that when they sing about the burdens and sorrows of the Negro, for example, they are singing out of their own state of mind as well."[26]

"Many of them," Montgomery observed of the early folksong revivalists on Washington Square, "in some small detail of their appearance, looked ever so slightly beat. The badge of identity was sometimes a beard, worn as if in defiance of its owner's Shetland sweater or expensively tailored Madras shorts, or a workman's blue shirt tucked carelessly into faded jeans. Or a girl might go in for wrought-iron jewelry or long straight hair or a

Mexican cotton skirt or handsome hand-crafted leather sandals." Folk music, she understood, had "come to represent a slight loosening of the inhibitions, a tentative step in the direction of the open road, the knapsack, the hostel."[27]

What can have been the origin of this culture, if indeed it can be called a culture, this precise synthesis of attitude, avocation, and style, with folksong as its medium? Observers detected in it the traces of Left Bank and North Beach bohemianism, motorcycle errantry, left-wing politics, and the rest; but the folk revival that emerged out of the folksong movement of the postwar period could not really be identified with any of these. Montgomery, calling attention to the "open road, the knapsack, the hostel," was closer, I think, to the essential spirit of the emergent folk revival, with its peculiar mix of youth, Ivy League collegiality, communalism, recreation, rebellion, adventure, and idealism, and might have found it instructive to peruse the songbook from which the Kingston Trio had learned the words to "Tom Dooley," Dick and Beth Best's *New Song Fest*. Originally issued in mimeograph, *New Song Fest* was a publication of the Intercollegiate Outing Club Association, an organization founded in 1932 "to bring together students with a mutual interest in the out of doors"—students who, it appears, took special delight in singing folksongs together around the campfire, very likely to the strumming of a guitar or banjo. The authors of this collection appended to their signatures their class and college— "Cornell '44" and "Radcliffe '47"—and in a prefatory statement announced that "A reward of one dungaree patch, guaranteed not to rip, run, rust, tear, split, melt, break, etc.[,] is hereby offered for the pelt of the first bohunk caught surreptitiously using this book at a songfest."[28]

Are we catching here an essence from an esoteric but seminal phase of the folk revival as we had it in the early 1960s? Consider the IOCA song, which pictures the young "bohunks" in "old dungarees, patched in the rear and on the knee," tramping high in the Adirondacks, "crashing through brush with heart so free," reveling in their disdain of hierarchy, manners, and rule:

> Our disorganization is perfect;
> Figureheads we have but a few,
> But no meetings among 'em, for we have hamstrung 'em
> 'Cause organization's taboo.[29]

Collegiate as they are, they seem to prefer a vision of a simpler life to the fraternity mixer:

> Give us an old-fashioned barn dance
> With the village's best orchestry,

And we'll whirl and gyrate while the walls all vibrate
In echo to our jollity.

By 1965, in any case, as music critic Paul Nelson noted, the folksinger's *persona* had evolved into a loosely conventional form, that of the "casually road-weary" traveler in jeans and boots or peasant frocks, unclipped hair, speaking a pidgin idiom neither South nor West but vaguely regional and proletarian and, with a touch of the library in it, "highly humane."[30]

John Cohen, himself a "highly humane" Yale graduate and banjo player who became one of the leaders in the revival of old-time string-band music, remarked on the "intensity" arising "from the struggle with forces in the music itself—which become as real as any other problem of life."[31] Many students abandoned their studies, and their medical or legal careers with them, in response to those forces: to the demands of the bluegrass banjo style, the blues guitar, or the Appalachian fiddle. These were "bedeviled people," Montgomery concluded, "who should be counted among the casualties of contemporary American life."[32]

One such casualty was Cohen himself, a photographer by vocation; he joined with Tom Paley, a City College old-time music enthusiast, and Mike Seeger, Pete's younger half-brother and the son of the ethnomusicologist Charles Seeger, to form the pioneer revivalist string band, the New Lost City Ramblers. Setting the pattern for the hundreds of amateur bands that followed their example, the New Lost City Ramblers offered concerts of old-time music painstakingly reconstructed from rare commercial discs recorded in the 1920s by such bands as Charlie Poole and the North Carolina Ramblers, Gid Tanner and His Skillet Lickers, or J. E. Mainer's Mountaineers, raising the nap of the revival with newly esoteric discographical sources and a performance style almost as exotic as a Tibetan prayer. In addition to their expert musicianship, arcane scholarship, and a demeanor sober enough for the recital hall, the New Lost City Ramblers presented themselves like railroad station-masters or telegraph operators of 1885, in vests, shirtsleeves, and neckties, and posed for an album cover photograph, its surface artificially mottled and cracked, with the blank faces and straight spines familiar in a small-town portrait studio of the last century. Yet they were not above self-parody: clowning with their many instrument-changes on stage, which their own versatility—and accuracy to their sources—demanded, and identifying themselves to nightclub audiences as an "underground" version of the Kingston Trio.[33]

But no career better embodies the folk revival than that of Bob Dylan, whose audacious self-invention sanctioned and consolidated the movement already abroad in youth culture. Dylan was born Robert Zimmerman in 1941 and grew up in working-class, predominantly Catholic, Hibbing, Minnesota, the son of a Jewish hardware merchant. As his biographer Anthony Scaduto points out,[34] Zimmerman was subject to all the influences that marked the period for people his age: films such as *Blackboard Jungle* with its theme song "Rock Around the Clock," a rhythm-and-blues cover by Bill Haley and the Comets; James Dean's *Rebel without a Cause* and *East of Eden;* and the rock-and-roll shouter Little Richard, the first to bring the emotional energy of black gospel singing uncompromisingly into secular music. Zimmerman heard honky-tonk singer Hank Williams on the radio, however, as well as blues singers such as Muddy Waters and Howlin' Wolf broadcast from Little Rock. Listening to them and imitating them, Zimmerman gained a deeper understanding of the roots of rock and roll, perhaps, than suburban youth who first encountered it in Elvis Presley.

It is certain in any case that life on the Mesabi Iron Range, in a community of open-pit miners, differed from life in Great Neck. In order to find acceptance among his schoolmates Zimmerman strove to efface his family background, which was neither working class nor Catholic but mercantile and German-Jewish, and by the time he was sixteen he was riding with the local "greasers" and fronting at the piano a rock-and-roll band modeled on Little Richard's. When in September 1959 he pledged the Jewish fraternity at the University of Minnesota, Zimmerman had abandoned his leather jacket and jeans for the collegiate button-down shirt, chinos, and white bucks of the day; but in a matter of months, having encountered the beatniks and folksingers in Dinkytown, the Minneapolis riverfront bohemia, and having read Woody Guthrie's autobiography, *Bound for Glory,* he had become "Bob Dylan": an orphan raised in Oklahoma, or in Gallup or Sioux Falls; a former pianist for Bobby Vee, or a circus hand, or carnie, or railroad bum, or streetsinger—or so he claimed to anyone who asked—but ultimately the youth in the fleece-lined jacket and corduroy cap who, sizing up his new audience from the cover of his first record album like a suitor who thinks he may be in love, had dared to offer himself, after his pilgrimage to Woody Guthrie's bedside, as the lad upon whom Guthrie's mantle would, and did, fall. Who Bob Dylan was was anybody's guess; but Columbia's high-fidelity microgrooves brought his callow voice, wretchedly overwrought, his stagey Panhandle dialect, his untutored guitar and harmonica—all of his gallant fraudulence—into dormitory rooms with shocking immediacy. And when, in the spoken preface to his shattering "Baby Let Me Follow You Down," he waggishly reported he had learned the song from one "Rick Von Schmidt," a "blues guitar player" from Cambridge, whom he had "met one day in the green pastures of ... ah ... Harvard University," the folk revival knew it had found one of its own.

To the parent generation, a folk revivalist like Dylan could scarcely be distinguished, on the one hand, from the motorcyclists and street gangs of the 1950s whose crypto-fascist style was rooted in postwar social dislocations, or, on the other, from the Beatniks—the jazz-centered urban bohemian subculture that after the war had modeled itself loosely on the life of the Left Bank of Paris, finding in the underground resistance to the official culture of wartime France a metaphor for the conduct of an awakened mind in postwar consumer America. In fact, as Dylan's career illustrates, the folk revivalists *had* adapted, quite early, these styles of youthful dissent, the one belonging to a displaced and disenfranchised class and the other largely to the wealthy, educated, and well-traveled—but not without subtle displacements and sublimations. The aggressive black leather and silver chains of the motorcycle highwayman softened, and became a kind of dry-goods or surplus-store outfit of coarse textures and natural hues, strongly influenced by Clint Eastwood, James Arness, and other "adult" television cowboys—Wellington boots, chamois jackets, work shirts, and wheat jeans—while the motorcycle itself remained: motorcycle accidents, in fact, seriously injured both John Hammond, Jr., a revivalist blues singer, and Bob Dylan; a motorcycle killed singer-songwriter Richard Farina. Much of Beat culture survived in the folk revival, too: the coffeehouse, existentialist philosophy, symbolist poetry, paperback science fiction, and the rest—the world, as one commentator saw it, of "barren lofts, damp cellars, bearded men, candles in bottles, wine, free love, intellectuals, pseudo-intellectuals and total disagreement with the Dale Carnegie system."[35]

But while jazz, as Alan Lomax put it, had "wandered into the harmonic jungles of Schönberg and Stravinsky,"[36] a search for the primitive *origins* of jazz, begun years earlier by anthropologists and musicologists, had made a niche in bohemian culture for folk music to enter and displace it. Jazz impresario John Hammond, father of the aforementioned revivalist, for many years a champion of racial integration in the music, discoverer of Billie Holliday, Count Basie, and Charlie Christian among others, had brought the North Carolina blues harmonica player Sonny Terry and the Arkansas country blues singer Big Bill Broonzy to New York in 1938 for his historic "Spirituals to Swing" concert at Carnegie Hall; in 1962 this same man convinced skeptical Columbia executives to sign Bob Dylan, whose first album Hammond produced.[37]

The triumph of Bob Dylan's first album was a triumph for all. Playing the desperado, the tramp, the poet, peasant, earth mother, or May Queen had been nursed and protected on the college campus and sanctioned by the broad complicity of one's peers; now it was conspicuously ratified by the commercial establishment. Play had become an instrument for shaping reality and hence a means of laying claim to the social and historical initiative. This was the contribution of the folk revival to the 1960s' counterculture, which, with its social coherence and consistency, its relative freedom from social and economic constraints, and of course its youthfulness—this above all—acquired an enchanted, primitive, tribal quality that carnivalized the existing world with roles rooted in the imaginative life, which, like all things imaginative, urged their own actualization.

The folk revival, then, historically speaking, is really a moment of transformation in which an unprecedented convergence of postwar economic and demographic forces carried a culture of personal rebellion, with its expressive forms, including rock-and-roll music, certain dances, sartorial and kinesic styles, forms of association, and the like, across normally impermeable social and cultural barriers under the influence and authority of folk music, with its connections to southern folk culture on the one hand and its association with various esoteric and learned folksong movements on the other already imbued with a spirit of social or political protest. This passage across social lines, again, transformed this culture of personal rebellion, endowing it with new expressive forms, the forms of the folk revival, and with a legitimacy at once wonderful and terrible—terrible because the massively politicizing issue of the Vietnam War, beginning in 1965, would swell it to a tidal wave of resistance and protest that swept over the cultural landscape, leaving behind deep divisions of race, class, sex, and other social and economic conditions.

On the sources of that culture of rebellion one can only speculate. Angry, inarticulate, sullen, largely Anglo-American, it seems to have begun in the South, among the urban poor, though it trespassed regional boundaries swiftly and with impunity, following the wartime migrations of workers to the North and West. Was it, perhaps, rooted in the subversion of the economically fragile post-Depression household by a war that drew young fathers into the military service and young mothers into the defense plant? Or is it something much older, a cultural relic of the Civil War and particularly of Reconstruction, in which a feudal and agrarian order based in slavery fell to a democratic and industrial society with its subtler forms of servitude founded in mechanization?

Its first visible stirrings after World War II, in any case, seem to be in the early 1950s when Hollywood idols such as Marlon Brando and James Dean made heroes of the teenagers hanging around the soda fountain and cruising the streets on motorcycles, the brooding sons and daughters who could neither understand nor were understood by their parents. In 1954, the year both films were released, Brando's roles wedded the identity of Elia Kazan's moody, inarticulate working-class hero Terry Malloy of *On the Waterfront* to the implacable motorcycle outlaw of *The Wild One*, forging the public persona with which Brando made his reputation. But James Dean—restless but not warlike, diffident but not defiant, isolated but capable of love, with more than a trace of Steinbeck's Tom Joad in him—was, perhaps, the transitional figure: his *Rebel without a Cause,* released in 1955 and shortly followed by *East of Eden,* was directed by Nicholas Ray, a folksong enthusiast who was closely associated as a radio producer in the 1940s with the left-wing folksong movement in New York, and who perhaps detected in, or contributed to, the film's theme of a young man's personal rebellion the messianic glow of New Deal populism.[38]

This subtle drift of the moral center of gravity—from Brando to Dean, Zimmerman to Dylan, bandit to balladeer—reflects, I think, a deeper shift in the strata of our postwar cultural life. The Hell's Angel aboard his motorcycle has declared war on authority by mounting a parody of its presiding symbol, the motorcycle cop. But he recalls, and perhaps lineally descends from the war-bereft Rebel without a cause, who like Tom Dula will not "conform to rules," and, still earlier, from the Ringtail Roarer, the fiercely independent Scots-Irish frontiersman of Old Kentucky, who partakes of early America's persistent and contentious repudiation of privilege: his identity is formed from resistance. But the sandy-haired, solitary son of the California grower that we saw in *East of Eden,* abandoned by his mother and unable to please his father, descends from the egalitarian West, with its family-bound and community-building immigrant pioneers from central and northern Europe; James Dean, in fact, had lost his own mother as a boy, and afterward he was raised on an Iowa farm. One is wild, and will not be contained in representations—he becomes James Fenimore Cooper's noble savage, minstrelsy's buffoon, the magazine writer's caricature, Hollywood's rustler, outlaw, or misfit; the other abides with the possible in Willa Cather and John Steinbeck. One is parochial, born out of regional America, at once hallowed and despised, always the rebel, always the outsider; the other is popular, the image of a youth in search of the human ties that tell him who he is. It is a westward migration of the spirit, betokening what such movement always has meant in America, a retreat from a society corrupted by entrenched cultural, social, and economic power toward a vision of social harmony, cultural independence, and personal fulfillment.

Reflecting on the popularity of the Kingston Trio's "Tom Dooley," Dave Guard recalls that the title of the song coincidentally resonated with the name of a then-famous Navy doctor, Dr. Tom Dooley, who had left the military to build hospitals in northern Laos. This is fitting, for Dooley's moral awakening, and his sense of mission, recalls the hundreds of young Peace Corps volunteers who followed the good doctor into the jungles of Southeast Asia a few years later, a great proportion of them with guitars and banjos on their backs, as well as the many who would not go as soldiers. Dooley in fact exemplifies the fundamental shift in consciousness that lies at the heart of the folk revival. Like the utopian or internal missionary movements, social and artistic programs, religious revivals and political crusades before it, the revival made the romantic claim of folk culture—oral, immediate, traditional, idiomatic, communal, a culture of characters, of rights, obligations, and beliefs, against a centrist, specialist, impersonal technocratic culture, a culture of types, functions, jobs, and goals.

Folksong, shaped over time by the life of a people, sends out its influences to shape life anew. Well after the commercial popularity of folksong had faded, many diehard revivalists, becoming now parents and householders, endeavored, after the cataclysms of the 1960s, to create a life that might somehow reverberate morally to folk music: a life radically less reliant upon money and the accumulation of it; a life of participatory, not vicarious, recreation, with a recognition of the importance of small community to such enjoyment; a life, above all, that in the personal and domestic realms reflected an awareness of our involvement in the global ecological, economic, and political order. Chickens and goats, cottage crafts, organic gardening, home canning and preserving, wood heating, natural foods, natural fibers, natural childbirth—though inflation undercut most of these experiments, or sent them along commercial routes into exurbia to occupy the weekends of the rich—were the late contributions to American life by young adults for whom folk music had become, in Raymond Williams's phrase, "the site of resistance to the centralization of power."[39] Some, like conservatory-trained Andy Cahan, who left Oberlin for Low Gap, North Carolina, in order to apprentice himself to the great old-time fiddler and banjo player Tommy Jarrell, adopted not only the music of their mentors but their way of life—it having at last been understood that only from a way of life can folk music, or any music, genuinely proceed.

Through the folk revival the broad typology of the American character, and with it the principle of cultural democracy, long established in literature, journalism, theater, film, and elsewhere—what Walt Whitman called the "democratic identity" and Kenneth Rexroth "the old free America"—sought a new apotheosis on the social landscape. The "old free America" was of course an artifact too, of the poetic imagination—but one without which we have only a winter of naked "society" to live in. It had emerged on the minstrel stage and in regionalist journalism and literature, in tent shows, vaudeville, and Hollywood film, out of the traffic in human encounter that transpires across the intricate network of America's social boundaries, particularly those that lie between urban and provincial cultures. During the 1930s, in the great documentary project of the New Deal, the "old free America" proliferated in guidebooks and photographs, in field recordings of folksong and oral history, in theater, dance, painting, and in the *Index of American Design*. All of these strove not only to document the scenes, the faces, the music and art of the American people, but to embody them in cultural heroes such as Abraham Lincoln, to whose mythology Carl Sandburg devoted over ten years of his life, or in Woody Guthrie, the "dustbowl balladeer" whose influence, through his companions and friends such as Pete Seeger, as well as through his many conscious and unconscious imitators, spread to hundreds of young people in schools, colleges, and summer camps throughout the 1950s. Even after his disappearance from Washington Square hootenannies, where he had lingered long after Huntington's chorea had begun its grim encroachment, the unkempt figure of Woody Guthrie survived to shape the personae of numberless young balladeers, including, of course, Bob Dylan, who in his touching "Song to Woody" placed him among the folk heroes who had "come with the dust and are gone with the wind."

The supreme moment in this national seance, in which the summons of folksong to the cultural dead populated the stage with a reunited family of heroes and heroines of the past, occurred at the closing concert of the Newport Folk Festival of 1963. Pete Seeger, Bob Dylan, Joan Baez, and the popular trio Peter, Paul, and Mary linked arms with the Student Nonviolent Coordinating Committee's Freedom Singers to sing an old Baptist hymn, anthem of the civil rights movement, "We Shall Overcome," and a parable of apocalypse, Bob Dylan's "Blowin' in the Wind"—litanies of the revival's dream of freedom, brotherhood, and peace. It was a moment in which, like a celestial syzygy, many independent forces of tradition and culture, wandering at large in time, some of them in historical deep space and others only transient displays in the contemporary cultural atmosphere, briefly converged to reveal, though inscrutably, the truth of our national life. Peter, Paul, and Mary, for example, who looked like seminarians and bore New Testament names, might have flourished on the Christian Missionary Youth circuit, though their music was thoroughly ecumenical. At a deeper level, the Dustbowl Balladeer, Woody Guthrie, was of course present in spirit, as was John Chapman, the roving Swedenborgian called Johnny Appleseed to whom Pete Seeger had aptly compared himself. But so were the Fisk Jubilee Singers of the 1870s, and the Almanacs, labor songsters of the 1940s, after whom the Freedom Singers, at Seeger's suggestion, had modeled themselves; Tom Joad and James Dean were present in spirit, as was a dark Pocahontas with a Spanish name in the guise of a demure convent-school girl singing an Elizabethan ballad and dreaming of its hero, a dashing Gypsy Laddie-o. Perhaps Holden Caufield, from Pencey Prep, was in attendance, too: not out of Salinger's novel, but in its unwritten sequel that Bob Dylan, who once dreamed of playing Holden in a movie,[40] was enacting in his own life.

Others, less palpable, perhaps, lingered around the group–a Calvinist, Yankee man of the cloth; a plantation slave; a Jehovah's Witness; a black-face minstrel with a banjo; and a yeshiva boy—all of them held together with the vast chorus of the audience whose fifteen thousand voices ascended into the summer night while "thousands of fans milled in the darkened streets outside, listening to the music drift over the stone walls of the arena."[41] They were telling their own story; and for the space of a few years, innocent of the last world war and united against the next, largely free of ideology, still protected from the realities of money, privilege, and power in which they were already unconsciously swept up, they let it flow from their own voices, and their own hands, into the lives they had yet to live.

NOTES

"When We Were Good: Class and Culture in the Folk Revival" is based on an earlier essay by Robert Cantwell, "When We Were Good: The Folk Revival," in *Folk Roots, New Roots: Folklore in American Life,* ed. Jane S. Becker and Barbara Franco (Lexington, Mass.: Museum of Our National Heritage, 1988), pp. 176–93. Used with permission of the Museum of Our National Heritage, Lexington, Massachusetts.

1. Warner, *Traditional American Folksongs,* p. 290.

2. Ibid., pp. 251–61.

3. Ibid., p. 35. Warner's recording of "Tom Dooley" appeared on a 10" album called *Frank Warner Sings American Folksongs and Ballads.*

4. Ibid., p. 9.

5. Ibid., p. xii.

6. Ibid., p. 29.

7. John A. and Alan Lomax, eds., *Folk Song U.S.A.,* p. 285.

8. Author's interview with Joe Hickerson, 31 March 1988. The Folksay Trio's rendition appeared on the 10" album *Folksay: Volume II.*

9. Best and Best, *New Song Fest,* p. i. For the information that "Tom Dooley" was in oral circulation on the West Coast in the 1950s, and for other helpful suggestions whose fruits are scattered about the text of this essay, I am indebted to the editor of this volume, Neil Rosenberg.

10. Author's interview with Dave Guard, 1 September 1989.

11. Author's interview with Dave Guard, 15 June 1989. The Weavers' 1950 recording of "Goodnight, Irene" with the Gordon Jenkins Orchestra was issued on Decca 27077.

12. Brand, *The Ballad Mongers,* p. 140.

13. See Wolfe, *Tennessee Strings,* pp. 46–47. The terrific success of the Kingston Trio's "Tom Dooley" eventually provoked a lawsuit involving Ludlow Music,

which held Lomax's and Warner's rights to the song, and Capitol Records; its outcome was an equal division of royalties on the song after 1962, well after its popularity had peaked. See Coon, "Some Problems with Musical Public-Domain Materials," pp. 189ff. Coon observes that John A. Lomax, while director of the Archive of Folk Song at the Library of Congress, had coincidentally collected a version of "Tom Dula" in North Carolina in 1936, and that the Music Division's *Check List of Recorded Songs* includes three additional versions collected by others as early as 1935. Thanks to Neil Rosenberg for the reference.

14. See Wolfe, *Tennessee Strings*. The account of Rinzler's visit to North Carolina is a summary of his own, from an interview with the author on 19 January 1986.

15. *Doc Watson*, Vanguard 9152.

16. Author's interview with Joe Hickerson, 31 March 1988.

17. Warner, *Traditional American Folksongs*, p. 290.

18. Author's interview with Dave Guard, 15 June 1989.

19. Author's interview with Dave Guard, 1 September 1989.

20. Botkin, "Notes."

21. Brand, *The Ballad Mongers*, p. 84.

22. Alan Lomax, "The 'Folkniks.'" Israel Young, of the Folklore Center in Greenwich Village, claims to have coined this term; see Montgomery, "The Folk Furor," p. 118. It is, obviously, a Yiddish-inspired back-formation from San Francisco columnist Herb Caen's "beatnik."

23. Nelson, "Newport," p. 53.

24. Sandburg, *American Songbag*, p. ix.

25. Quoted in Montgomery, "The Folk Furor," p. 118.

26. Ibid.

27. Ibid., p. 99.

28. Will Brown and Gerry Richmond in Best and Best, *New Song Fest*, p. i.

29. Best and Best, *New Song Fest* (1948), p. 1. The IOCA song was deleted from the 1955 edition.

30. Nelson, "Newport," p. 51.

31. John Cohen, "In Defense of City Folksingers."

32. Montgomery, "The Folk Furor," p. 118.

33. Neil Rosenberg refreshed my memory here.

34. Scaduto, *Bob Dylan*.

35. Sherman, liner notes.

36. Alan Lomax, "Bluegrass Background."

37. See "John Hammond."

38. Klein, *Woody Guthrie*, p. 206.

39. Quoted by Kirshenblatt-Gimblett in "Mistaken Dichotomies," p. 151.

40. See Shelton, *No Direction Home*, p. 147. Thanks to Neil Rosenberg for the reference.

41. Brauner, "A Study of the Newport Folk Festival," pp. 86–87.

The Campus Folksong Club:
A Glimpse at the Past

Archie Green

Memory's camera eye focuses upon past scenes: concert, folksing, workshop, party, jam session, album production, cultural debate. After long commitment to folksong—listening, gathering, presenting—and after time's clouding of vision, I remain exhilarated by the years 1961–70 when a folksong club flourished at the University of Illinois at Urbana-Champaign. Two adventurous students, Vic Lucas and Dick Kanar, conceived the group; I served as faculty adviser. "Tradition" became our talismanic keyword. We used it variously to describe process (a tale handed down traditionally); substance (customary material as in traditions of a people); meliorative norm ("Sarah's more traditional than Joan").

As good words do, "tradition" altered, expanded, and contracted to fill needs. This word made Campus Folksong Club members brave partisans in a noble cause: to bring distant performers to the prairie, to overcome town/gown tension by encouraging local singers to treasure their wares, to wean fellow students away from "Mickey Mouse" sounds to authentic styles. Thirty years have passed since the club's inception. Here, I recall a few events and persons with special attention to guiding templates. This latter term itself translates as gauge, pattern, mold, overlay. Metaphorically, Illinois students used the club as a vibrant template in constructing their 1960s culture.

A personal flashback opens this glimpse at the past. Through the 1950s, I had worked as a shipwright on the San Francisco waterfront and as a carpenter in the "uptown" building trades. During those years, fans seriously interested in blues or old-time music gathered at Jack's Record Cellar. Norman Pierce, a retired longshoreman, presided at Jack's (really Norm's shop in the Fillmore District). There, I met Bob Pinson and Fred

Hoeptner, together immersed in western swing music and cowboy lore. Bob hailed from Wichita Falls, Texas, and worked in a San Jose lithography plant. Fred, a civil engineer, was on Navy duty at Moffett Field. Chris Strachwitz, a Berkeley "GI" student, searched for blues rarities. Peter Tamony, a local etymologist, purchased race records as tools in dialect studies. Ralph Gleason, the San Francisco *Chronicle* jazz critic, used the Cellar to anticipate musical trends. Pierce encouraged me to correspond with Joe Nicholas in Palmer, Michigan, who edited *Disc Collector,* and with Gene Earle, a space engineer and discographer, in far-off Cape Canaveral.

I mention few of the Cellar's crew. In the early 1950s, we could but dimly anticipate the contour of the coming "folksong revival." In time, we all made contributions: Peter penned etymologies of "jazz" and "hootenanny." Gene became president of the John Edwards Memorial Foundation. Chris now heads Arhoolie Records. Bob leads the study team at Nashville's Country Music Foundation. However, at Jack's, we saw our roles mainly as collectors of 78 rpm discs, and, secondarily, as oracles of vernacular music.

By 1954, I had undertaken a coal-mining song discography holding formal lists as well as explanatory case studies. Delving into particular ballad histories required finding rare records, extensive reading in language and literature, piecing together disparate texts and tunes. About the time that my case study on Gene Autry's "Death of Mother Jones" shaped itself in mind, I also heard a mournful narrative by the Blue Sky Boys, "In the Hills of Roane County." Convicts who dug coal at Tennessee's Brushy Mountain State Prison knew this song. Did it belong in a coal discography, or did its themes of murder and penance place it in a category beyond my special concerns?

Today, with a wide range of fine country-music books at hand, readers cannot comprehend a previous period that did not have reference volumes treating such music. Literally, during the 1950s, one did not locate in academic libraries data on Gene Autry or the Blue Sky Boys. In time, I corresponded with Autry on the Mother Jones song. Also, on a trip to Greensboro, North Carolina, I met Bill and Earl Bolick, the Blue Sky Boys. Fortunately, I was far from alone in searching for pioneer recording artists and traditional exemplars. Actually, the individuals who dropped into Jack's Record Cellar represented similar collectors across the land. Serendipity and letter writing gradually brought us together, coast to coast.

Throughout the 1960s, from Cambridge to Berkeley, the New Lost City Ramblers interpreted mountain songs and inspired students to undertake collection and performance. Mike Seeger valued old-time styles, vocal and instrumental. Ralph Rinzler spoke for authenticity at the influential Newport Folk Festival. David Freeman and Chris Strachwitz reissued classic 78 rpm discs on LP albums. Ed Kahn interviewed Sarah, Maybelle, and A. P. Carter for a UCLA dissertation on the Carter Family. D. K. Wilgus pointed academic folklorists to hillbilly idioms. Norm Cohen nurtured the *JEMF Quarterly*. This handful of fans and teachers (as well as others named elsewhere) championed southern, rural-based, Anglo- and African-American music.

Circumstances in 1960 led me away from San Francisco to Urbana, where I served as librarian of the Institute of Labor and Industrial Relations, University of Illinois. Literally two UI students, Vic Lukas and Dick Kanar, tracked me down after having attended the first University of Chicago Folk Festival in February 1961. There, they had heard me comment on the college folk scene, and they wondered why downstate Illinois students should be left behind peers in Hyde Park. At that time, the UI faculty offered but a solitary course in folk literature—nothing in ethnomusicology or anthropology. The university's Star Course imported big-name talent indifferent or hostile to folk style. A Folk Arts Society at the friendly Unitarian Church featured folk dancing and citified "hoots." In this bleak campuswide setting, Vic and Dick appeared as crusading knights championing deep tradition. Nominally, they built a club; in reality, they helped pull a staid Big Ten school into the turbulent 1960s.

Because of student origin, the Campus Folksong Club remained unattached to any academic department. Nor did it draw strength from recognized power blocks, right or left, in student government. Such freedom challenged members to innovate with structure and technique. Biweekly Friday-night folksings—free, open, casual—attracted townspeople, university employees, and students in great numbers.

Two members from the community represented the many who performed at folksings and joined the club. Lyle Mayfield, a journeyman printer on the campus newspaper, and John Hartford, a disc jockey at nearby Clinton station WHOW, symbolized key areas of appeal to the club's core membership. Students left the club as they graduated. Eventually, Lyle returned to printing work at his downstate home. John found his way to Nashville, song composition, and his own role in trumpeting old-time music.

Folksing planners favored "pure" representation of traditional material but exercised no censorship over those who burlesqued or sanitized folksong. One night, a fraternity duo coupled a saccharine "Johnny, I Hardly Knew You" with a Chad Mitchell–flavored "Lizzie Borden." Club partisans felt that they had been dragged to the precipice of vulgarity, but they tempered outrage in the knowledge that "obnoxious" Fijis (Phi Gamma Delta members) courageously offered then-current majority views of folksong. Although our club grew to more than five hundred members, sober leaders know that they formed but a tiny enclave within a huge campus geared to elite and popular culture.

The heady days of the "folksong revival" have long vanished, yet I am confident that all the club activists—as they planned folksings—learned something of the then-new formulation "politics of culture." Engaging in dialogue over political force and cultural ambience energized members. Clearly, I do not refer to the "sandbox politics" in the Illini Union, nor to Greek/Barbarian rivalry. Rather, I note the then-new club's search for space—physical stages for folksings, conceptual room for neglected sounds.

On campus, we found it relatively easy to secure small auditoriums, to issue flyers and posters, to write publicity releases, and to arrange for custodial help after the sings. (I firmly believe that the entire campus janitorial force loved our music.) It proved difficult to convince campus police that we could maintain order at events. Several heated disputes with deans took place before we persuaded the administration to remove armed police from our casual folksings. In such dealings with authority, I saw myself as an adviser/advocate of those students then feeling their way into positions of personal autonomy and cultural pluralism.

Club members produced three fine LPs: a) *The Philo Glee & Mandolin Society* (Doyle Moore, Jim Hockenhull, Paul Adkins—a student-staff trio favoring Appalachian music); b) *Green Fields of Illinois* (downstate traditional performers); c) *The Hell-Bound Train* (Glenn Ohrlin, a working cowboy, in his first LP). Doyle Moore, autoharpist and graphic-arts professor, designed eye-catching jacket covers for the albums. Reviewers praised these club efforts; album copies can be found in major sound archives.

On 7 April 1961, the club introduced its mimeographed newsletter, *Autoharp*. Running for thirty-three issues through 1968, it has become a documentary source for "revival" concerns. Each issue held some artwork; we solicited no ads. Over the years, nearly a hundred members contributed articles, reviews, discographies, drawings, and news reports. No facile way exists to list all contributors or to credit their verve. I isolate a representative handful: Dick Adams—a detailed report on LP production, "Our First Record: CFC 101" (issue 11); Ronald Foreman—a sophisticated set of disc reviews, "Blues A to Z" (beginning issue 16); Kandee Trefil—a polemical challenge, "Ethnics vs Folkniks" (issue 12); Jont Allen—a tablature of C-scale notes, "An Interesting Approach to Advanced Guitar Playing" (issue 22); Fritz Plous—a visit with Chicagoan Kevin Henry, uillean piper and structural ironworker, "The Irish Again" (issue 29).

Throughout the 1960s, the club scheduled many seminars and lectures by distinguished scholars: among others—MacEdward Leach, Francis

Utley, Wayland Hand, Bruno Nettl, D. K. Wilgus, Roger Abrahams, Ellen Stekert, Harry Oster, Américo Paredes. Mayne Smith, then a graduate student at Indiana University, presented his early findings on bluegrass music to an attentive club audience. In such programs, we filled an academic vacuum and, more important, introduced students from science, commerce, or engineering to humanistic discourse.

The activity best remembered by club alumni remains our series of CFC concerts. I recall: Dock Boggs, Sarah Gunning, Sonny Terry, the Blue Sky Boys, Buell Kazee, Emmanuel Dunn, Almeda Riddle, Flatt and Scruggs, Doc Watson, Clayton McMichen, Muddy Waters, Robert Pete Williams, Big Joe Williams, Johnny Shines, Bukka White, the Balfa Brothers, the Stoneman Family, Lloyd and Cathy Reynolds, Lyle and Doris Mayfield, Stelle Elam, John White, Hobart Smith, A. L. Lloyd, Seamus Ennis, Kevin Henry, Elizabeth Stewart, Mike Seeger, Norman Kennedy, Jack Elliott, Frank Proffitt, Jimmie Tarleton, Glenn Ohrlin, Heddy West, Jimmy Driftwood, Robert Johnson, Sleepy John Estes, Curtis Jones, Jean Redpath, the Holy Zioneers, the Cook County Singing Convention.

A few of these performers live in "revival" annals; most remain obscure. Many are now dead. Our Robert Johnson was not the great Delta bluesman of the same name. I can only speculate as to whether a historian will ever trace the stories of the many campus guests who introduced college students, coast to coast, to folksong.

I mean no dishonor to artists not cited above, for I am unaware of any full compilation of all the club's concert guests. Thus, I pause to pay tribute to the students who honed tastes, sought artists, raised funds, arranged travel, and managed the countless mechanical details in concert presentation, semester after semester. Essentially, our list comments upon the "folksong revival's" geography. We ranged through the Ozarks, the Mississippi Delta, and Appalachia, reaching across the Pacific to India and across the Atlantic to England, Scotland, and Ireland.

Professor Américo Paredes, from Austin, Texas, brought Mexican border corridos as well as a formal lecture. In linked evenings, he introduced us to ballad hero Gregorio Cortez and his era. Paredes revealed the world of folksong beyond English-language bounds. Rangaramanujan Ayyangar, a South India veena player and editor of the six-volume Tamil anthology, *Kriti Mani Malai,* brought to the surface some of the thorny problems in our growth. As a Brahmin and classicist, he resented performing under a folksong banner, for he saw "the folk" as the province of lowly fishermen and streetsweepers. Within the audience, we had to learn that not all "ethnic" or "foreign" artists fell comfortably into American "folk" bins.

Although this essay appears in an anthology on the "folksong revival," I must confess that in my years at Illinois, I remained uncomfortable with the "revival" rubric. Yet, at that time, no better name emerged to encompass a cultural explosion, sales boom, and expansion in consciousness about expressive matters. Reaching from coffeehouse to fiddlers' convention, lecture hall to sound studio, activists had established a leisure-market "folk" circuit. Participants sought tags to describe their new cosmos: "folk scene," "cult," "movement," "revival." I tried a circular metaphor—a wheel with spokes; each spoke functioned as a venue: mart, circus, carnival, rodeo, bazaar, little theater, county fair, craft show. Domestic and ethnic performers stood at this wheel's hub; Bob Dylan and Joan Baez dazzled at the rim; the radiating spokes bound center to periphery.

No lone symbol, no beacon light, then, fits all "revival" components. Sarah Gunning and Glenn Ohrlin came to Urbana from tightly structured regional and occupational communities. Sarah sang of her Kentucky coal-camp home; Glenn personified western cowboys. This pair lived at folksong's hub. By contrast, countless fraternity/sorority groups came together briefly—emulating the Kingston Trio, and other stars. And how do we now locate the children of urban intellectuals and professional radicals who learned their parents' songs—protests stemming from Weavers' concerts? Those of us active in the Campus Folksong Club did not wish to surrender the term "folksinger" to "revival" grandchildren.

Normally, words rush into vacuums to fit social configurations. In the 1960s, we lacked precise language to denominate total absorption in folksong. We needed light, but no linguistic comet lit the sky. While attending to myriad club details, I toyed with a term that might combine "survival," "revival," and "arrival." Awkward coinages, like "rasboom" or "sarcene" seemed useless. We knew then of interconnections: singers within enclaved societies do retain material; lore *survives*. At times, folk artists do *revive* elements of their own culture. Other cultural material moves (*arrives*) from special group to large society, or, reversing direction, travels from national center to folk margins.

Many concert guests at Illinois offered song examples, musical techniques, and a moral worldview that combined survival, revival, and arrival processes. To illustrate: in March 1989, Rounder Records issued an album (LP disc, cassette tape, CD disc) of a Blue Sky Boys concert at the University of Illinois's Lincoln Hall on 17 October 1964. The album ably displays the Bolicks' own nomenclature and sources: true songs, old ballads, tragic stories, or favorite tunes learned from parents, neighbors, songbooks, and phonograph records. (I leave to others the matter of reviewing this quarter-century-old evening.) At this juncture, I stress the beliefs that prompted us to invite concert guests to Illinois.

In our eyes, most of the performers coming to Urbana represented authentic cultural experience. Further, we asserted that citizens in folk societies held rights to their own material superior to the claims of out-siders, interpreters, and merchandisers. Beyond the matter of rights, as traditionalists cleaved to deep styles they helped ward off large society's hegemonic thrust. Agents of change in the United States, a transcontinental and multicultural giant, had been granted state privilege. Ultimately, this privilege became a license to drive underground time-tested themes and styles. No matter how abstract or contentious these beliefs seem in ret-rospect, we discussed their substance in the 1960s. Of course, such in-tractable matters continue to this day to concern arbiters of national taste and critics of public policy.

In a total history of the American "folksong revival," our club might occupy but a few paragraphs. However, students who grouped together to foster authentic performance gave themselves fully to the club. It seemed, then, that we filled volumes of history each year. Truly, we lived in the eye of a cultural storm. Today, I marvel that any of the club's stalwarts graduated. When did they put their banjos and guitars aside to study? What gave them the confidence to issue a newsletter, edit LPs, tape concerts, plan guitar- and banjo-playing workshops, engage the adminis-tration in dialogue over onerous rules, and educate themselves in the nu-ances of folkloric conceptualization?

Coming to Illinois from San Francisco, I adjusted slowly to the prairie landscape. I longed for Twin Peaks and Telegraph Hill; I missed the waterfront's loading docks and boatyards. Curiously, the Campus Folksong Club formed a near–self-contained community with its own hills and dales, tasks and rewards. A few students exhibited gauche behavior. Caught be-tween libertarian respect for their choices and a felt need to help them build a club by accepting some university demands, I debated, cajoled, and exampled. Even with the passage of decades, I remember painful attention to rules—a bulletin-board poster could not exceed 8 1/2″ x 11″ in size; a folksing announcement had to be submitted a week in advance of printing the campus calendar. These rules are etched in memory.

Essentially, I taught students to work shoulder-to-shoulder in common cause, urging them to articulate and act upon their esthetic preferences. For example, several members "discovered" Red Cravens and the Bray Brothers playing in local Champaign-Urbana watering holes. The club presented these dynamic bluegrassers in our very first concert, 26 May 1961. Students felt rewarded that they had handled this opening event on a do-it-yourself basis. Similarly, they found fiddlers at the local Greyhound station, and diverted or kidnapped them to our folksings. Members re-viewed concerts and records for the campus newspaper, the *Daily Illini.* (To this day, when I see Chicago film critic Roger Ebert on television, I hark back to his CFC apprenticeship.)

Club members held stapling parties to assemble *Autoharp*'s mimeo-graphed pages. Students assisted Louanne and Archie in regular receptions and late-night fetes before and after concerts. We held no monopoly on hard work and good times at Illinois; we knew that similar groups thrived elsewhere. Traditionalists traveled from Atlantic to Pacific, exchanging gossip with guitar licks. Illinois students rejoiced that they had built a "far-out" club on a "straight" campus, that they had conjured a rainbow over one multiversity.

I have already suggested that we invested the word *tradition* with diverse meanings—signpost, passport, template. How will anyone in coming years make any sense of the "folksong revival" without viewing the governing paradigms of Illinois students, and their cohorts in other schools? In ret-rospect, the Campus Folksong Club functioned as a decade-long seminar in definition: folk, lore, song, ballad, text, tune, texture, style, code, com-munity, survival, arrival, revival, authentic, ethnic, tradition.

To this day, old verbal figures shaped at Illinois resonate in mind. I saw "folksong revival" as an unstable semantic combination, knowing that Americans had long been ambivalent about actual religious revivals. We associate one kind of a revivalist positively as a lifeguard—tanned, keen-eyed, alert—who pulls drowning survivors from the water. Metaphorically, preachers at early camp-meeting revivals threw out lifelines to pull lost souls to safety. We applaud vivifying acts, curative skills, and redemptive powers. However, we know, sadly, that camp-meeting participants faced temptations of backsliding. Satan did compete at revivals by staging pas-sionate attacks on believers.

Although most Illinois club members did not study theology, nor follow arcane camp-meeting history, they did take up religious rhetoric in estab-lishing dichotomies of purity and pollution. We anguished over the roles of Bob Dylan, Joan Baez, the Kingston Trio, the New Christie Minstrels; we sought critical tools to demystify these cult figures. Caught up by "revival" pyrotechnics, we held our little fort with attention to organi-zational responsibilities, as well as to a formula favoring traditional per-formers and faithful interpreters.

Juggling emblems of lifeguard, evangelist, cheerleader, snake-oil sales-man, and superstar, I sought practices mixing group discipline (drawing on former trade-union behavior) with conceptual analysis of folkloric key-words. Sensing the "revival" as a boom (as in oil/land), I called attention to alternate tides of national experience that might serve students in com-prehending their scene.

Fortunately, several of the club activists had come to Urbana with fine record collections and an interest in sound-recording technology. Some-how, they had found their parallels to Jack's Record Cellar. In the summers of 1961–63, I did fieldwork in the South for a paper, "Hillbilly Music: Source and Symbol." Writing in my office, I shared ideas with club members who seemed constantly at the door, if not underfoot. We talked about "lost" pioneer recording personalities, changes in style induced by Nashville and Motown, the commodification of folk culture, the music industry's double-edged swords. Our discussions usually began with specifics—poster design, press release, concert funding. At times, I turned such dialogue from substance to theory, raising questions about the University of Illinois's cultural policy.

A discographical query might elicit an out-of-the-ballpark response. I avoided overt political clichés, but did not neglect the values implicit in sound recordings. I had no wish to radicalize students, for others on campus lived at the barricade's edge. I assumed that students attracted to Old Left dogma, or New Left spirit, would find their way to these causes. Some club members found my politics difficult; others saw little connection between traditional performance and state ideology. My message consisted mainly of calling attention to American diversity and pluralism, as well as to the roles of marginal and enclaved communities within large society.

A speech figure from club discourse illustrates the connections we tried to establish. America's melting-pot image generally connotes stainless, if not red-white-and-blue, steel. This melting-pot symbol ignores foundry and steel-mill slag, industrial waste destined for railroad ballast, and stream pollutant. How does one fit any metaphor into student consciousness? When John Schmidt, the club's sound engineer, recorded Stelle Elam, an elderly fiddler from Brownstown, Illinois, I knew that we had met a quintessential American, a "daughter" of Betsy Ross. Stelle's fiddling is preserved on the club's LP *Green Fields of Illinois,* an ethnographic document. I look back at Stelle and her neighbors, not only as musicians, but also as friends who helped Illinois students address melting-pot questions of stainless steel and slag.

I do not know how best to judge my teaching role in the club. We gave no grades; required no exams. It seemed "natural" to raise "outside" issues in the 1960s. Many students on campus took up matters of discrimination, civil rights, peace, personal freedom. Club members responded to national storms; John Kennedy and Martin Luther King cast large shadows. However, our special stress on traditional folksong restricted the lens through which we viewed the world.

As a shipwright, I had not planned to become a folksong club advisor; in fact, I had never heard this term before reaching Illinois. Hence, I improvised as problems surfaced, or fell back on early positions. Clearly, my interest in commercially recorded vernacular music preceded Illinois years. Similarly, while working on the San Francisco waterfront, I had begun to puzzle the contradictions between populist vistas and folksong's conservative nature. These matters of vernacularity, democratic impulse, and tradition's resilience became planks in the platform from which I addressed club needs.

The platform analogy served well. Students mounted folksing stages in their performance; I used these forums to comment upon American concepts of individualism dating back to John Locke and Thomas Jefferson. In our own era, corporate nabobs and television evangelists could not be trusted as the sole guardians of personal freedom. When appropriate, I talked to club members about the contributions to American polity of abolitionists, Indian-rights champions, nature conservationists, populists, and left-libertarians.

Many students, during the 1960s, seemed better acquainted with Freudian nomenclature than with Jeffersonian language. Club members casually enlisted helpful locutions—ego, repression, sublimation, identity, self-actualization—in acting out their own transformations. Youngsters from comfortable mercantile or professional families donned Huck Finn or Jesse James garb. In drawling voices, they recited boxcar adventures that put Jack Kerouac's continental auto drivers to shame. Students who rejected parental or puritanical notions often asserted that guitars and banjos had become instruments of liberation. The rhetoric of individuality couched as "doing your own thing" and "taking charge of your own life" seemed ever present.

By probing individualism's meaning and by seeking limits, I tried to assist in articulating student values. Some questioned my Wobbly (Industrial Workers of the World) stance, or my falling back on shipwright lore. Some expressed curiosity about New Deal cultural strategies—WPA plays seen, post office murals enjoyed. Did Franklin Roosevelt democratize the arts? Duty, of course, demanded attention to all club members, not to those alone interested in social theory or critical analysis.

During the 1960s, in sessions with club members, I used ideas gleaned from literary and philosophical disciplines. The figure "culture authentic versus culture spurious" appeared frequently. However, I did not usually cite Edward Sapir as this formulation's proponent. Similarly, I did not mention Horace Kallen in dealing with cultural pluralism. When urging students to explicate the texts of their favorite songs, or to transcribe difficult blues, I did not credit Northrop Frye, the Vanderbilt Fugitives, or other new critics. At times, I did use Robert Redfield's name in describing the bounds of face-to-face (folk) societies. Although I respected figures such as John Muir and Rachel Carson, I did not always name them while asserting the need to preserve living cultural forces within walking distance of the campus. Yet, Rachel Carson (as well as exemplars before her) strode figuratively upon the stage at club concerts and sings.

Perhaps this glimpse at the past will be read by a few former club members. Perhaps some will wish to compare notes, to place their response alongside mine. In drawing this camera-eye picture to a close, I must credit four individuals at the University of Illinois who encouraged me in club activity: Martin Wagner, director of the Institute of Labor and Industrial Relations; Robert Downs, librarian, University of Illinois; Cliff DeLong, university bursar; and Dan Perrino, dean of students. These four grasped the club's basic role in enlarging Illini life; they tolerated my intense involvement in an extracurricular happening.

Ultimately, the club's dynamism stemmed from the hundreds of students who paid modest dues and accepted responsibility for horizon-stretching projects. One such project hardly mentioned in "revival" reports touches volunteerism. Club members entertained at local schools, senior centers, churches, and hospitals. It is difficult to convey the admiration I felt for students who "clowned" at folksings and "turned serious" on a quiet visit to perform for shut-ins.

In reporting various club activities, I have already named several of the members in pages above. It would take a separate paper to credit all others. Here, I name those who jump to mind while writing this essay: Bill Becker, Jarvis Rich, Larry Klingman, April Applequist, Rita Merkelis, Bob Sayers, Bill Bush, Page Stephens, Benette Rottman, Preston Martin, Martha Davis, Cathy Corl, Tom Adler, Dave Huehner, John Munday, Marci Sayers, Bruce Hector, Cathy Crowley, John Walsh, Sue Wasserman, Rich Warren, Ardy Broderick, Dave Samuelson, Suzy Levin, Patricia Wilson, Judy McCulloh.

No magic wand can complete the scroll; time does cloud vision. The Campus Folksong Club remained active throughout the 1960s, spanning three student generations. At the inception, a few members had recently returned to school from Korea. I see them visually in Eisenhower jackets. By 1970, some had sailed to Vietnam or marched against the war. In the club's decade, many students switched loyalty from folk to rock music as Sergeant Pepper triumphed over Tom Dooley.

Decline came slowly, not in a single day, but rather, over the span of semesters. A number of creative members turned especially to film making. One of them caught the new mood in a song parody, "I'm Trading My Banjo for a Bolex." Tim Leary, Gene McCarthy, and Jane Fonda beckoned from their respective corners. Not all compass needles point north; students dispersed in many directions.

From time to time, I meet former club members at festival ground, university press, anthropology museum, radio station, or memorial service.

As we pause to reminisce, one calls up a favorite concert, another relives the exact moment of learning a song, still another asks for the location of a lost friend. Our memories tend to be concrete. We dwell on concert, song, friend. Behind this specificity stand templates of tradition so important in helping us into the 1960s, in altering campus patterns, and in transforming our lives.

The Folksong Revival

Bruce Jackson

A folksong revival occurred in America thirty years ago. Like many revivals, it appealed primarily to individuals who celebrated traditions not their own. Blues were popular in the folksong revival, but the audiences were mostly whites; rural songs and performers were popular, but the audiences were mostly urban; labor songs were popular, but the audiences were mostly middle-class students. Many of the traditional performers were in their fifties, sixties, and even their seventies—but the audiences were primarily under twenty-five. Scholars were involved but it was not a scholarly revival. Topical and political songwriters figured prominently, but by and large the audiences were apolitical. Walt Whitman provided a century earlier what is perhaps the best approach to the revival: "Do I contradict myself? I contradict myself then. I contain multitudes."

Many writers and festival fans claimed the revival provided an opportunity for millions of modern Americans to better understand their country's musical roots, as well as an opportunity to honor the musicians who still represented those traditions. Others—often disparagingly referred to as "purists"—were certain the revival and its attendant commercialism would provide the death stroke for whatever fragile rural and ethnic traditions still survived.

In retrospect, the fears seem inordinate and the anxieties misplaced. On the whole, the movement was benign. I think the revival can be fairly characterized as romantic, naive, nostalgic, and idealistic; it was also, in small part, venal, opportunistic, and colonialistic. I do not include in the revival most ethnic or regional folklore celebrations or performances that went on within the communities of regions that were the source of the materials. It is not, in my view, a revival when a group of Arkansas musicians in Arkansas sings Arkansas songs for fellow Arkansans—not unless these songs are self-consciously learned in order to put on such a performance. On the other hand, middle-class Italians in Buffalo, New York, using federal funds to hire Italian traditional singers from Philadelphia, Pennsylvania, to put on concerts for them, as happened recently, *are* part of the revival. The same performer might have at once been both inside and outside the revival. Instrumentalist and ballad singer Hobart Smith participated in the Newport and other large folk festivals; he also sang with his family and friends in Saltville, Virginia. Blues performer Big Bill Broonzy performed for white students at the University of Chicago Folksong Club and, often on the same weekend, performed for blacks in ethnic southside Chicago bars. When he performed in the black clubs, he used an amplified guitar, but he used an acoustic guitar for the white university audiences because they let him know they thought the acoustic guitar more "folksy."

The complex of events called the Folksong Revival probably dates from 1958 and 1959. Like most social movements, the beginning boundary is soft and slightly arbitrary. The Weavers, an influential urban eclectic folksinging group, had hit records as early as 1950 and 1951, and even after they were blacklisted for being too far on the political left they continued for a while to perform on campuses. Their records were widely shared by folk music enthusiasts long after those records became unavailable in stores. But the great expansion in folksong activity happened toward the end of the decade.

Although university students and some faculty members were central to the revival, the revival had little direct impact on university teaching or research in the 1950s and 1960s. Many students, for example, who entered the Indiana University folklore Ph.D. program in those years (it was the only Ph.D. program in folklore in America at the time) were drawn to the field by their interest in folksinging, but that aspect of their lives was kept totally separate from their formal studies. Richard Dorson, who directed the program, was uninterested in music in general and he loathed in particular nonacademic popularization of folklore.[1] Nothing that went on in the folklore program gives any indication of the revival involvement by Bruce Buckley, Joe Hickerson, Neil Rosenberg, Ellen Stekert, Edward D. Ives, and many others.[2] Typical of such student singers was Roger D. Abrahams, who did his graduate work at the University of Pennsylvania: "... I began to study the background of the songs which I was singing (this leading to a study of folklore in general). ..."[3] Some faculty members at other universities took part in some of the folk festivals—University of California professors D. K. Wilgus, Bertrand Bronson, and Charles Seeger were all involved in the 1958 Berkeley Folk Festival—but so far as I know that enterprise was totally separate from any of their classes. It was like a mildly embarrassing hobby one tolerates in a friend who is otherwise virtuous.

Three commercial artists of the 1950s helped set the stage for the folk revival: Harry Belafonte (an actor who performed carefully arranged and orchestrated folk songs), the Kingston Trio (a slick group that took their songs completely out of context and sometimes parodied the traditions), and the Weavers. All were enormously popular, especially with white, middle-class audiences.

The folksong magazine *Sing Out!* began publication in 1950, but its circulation remained small for most of the decade. Like the Weavers, it was very much indebted to Pete Seeger's inspiration. In its early years *Sing Out!* was heavily political. It published words and music to traditional songs, but there were also anti-Korean War peace songs, civil rights songs, anti-draft songs, Ethel Rosenberg's death song, and songs from Soviet Bloc countries. Special issues were devoted to Paul Robeson, the Rosenbergs, Pete Seeger, IWW organizer Joe Hill, and the Progressive Party campaign. Toward the end of the decade, *Sing Out!*'s politics became less strident as its editors attempted to reach the large audience developing for folk music and topical songs. This audience seemed more willing to sing about political causes than it was willing to be involved in any of them. The first two issues of *Sing Out!* in 1959 had, in addition to many traditional and topical songs, articles on counter-tenor Richard Dyer-Bennet, commercialism and the folksong revival, folksongs and summer camp, and an article by Alan Lomax on "folkniks" with a reply by John Cohen. The revival had become self-conscious enough to begin looking at itself.

In 1959 and 1960, jazz concert producer George Wein and promoter Albert Grossman put on two commercial folk festivals at Newport, Rhode Island. The concerts featured what Wein and Grossman thought important stars of the revival, but both festivals were financial failures. The two promoters had missed the point: stars weren't enough to attract big audiences in this phase of the revival. Audiences were beginning to demand significant participation by traditional performers. The first University of Chicago Folk Festival, held in 1961, avoided name performers almost entirely in a conscious attempt to avoid the errors of Newport.

It is always, in cultural matters, difficult to separate causes and effects. How do we know if something starts a trend or is instead just an early representative of a trend already in motion? If an artist is spectacularly successful with something apparently new, we should assume that an audience was, for whatever reasons, ready to receive that something new, and that the "something new" fitted a slot or fulfilled a need already there.[4]

The Newport festivals *would* become central to the folksong revival, but not in the commercial form designed by Wein and Grossman and not before the occurrence of a spectacular and sometimes traumatic sequence of political and cultural events.

In 1959, the Cuban dictator Battista fled Havana and was replaced by Fidel Castro, then still a hero in America. In 1960, John F. Kennedy, young, charming, and literate, was elected president. In 1961, the Bay of Pigs fiasco occurred, the Berlin Wall was erected, the idealistic Peace Corps attracted thousands of volunteers, and the cult novels *Catch-22* and *Stranger in a Strange Land* were published and became best-sellers, especially on college campuses. Freedom riders trying to integrate buses in Alabama were attacked by racist mobs. In 1962 the Cuban Missile Crisis brought the world for the first time to the edge of nuclear war. William Faulkner, e. e. cummings, Eleanor Roosevelt, and Marilyn Monroe died. The hit songs were "Days of Wine and Roses," "Go Away Little Girl," and Bob Dylan's "Blowin' in the Wind." James Meredith, a black, was denied admission to the segregated University of Mississippi by Governor Ross Barnett, and U.S. marshals and three thousand soldiers suppressed riots on the campus. In 1963, civil rights leader Martin Luther King was arrested in Birmingham and President Kennedy was obliged to call out three thousand federal troops to restore order. Two hundred thousand people demonstrated against racism in Washington, D.C. *The Spy Who Came in from the Cold*, a novel that delineates the cynical inhumanity of bureaucracies on both sides of the Iron Curtain, was a best-seller. The Guggenheim Museum in New York mounted the first major show of the antiestablishment pop art by Andy Warhol, Robert Rauschenberg, Jasper Johns, and others. *Dr. Strangelove* was one of the year's top movies. By year's end, fifteen thousand American advisers were in Vietnam, Diem and Nhu had been overthrown and murdered in Saigon, and John F. Kennedy had been murdered in Dallas. Lyndon Johnson became president and the American Congress was about to pass the most sweeping welfare and civil rights legislation in the nation's history. The list of most popular singers in America included folk revival performers Joan Baez and Bob Dylan.

And the *new* Newport Folk Festival, which until the establishment of the Smithsonian Folklife Festival four years later, would be the largest and most influential of the revival folk festivals, was born.

Once again, it was Pete Seeger who was instrumental in engineering what happened. Seeger knew about the financial disaster of George Wein's commercial folk festivals of 1959 and 1960. Seeger had the idea of starting over as a nonprofit foundation. Wein, Seeger, and actor/singer Theodore Bikel developed Seeger's idea of a Newport Folk Festival that would be a forum for folk music programmed and directed entirely by performers (they later added one scholar), a festival which was not grounded in profit. If all performers worked for the minimum, Seeger said, there would be enough money to invite more traditional performers than any other festival had so far been able to afford. The big names would draw the crowds which would then be able to hear the traditional musicians. The festival was to be as much an educational as an entertainment event. In addition to the usual large concerts on a center stage, there would be smaller workshops where performers could have more time to perform and audience members could get closer. (The number of workshops steadily increased during the seven years the festival survived. In 1964, no more than three workshops went on simultaneously; the crowds were large and electrical amplification systems were necessary. In 1968, twenty-two workshops went on simultaneously and microphones were banned in order to keep the groups around the performers as small as possible.) Year by year the directors increased the proportion of traditional performers. In 1963, there were around twice as many urban as traditional and ethnic performers; in 1967 and 1968, it was just the other way around.

The largest audience for a single Newport concert was slightly over eighteen thousand people. The largest profit after all expenses was about seventy thousand dollars. The festival used all its profits to sponsor fieldwork, produce regional concerts of folk music, and make grants that would be beneficial to what the directors thought were the revival's roots. Grants were awarded to the John Edwards Memorial Foundation, *Foxfire*, Highlander Research Center, Old Town School of Folk Music, the folklore program at UCLA, cowboy singer Glenn Ohrlin, public radio station WGBH in Boston, and other organizations and individuals. Newport profits paid for a Cajun festival in Louisiana (later credited with directly leading to a regional revival of Cajun music), a Georgia Sea Island Christmas festival, Native American projects in New Mexico and Florida, and music programs for Resurrection City and the Poor People's Campaign. Newport profits bought guitars for blues musicians Skip James, Pearly Brown, and John Hurt, and Ampex tape recorders for the University of Pennsylvania for copying archive tapes.

Newport wasn't the earliest folk festival in the revival and neither was it always the biggest. But it was the best known and it had in abundance the virtues and faults of the revival.

By 1966, the revival was booming. *Sing Out!* doubled its page size and began newsstand sales for the first time. Its circulation reached twenty-five thousand. Other magazines reached wider and wider audiences. Robert Shelton, folk music critic of the *New York Times*, edited *Hootenanny: The National Folk Singing Magazine,* which started publishing in 1964. A nationally broadcast television show, *Hootenanny,* featured many folk performers (but not Seeger and others who were still being blacklisted).

Then political events overwhelmed the revival. By the end of 1967 nearly 500,000 U.S. troops were in Vietnam and even the *Wall Street Journal* was predicting that the war could not be won. Riots erupted in the black ghettoes of Cleveland, Newark, Detroit, and other cities. Antiwar demonstrations were held all over the country. Many of the kids who had formed the audiences for the folk festivals became eligible for the draft as student deferments were lifted. Nineteen sixty-eight brought the Tet Offensive, Eugene McCarthy's astounding near-victory in the New Hampshire primary, Lyndon Johnson's surprise announcement in March that he would not run for reelection, and the murders of Martin Luther King and Robert Kennedy. American troop strength reached 540,000 and there were hundreds of student riots across the country. The top performers were soul-singer Aretha Franklin and acid-rock guitarist Jimi Hendrix. The romantic idealism so much a part of the folk festivals was, I think, inappropriate in the climate of continually escalating violence. For many individuals who had formed a large part of the festival audiences, singing about social and political problems was no longer adequate. The late 1960s and early 1970s were years of increasing political activism.

The 1969 festival was a financial disaster from which the Newport Folk Foundation never recovered. Nor did many of the other large festivals. The big successful festival of 1969 was Woodstock, with well over a *quarter-million* fans jammed into the fields of a New York State farm. Woodstock starred rock groups such as Jefferson Airplane, The Who, Joe Cocker, Crosby Stills Nash and Young, and Jimi Hendrix, and former folk revival performers Canned Heat, Arlo Guthrie, and Joan Baez. The mixture wouldn't happen again: Woodstock was the only large rock festival in which folk revival singers were a major element. With a single exception, all the big music festivals of the seventies were rock festivals. The exception was the Smithsonian Institution's Festival of American Folklife, directed by Ralph Rinzler.

Rinzler, in a far quieter and less public way, is to the federal festival what Seeger was to Newport. Rinzler was a member of an excellent revival group, the Greenbriar Boys, then he worked for Newport as a fieldworker, talent coordinator, and board member. In 1966 and 1967, Newport "lent" him to the Smithsonian to do fieldwork. He traveled the country seeking performers for both festivals. The job at first was temporary, then it became permanent.

The first Smithsonian Festival of American Folklife was in 1967. It was free, it was accessible, it was broadly conceived—and it was a smashing success. The folk festivals of the earlier phase of the revival had appealed primarily to younger people; the Smithsonian festival appealed to people of all ages, and it seems to have been especially attractive to vacationing families. Unlike all the other festivals, the Smithsonian's never had to turn a profit and it never had to find grants; it just had to continue to make political sense to the bureaucrats in the Smithsonian and the congressmen on Capitol Hill. It was the only festival, then, that could afford to ignore the usual marketplace demands, and it therefore became the most traditionally based and responsible of all the large festivals. The Smithsonian Festival of American Folklife could not have developed as it did without the groundwork laid by Newport and the other festivals. It has been able to afford a depth of representation and seriousness of concern none of the others could ever attempt.

The federal government, through the Folk Arts Program of the National Endowment for the Arts, controlled funding for many of the local festivals that went on in the 1970s and 1980s. Folk Arts was established in 1974 with Alan Jabbour as its first director. In 1975, the program awarded about a half-million dollars in grants. That amount doubled the next year. In 1979, Folk Arts gave $1.33 million, in 1980 $2.27 million, in 1981 $3.1 million, and in 1982, a year in which many agencies were suffering the first of the drastic Reagan cuts to the arts, Folk Arts gave away $2.64 million.[5]

Rinzler directed the Smithsonian festivals until 1984. Alan Jabbour became the first director of the American Folklife Center in 1976. Since its third year, the Folk Arts program has been run by Bess Lomax Hawes, the daughter of John A. Lomax and sister of Alan Lomax. All Folk Arts grants are voted on by a panel, but Hawes selects all panel members herself. Federal folklore power, then, has been wielded by a small group of people for more than a decade. (Hawes, by the way, was a participant in the 1963 Newport Folk Festival.)

As federal involvement increased, the folk revival changed form. The large festivals gave way to many more smaller festivals. So far as I can tell most of these are without politics except in the sense that the nostalgia they articulate reflects a kind of romantic conservatism. It is a kind strongly endorsed by the Folk Arts Program of the National Endowment for the Arts, which, as I noted earlier, provides funding for many of them.

I don't think the folksong revival of the 1960s died so much as it became ordinary. Much of the revival was fad or fashion, and it should be no more surprise that the youths went somewhere else than it was when disco came and went or when the recent fad of breakdancing is replaced by something else. The nice thing about the folksong revival is how much of it survived and became part of the general culture, how much of it is still accessible. I doubt that rock music would have developed the way it has were it not for the folksong revival. More folk festivals go on now than ever went on during the 1950s and 1960s, and many of them reflect real sensitivity and sophistication in programming. Many are directed by graduates of folklore Ph.D. programs—men and women who themselves had often been in the audiences of the folk festivals of the 1960s.

One of the best assessments of the revival was written by B. A. Botkin in 1964, well before the popular phase had run its course:

> Every revival contains within itself the seed not only of its own destruction (in our mass entertainment the destruction proceeds from repetition and dullness as much as from catering to the lowest common denominator) but also of the new revivals. Thus, the revival has already gone through British and native American balladry, gospel songs, and jug bands and has started on the blues, minstrel song, and ragtime, and the popular songs of the twenties and thirties. What is being revived, in other words, or rediscovered, is not so much American folk music as the musical past of America, with the young folkniks running ahead of some of the professors who got stuck in the ballads, and behind other professors and scholars (Newman I. White, Robert W. Gordon, and Phillips Barry, for example) who were ahead of many of their colleagues in the diversity of their folksong interests. Any revival that can accomplish this kind of rediscovery has earned its name.[6]

There has been a great deal of journalistic writing about the folksong revival, but very little scholarly attention has been paid to it thus far. It did not fit the academic models of folkloric behavior fashionable in the 1950s, 1960s, and 1970s. Perhaps the revival was too closely linked to popular movements, perhaps it was too close to contemporary political and social events for the taste of American folklorists. One can read every issue of the *Journal of American Folklore* published between 1963 and 1983 and get no idea from them that the United States had for ten years in that period been engaged in a massive land and air war in Asia, so it is hardly surprising that what seemed a transient and popular phenomenon escaped scholarly notice.

Professor Alan Dundes has suggested that the folksong revival, since it consisted of performers and audience members who had little in common with one another outside the festival, wasn't a matter of folklore concern so much as it was an example of *folklorismus*.[7] I disagree. As the Broonzy anecdote I recounted earlier illustrates, the revival, over a period of years, developed aesthetics clear enough to influence performers from tradition. I would suppose that all the performers to some extent modified their presentations to fit their image of the festival context—a musical instance of what linguists call "code switching." The events involved three groups— performers, audience, organizers—but there was continuity in the membership of those groups over a period of years. I doubt that many performers, organizers, or audience members were simple-minded enough to think they were seeing and hearing folk music performed in an original context. But they *were* seeing and hearing folk music performed in a real context, a real community: that of the folk revival. Transitory as it may have been, the folk revival community was as real and as legitimate as any other based on shared interest and knowledge. Performers and audience members learned songs and performance styles from one another; they exchanged narratives about folk music, folk revival music, revival performers, and about the revival itself. If the folklorists' models cannot account for that kind of learning, and for that kind of tradition, the defect is in the model, not in the event.

The social vision of American folklorists is broader now, and it is more catholic, but the moment when direct observation of the revival might have occurred is long past. Folklorists can examine the revival as an historical event, but not, alas, as the vital season it in fact was.

NOTES

These remarks were presented on 26 March 1984 as part of "Culture, Tradition, Identity," a symposium sponsored by the Joint Commission on the Humanities and Social Sciences of the American Council of Learned Societies and the Hungarian Academy of Sciences, held at Indiana University, Bloomington, Indiana, 26–28 March 1984. They were subsequently published as "The Folksong Revival" in *New York Folklore Quarterly* 11 (1985): 195–203. Reprinted with the permission of *New York Folklore* and the New York Folklore Society.

1. According to Roger D. Abrahams, Sandra Dolby-Stahl, and Ralph Rinzler, Dorson's interest in and attitude toward revival folksinging, festivals, and popularization changed significantly near the end of his life. He published a popularizing folklore collection targeted for a general audience (*America in Legend*, 1973), developed a few years after that an interest in the Smithsonian's Festival of Folklife, and he began to enjoy parties where students performed musically.

2. Buckley subsequently became director of the graduate program in folklife at Cooperstown, Hickerson became head of the Archive of Folk Culture in the Library of Congress; Rosenberg, Stekert, and Ives became professors of folklore at Memorial University of Newfoundland, the University of Minnesota, and the University of Maine, respectively.

3. Abrahams, "Folk Songs and the Top 40," p. 12.

4. For an excellent recent study of the relationship between artists, technologies, audiences, and social and political contexts, see Howard S. Becker, *Art Worlds*. For an involved participant's autobiographical observations on the revival, see Brand, *The Ballad Mongers*; DeTurk and Poulin's *The American Folk Scene* contains many contemporary articles about the revival by a wide range of critics and commentators.

5. Bess Hawes told me more funds were available for distribution that year, but they were not given out because she and the evaluation panel didn't find enough worthy projects.

6. Botkin, "The Folksong Revival: Cult or Culture?," p. 98.

7. Dundes's suggestion was made after the oral presentation of this paper at the "Culture, Tradition, Identity" symposium.

Author's Postscript

Neil Rosenberg offered me the opportunity to update "The Folksong Revival" if I thought it needed such updating, but on reflection I've decided to leave it as it was first published: the substance of the piece is historical and I pretty much agree with what I said in Bloomington in March 1984.

I'm delighted to see the piece appearing in its present company. "The Folksong Revival" was meant to be part of a conversation about what I thought a significant aspect of mid-century American cultural history; I never intended it to be a stand-alone statement seeming to put everything into neat boxes. I wrote it at the invitation of Professor Linda Dégh for a conference at Indiana University in 1984. When the conference ended, I asked her if there were any plans to publish the conference proceedings, perhaps in *Journal of Folklore Research*. "No," she said, "we're not going to do anything like that." About that time Phillips Stevens, Jr., asked me to contribute an article for the fortieth anniversary issue of *New York Folklore*, so I sent him a slightly revised version of the talk. A few weeks after Stevens accepted the article for publication I received a letter from the *Journal of Folklore Research* letting me know they planned to include "The Folksong Revival" in a special issue, which would consist of the proceedings of the IU conference. I told them that the manuscript had been accepted by another journal and I didn't think it right to ask for it back. That meant that the article appeared without *NYF* readers having any sense of the context for which it was written, and that the readers of the *JFI* special issue saw transcriptions of my comments in discussions without any sense of the talk that preceded and partially contextualized those comments. Now, nearly a decade later, Neil Rosenberg undoes those old confusions; his introductory notes describe the conference in which the talk was given, and the excellent host of articles he's commissioned and selected provide the kind of context I'd originally wanted.

I should mention that two months after the 1984 Indiana University conference, House Speaker T. P. O'Neill appointed me to a six-year term on the Board of Trustees of the American Folklife Center, so I had a chance to learn a great deal more about the workings of the federal folklore establishment. I developed a great deal of respect for the many individuals who work so hard to continue presenting folklore performances to a public that would not otherwise have access to such art, and I continue to be impressed at how, even with the Byzantine constraints of Washington bureaucracy, dedicated individuals are capable of imposing their unique vision on complex public programs. I'd also note that at the time of this writing Bess Hawes still directs the Folk Arts Program at NEA and Alan Jabbour still directs the American Folklife Center. Ralph Rinzler, in a special emeritus position, continues to use his great expertise to influence folk program policy at the Smithsonian Institution.

Cents and Nonsense in the Urban Folksong Movement: 1930–66

Ellen J. Stekert

Author's Introduction

My initial reaction upon re-reading this essay was, "Did I write *that?*"
Well, I did, and while there is a tone about it that I do not like, there are
major points in it that remain sound. Authors seldom have the opportunity
to explain their past works. It is my hope that what I say here will allow
the reader to situate this essay in both personal and historical time. Writing
this introduction has helped me understand the judgments, the snide tones,
the points that are well taken, and those that are the product of anger,
naiveté, or other factors. Ultimately we are all part of our texts, and given
the chance we could probably explicate ourselves into infinity. I am grateful
for the opportunity to critique my own artifact.

I have written elsewhere about my career as a folklorist.[1] I must now
speak of my career as a folksinger, because it helps to explain my perspective when I wrote this essay. At that time I was an assistant professor
of English, hired by my university as a folklorist. I had been raised in a
middle-class, white suburb of New York City, and with many others of
my generation and background, I took up folksinging. Between 1952 and
1959 I made a number of LP recordings. I had learned to play the guitar
and sing in relative isolation. It was shortly after 1949, and I had just
survived a bout with polio. In those difficult years I spent hours each day
with my brother's abandoned guitar poring over a gift from my father, the
four volumes of Vance Randolph's newly published *Ozark Folksongs.* The
work was a wondrous mystery to me; I struggled to understand, harmonize,
play, and sing those songs from another world. They were my first lesson
in the subjectivity of culture.

In high school I was befriended by a slightly older set, a group dedicated to singing folksongs. Among them was John Cohen, who would later be a founding member of the New Lost City Ramblers. We made forays into the city to attend hootenannies. We were the first to "discover" Reverend Gary Davis and made some private recordings of him. In 1952 we visited with Woody Guthrie in Bob Harris's record store on Union Square.[2]

When I wrote this essay in 1966 I was a folksinger who was satisfied with her decision to be a scholar. There had been numerous opportunities in the previous years for me to become a professional performer. In 1956, after I made a record for Riverside in New York City with Milt Okun, he took to introducing me as a new voice with as much potential as that of Ronnie Gilbert, the only woman singer with the newly reactivated Weavers. Not long after that the Tarriers were just forming as a group with hopes of achieving success in the musical idiom being popularized by the Weavers. They asked me to join them, but I declined. In 1958, after I performed with Jean Ritchie, Oscar Brand, the New Lost City Ramblers, and others along with guest host Harry Reasoner on "Camera Three," a network TV series, the director urged me to audition for a new musical that a friend of his was developing, *The Sound of Music*, starring Theodore Bikel. No, I told him, I had to return and finish my doctoral studies in folklore. By the time such opportunities presented themselves, I already knew that my talents lay more in my intellect than in my musicality. I anticipated that folksong would eventually break into the monied entertainment world, but I was ill-equipped and not in the least inclined to cope with the evanescent life of that profession. An academic career, I figured, would be more fulfilling than one as a singer. In retrospect I think that I was realistic about life in show business but a tad idealistic about life in the academy.

But I did not give up singing; when I wrote this essay, I was still giving concerts. My performances were vastly improved compared to those on my early, poorly conceived recordings. In my own classification scheme I was a singer of folksongs, not an emulator. I sang in a way that was "natural" to me, clearly influenced by urban pop singers such as Jo Stafford. I never claimed to be anything other than a product of suburban New York City. I learned guitar by watching and questioning other players. I was part of a changing urban folk aesthetic that in this article I call "the new aesthetic."

Since I was a part-time entertainer who did not aspire to fame or fortune, and since I moved easily in folksinging circles, I felt that I could offer insights into a significant social and political movement that was being given little or no attention by academics. As a singer, I felt I could offer the possibility for peace among warring factions. From the beginning of my years as a performer there had been heated squabbles among singers of folksongs. I watched people put one another down or approve of a performance by using charged (but never defined) terms such as "authentic," "popular," or "ethnic."[3] What I hoped to do in this article was to introduce new ways of talking about performances, ways to describe them that were as devoid as possible of previous value-ridden language. Realizing that no one is bias-free, I still felt qualified to tackle the job.

While the late 1960s might have been a time of burgeoning success for urban folksingers, it was a lean time for those of us who wished to study the folksong at universities. The academic folklore establishment was manifestly uninterested in folksong, in part because it had been used as a voice by the political left, and also because it was becoming popularized and reified into an emerging new urban tradition. It was a time when established academic voices insisted that politics had no place in art or scholarship. In reality, the only *acceptable* politics in academe was that of "anticommunism" (the McCarthy era was still very much with us). It was also a time when folklore as a discipline was struggling with the related issue of "applied folklore." Many academicians looked down upon "applied" anything as a lesser form of human activity. Just as Shakespearean scholars were viewed with suspicion if they were also actors, so folklorists who sang or who were involved in other kinds of popular or ("left-wing") political performances were viewed as dubious scholars. In part I wrote this piece to say to academics that there was something important happening in the "pop" urban world that was both exciting and absolutely necessary to study. I did not see that sarcastic tones and jumps of logic would destine this piece to obscurity among academicians and to disappointment among scholar-populists.[4]

When I wrote this essay, my understanding of art vis-à-vis life was on the cusp between belief in an absolute art-for-art's-sake and a recognition that "art" is a relative cultural construct, inherently political. I thought my painful shift from belief in a universal aesthetic to my recognition of relative ones had been complete by the early 1960s, but I see it creeping about in the words of this piece, in the unconsciously disparaging ways in which I discuss the "imitators" and in the manner in which I condemn Dylan's artistic efforts or hold Woody Guthrie responsible for the fact that he was used by others. The judgmental aspects of this piece stem, in part, from that unresolved absolutism and its naive corollary that demanded complete separation between the realms of aesthetics and politics.

I had held mixed feelings about the performances of some friends who had introduced me to folksongs and who had encouraged me to perform. In the 1950s I was impatient with what I considered Pete Seeger's preaching from the concert stage, little realizing that almost forty years later I would firmly hold that politics are inevitably part of any artistic expression. What I differed with Pete about was *how*, not *what* to proclaim in those days of red-baiting. In the early 1960s I had been puzzled by people such as John Cohen and Mike Seeger, who were beginning to take on the mannerisms of the southern mountaineers whose music they were beginning to master. After all, that was where I had done much fieldwork for my dissertation, and if I certainly was not a southern mountaineer, how could middle-class, suburban John or Mike be? At first I wondered whether or not such emulation was a cruel charade. By the time I wrote this article I was only beginning to come to terms with the emulators. I was coming to the realization that one could be creative in numerous cultural vocabularies. However, I still had a way to go in order to see beyond imitation to the potentials for creativity in their approach.

I was aware in 1966 that the leverage of mass-media aesthetics could be used either to overthrow the establishment or to gain its power. Guthrie, Dylan, and, more important, their supporters also realized this. But I was offended seeing people and the cultures of the folk, those "others,"[5] manipulated in ways that I considered unethical. I was annoyed at what I considered benevolent paternalism: the moving of traditional singers to places like New York City (where they often wished to go), having them sing for the well-meant causes of the Progressive Movement, and then leaving them to wander unprepared in the strange landscape of urban poverty. I had never believed that the political left could be culturally naive. In 1966 I had been working closely for years with Sarah Ogan Gunning, recording her repertoire and her life story, and she made it clear to me that she regarded herself as living testimony to this treatment.[6]

I think that my concern about how traditional folksingers were treated by many who championed them was the reason that the second half of this essay breaks abruptly from the more descriptive first half. This second section is replete with judgmental thrashing. However, if read carefully, especially the last sentence of the essay, the piece is not as extreme as the tone implies. Had David Whisnant written his superb work *All That Is Native and Fine* a few decades earlier, I would have discussed the political left—which encouraged Woody Guthrie and which gave Bob Dylan his springboard—in terms of a complex "intervention."[7] By "intervention" I mean the *imposition* of some aspect of a culture upon a people by those in a position of power. I use the term *advocacy* to suggest the *support* of a given culture in order to "preserve" it.[8] Advocacy (like intervention) can succeed only for those who have power. Basically, it, like "intervention," is an intrusion. Setting aside the questions of whether or not some people invite either intervention or advocacy, it remains that neither is a benign activity. They both have consequences—consequences selected by the empowered. Advocates valorize a particular aspect of culture at a given point in history, marking forever future change. Just like intervention, advocacy easily turns into preservation and then into petrification. It derives its strength from a misapplication by metaphor of the biological concept of "endangered species." Both intervention and advocacy need be approached with care; they both alter history. And who is it that should be in charge of whose cultural history? Although I do not yet have an easy answer to this question, I am far clearer today about the issues than I was in 1966.

As I have said above, when I wrote this essay I was bothered by what I saw as either the intentional or unintentional appropriation of performers by advocates. These folksingers had developed and practiced their art in cultures whose aesthetics and politics were vastly different from those of their more powerful champions. I felt that there was an unacknowledged exploitation and romanticizing of a class of people, the economically "underprivileged" traditional performers. These artists were heard by urban(e) audiences mainly because of the efforts of their advocates, earnest men and women who often had personal and political agendas quite different from those whom they championed. It was a time when many young, urban, middle-class white males "discovered" forgotten African-American male folksingers and set themselves up as the agents of those singers, traveling the coffeehouse and festival route with them. Such "advocacy" often (although not always) masked a large measure of unconscious exploitation, a fact that did not go unnoticed by many of the performers.

Most urban audiences at the time were hard pressed to understand the aesthetic of a traditional performance. I suspected that they substituted political and social judgments for aesthetic ones in an absolute and unconscious switch. I now believe that they, like I, failed to realize how complex the appreciation of another culture's aesthetic can be. But I was *not* arguing against change, nor was I unaware that many a traditional performer held the fond hope of some day being "discovered" by powerful and more privileged America. I was arguing for an understanding of both the aesthetics and the politics of traditional performance on its own terms, not on the terms of the advocates.

In 1966 I wanted this essay to clarify the squabbles within folksinging circles about who was "valid" and who was not, who "should" sing folksongs, and how they "ought" to be sung. In my effort to establish that much-needed dialogue and to develop a coherent way of looking at song performance, I unknowingly inserted my own "shoulds" and "oughts." But even with that, and even though the first half of this essay is peppered with unneeded sarcasms, I feel that it is conceptually solid. It is the second section that needs more explaining and expanding.

I now realize that I had not read enough of Guthrie's early and developing work. Guthrie *had* learned the urban intellectual aesthetic within which his promoters existed. He had a genius for playing games with its language; his music and his style of presentation raise other issues. I believe that Guthrie was used by those with power, and that, in turn, he (to a limited extent) used the powerful. He had some idea of Marxism, but as Joe Klein points out, he expressed his understanding in a "good guys vs. bad guys" scenario.[9] I know that Sarah Ogan Gunning, a friend of Woody's in New York City, also did not understand the politics of these intervenors any more than they understood hers.[10]

Guthrie often wrote skillfully, and he succeeded in indicting the capitalist system while at the same time parodying the valued "literature" of the intellectual left. His advocates did not seem to recognize an important part of *his* political message, that part that parodied them. Guthrie's art still has not been understood fully. I would now say that Guthrie—who like Dylan could have used a good editor—was a poet who attempted to create an aesthetic of words from both his traditional base and from the aesthetic he learned from the elite (albeit "left-wing") culture that had given him the opportunity to both create and be heard. Many who did and do idolize him do so with little understanding of his complexity. Even Joe Klein does not grasp the essentials of Guthrie's craft.[11] The anger that triggered my overstatements about Guthrie's work in this essay was directed at those who took every scrap of what Guthrie wrote and called it remarkable according to canonical (i.e., Whitmanesque)[12] standards. Alan Lomax equated Guthrie's writing to that of James Joyce in *Ulysses*.[13]

Dylan, on the other hand, used—rather than was used by—others. For a while he became his own moving force. Unlike Guthrie, he came from the middle-class heart of the advocate's culture. He used the persona of the "folk" as part of his message. He was a performer who took hold of the reins of mass media and made it do what he wanted. His was the voice of young America—at first only when his songs were sung by more palatable groups such as Peter, Paul, and Mary. But Dylan's *verbal* creativity was not as stunning as was Guthrie's. His lyrics, to me, were shallow; his themes simplistic. They signaled an America turning inward, unconcerned about others, anti-intellectual, and gravitating toward one-issue causes. Dylan affected poverty in order to speak to middle-class youth. The critics who praised his work never convinced me that his lyrics were "poetry," even though they claimed it. As the innovator of a new musicality and a new sound of performance, he was brilliant. Perhaps those who prized his work felt they had to call him a poet in order to justify him as an artist. It was not a time when pop musicians were regarded "seriously."

It is ironic that in an essay aimed at minimizing the use of judgmental words to describe singing events, I concluded by hop-scotching from judgment to judgment about Guthrie and Dylan. It is even more ironic that I appear to criticize Guthrie and Dylan rather than the advocates who judged them by inapplicable values. But I was angry and galled by the politics of culture. I saw people who had power and a cause exploiting a less powerful "folk," recreating them by and for their own empowered vision. I saw the edge of advocacy overlapping exploitation.

Today I mind far less being called part of a "dim-witted band of academic folklorists"[14] who thought Guthrie was totally manipulated by the "big city radicals" than being thought a reactionary. Few scholars were more committed to the "left" than I. But rereading this essay, I see how my elitist and judgmental tone placed me in the "right-wing" camp to scholars such as R. Serge Denisoff.[15]

Certainly there are some other things I would change were I to write this essay today. I would omit the unhelpful reference to my ethnic bagels and lox (and warm bath). I would discuss at length the reasons why and ways in which middle-class America idealized the cultures of white and African-American southern poverty. I would call "imitators" *emulators,* and I would change "tune" to *music,* a loss of alliteration I was loath to allow in 1966. I would rewrite my use of the period's gender-specific language, and I would change the term "Negro" (which was just about to become "black" in general usage). I would also decry Guthrie's sexism, a recurrent motif in his writings and in his life, albeit a reflection of the times (even within the political left). And I would talk about the politics of art in order to expand and clarify what Guthrie and Dylan represented of and to the folksong revival.

When I am sympathetic to myself, I read the essay again and say "I wrote that" (no appalled emphasis this time). I can now see that I often left out major assumptions underlying passionate opinions. I seemed to be against the very changes I was trying to clarify and describe. And while I clearly had personal likes and dislikes for certain singers, songs, and performances, I never saw that I appeared to be railing against change itself. Today I agree with, disagree with, and would modify, some of the ideas in this piece, but I still hold to my initial conviction that it is important to write about the present *in* the present, no matter how harshly you may judge yourself in the future. We have to study ourselves as well as those "others" if we are to learn anything.

At the time I wrote this essay, it was my hope that it could offer a new and helpful way of looking at the much-beleaguered folksong revival—if not at song performance in general. I think I accomplished that even though I have reservations about the split in the piece. While my involvement in the movement clouded my writing and some of my judgments, it also informed them. I feel fortunate to have been allowed the chance to place my past work in context and to view myself with a degree of fond irony.

NOTES

1. Stekert, "Autobiography," pp. 580, 584–85.
2. Klein, *Woody Guthrie,* pp. 397ff. This is a sympathetic though flawed review of Guthrie's complex life.
3. See the folk-music fan magazines published during the 1950s and 1960s; for example, *Sing Out!* or *Little Sandy Review.*
4. I was told in a private communication by Bruce Jackson that my mentor and close friend Ben Botkin felt that this essay argued against the popularization of folk song. That had never been my intent, but I can now see how tone and illogical jumps within my discussion would have led Botkin to believe that. For the respect I felt for Ben Botkin and his work, see my obituary "Benjamin Albert Botkin."
5. The term "other" is used here as suggested in Said's *Orientalism.*
6. I worked with Sarah Gunning from 1964 through the late 1970s conducting many in-depth interviews and recording her repertoire.
7. The parallel between the missionary-school "intervenor" in the southern mountains and the political-left intervenors in this same region is striking. Regardless of region, Whisnant's observations in his "Afterword" (pp. 259–60) pertain to endeavors far beyond the mountains: "Just as every act in a complex social order is inescapably political in character, so is it also bound up—in origin, intent, and effect—with culture. . . . An intervenor, by virtue of his or her status, power, and established credibility, is frequently able to define what the culture *is,* to normalize and legitimize that definition in the larger society, and even to feed it back into the culture itself, where it may be internalized as 'real.' "
8. Whisnant does not make this distinction. He would incorporate what I am calling "advocacy" under "intervention." See pp. 12–13.
9. Klein, *Woody Guthrie,* p. 270.
10. It was clear that she understood only vaguely what her advocates meant by the expression "the capitalist system," a phrase she used prominently in several songs she composed after she moved to New York City. Depending upon what she felt that her audience wanted, she would sing either that phrase or replace it with "the company bosses." Many times she said that she had no quarrel with the system, but she did have one with the people who kept her from having food to feed her baby. I should also mention here that those who encouraged the "folk" such as Leadbelly, Guthrie, and others to compose and perform in the 1940s, 1950s, and 1960s were mostly white middle-class males. They encouraged almost no women to the extent they encouraged the men. Sarah's vast musical talent and intelligence was not recognized by them as much as was that of her musically untalented brother, Jim Garland. Her half sister, Aunt Molly Jackson, was an exception to this rule, but even her "fame" was more complex, and it nowhere approached that of the men.

11. Klein, *Woody Guthrie*. There is almost no discussion of Guthrie's singing style of presentation or of his musicality in this work. Klein is wise to avoid discussion of these elements, for it minimizes the type of misstatements he makes when he describes Guthrie's acceptance by the political left. He says that the Left was displeased with "New Orleans Jazz [that] had been bleached and diluted into swing music [and the] mountain and cowboy songs [that were] becoming 'country and western,' " yet in the next paragraph he speaks of Guthrie as untouched by "popular styles," even though he says that Guthrie was influenced by "a little Jimmie Rodgers, maybe, and certainly he borrowed heavily from the Carter Family's more traditional material" (p. 149).

12. Ibid., p. 195.

13. Ibid., p. 151. Also see my review.

14. Ibid., p. 434.

15. "The Proletarian Renascence," p. 51.

Cents and Nonsense in the Urban Folksong Movement: 1930–66

The entrance of "folksong" into the mainstream of popular entertainment in the United States has been a spectacular one. Ever since the Kingston Trio produced its record of "Tom Dooley," and Joan Baez made the cover of *Time* magazine,[1] the term "folk" has ceased being nonsense to the American public and has become a matter of dollars and cents. This popular acceptance of folksong bears close study, for like most mass movements, it will undoubtedly feed back into oral tradition.[2] The folksong scholar, finding "his" material accosting him from all manner of unlikely places, transistor radios to Muzak, is caught in the whirlwind created by the capricious spirit of modern mass entertainment. The frenetic and off-handedly nihilistic young generation which dominates our times, unlike the bovine and silent 1950s, holds little truck with intellectual distinctions, and uses all things, from soup cans to folksongs, as a means of expression. The eye and the ear seem more important than print; the silver screen and the LP have become the books of the present young generation, an irony for such an impatient time since one can read much more quickly than hear or view. But in the hearing and the viewing are the sensation, and perhaps above all else, this is a hedonistic and sensual age in which living with all the senses is the goal. The modern folksong movement at one time both stimulates the senses and celebrates them.

Certainly it is difficult to write about the present, but in part that is exactly what the folklorist must do. He must be able to see the major currents of his day as well as ones of the past. Just as broadsides were a part of popular and mass entertainment of their time, scorned by scholars as recent as Child and Gerould, so the present records, radio programs, and festivals speak for and are symptoms of the contemporary urban folksong movement, a popular movement at which many contemporary folklorists dislike looking. Instead of leaving the present to be picked over in the future, allowing it to fragment into myriad pieces for subsequent tedious reconstruction, we must investigate it now. In this article I shall attempt to delineate the major groups of the urban folksong movement from the late 1930s to the present, and show how the movement actually helped create a new idiom of popular entertainment, one epitomized by the products of Bob Dylan.

Folksongs are not simple things, and in discussing them it is important to remember that they are not only texts or "poems" as Bishop Percy and the circle of Samuel Johnson regarded them in the eighteenth century. A folksong is a blend of text, tune, style of presentation, and function. The uses that have been made of folksong in the cities of the United States during this century have been complex, and in order to understand them, one must look carefully at these four ingredients and note which ones have been altered, when, and how. So that the 1950s and 1960s can best be understood, it is profitable here to present first a brief history of the folksong movement in the cities and then to cut across historical lines and delineate the different types of "folksingers" and "folksongs" which appear, and have appeared, on the scene.

In the 1930s and 1940s, folksongs were brought to the attention of the cities mostly by conscientious and adamant left-wing political groups. Both songs from oral tradition and songs composed by urban and rural singers were sung at "hoots"[3] and at union meetings. Not only were the songs from oppressed cultures brought to the cities, so were the singers themselves. In a subtle and unwitting way, these singers were regarded as "noble savages" by their patrons: Woody Guthrie, Aunt Molly Jackson, Jim Garland, and many others were celebrated as the living voice of folk tradition whether or not they sang traditional songs, or could even sing well in their own traditional style. It was an urban generation blind to its own naive prejudices which avidly and sincerely brought folksong, and what was taken for folksong, to the cities.

Many of the "folk" who were celebrated by folksong enthusiasts during this period were unskilled performers both in terms of the traditional aesthetic with which they were raised, and in terms of the urban aesthetic within which they were subtly required to produce. The vast majority of Woody Guthrie's work, for example, is meandering, unstructured, and politically forced, satisfying neither the traditional standards of his Oklahoma background, nor the urban standards of his supporters. He was, and still is, touted as a great artist by his city friends, but, as the latest book of his work shows most tragically,[4] he was not a "poet," and in his more lucid moments realized he did not even know what a poet was.[5] Aunt Molly Jackson, never considered even a mediocre traditional singer by her own cultural group,[6] was used as a spokesman for social and political movements, often composing her own "protest" songs out of nearly whole cloth, and singing in her "traditional" manner for her city discoverers.[7] Both Woody Guthrie and Aunt Molly Jackson were lauded for their great art; it was a pitiful confusion much like that which Katherine Anne Porter states in her short story "Flowering Judas": "It is monstrous to confuse love with revolution."[8] So, with many of the people brought to the cities by the politically oriented folksong movement of the 1930s, it was monstrous for urbanites to confuse poverty with art.

Still, in the 1960s we can hear echoes of the idea that what comes from the working class—the poor—is necessarily art and folklore. Peggy Seeger, in an interview for the fan magazine *Sing Out!* in 1962, was quoted:

> And that's what's wrong in America. There is a lack of recognition of the essential working-class character of folk music—and a lack of pride in the working-class character of the music.[9]

Although we should not forget that the period of the 1930s and early 1940s brought many good singers to the cities and laid the groundwork there for a genuine appreciation of traditional material, we should also recognize that the era encouraged subtle and easy prejudices, ones which still linger and are difficult to overcome.

In the silent frightened years of the late 1940s and early 1950s, only a few stubborn and dedicated voices from the previous decades remained. But interest in folksong slowly grew, especially on the campuses of American colleges and universities. Pete Seeger's political voice was still influential, but so were those of essentially nonpolitical singers such as John Jacob Niles and Burl Ives. Niles, with his fine aesthetic taste and early superb control of a less than mediocre countertenor, drew to folk music those who were interested in the possibilities folk material held for aesthetic expression. Burl Ives dissociated himself from the political 1930s and early 1940s and became essentially a pop-tenor who charmed middle-class hearts. Thus, the 1950s saw a shift from political use of folksong to an interest in original texts and tunes of folk material as collected from the folk's (rural) mouth. Singers from the cities often went to academic collections for their songs. It was in these years that the distinction between "folksinger"[10] and "singer of folksong"[11] became important, and it was a time when singers searched traditional folksong collections for songs which expressed their own personal feelings and pleased their personal taste. In this cowardly and intimidated era, the city sought expression behind the words of other—perhaps more "natural"—folk.

But while the original words and melodic line of the folksong were easy for urban America to accept, it took a bit longer for the performing style of the traditional folksong to reach the cities. Some idioms, such as American Negro blues, had always been there, but it took Caucasian America much agonizing to accept such singers as Jean Ritchie,[12] Hobart Smith, and Frank Proffitt. Slowly, toward the middle and end of the 1950s, urban America became aware of traditional style as well as traditional texts and music.

The 1960s produced creative accomplishments that summarized the development of the preceding three decades. The freedom movement revived the genre of the political protest song—at last there was another definite

cause about which to sing—but with a difference. No longer did the traditionally collected or traditionally composed songs speak for the young
singers who had known neither the intimidation of the 1950s nor the
Guthries and Aunt Mollys of the 1930s and 1940s. Seeger was winning his
battle with the courts, and young people were feeling very different from
the mountain folk who sang of corn liquor and distant murders. The concept of the folk, or "natural man," remained meaningful to the city singer
only in terms of himself as an individual. As Josh Dunson points out,

> it was in the years 1960 and 1961 that the pronoun "I" replaced "we"
> in topical songs, and that a new group of songwriters emerged, influ-
> enced by, yet very different from, their less spiritual fathers.[13]

The young singer of folksongs was becoming more self-concerned and
less socially concerned, despite the irony that social (protest) movements
introduced many to their first folk, or folk-like, song.

In the early 1950s traditional songs had been adapted to urban singing
styles and by the end of the decade new sounds began to emerge in the
cities—sounds with traces of jazz, folk tradition, classical music, and pop
music. By the 1960s, the young singers found it necessary to create their
own songs, and they did it first, as Bob Dylan originally did, in the image
of the folk song as it was sung in the 1940s and 1950s.

When one looks about today at the folksong world in the cities, four
clear groups stand out, some reflections of the present, some vestiges of
the past. The lines between these groups are not always sharp, but the
general contours remain. The first group I shall discuss is composed of
the traditional singers—singers who have learned their songs and their style
of presentation from oral tradition as they grew up. Such singers usually
appear at festivals and on college campuses for small programs, and seldom
face the spoiled coffeehouse audience. Most often they are from an im-
poverished group, one in which the native language is English. The two
groups best represented are the white Southern Mountaineer and the Negro
blues singer. Just as in the 1930s when Woody Guthrie and Leadbelly were
the demigods of the folk-political scene, today numerous traditional singers
such as Almeda Riddle, Sarah Ogan Gunning, Reverend Gary Davis, and
Son House are the darlings of the folk enthusiasts interested in the traditional sound. Interestingly, few foreign-speaking traditional groups have
found their way into the resurgence of interest in folksong. Perhaps we
can look for part of the reason in the fact that most folksong enthusiasts
today are young people of comfortable means from second and third generation American homes. They prefer to identify their agonies with those
of the downtrodden Negro and Southern Mountaineer, two of the most
"American" groups by lineage, who have suffered at the hands of Big White

Authority. Perhaps to many of these youngsters, authority is not far removed from the foreign accents and traditions of their grandparents. After all, proportionately few "hillbilly" or Negro youth compose the audience of these traditional singers. For the middle-class white (sub)urban youth, to "suffer" with the downtrodden has become the ideal; in a society where there is little left that is not synthetic, aping the "natural man" has become an end in itself. Thus, as in the 1930s and 1940s, one can belong and be angry at the same time; one may live the life of the traditional singer for a while with great ease if he knows that at the end of the trip there is a warm bath and lox and bagel.

The second clearly distinguishable group of performers in the urban folksong movement is what I call, for want of a better label, the "imitators." This group consists of much the same type of young people as compose the audiences of the traditional singers, although they are a bit older. They have taken time to learn the skills of those whom they have admired. These imitators have found meaning in the traditional songs and style of presentation of the authentic folksingers, and have sought to totally absorb themselves in their chosen style. Learning a traditional style is infinitely more difficult than learning only traditional melodies or texts, and these performers have dedicated their lives to practically becoming part of that style and culture from which they have chosen to learn. Since it is so difficult to learn a style, imitators usually learn only a single one. For example, learning how to sing with the pinched flat tone of the Kentucky mountaineer takes years, and it is just as difficult for a trained opera singer to imitate the scooping melodic figures and dynamic staccatos of traditional Scottish-Irish Southern Mountaineers as it is for the mountain singers to sing opera. In her early recordings Joan Baez, influenced by the excellent imitator group "The Greenbriar Boys," attempted a few semi-hill-sounding songs which badly fell short of any type of emotional impact, and almost approached parody.[14]

The cultural expressions which seem to be most popular with the imitative group are the Southern Mountain instrumental tradition (bluegrass and old-timey music) and the Negro blues. Interestingly, once again, most of these performers who have immersed themselves in the aesthetic of a culture different from their own, these same young people who have found a creative voice in the traditional music of others, have been mostly from the middle-class, educated, white city. Think twice, and nothing seems more incongruous than John Cohen of the posh suburbs of New York City's "West Egg"[15] singing in old-timey style with the New Lost City Ramblers, or young, blond, and blue-eyed Doctor Kildare in the form of John Hammond, son of a Columbia Records executive, grinding out a Negro blues, defying the ear with the eye. At their best, the imitative groups have learned to speak eloquently in a form of aesthetic expression not offered them in their city. Many singers have taken almost every aspect of their chosen culture into their private lives, even to the point of an alteration of speech patterns. The work that imitators do can be impressive and meaningful; but the question still remains why such expression was not possible within the aesthetics offered by their own city environment.

The third city group of the 1960s I call the "utilizers." This conglomeration of people is loosely held together by the fact that they have taken folk material and have altered it in the light of accepted city aesthetics. They usually change three elements of folksong: tune, text, and style of presentation. Sometimes they retain only one of the original folk elements. Broadly speaking, there are two sets of singers which have taken traditional material from other cultures and have remolded it, changing words and changing style, and often changing melody lines: the "urban pop" groups, and the "urban art" groups. After the Weavers' brief success in the early 1950s, the Kingston Trio was the first nationally known group to utilize folk materials and alter them according to a pop aesthetic. More than the Weavers, they altered material to city tastes; they would sing "Jesse James" as a joke[16] or take a song, such as the Southern Mountain "Bury Me Beneath the Willow," put it to a calypso beat, pump their sound through an echo chamber creating a syrupy vibrato as far from the flat Southern Mountain sound as possible, and generally reshape both words and style of presentation to conform to pop musical and textual standards.[17] Endings of musical lines are drawn out, dynamics are exaggerated, tempos altered, and in general the originally understated folksong is given the overstated pop treatment. If one does not like what the Kingston Trio does, it could not be on the grounds of "not authentic," for no culture has a monopoly on folksong, and the Kingston Trio and its imitators never claimed to be the real thing. One can only object to the Trio on personal grounds—either one likes pop or one doesn't; and if you don't, but only on the grounds that they are or are not good pop. Much heat has been lost over "purist" vs. "popularizer" arguments which are appeals to the wrong prejudices.

The newest pop utilization of folk and folk-like material and style is the army led by Bob Dylan and the Beatles. Here a blending of Southern Mountain and Negro traditional style is the strongest tie to folk music. Whereas the Kingston Trio often kept words and tunes recognizable, and primarily changed style, the folk-rock sound centers about a folk-like vocal style, and is further related to the folk music movement as a result of the historical accident that Bob Dylan, one of its leaders, made the scene through the folk ranks by writing traditional-sounding protest songs, the writing of protest songs itself being a tradition.[18] But eventually Dylan left the imitative textual style and discarded his social conscience in order to explore the depths of his own chaotic soul to the metallic beat of an electric guitar and the rasping vocal style of the rural and urban Negro and Southern Mountaineer. As with Kingston Trio adaptations and utilization of folk material, one cannot judge "folk-rock" good or bad *a priori*. One can only judge each song or each performing group for its worth. Even if one does not like the aesthetic vocabulary of the folk-rock groups, one can at least distinguish between good and bad folk-rock in its own terms. Folk material is not sacred, and it is imperative that in time we come to tolerate and understand sociologically all manner of styles and texts and tunes.

The same value-judgments must hold true for art utilizers, such as Richard Dyer-Bennet and Alfred Deller. Both men, schooled in classical song performance, have picked and utilized their material in the light of art song performance. The art performer, just like the pop utilizer, must be judged on his own terms. One can complain that Dyer-Bennet's polite guitar and countertenor rendition of "John Henry"[19] grates on the listener who has heard Negro blues performers render the song, but one can only hold that Dyer-Bennet falls short as a classical singer and guitarist, and that his interpretation of the song is poor. Ideally, it possible for a good classical arranger and good countertenor and classical guitarist to render "John Henry" well in a classical adaptation. Certainly Dyer-Bennet's tasteful renditions of such songs as "The Vicar of Bray" show that he can be extremely expressive through his style.

The fourth group of folksingers to appear on the urban scene at first seems to belong to the classification "urban utilizers," but I have hesitated to place them there since part of the definition of the utilizers is that they remold material to an already extant urban aesthetic (for style of presentation, text, and tunes). The remarkable thing about this fourth group is that it has developed its own set of aesthetic criteria, and so, imaginatively or not, I call this group the "new aesthetic." It is not an easy task to define this group, but the sound they make is that which in the early sixties could be heard coming from coffeehouses whose clientele scorned the Kingston Trio and felt art singing too sterile and inhibited. Peggy Seeger was one of the first outstanding practitioners of this group,[20] the list of which would be long, if not prominent in "show biz." The sound of the new aesthetic group is one which developed from a merger of vocal and instrumental folk, classical, jazz, and pop styles. Almost all of the singers sing with accompaniment; they have learned to chord modal tunes, creating a bizarre and pleasing new texture to their songs, not unlike pre-Bach music. Compared to traditional singers their style is overstated, but compared with art and pop singers, they are the traditional embodiment of understatement.[21] Their instrumental techniques combine the traditional and classical devices.

It is the sound of this new aesthetic, a sound which became widely recognizable in the early 1960s with Joan Baez's meteoric popular success, that has become the folk sound in the cities. Peter, Paul, and Mary use the musicality of the new aesthetic in their arrangements. I would venture to say that if the folksong movement in the cities can be said to have given anything new to urban culture, it would not be folk-rock, which actually is another branch of what the Beatles have done to rock and roll, but the new aesthetic. The early brittle vibrato of Joan Baez, whose voice is essentially lacking in emotional range, is being replaced by numerous new voices such as Judy Collins who exploit the new sound to its fullest. Most singers of folksongs in the cities who have not attempted to be pop, arty, or imitators of style fit into this category. Pete Seeger, although at times he attempts half-hearted imitations, remains a talented and versatile arranger of folk and folk-like materials in the new aesthetic. In a sense, this new sound is the urban revival's traditional sound—certainly no handbooks tell you how to sing like Baez or Seeger—it is a new vocabulary for emotional expression and one that is being widely used.

Painted with a wide brush, these are the four major groups that exist in the urban folk scene today: the traditional singers, the imitators, the utilizers, and the new aesthetic. Some people use one, others use many of the idioms with which to express themselves. Usually, however, as with Joan Baez on her first recordings, attempting two idioms leads to inferiority in one.

But having outlined the major groups in the urban movement is not enough; we must also ask ourselves what the movement means. Let us take two figures—one from the early years and one from the present—Woody Guthrie and Bob Dylan, and see how in their respective times they were representative of major currents in the urban folksong world.

Woody Guthrie, born in 1912 in Oklahoma, sang, drank, and fought his way through most of the 1930s and 1940s in the company of the most active folksingers and folk enthusiasts of his time: Cisco Houston, Pete Seeger, Leadbelly, Alan Lomax, Will Geer, to name just a few. He, like most of these people, was caught up in the union and socialist-oriented movements of the time before the Second World War and after. He was an Okie, poor, and a compulsive writer. These qualities in themselves were enough to make him almost an idol to those with whom he kept company in the cities. It was an age of socialist sentimentalism, one in which it was far better to have discovered a noble rural savage than to have helped a starving poet in a garret. Ironically, it was not far from the time John Jacob Niles claimed to have collected "I Wonder As I Wander" and many other superb creations of his own, for to have discovered the natural gem was then far better than to admit having produced it artificially.

Guthrie created nothing artificially; he simply wrote and seldom (it seems) rewrote. He said he could never write like Whitman "because I can't set here and look at my paper a half a day between each word."[22] It was whispered in his ear that he was "the best ballad-maker to come down the American 'pike, and in many ways the most truthful and most talented man of his generation."[23] Robert Shelton has waxed enthusiastic to the absurd point of calling Guthrie "a major American literary figure."[24] The sad fact is that Guthrie produced reams of abominable prose and ditties, only the smallest fraction of which is aesthetically worth anything either in the folk culture from which he came or in the urban culture to which he wanted at times to belong.

Like Joe Hill, who was executed when Woody was three years old, Guthrie was a songwriter and cartoonist who gave a great deal to the labor movement. Like Bob Dylan, who was originally inspired by Woody's image and work, Guthrie was a tormented adolescent soul trying to cope with the chaos about him. He resembled Hill in that he turned outward and advocated the one cure for all the ills of the world, as in a pathetic letter to "Attny. Gen'l. Tom Clark,"

> There is only one cure for all of this, and that cure has already been found in millions of windows and streets around the world. That cure is socialized healing. Socialized medicine. Socialized living, socialized working, socialized thinking, and socialized resting, sleeping, seeding, breeding, which you may or may not be fearful about.[25]

Guthrie thrived on the simplistic answer; like a child he often wished for the "one word" which would make everything right.[26] The Second World War deprived him of his word. He knew he was unstable and admitted his personal and childlike agony: "And, well, to be right honest with you, I've been one of the mixed-uppest men out of all the others all the way around this planet."[27] But his city friends told him he could write— for after all what could be a better mixture than a real noble savage with a bit of neurotic sensitivity? At times he admitted he was no poet:

> And back and back, and on back, to the love life I crave and am not man enough nor [sic] genius nor [sic] poet nor husband enough to get.[28]

At times he produced a bizarre and arresting line, so typical of Dylan's equally undisciplined craft:

> This is the time of the year when birds fly down
> And pick up seeds with people off of the ground.[29]

Guthrie at his most candid, admitted he knew what was being asked of him, and so he played the poet to the cause and to his friends, never really loving or understanding poetry; for reading for a poet in training, he recommends Darwin's *Evolution of the Species*.[30] He brags "I'm a profit,"[31] and speaks of "my deathless books, songs, stories,"[32] yet mocks those who consider him a poet. His idea of the poet's work can be gleaned from one of his more coherent and revealing poems, "My Job as a Poet":

> I love my job as a poet
> It gets me in and out real easy
> Woman go for it
> Girls run and fall and roll for it
> Men get mixed up about it
>
> The world has already built me a legend
>
> I love my job of being your poet
> Because I can drink your liquor and your beer
> And drink your good wine and your wife's blood
> And call it a poem and say I'll mention your name in my poems
> And you ask me to sleep with your daughters and your wives
> And to eat at your tables and your boards
> Just so long as I mention your name in my next book of poems
>
> Don't you turn out to be a poet and come and sleep with my wife.[33]

Guthrie wrote, became the city's idealization of the folk poet, but his writings reflect his name, not his art; his works are social documents, not literature, while at times one can see in his writing the future bitter, confused anti-singer, anti-poet, Bob Dylan.

Guthrie lived and wrote past the tragic and disillusioning years of the Second World War. By the time the war ended, right and wrong, good and evil were much more complex; the good guys and the bad guys had been lost in the shuffle. Guthrie's best works were written for the "cause." Joe Hill died for his cause in 1915; Guthrie lived to see his cause die, and Dylan sings to eulogize the chaos of his own private hell, a hell he feels reflects the ambiguous and hypocritical world about him. The sad fact is that if one takes any of these three from their environments and prejudices, and attempts to look understandingly at their works, one finds precious little of any literary worth. Unfortunately, especially in the cases of Guthrie and Dylan, many of their followers have claimed a major place for them in the hall of American letters. Ideally, there is no reason why a songwriter cannot eventually claim such a place, for there is nothing to stop the merging of good poetry with good music so that a blended aesthetic effect is obtained.

The fact that Guthrie and Dylan are the folksinger-writer heroes of their times is living proof of the undercurrent of anti-intellectualism that has run throughout the urban folksong movement. For although many scholars have come from the ranks of folksingers, there is generally a profound distrust of academia amongst the great majority of city folksingers. Too often the goal of the academic is misunderstood by these singers, who see only petty dissection where the good academic attempts to use discipline and sympathetic analysis to further his appreciation and experience of the art product. With just a smidgen of understanding about how to read a literary endeavor, even a child can see that most of Guthrie's and Dylan's work is doggerel. Dylan Thomas, after whom Bob Dylan took his name, sweated blood for each word.[34] Bob Dylan, like Guthrie, surrounded essentially by people who idolize the poet and not his work, people who have not felt the need to learn to distinguish between art and artifice, spews out words as though each came from the lips of a divinely inspired Hesiod. One dares not question the gods, nor the emperor, but if he did, he might find that he has been living in a fairy-tale world; in the real world the droppings of the donkey are no longer gleaming gold.[35]

Guthrie spoke for his age as the worker and "natural man"; his works praise "naturalness,"[36] and while he had no job, he felt compelled to speak of his work as a poet. Dylan also speaks to his age as a "natural man," but no longer is the worker the idol, and the causes are too confusing. Dylan first attempted to fill the "social protest" role, but even his socially and politically conscious songs are heavy laden with his own personal problems. He, too, is anti-intellectual, anti-discipline, despite all the often meaningless references to art and literary figures in his songs. He is, in a phrase, full of hate and nihilistic fury. His very voice is as far from "accepted" style as he could have gotten. He has gone from the acoustic guitar to the harsh metallic frenzy of the folk-rock sound. The medium he has picked for his expression of disgust and disillusionment is the song. In an age which sees no future and to which the past means little more than restrictions and war, the rule of life is to live in the present, to make the most of the moment, and what art form could be more momentary than the song? It exists around you in space and disappears in time; it *is* the moment. As Bruce Jackson has observed, "The singing of the song is an act of value, somehow."[37] The song is the natural medium for Dylan, and as Dylan progresses in his introspection and rejection of the world, his songs become more and more meaningless.

From the beginning of his career, most of Dylan's poems were weak as poetry. They contain flashes of insight, bits of all the adolescent poetry we ever wanted to have written, but they are not controlled, and fall apart under inspection rather than yielding up greater riches of understanding and experience. We react to him on an emotional level rather than an aesthetic-emotional level. Dylan never was a great poet, although he is undoubtedly a talented man, and as he has progressed to the present his songs no longer have content, they simply have style. It is the Dylan style[38] that is now doing the talking, not the content. He is fast becoming one of the greatest (at least richest) pseudo-poets of our age.[39] He is sowing the field with millions of young anti-intellectuals who will never want to learn what the experience of a good poem is all about. Dylan, like the gyrating dancer doing the frug, monkey, or whatever, is almost completely self-involved. He apparently cares little about the products of his imagination and sees no social responsibility for himself. He is, essentially, an existentialist who has lost the sense of his own absurdity. Like many of his generation he is a nihilist without a sense of humor. As Dylan and the folk-rock singers have progressed, they have lost their ability to laugh at themselves; they have become "cool" and have developed the "mute sound."

With the advent of folk-rock, which blends urban "folk" and pop idioms, we have the epitome of subjectivization of the urban folk movement. Concern with groups of people, such as in the thirties and forties, or with people within groups, such as in the late fifties and early sixties, has passed, and the modern, self-involved, self-isolated folk-rock singer has won the day. Today "folksong" to most young urban people is almost completely equated to personal protest song and with pop professional entertainment. Folksong to the scholar is a matter of oral tradition, change, and generally non-professional transmission. We are in a humpty-dumpty age of ambivalent and misapplied words and although it is not our province to dictate usage, at the very least we can clarify what is happening.

NOTES

This essay appeared originally in *Folklore and Society: Essays in Honor of Benjamin A. Botkin*, ed. Bruce Jackson (Hatboro, Pa., Folklore Associates, 1966), pp. 153–68. Reprinted with permission of Legacy Books.

1. The Kingston Trio record made its big impact in 1958–59. Joan Baez, for better or worse, was graced by *Time*—see "Sibyl with Guitar." See also my "Views and Reviews" for a review of the *Time* article.

2. It would be foolish for folklorists, who have come to accept the influence of records, broadsides, and songsters upon folk tradition, to ignore the influence of modern mass culture. Furthermore, they should regard the influence as important whether it be temporal or only spatial, that is, whether the songs spread quickly and widely, or last through time. For a discussion of "tradition in time and tradition in space," see Barry, "What Is Tradition?"

3. See Tamony, " 'Hootenanny.' "

4. Guthrie, *Born to Win*.

5. See, for example, his poem, "My Job as Poet," ibid., pp. 68–70.

6. This information was gathered during my collecting with Aunt Molly's half sister, Mrs. Sarah Ogan Gunning, in 1963–64.

7. According to Mrs. Gunning and others in Aunt Molly's family, Molly did not hesitate to fabricate stories for her city friends, often using incidents which happened to her brothers and sisters rather than herself. Wilgus, in "Aunt Molly's Big Record," p. 171, states on that she was "not a good singer—merely a great one. Aunt Molly's singing contained the essence of Appalachian tradition." Perhaps Aunt Molly's singing had the characteristics of Southern Mountain style, but that still does not mean she was regarded as "great" by her own cultural group. In addition, simply because she was from the Appalachian tradition does not mean that everything she recast was a part of folk tradition. One must make distinctions somewhere, and although in recasting an item such as Child 192B ("Willie and Earl Richard's Daughter") a person is bound to use some of the elements of one's traditional culture, the item must be defined and not regarded in the same light as a traditional song from that culture—especially when the singer, like Aunt Molly, had been influenced by traditions other than their original one. Listen to "The Birth of Robin Hood," introduced by Aunt Molly, on Greenway, *The Songs and Stories of Aunt Molly Jackson*.

8. Katherine Anne Porter, "Flowering Judas," p. 397.

9. Silber, "Peggy Seeger," p. 7.

10. The traditional singer who learned both the content and style of the folklore from his original culture.

11. A person (usually from the city) who learned songs from traditions other than his own, and who performed them in a style other than that of the traditional culture from which the songs came.

12. Jean Ritchie actually had many urban pop and art elements in her early presentation of folksongs. In a sense, she had to relearn her traditional style. Listen, for example, to her 1946 rendition of "The Two Sisters" on *Child Ballads Traditional in the United States* (I), and compare it to her records of the 1960s. The records she made between these times show her transition to "traditional" style.

13. Dunson, *Freedom in the Air*, p. 33.

14. Listen to "Wildwood Flower" and contrast it with "Mary Hamilton"—both are on *Joan Baez*.

15. West Egg is F. Scott Fitzgerald's name for the New York City suburb of Great Neck, approximately sixteen miles east of the city on the North Shore of Long Island.

16. Listen to "Jesse James," complete with spoken introduction, on *The Kingston Trio: Close-up*.

17. Ibid., "Bury Me Beneath the Willow."

18. Dylan's "development" has taken him through almost all historical and stylistic aspects of the modern urban folksong revival. He began in the image of Guthrie, actually singing traditional songs in a fair imitative style, wrote folk-like protest songs, and then shifted to his more introspective lyrics and the urban "folksong" sound, and eventually became "folk-rock."

19. Listen to "John Henry" on *Folksongs: Richard Dyer-Bennet*.

20. Listen to *Courting and Complaining Songs: Peggy Seeger*.

21. Compare, for example, the Kingston Trio's pop-utilization of "The Whistling Gypsy" (Child 200) on *Close-up*, for the pop overstatement, and then compare that rendition with the traditionally understated one of "The Three Babes" (Child 79), *Child Ballads Traditional in the United States* (II). If, after listening to these two performances, one then listens to Joan Baez singing "Mary Hamilton," on *Joan Baez*, it can be seen how the "new aesthetic" style, to which Baez belongs, fits between the two dramatic poles.

22. Guthrie, *Born to Win*, p. 25.

23. Ibid. A quote of Alan Lomax, p. 13.

24. Ibid., p. 11.

25. Ibid., p. 68.

26. Ibid., p. 31, "The Word I Want to Say."

27. Ibid., p. 71.

28. Ibid., p. 116. Note the literary usage of "nor."

29. Ibid., p. 87.

30. Ibid., p. 29.

31. Ibid., p. 28.

32. Ibid., p. 38.

33. Ibid., pp. 69–70.

34. Dylan told Robert Shelton: "Straighten out in your book that I did not take my name from Dylan Thomas." See Shelton, *No Direction Home*, pp. 44–45—Editor.

35. Motif B103.1.1, Tale Type 563.

36. As in his poem "My Best Songs," Guthrie, *Bound For Glory*, pp. 46–63, one feels he is a bit self-conscious about his attempt at such naturalness.

37. Jackson, "Sanitary Signifying," p. 6.

38. See Wain, "In the Echo Chamber," for a discussion of how style seems to be speaking instead of content in many aspects of our "mass" culture.

39. Meehan, in "Public Writer," an ignorant and misinformed article, treats Dylan seriously as a great poet.

A Future Folklorist in the
Record Business

Kenneth S. Goldstein

There's a whole set of philosophical questions that I've always had to face up to. At the beginning, in many cases, the records were prerecorded for me, or they were already material that had been issued. I simply had to put together the album: what to select and what is representative? My aesthetic was changing, my interest was changing, and my idea of an intellectual approach to content was changing. In the Stinson stage especially. I never had any hang-ups about issuing traditional albums or revival albums for a very simple reason. I was a well-trained B.B.A. and M.B.A., and a pragmatic businessman at all times. To be able to put out the records of "traditional singers" and of more or less "authentic music," I knew it was necessary also to put out commercial records. One Oscar Brand record would pay for four Jeannie Robertson records, it was that simple. So at that time there was never any question in my mind about responsibility to my discipline. I was not yet a member of the discipline. Think about it: if I wanted people to listen to unaccompanied singing, and we know unaccompanied singing wasn't going to sell, we issued only five hundred records and it took three and a half years to get rid of those five hundred records. That was a statement in itself about what our intentions were. We knew the stuff couldn't sell and we were still going to issue it, because we could come out with an Oscar Brand, semi-bawdy songs or war songs or whatever. I knew that was going to sell three thousand records. By the way, those were large figures at that time, huge figures as a matter of fact.[1]

And that would balance it off. So I never had to worry about that issue. I still think there is a relationship between the two. Now I understand intellectually the relationship of the revival (and the fact that there have been nothing but revivals in this country) to, if you want to call it that, tradition, unaffected tradition, and there hasn't been unaffected tradition for a long time.

I was a member of the revival market. You see, I was a purchaser of records before I became a producer of records. And I understood which kind of records had been issued and for what reasons they had been issued. Therefore it was very simple to translate that into wearing the other hat.

Okay, that's where you started.

Yeah.

But you've alluded to setting up small concerts in New York, to being involved in the Philadelphia Folk Festival and so on. So were you involved in the booking of talent to some extent as well?

Yes, actually I was an agent for only one singer for a very short while and decided that I couldn't do her justice because I didn't have the time. That was Odetta. It was the only time that I ever tried, otherwise it was always something done as favors. People would call me up and say, "Hey, we need to get some people together for a concert, who's in town? Who can you get?" So I was always recommending to people, especially when I moved out to Philadelphia where I entered the University of Pennsylvania and was immediately corralled into the Philadelphia Folksong Society. The first year I was made the program director for the society for the monthly meetings, for concerts and everything else, and for the festival, too. I did that for thirteen years, don't forget. But none of that was done for money.

This was just a kind of a spin-off of your knowledge?

That's right. Since I knew the performers—I was directly and intimately involved with so many of them that it seemed logical for me to be called on by a lot of people and I would help them immediately. I also had the feeling, partly because I was in the recording industry, one of the most capitalistic industries in the world—I was a socialist (with a small "s")— and I felt that if I don't do it, somebody else is going to do it and rip them off. I really felt that. I would fight with radio and television people continuously, including educational TV and WHYY, that they can't just put on performers and festivals and other performances and not pay the performers. I insisted upon at least nominal payment for them. For two years they wouldn't use me on any programs; they always had asked me before that, but because I now insisted upon nominal payment for the performers they said I was breaking them financially. I said the producer of the program gets paid and the guy who sweeps up the studio gets paid, why should the people who make it all possible, the performers themselves, not get paid. It was a moral issue to me, an ethical issue.

I've always felt that the folksong revival—especially those people who are not thinking about it in such pragmatic terms—is seen as nonprofessional.

That's one of the worst things of course. As Lomax and others have pointed out, American folk music will never be treated the same as other musics. A performer of classical, art, or pop music can get five thousand dollars when he builds up a certain name reputation. In folk music you can't do that. Even when the performer develops the same level of name, he can't make it big unless he changes his musical format. There is no way he can do it. What they're saying is that folk music is incidental, nonprofessional or whatever else they want to call it. Therefore it's not worth the same as other kinds of music. That's ridiculous.

When you started writing liner notes, what models did you have besides classical—or was it just classical?

No, I didn't even have classical. All I knew was that on classical records they talked about the music and they talked about the issues of the music. There was an attempt in terms of actual knowledge, to put down information that somebody else could read and learn from. And I thought of the record as a teaching device. You remember I mentioned before that I was going to affect people by letting them listen to music that would grow on them. To me, that was a learning process. In order to assist in that learning process I had to supply information to go along with the record, information they couldn't just pick up out of the air. The chances were that most of the people buying the records would never have met a member of "the folk" or personally have known a revival singer of the category or caliber that was being recorded. Therefore I thought that you had to have information on the records, at least about the songs, if you knew nothing else, but that there should be something about the singer as well. I saw it as an educational thing and I had no real models. An occasional Folkways record that had come out earlier suggested a model to me. The pasted inside liners on Moe Asch's records, on Asch records, Disc records, and so forth, indicated what was possible; also Keynote Records did some of the same things. The interesting thing that I find is that the people who produced those kinds of records had a propagandistic or an educational perspective to begin with and that's why they put in those notes. Maybe it was because of their political biases or social educational biases or maybe a combination of both of those. They thought that the record and every other part of the medium must inform; not just what you hear but what you see as well. And I think that's probably the unconscious model that I used. I can't remember actually following a model, however. Essentially I established my own model because nobody had done notes on the back-liners for folk music on LPs, and I started with LPs, so I couldn't use the 78 model very effectively at all. I think that's where it may have come from, probably from reading the 78 liners and/or booklets. Lomax had had booklets, John Jacob Niles had had booklets, and probably those booklets suggested it to me. But I had to encapsulate it still further, to put it into a much smaller space, because I had a limited area with a much greater number of songs. Whereas a three-record 78 rpm set would have six to eight songs on it (one record might have two songs or short pieces). You still only had to worry about two sides to use, the front inside and the back inside album covers, maybe three including the back outside cover. I had only one side to use and I quite often had notes on from twelve songs and up to put into it, so I had to encapsulate a great deal of information.

By the time I was in my third summer of field recording in North Carolina (which would have been around 1954 or 1955) I had begun to lose my ethnocentricity; that is, not that I knew better than the singers what was good, but that they could tell me what it was *they* liked, and that belief in the value of the singers' aesthetic always held up well, later on in Britain and other places. But it also held up very well in the studio. I was taught by other people who worked in the studio, especially by Esman Edwards (of Prestige Records) and Bill Grauer (of Riverside) that as an A & R man you have to be very strong, you have to make the decisions. I took it with a grain of salt. I was not a musician. If I had been a musician I might have felt stronger about it. I was not a musician, therefore my idea of what was good and what was bad was based on principles other than purely musical ones. I had a very good ear, but I didn't know technically what I was listening to. Therefore I would defer to the musician for the final decision of what was a good or a bad take. Or I would call on somebody else if I had any doubt about it. This attitude remained with me later on, for example when I asked singers to write their own notes. Though that cut out part of my income (I was always paid separately for liner notes), I thought it was important because what was missing was the dimension of the singer telling you what they felt, of the singer telling you what was important to *them,* telling you what were *their* favorite songs. I could have interviewed them, I could have put down some of that information, but I couldn't do it as effectively as they could. Now for a lot of the singers this was strange. For example, Bonnie Dobson, who felt she couldn't write a sentence. Well, that simply was not true. She's a very poetic person who at that time didn't appreciate how poetic she was. To other people it came easier. Ewan MacColl and Peggy Seeger liked to write. They were professional writers, so it was easy. But in each case I decided that the perspective the revival singers could add was important. Make them write their notes, containing whatever they wanted put on the back liner, whether it was about their background or about their songs. Give them a model in case they asked you, have one ready with the kinds of information that could go on the back liner, and help them if they needed information about the songs, but *they* had to write the back liner. I think some of the best statements made by the revival about the revival are in those notes.

On that Prestige series.

Yes, in the Prestige series.

So that's one kind of liner or note concept that you developed over a period of time.

Partly it came through inspiration from Alan Lomax. Alan Lomax, when he was commenting to me on my *Guide for Fieldworkers,* repeated something that he had written earlier, which was essentially that the traditional singer is attempting to communicate with the rest of the world, and that it's your job to give the singer that opportunity, giving him the platform for doing it. This is one of the reasons why you do your work and you do it as well and as carefully as possible. You're acting as the medium for the singer to reach that larger public. I decided the revival singers were no different. Because of their training, background, ego involvement in everything they did, which may be more self-consciously intense than that of the traditional singer, why shouldn't the revival singers, the nontraditional singers, be given access to that same audience? In this particular case you don't have to translate for them; let them say what they want in their own words. And that was where the idea came for their writing their own notes. I wouldn't let them get away with a paragraph, which would have been a tendency on the part of some of them. Make them write a full set of notes. I expected a minimum of four hundred words dealing either with songs, or dealing with their experience in working on the songs. Maybe there might be only one sentence on a song, if that's all they thought it deserved; they would, however, comment on what the songs meant to them. And I would give them certain kinds of guidelines—basically they were not that different from the guidelines I later used in my *Guide for Fieldworkers*—of the kinds of questions that you ask on the history of a song, or on their personal history.

You said you had a hang-up on singers. What do you mean?

I had my favorite kind of singers. For example, I liked bland singers. I really thought even before I read anything about it that the story of the song was more important than the singers. There were certain singers who presented the story more effectively; that's why I put out so many records of Ewan MacColl and A. L. Lloyd, who I thought were great storytellers, you see, and who didn't interfere with the storyline. MacColl was far more histrionic as a singer than was Lloyd. Still I thought he told it very, very effectively. The ideal singer for American songs as far as I was concerned was Paul Clayton, which explains why I put out so many albums with him. And he couldn't have been more bland. I mean you never really *listen* to Paul Clayton. When you listen to Paul Clayton you're listening to the song and that's all. I liked Ed McCurdy for a different reason. He was an art singer but he did his art with sense, and he had a tendency to put the proper emphasis where it belonged, as did of course Richard Dyer-Bennet on a different artistic plane. My taste was very eclectic, but I can remember why I liked each one of them. There were a few singers that I issued whom I didn't like, and I won't bother mentioning them since some of them are still alive. But I put them out for pragmatic reasons. I put out one singer because I wanted his family to record but he wouldn't let me record them unless I first put out a solo record of him. I didn't think he was a solo singer—I thought he was a great family singer and I thought everybody else in the family was a better singer.

And then there were singers I recorded for purely academic purposes; they had the texts, or they had the music, and they were available to me. For example, I knew no Irish singers at the time. Patrick Galvin was interested in this material, wanted to do it, and was academically enough inclined to go look up what he didn't have. And that worked out fine. Those were among the first Irish songs recorded in the revival of the 1950s, of which fact Galvin reminded me just a couple of years ago when I last saw him.

There was sort of another issue, I don't know whether to call it an academic issue or not. The whole idea of organizing records by themes—I think I was one of the first people to do that intensely. Folkways may have had one or two before that but the idea of having street songs, of having protest songs, of having mining songs, this kind of a thing, was mine. I think I was one of the first to take themes—love songs, street songs, drinking songs—to have whole albums devoted to a single topic rather than to the singer or to the country that was involved.

The other thing I will take direct credit for is that I introduced British folk music to America. Through my recordings of A. L. Lloyd, Ewan MacColl, and Patrick Galvin, British and Irish folk music was introduced to the revival. Then these performers were brought over to festivals and Americans started copying them and developing their own repertory of British songs by looking up such songs. There wasn't much of a market for it early on, but it was my hang-up.

So I catered to my own tastes at the same time that I tried to see that it was financially viable for the companies to issue the records, and when necessary I would issue other things that could make money for them.

And this eventually had an effect in Britain, because there was a lot more available in the United States than there was in Britain?

That's right, what happened was I made the market for British singers because they were able to make some money by recording for American companies. But it can't be taken separately from Lomax's influence. Lomax's influence was far greater. Lomax introduced the British to their own singing and their own songs. The record part was in effect supplemented by me. That is, more British singers would write to me and ask to be issued in this country on records when they couldn't get issued in their own country. It also produced money for Topic, for the Workers Music Association, which was the original owner of Topic Records. When they would produce albums for me that would give them enough money to produce their own albums of the same singers. That made money, so they could issue more records. The more records they issued there, the more material I had to select from. So it was a symbiotic relationship. It's still funny when I go to Britain and I find out how well known I am in folk music circles there. Some of my records are classics now; they're pieces of legend because I haven't produced any recent British material for some time. For example, I find that people remember the Alf Edwards record that was issued only in the United States. It wasn't even issued in England, as far as I know, and it should have been but nobody even thought of putting out an album of concertina music at that time.

Would it be proper to say that there were hits and stars in this revival music during the period that you were active? To what extent were you aware of this sort of thing, how did this work? Did you get feedback on this sort of thing?

Sure, we got feedback on it continuously. First of all I got it in several ways. One, I got it because companies would immediately ask you, once they saw their own sales figures, go and do another one. There's nothing that succeeds like success and that's *immediate* in the music industry, no matter where or at whatever level, as well as in most parts of American business. Instead of trying to find out what the formula is and to go and distill the formula and work it out and improve it, all they want you to do is to repeat the formula whether you know what the formula is or not; for example, the idea of recording two singers, if two singers made it on one record, use the same two singers; if one singer made it, use that singer. That certainly seems to be the case in the American business sense. But it also had to do with the fact that I would be called by people who knew I had produced such and such a record; they would say, "Listen, can you get them for our festival?" That gave me a chance to book these people into festivals that would promote the record, which in turn would give them a bigger market, resulting in my getting them a second or follow-up record, or even third or fourth records. And I was a well-trained M.B.A. I knew how to deal with markets, with sales, with market research, and I knew that promotion was a big part of it all. I had worked for Fairchild Publications, first in the advertising-production department, then in the market research department, so I knew both sides of that, as well. And, as I said, *all* my training has always stood me in very, very good stead. I'm a very, very pragmatic person. And I manipulate what is there to be manipulated. My interest lay in protecting the interest of the performers, in almost every case, and in developing their careers further. Aside from that seemingly altruistic stance, my idea was that if something is good, how do you find out what's good? I was always disturbed by the way the industry went about it but there was nothing much I could do about it.

I've always wondered how you felt about Riverside Records' two series, the Folklore (600), which presented traditional performers, and the Specialty (800), which featured revivalists.

I really liked the revival; I always liked singers of folksongs as well as traditional singers. I also liked people who did almost anything with folk-song, basically; my taste included art singers—[Richard] Dyer-Bennet, [Ed] McCurdy; and I always liked sweet-voiced women singers like Evelyn Beers, and Bonnie Dobson. These were sort of another subcategory in my head, as well as liking traditional singers. I like Woody because I liked people who had rough voices and weren't polished. I saw them all as somehow connected to each other and feeding on each other and I think that in that sense I was correct. Though my later training in folklore indicated these are different kinds of singers, I'm now beginning to think again that they're not so different after all. They're just treated separately and we therefore pretend that they're separate and different, but ultimately they really aren't all that different.

I produced what there was. I also had a sense that I had a responsibility to the company, not because I was well paid, since that was never the case, nor because I made my living from it. If I didn't make it there I could have gone back into market research and I'd be making a lot more money. So that wasn't the issue either. It had to do with my sense of responsibility to the company, to the performers and, in a sense, a responsibility to myself as well, for how I dealt with people, as a moral and ethical human being. I saw the issue of the pragmatics and the business promotion of performers as being related to the end of furthering folk music and I was really gung-ho on promoting folk music. My friends who I meet now, who knew me when I was in the recording industry, said that I talked about nothing except folk music at the time and that there was no way that they could turn me off. After a while they couldn't even listen any more. Not that I was repeating myself, but that I was so intense that unless they shared that intensity, it was impossible to really communicate with me. This intensity had to do with my attitude that whatever you do you do full-heartedly, that is, you go into it gung-ho, there's no other way. At least that's my approach to it. Maybe I'm rationalizing the fact that that's the way it is, but I don't know of any other way. If I promote one kind of folk music it will promote another kind, I was absolutely convinced of it.

I had an exchange of letters with John Edwards in which we argued about the definitions of folksong. He was much narrower; he was only interested in one kind of music, he saw it as one kind of thing. Our letters were on defining what it was that we were respectively interested in. I saw folk music as being a special thing at the time but that the revival singers (whom I still hadn't called revival singers, and who weren't being called revival singers at the time) were important because they introduced people like me to folk music who could then listen to traditional singers, who could then listen to hillbilly music, which they otherwise wouldn't have. That is, that folk music itself was so alien to most Americans that you had to introduce them to it, you had to soften them up for it. The best way was in the musical forms that were closest to the ones that they were most familiar with. Pop music, whether they liked it or not, was what they heard on the radio. Therefore you introduced folk music to them, which was certainly alien to them through the medium they knew, through the expressive form they knew, which was pop music. So you have folk songs sung by pop singers, then you introduce them to folk songs sung by hillbilly singers, which is what I saw as the next stage. I don't know whether Charlie Seeger had yet written his article on the continuum from hillbilly to the citybilly.

That's something that you discovered later, and it made sense?

Yes, oh, it made absolute sense. And the idea that, then you could wean them away from instruments and issue unaccompanied singing by nontraditional singers and then you could introduce them to traditional singers. That way you could cover the whole spectrum of all the kinds of music by simply leading them from one kind of music to another. That was my own experience; that's how I had gotten to like traditional singing. It was by listening to music and identifying with the previous stage of music that I was interested in, and then carrying over some of that interest into the next stage that I was listening to. In other words, music grows on you, you aren't born to like a specific kind of music, you may like one kind because you hear a lot of it and you dislike some other kind. But you can learn to like the kind that you dislike if you hear enough of it and if enough of it is good in whatever framework "good" means for that particular aesthetic as you employ it.

In a sense your editing, it seems to me, has a kind of a political dimension.

Yes, that's a good word, political is a good word, ideational, it was; it was my idea to sell folk music to people. The way to do it was a fairly conscious one, that the only way I could do it was by letting everybody come to it through their own particular interest, including even classical performance of folksong. I never got into instrumental music until much later (I became interested in instrumental music only in Ireland), but in singing I was convinced that art singers could introduce people to non-art singing of folk song, that pop singers could introduce people to hillbilly singing, that hillbilly singing could introduce them to traditional singing of folksongs; that all of these fed on each other ultimately in the larger scheme, though there was no real scheme in my head at that time. The idea was that this was all beautiful music and I didn't care how people get to it. Every music serves that particular end, and I think that my records, the kinds of records that I produced, showed this kind of eclectic philosophical approach—all musics are viable. The first records were reissues of nontraditional singers singing folksongs, then I looked for singers who would sing unaccompanied but who were still revival singers, like MacColl and Lloyd, who knew the tradition very, very well. All of these were mixed up; if you attempted to plot it you couldn't find that I did one kind of singer first, then another kind of singer. It's what was available to me at the time. There was a certain amount of pure chance occurrence as well—who made themselves available to me or whom could I draw on. And this would include anybody and everybody, so that when I was working with Jac Holzman, I met Jean Ritchie and then Frank Warner, and that didn't mean that I could no longer go back to an Oscar Brand or a Bob Gibson.

There's a certain amount of serendipity to all of this too. The order of things that happen to you and therefore become part of your input whether you like it or not, is not always controllable by you. And you respond to the individual issue when it comes up and presents itself so that there doesn't appear to be any organized philosophical sense. Now when I sat down, however, to edit or record a tape, that was a different issue. Now that to me was philosophically controlled and was in a larger sense a set of issues from the very, very beginning.

Just as I was interested in fieldwork and even prior to going back to school had become interested in technical issues and in philosophical and theoretical issues of fieldwork, I was always interested in how was the best way to get somebody to sing? What is the best way to get a response, how do you do this kind of a thing with a person? I was concerned with the human interaction that would produce the folkloric situation, which are all big words now, and while I did not use them at that time I was concerned with what it was.

I had the same problem in recording tapes. For example, I record in the field, I go down to North Carolina and I'm recording people who I met through Bascom Lamar Lunsford—Pegram, Parham, Aunt Samantha Bumgardner—the people who were at the Asheville Folk Festival. How do I put out a record of them? Because this isn't the same thing you do in a studio. You go into a studio, you record in a studio, and you have the singer do it over and over until you get the take you like, if you don't get a take you like, you put it off until the next day and then you have to do it again until eventually you get a take you like or you decide not to use the song. You can't quite do the same thing with traditional singers.

I saw very, very serious results from such an approach. A singer-collector whom I knew, for example, would go down and badger the shit out of a traditional singer. Now that person screwed up a couple of singers that I worked with in North Carolina, by going down later on to record them and getting them to rerecord, rerecord, rerecord, and rerecord until this person got the recording out of them that this person wanted. Now I knew that you couldn't do this with people who were not trained singers, people who sang for reasons other than perfection, that is, where they had a sense of perfection—it was a different sense than our sense of perfection. They were looking to tell a story well. They didn't care about if their voice broke, whereas this person did. They didn't care if they missed a note on an instrument if they were accompanying themselves, that wasn't important. It had to do with the effectiveness of communication, though they wouldn't have used terms like that, but that's essentially what they were concerned with. And this person's definition of effectiveness of communication had to do with perfection of media use and language, which was not of the same order as theirs. And I became interested in those problems as I wrote up in some of my album notes later on, like what is a good singer, in the cowboy-song album where I discussed what different singers had told me. And I was using the records really as my platform for the ideas that I was developing. So that if you want to see the development of a folklorist before he becomes a folklorist, read his album notes.

I wouldn't swear to some of those things today but I'm fascinated by reading them now and seeing how right I was because I was naive and therefore didn't have any academic prejudices. I have to rethink those issues now before I come out straight on them. That is, I had good intuition and I was listening to what people were saying then.

Plus you also had to explain to people who are not academics and don't care about what the previous thought is—they want to know "what does this all mean?"

And I had to find the words to do it. And I wrote a lot easier then because I didn't have academic problems, I didn't have to worry about, was that a good English sentence? As long as it communicated what I wanted to say, which is still the most effective way of writing, I just was able to zip off what I wanted to say and do it well. Now, when you rethink for papers you have to be grammatically correct as well as communicating theory, now that's another issue. Anyway, I don't think I should go into that matter further because I still have to deal with students whom I have to take to task for things like that. The question of when you record in the field, a singer who stops in the middle of a song and redoes a verse, do you get the singer to sing over the songs, as this person I was talking about would say, "take it from the top," or, when I'm working with Baxter [Wareham], "let's do it over." Instead, I'll splice the tape together. The whole issue of splicing became an important issue then. It's not a record of a folk performance, it's a record of an edited performance, when I do it. And I had to figure out what my responsibilities were to (1) the public, which is a record that is good to listen to, easy to listen to, straight through; (2) to the folklorist, an actual representation, an ethnographic record, if you will; and (3) to the singer, which is the best that he bloody well can do, which is what the singer wants to present to the world, wants to communicate with the larger world, and his interest in doing it as effectively as he thinks he can, which he may not be able to achieve without the help of the recording engineer. Therefore I considered my commitment to the folklorist less important than commitment to the performer.

If there has been a single line that has run through my rationalizing of what I've done, either while it was going on or now in looking back at it, it's that ultimately the person who makes all the wheels go is the performer. Therefore your primary responsibility, your primary concern—because nothing else can follow without him—has to be that performer. A record that I issue of a singer, which is supposed to represent the best of that singer, whatever it is he or she thinks would be the best, leaves me with no compunction whatsoever about editing a tape and splicing together two verses or splicing out a verse if they've repeated something. I will not go so far as to correct individual words though I could do that, too. I used to laugh myself sick when I read what was going on with the Nixon tapes.

Because of all my experience with editing, I knew I could put together any two or three things, where to make the splice so that you can't even hear the splice, how to splice in the middle of a word or in the middle of a sound, instrumental or vocal, and to produce a continuous sound as if it was a stream of activity that actually occurred.

When it came to the traditional singer there was never a question to me about splicing if it made the performance better. Now there were times that I left an error in because the error made an ethnographic point. I view an ethnographic record and an aesthetic record as two different things, that is, the aesthetic record is not meant to be a document of an actual ongoing happening, a stream of activity. But sometimes I leave errors in to show what happens in the singer's mind; for example, he sings a verse out of order, or he sings the verse from another song, or he begins a verse from another song and it makes a folkloric point. When I'm interested in a folkloric record, that's fine, otherwise I don't think I have the right to do it, and I do it only with the permission of the singer. You have the same responsibility to the singer whether you do it for an academic article or whether you do it for a commercial record. It's his final say that permits you to go ahead and do it. Otherwise, you ruin your position with that performer, you ruin it for all other folklorists with that and related performers. Those are pragmatic reasons, but there is a moral reason too: you owe it to your informant to do the best that you can for him or her.

Did you in fact take your final test pressings back to your informants?

Oh yes, I would send them copies of the tapes in some cases where they had proper equipment, or if I knew I was going down the following summer (and records never came out the same year so I didn't have that problem) I would play the tapes for them. If I couldn't do any of those things and if there was an issue of time, I would write to them and tell them what I was doing. The only time I didn't do that, interestingly enough, was with revival singers. Sometimes I didn't check with them and I got my ass eaten for that. But I always did it with traditional singers—every time, there was never a time that I didn't do it. It just seemed so right, so necessary, as there were things that I couldn't understand that they could, about what it was that they were doing, and I thought that to keep me straight they had to review it, to keep me from making a serious error.

So there was never any question about my editing the tapes and letting them listen to the edited materials. There were a number of interesting sort of side issues here as well. The record companies wanted perfect records and perfect recordings. For that reason I had to become a good engineer. I had to learn how to use the best field equipment or the best portable studio equipment to make good recordings. And, unlike the concept of the documentary record, which is to record in context (and nobody has done more writing about recording in context than I in my *Guide for Fieldworkers*), I did not see the commercial record as that kind of document. There were documents of that type recorded by Carl Fleischhauer and Alan Jabbour in which the idea was to record in context, and that it's meaningless unless recorded in context, that the effect is so much better when, for example, you have background sounds. I want to know if they really believed the performers thought so. For example, I produced a tape of a storyteller/singer and I brought it to them. They said, why don't you record this person in front of an audience, not because the storytelling isn't effective, or the singing isn't effective but because it would be better for the record. That's as false in its own way as what I did; but what I did, I did consciously. When I was producing a record for a commercial *record company,* quite often I would play back a tape for a singer in which a kid had just opened up the door and somebody in the background said "ssh," and they had continued singing. They said let's do it over. That is *they* had the sense of wanting to replicate a studio recording. They had heard records, all of them had heard records. They didn't hear background noises on those records. That became the standard to them for what a good record was. Right or wrong is not the point, that became the standard, therefore they wanted a record that sounded like it was in a studio, or sounded quiet, or the best possible sound without interruption by exterior noises, and that has been the model essentially that I work with for most records. Now I do use introductory comments, because I interview the singers before and after and I will sometimes add that to the record. I think that the best kind of record is one that Ewan MacColl and Peggy Seeger did with Sam Larner, for example, where they did intensive interviewing, where they worked in the contextual statements of meaning, but did it with room sound, which was quiet, rather than the contextual sound of an audience. I just found, when I asked, that singers prefer it that way.

The other situation is like this: how do you take pictures of people? Is it best to take a picture of a person while they're doing something or while they're still? Well, I'll tell you the best way—the best way is the way your informant wants it, and if your informant wants to be formal, if he wants to be looking into the camera, if he wants to be dressed properly, if he wants to be as good looking and as effective looking and as nice looking as his ideal of what he should look like should be, then that's how he should be photographed. He doesn't want to be shown with his hair down. These photographs that photographers take in context, in midstream activity, are sometimes offensive to those being photographed. If they're going to do informal shooting and the candid shot, they must also take the noncandid shot, the formal shot. My experience has been that most people want to present themselves to the world formally, not informally; they may learn to manipulate the informal to make it formal, as, for example, the country singer who would never think of going on stage in anything less than his best clothing, who finds out that the best way to get attention on stage is to wear stereotypical country bumpkin clothing and therefore dresses up that way. Whatever it is, it doesn't matter, whether it's in revival or in the tradition, that's the way people want to present themselves. There's a philosophical issue here. Which is the real truth? Is the real truth for us to tell them how to pose, for us to tell them what to wear, for us to tell them to be natural, or for us to say how would you like to be recorded? How would you like to look? And then using that as a model, to do it that way and then check back with them to see if its suits them.

NOTE

1. These remarks are excerpts from an interview with Kenneth S. Goldstein conducted by Neil V. Rosenberg on 2 January 1979. Rosenberg's questions appear in italics.

PART 2

The New Aesthetic

We turn next to a North American revival milieu that might be termed "post-boom" but which also fits under Stekert's rubric of "new aesthetic." Present-day in-group terms for this music-culture link the word "music" with "alternate," "contemporary," or "acoustic." As this is written, the leading popular figures are acoustic-guitar-playing composer-performers like Tracey Chapman and Michelle Shocked. This music-culture, although an outgrowth of the great boom, was strongly influenced by the British revival. Its early American manifestations were outlined by John Cohen for the readers of *Sing Out!* in 1971.[1] Its parallel Canadian roots are described by I. Sheldon Posen in the first article in this section. The two ethnographic studies that follow examine a song that began in the same Canadian sector of this revival.

Included in Stekert's formulation of the new-aesthetic approach was the idea that this was a kind of tradition in itself. This is echoed in Jackson's suggestion that the folk revival created its own traditions and—as the authors suggest in this section—can be and has been studied from an ethnographic perspective. This dimension of revivalism exists in its own cultural contexts of the club, coffeehouse, festival, and other essentially urban middle-class performance venues. There are significant differences between this type of revival and the named-system revivals that form the focus of Part 3. The new-aesthetic involvement in folk music is viewed by some as fickle and dilettantish. Conversely, the way in which new-aesthetic revivalists situate themselves in their own cultural milieu rather than in some romantic conception of another culture can be interpreted as a more open and honest way of expressing fundamentally middle-class values. But the new-aesthetic revivalists may also be less tolerant of the working-class roots of the music on which the new aesthetic is based, a point that emerges in Lederman's paper.

In "On Folk Festivals and Kitchens: Questions of Authenticity in the Folksong Revival," first published in a revival magazine, I. Sheldon Posen explained to revivalists how his perceptions of revival activity changed as he moved from being a revivalist musician to becoming an academic folk-lorist. Like Stekert, he recognized revivalist-scholar tensions between the two camps as he worked to justify his own involvement in the revival. This article can be seen as his final statement as a performer, the kind of state-ment I discuss in my article on bluegrass revivalism later in this volume.

Not surprisingly, Posen's explication of revival was couched in terms of his new academic profession: it could be considered authentic in terms of context. This reflects the folkloric "state of the art" when Posen wrote in 1979. With this reprinting of the article he offers a new introduction that shows that his thinking on this issue has shifted, particularly with respect to the question of authenticity. In a sense he has come to accept a "new aesthetic" position on this issue, one in which contemporary art and life take a more prominent position than do the histories of the music's former existences.

The idea of studying the revival as a separate social group has occurred not just to folklorists; in fact there are ways in which scholars from other disciplines can approach this topic with more "objectivity" than folklorists. But all academics tend to couch their analyses in terms of the theoretical baggage and terminology of their discipline. So Arlene Kaplan, a sociologist writing about the California Bay Area scene of the early 1950s, found social "deviance" at the center of the bohemian proto-beatnik scene she investi-gated.[2] And the social psychologist John L. Smith, examining a British folk club in the early eighties, described it in terms of what he called "the 'new' paradigm of ethogenic social psychology."[3] For the concerned intellectual who is outside the discipline such specialized language may seem unneces-sarily obscure. But ongoing debate in any rigorous academic discipline re-quires at least some of this philosophical and linguistic scaffolding. Scholars interested in ideas about folk-music revivals—which so often involve cul-tural and artistic alternatives—ultimately benefit from these alternative per-spectives from various disciplines.

Although not a performer, Pauline Greenhill, a Canadian folklorist, grew up listening to folk music in the context of revival interests within her family. The decision as a folklorist to study a revival song reflects her research on the popular community poetry of Canada, which revealed a broad range of types of involvement in such creation. In " 'The Folk Pro-cess' in the Revival: 'Barrett's Privateers' and 'Baratt's Privateers,' " Green-hill follows in the path of her mentor, Roger deV. Renwick,[4] in examining a revival product utilizing the analytical tools of her discipline instead of making a priori judgments about the nature of tradition or context. But she carries the approach a step further by dealing entirely with revival products.[5]

What in fact are the differences between revival and nonrevival products and processes? Emerging from Greenhill's careful examination is the conclusion that cultural differences between Canadian and British values can be seen when one looks at the career of a revival song in the two cultures. Thus the issue of group identity, so central to many definitions of folklore, remains as relevant inside revival contexts as it does outside, although it is to some extent transmuted into a characteristically middle-class concern, that of national identity.

Anne Lederman's " 'Barrett's Privateers': Performance and Participation in the Folk Revival" parallels and complements Greenhill's study by focusing on the performance dimensions of the song in its revival contexts. She finds that within this milieu lie unresolved paradoxes concerning the values of communal participation and solo (or ensemble) concertizing. These paradoxes can be seen in the ways in which this song was created and moved from Canada to England.

NOTES

1. John Cohen, "What Happened?"

2. Kaplan, "A Study of Folksinging." This article was based on her M.A. thesis of the same title, done in the Department of Sociology and Social Institutions at the University of California, Berkeley, in 1954.

3. Smith, "The Ethogenics of Music Performance," p. 154.

4. Renwick, "Two Yorkshire Poets." One of the two performed primarily in "what is often known as the 'folksong revival scene' " (p. 244).

5. "The Folk Process" was the title of a column of notes and queries that ran during the fifties and sixties in *Sing Out!*, the leading American revival magazine.

On Folk Festivals and Kitchens: Questions of Authenticity in the Folksong Revival

I. Sheldon Posen

Author's Introduction

This article was written around 1976 and appeared in the now defunct *Canada Folk Bulletin*. In agreeing to its republication, I decided to let the article stand substantially as written. I must admit on rereading it that some parts were hard even for me to absorb (I was a graduate student in folklore at the University of Pennsylvania when I wrote it, and Professor Ray Birdwhistell's uniquely phrased pronouncements on "context" were on my mind), but by and large I think what I wrote holds up as a worthwhile document of the mid-century folksong revival.

There are aspects of the article I would write differently now. There is much more to be said about "context," for instance: contrary to what I say in the article, contexts do mix, all the time, constantly interplaying and recontexting each other—in Newfoundland kitchens as well as on festival grounds. Not recognizing this when I wrote the article, I wasn't in a position to see festivals as the tourist experience they were and are: I might have been less hard on them and myself.

I would also try to open up the article's world a bit. *Why* so much harping on authenticity? In a way, "authentic" folksong was only one of the North American middle class's demands at the time for commodities of a certain perceived moral and aesthetic quality. (Others were organic foodstuffs, ethnic cuisine, blue jeans and work shirts, "industrial" cookware, and "professional" camping gear.) People were shopping for alternatives to what was offered them either by the marketplace or by their culture. Many were looking to give their lives new or expanded meaning by adopting aspects of the lives of others. With varying degrees of sincerity and innocence, people became tourists—or pilgrims—traveling in someone else's culture. They made choices from a menu they saw offered them by the rest of North America and the world, of music to play, food to cook, clothing to wear. The feeling was, the more "authentic" the item or emulation they found, the more valid their experience of it and the transformation it produced.

Among folksong revivalists, many who took the notion of "folk" as the basis of their quest for authenticity sooner or later decided they either couldn't or didn't have to go to "outside" groups for what they sought. Using criteria they had learned to apply to others, they could recontext and essentially validate a folk group they already belonged to, one that usually turned out to be their ethnic group. Their own authenticity was then built in or could be reconfigured. (I am thinking, for example, of the urban, Jewish, blues or bluegrass revival musicians who foregrounded their identity as the children of immigrants, invoked a small-town, East European, Jewish past, and founded Yiddish-singing klezmer bands.)

My own little mazeway resynthesis (if I may make free with that term of A. F. C. Wallace's) was of that order, helped along by the cultural schizophrenia that academic folklore induces in some of its students. But I took a *class* rather than *ethnic* route—the middle-income suburb, not the East European *shtetl*. I also maintained some academic distance, at least in the article, by allowing the process of the quest itself to stand as the chief sign of my membership.

The striving after authenticity is no longer a burning issue in whatever it is nowadays that occupies the folksong slot in popular culture (are we still in "the folksong revival"?). True, contemporary adherents have certain criteria for recognizing folk music—acoustic instruments (usually), audience participation (usually), and political or topical content (sometimes)— and directors of folk festivals justify their rosters (or not) in terms of these criteria. ("Folk music isn't just some old geezer sitting under a tree playing a banjo," said one organizer recently, defending his festival's importation of breakdancers.) But mostly, if it is given any shrift at all, authenticity for this generation of folkies is something to be satirized (the Kipper Family, an English revival group, comes to mind) or left for the folklorists to worry about (*viz.*, the sardonic comments about authenticity from many revival stage performers if they know there is a folklorist in the audience).

It is hard to say in a few sentences and in general terms just how this relaxation of *angst* came about. At some point in the 1970s, people seemed to tire of the whole argument about authenticity and just decided to play and listen to what they wanted. Very 1970s. Of course by that time, the folksong revival had ended as a popular-culture first run and was going into reruns, or spawning sequels. Where folk music was still played or listened to on a commercial basis, style had replaced context, had even *become* context, as performers got younger and grew farther away from "traditional" sources. A performer's connection with tradition—his "authenticity"—if it was promoted, became an emblem of that performer's persona, like the price tag dangling from Minnie Pearl's hat.

Now, in these postmodern, postfusion early 1990s, most folk performers offer a personalized collage of material, executed with references to all manner of past styles and sources. The elements are bound together by an overall sound—Celtic, say, or country, or singer/songwriter, or even "traditional" (another can of worms). If anything, "authentic" has become a "flavor" within that performance sound.

Maybe this casual approach to folksong, not to say life, is healthier than searching for a culture to be at home in and agonizing over how to be authentic. I must say I've tried to give that up myself.

On Folk Festivals and Kitchens: Questions of Authenticity in the Folksong Revival

It was a call from the Mariposa Folk Festival in Toronto several years ago for contributions to a book about the festival that got me thinking about my involvement with Mariposa over the years. I had come to think about my relationship with the festival as a singer, organizer, and researcher as a relatively pleasant and on the whole uncomplicated one. On reflection, however, I realized that there was one point in 1970, just as I finished my first year of formal studies in Folklore at Memorial University of Newfoundland, when I decided that the Mariposa Festival in particular, the folksong revival in general, and my participation in both, were a sham and a farce, and that I should sever my ties with both permanently. Because there may be other "folkies" who have suffered or who will suffer similar crises of purpose or identity, and because I think that my particular struggles with questions of "authenticity" in the folksong revival shed light on larger issues of context and the general notion of folklore, I offer this account of my problems and of how I reached an understanding of them at least with myself.

When I began working for Mariposa in 1968, I was what I would now call an "urban folkie." To me a folksong was any song that hadn't patently come off the pop charts or the Broadway stage, and that had an acoustic guitar or banjo accompaniment or could be given one. *Sing Out!* magazine, my bible at the time, told me that there were issues at stake which should govern my choice of songs: it talked about "authenticity" and "the people's songs," but I found that kind of polemic boring and I largely ignored it. If I liked a song's tune and/or the words (especially the "message"), I sang it. By 1968, most of the songs I was singing were ones composed by my contemporaries: Bob Dylan, Joni Mitchell, Leonard Cohen, Phil Ochs, Tom Paxton, Mike Settle, Mark Spoelstra, and the like. What I couldn't learn from the pages of *Sing Out!* I learned from recordings by performers such as the Weavers, the Kingston Trio, Pete Seeger, Theodore Bikel, and Tom Rush. Many of the songs they sang actually met *Sing Out!*'s criteria for authenticity, but mostly I learned them because I liked their melody or their message. I sang the old labor union and Spanish Civil War songs I'd learned at summer camp, as well as those which treated of the burning issues of the day: (American) civil rights and the peace movement. But I guess my preference was for "personal" songs about wandering and male-female relations.

All this changed with the appearance at Mariposa in 1968 of a young American singer named Michael Cooney and an exciting British group called the Young Tradition. Cooney, at the time, was a fresh, charming "singer of old songs" (as he billed himself), with a smiling, boyish manner which belied his essentially serious approach and helped him put across a huge store of historical information about his material. The songs were by and large "traditional," which to me came to mean that they were anonymously written and had been passed from one person to another, over time and space, till they had gotten to Michael Cooney. What hadn't come of its own accord, Cooney had got by dint of his own researches into collections of songs compiled by people called "folklorists," and through contact with folklorists themselves like Joe Hickerson of the Library of Congress Folksong Archive. Cooney called what he sang "neat songs," and he presented them to his audiences in a carefully casual, immensely entertaining program, ordered brilliantly to show family resemblances among them or to point up their different approaches to larger issues. I was fascinated by the materials he had turned up (many of the songs were quite beautiful, others simply very funny or just fun). More important for me, though, was his patter. I had always had a difficult time on stage trying to think of interesting things to say in between songs. Cooney's easygoing scholarship tracing song travels and transformations, and his accounts of his researches and delvings, gave me a performance model which would save me from comedy routines I was no good at, or from being bored and boring talking about my personal life.

The Young Tradition cast a spell quite different from Cooney's, but no less powerful. They too gave historical background for their songs, most of which they had found in the record, tape, cylinder, and book libraries of Cecil Sharp House in London. Their patter was refreshingly tart, probably the sharpest and driest of anyone's. But the Young Tradition's magic for me lay in the musical setting they devised for the songs: a crystal-hard harmony whose outlines were carved by Peter Bellamy's brittle tenor, filled out by Heather Wood's indomitable alto, and given a Gibraltar-like solidity by Royston Wood's bass. When the Young Tradition sang in the night concert at Mariposa that year, the stage seemed populated with medieval characters from their ballads; the trees on the island rang with hunting horns and the baying of hounds after foxes; and mundane, pleasure-boated and grain-betankered Toronto Harbour was transformed into the docks of the port of London a century ago, the air filled with creakings and groanings of sails being hoist aloft miles of masts by sweating, shanty-singing deck hands. This was my entrance into the world of British traditional song and unaccompanied harmony singing, and I was enthralled. While traveling in the British Isles the next year, I haunted folk clubs and Cecil Sharp House, and discovered and idolized singers on the English scene such as Lou Killen, the Watersons, and most of all, Martin Carthy.

When I returned to Toronto in the fall of 1969, my whole repertoire had changed, and with it my attitudes towards what I should sing and how. I wasn't alone: there was a whole traditional folksong revival scene under way in both Canada and the U.S. One of the central issues was the "authenticity" of song and performance style. As far as I was concerned now, a song had to be traditional for me even to consider it for my repertoire. Bob Dylan was out, Francis James Child was in. And the old standards for performance style were tightened and expanded at the same time. There was still what I would call a scale of "folkness" against which performance was measured, but it was modified to accommodate the new British repertoire and accompaniment instruments. For instance, singing an English song to concertina accompaniment was more "authentic" than singing the same song with a guitar; singing it *a capella* was more "valid" than either of those. Never mind that we were singing English sea shanties while doing no work, too fast and with too much harmony—we were singing them unaccompanied, affecting English accents, and our harmonies were in fifths. This was folkier than some clowns in a male glee club singing them to orchestra accompaniment and harmonizing in thirds. The traditional folksong revival created an environment in which performers vied with one another in being "folkier than thou," and audiences judged them on the same terms. (Just how seriously these matters were taken is discernible in the pages of *Sing Out!* at the time. See especially the letters from the editor to Bob Dylan during the mid 1960s, or Michael Cooney's advice to folksingers in his "General Delivery" column in the early 1970s.)

As a member of the traditional folksong revival, I felt it was my duty to learn as many traditional songs as I could, and as much about them as possible. Being from the sort of middle-class background that holds that if you want to learn about something, you take a course in it, I enrolled in the M.A. program in Folklore at Memorial University of Newfoundland ("M.U.N.") in the fall of 1970. Here I suffered a series of shocks. First, I discovered that there was more to folksong than pretty melodies and recondite histories, and that there was more to folklore than folksong. To my amazement, I saw that folklore students and scholars at the university were studying people and the way they lived. They were examining cultural issues and problems by looking at traditional ways of life including what and how they sang. My own desire simply to learn "neat songs" for performance began to look very trivial indeed.

My second discovery was that there was another set of criteria for gauging the "authenticity" of folklore. Folklore, I learned, is defined by many academics by the *context* of which it (any item—say, a song) is a part. Neither the style of performance nor the origin of the item alone serves to define it as folklore. Meaning lies not in the item, but in its function in the performing situation. For instance, so-called ethnic jokes take on widely variable meanings in different surrounds: "newfie"/"polack"/"Rastus"/priest-minister-rabbi jokes told by (respectively) a Newfoundlander/ Pole/Black/Jew to members of his own group, have different information flowing into them than would the same jokes told by that member to nonmembers of those groups, or by nonmembers among themselves. A U.S. government official some years ago told an "improper" joke about the Pope as part of one context (as if "among friends"), but its being reported publicly brought information from other contexts to bear ("told among friends" became "told by a non-Catholic to other non-Catholics"), and the official was forced to resign.

What I began to recognize during my first year in Newfoundland is that the context within which *I* sang folksongs, and within which Newfoundlanders sang folksongs, were worlds apart. This came home to me in an exhilarating and yet painful way on my first collecting trip. Wilf Wareham, a Newfoundlander and fellow student in the Folklore department, took me to the house of an old outport fisherman he had known as a boy, to record some of the man's songs. We sat at the table in this man's kitchen, and we talked and he sang for us while his children came and went, first hushed and awed, then smiling and bold, and his wife kneaded bread in a huge tin basin and baked it in her blackened oil stove. The air was warm and heavy with the smells of baking bread and stove oil, of cigarette smoke and the sweet dark rum that we had brought to drink. As the afternoon wore on, neighbors stopped in and had a drop of rum or tea, and asked for songs or gave us one themselves. When the old man sang it was to neighbors and friends (excepting us, of course, and really it was only I who was an outsider), songs that they all knew and which seemed in subject matter and style to be of a piece with—logical extensions of—their own lives. The singers were physically close enough to their listeners to touch them (and, I found out later, it sometimes happens that a Newfoundland singer and listener *will* hold hands and swing them gently in time to the singing) and continuously throughout the singing, singers and listeners could catch the expressions registered in each other's faces and bodies. Through this visual contact, as well as through comments made by listeners during the singing, all the participants were always aware of how the singer was doing and of how the song was going over. The whole event that afternoon was one of the most intensely involving I have ever been a part of, and I came away thinking, "This is the real thing; this is how it should be done."

That experience and others like it had a chilling effect on my attitude towards my own singing, and towards Mariposa. First of all, I wondered how I, a middle-class kid from Toronto, was warranted singing songs so removed from my own life—about nineteenth-century English sailors or seventeenth-century "lords and ladies fair," or of American cowboys and hill people, or even closer to home, of north Ontario shantyboys and Newfoundland fishermen. (This dilemma is the subject of a 1960s song by Shel Silverstein called "Folksinger's Lament," in which the singer agonizes over questions such as how you can sing about loading cotton on the levee "when you're young and white and Jewish ... and the only levee you know is the Levi who lives down the block.") And I wondered how I could reconcile singing such songs for other middle-class people like myself in coffeehouses and living rooms.

Worse still was the scene at Mariposa, where hundreds of strangers listened to other strangers performing on stages thousands of feet away, whom they couldn't see and who couldn't see them, whose only means of interaction was, on the one hand, talking and singing through a microphone, and on the other, applauding at the end of each song—how could this be remotely related to what I had seen in that Newfoundland kitchen? How could questions of "authenticity" obtain in such a situation? How could the festival boast of being more "traditional" than others? The whole situation struck me as ludicrous. I all but stopped singing in public for almost a year, and did not accept an invitation to sing at Mariposa in the summer of 1970. To paraphrase journalist Calvin Trillin, I had "authenticized myself out of the folksong business."

It took another year of thinking and studying before I was able to work some of this out. One of the first events that started my mind shifting was hearing Neil Rosenberg, a professor of mine at M.U.N. with whom I had begun to sing and play in a bluegrass band, explain to a radio interviewer why it was that our band did not perform traditional Newfoundland material. His answer hinged on "surround." He said that bluegrass music was a folk form which had originated on stage and always involved the use of microphones for performances to relatively large audiences. He therefore felt no compunction in presenting the same music under the same conditions—it was the way the music was meant to be performed. Newfoundland traditional music, on the other hand, was "kitchen music," and could not be done justice to, even if we were able to sing it right, in the bluegrass kind of situation.

So I had this concept to work with: items do not give meaning to contexts; rather, the reverse is true. And contexts do not mix, whatever the surround and however appropriate the singing. (It turns out that our band later *did* perform certain kinds of traditional Newfoundland songs in bars and on concert stages, because we began to see that Newfoundland bands were doing it and that Newfoundlanders expected it of them. Singing those songs under those conditions was, in fact, a popular traditional form, and we were violating no proprieties, theoretical or otherwise. But we had to be shown this first by members; we, as nonmembers, could not take the initiative.)

A second experience which enabled me to reconsider my thoughts about participating in the revival was researching and writing my M.A. thesis, a study of singing traditions at children's summer camps. I had selected camp for my study because it was the situation from my own urban background that I thought most resembled the Newfoundland outport community—my idea then of the ideal "folk society." One of the conclusions I came to in my thesis was that any songs sung in such a close little group had to be folksongs. My argument was as follows: items are not intrinsically "folk"; rather, their "folkness" lies in the functions and processes and ultimately the contexts of which they are a part. Camp exhibits all the qualities that have been traditionally associated with folk groups; its songs function as folksongs for the group; therefore campsongs, in fact any songs sung at camp (all things being equal), are folksongs. I was helped in this argument by an article by University of Pennsylvania folklorist Dan Ben Amos which defined folklore as "artistic communication in small groups."

Writing the campsong thesis finally freed me from thinking about folklore as old exotica which "belonged" to a "folk" whom I had until then (unconsciously) defined as uneducated, rural, peasant people. Instead, since "folklore" was the result of a process taking place within a certain order of context, then middle-class urban people like myself "had" folklore too, which we performed in appropriate surrounds involving interaction with peers and reflecting the values of our group. I had met the folk, and they were us. Furthermore, I reasoned, if we had done fifty years ago what we were doing today, folklorists would be studying us, and folkies singing our songs, right now.

These kinds of insights enabled me to resolve my doubts about Mariposa's "validity" and about my participation in the folksong revival. The resolution may be stated this way: given that folklore is defined according to how it functions within a certain order of context; and that folklore is therefore not the "property" of any one group of people however defined; it follows that "authenticity" is relative, and that the singing of a Newfoundlander in his kitchen to his neighbors, with all the norms, rules, and values operating in that situation, is relatively the same as the performer on a coffeehouse or festival stage to his audience, with all the norms, rules, and values operating in *that* situation. In other words, each takes place within a valid context which has to be taken on its own terms, with the singing seen as a different order of the same kind of event. "Festival singing" and "kitchen singing" are equivalent, though not identical, behaviors. They occur within different contexts which give different meanings to the activities taking place within them. But each is as "valid" as the other.

This leads me to questions concerning how the two contexts, festival and kitchen, relate to and cross over into each other, especially when they share participants. Obviously, in bringing kitchen singers to the festival, Mariposa is trying to bring the meanings of their context to bear on the festival context. My own opinion is that this happens in only a limited way. Just as I, singing in a Newfoundlander's kitchen, am not the same as I, singing on stage at Mariposa; so a Newfoundlander, singing on the stage at Mariposa, is not the same as that Newfoundlander singing in the kitchen at home. Each context gives its own meaning to the behavior occurring within it, even if the behaviors are "the same." As a folklore researcher, I would not go to Mariposa to find out about Newfoundland kitchen singing, though I might go there to see how Newfoundland kitchen singers fared at a large folk festival. I would also be more likely to go to see what kind of singers Mariposa was bringing in and why; in other words, to find out about Mariposa and the festival context, not about the context the singers come from or are asked to invoke. But this in no way "invalidates" Mariposa, or the folksong revival, as "authentic" contexts for singing. It just requires that one be aware of precisely what those contexts comprise and how they shape the meaning of the activities within them.

As far as my participation in the Toronto folksinging scene, I was now in a position to see that there I too was functioning within a group and adhering to that group's norms whenever I got up on a coffeehouse stage and sang English ballads. What I was doing was "authentic" not because I sang traditional songs unaccompanied or affected an English accent, but rather because I was doing those things in accordance with my group's belief that those things made me "authentic." In other words, I was doing what an urban folkie was supposed to be doing as a properly functioning member of the folksong revival.

Looking back on it, I can see that I had confused the accurate re-creation of the style of an original with the creation of that original, thinking in effect that my re-creation was part of the same phenomenon and shared the context which defined and gave meaning to the original. That was just not the case. What gave my re-creation its meaning was another context, within which it was held that if my re-creation was stylistically identical to the original, it would be part of it. That context was the traditional folksong revival of the late 1960s and early 1970s.

NOTE

This essay appeared originally in *Canada Folk Bulletin* 2.3 (May-June 1979): 3–11.

"The Folk Process" in the Revival: "Barrett's Privateers" and "Baratt's Privateers"

Pauline Greenhill

I don't remember when I first heard Stan Rogers's "Barrett's Privateers," but it was almost certainly at the Mariposa Folk Festival or at the Fiddlers' Green folk club. These were probably the most important institutions of the folk revival in Toronto when I was growing up in the 1960s and 1970s, and I periodically attended both. I do recall the summer of 1982, when I came across a new recording of this song, a version substantially different in text and tune from the one on Rogers's first album with which I was familiar. My immediate impression was that there was a telling similarity between the kinds of changes often seen as the hallmarks of traditional song and what had happened to "Barrett's Privateers."

Though the context of both recordings was the folk revival, I saw here an opportunity to examine with living composers some of the assumptions pertaining to change within traditional song. I looked forward to interviewing both Rogers and the performers of the new version, Alan Reid and Brian McNeill of Scotland's Battlefield Band, to discuss what had happened, and how it had taken place. Rogers's tragic death in a plane accident in July 1983, while returning to Canada from a folk festival in Texas, put an end to that idea. And ironically, the changes on Reid and McNeill's version were not as easy to trace as I hoped. I was no more successful at detailing the song's exact path from source to final version than were folklorists like Edward D. Ives who studied long-dead composers like Larry Gorman, Lawrence Doyle, and Joe Scott.[1] However, the issues remained, and I explore them here.

My contention is that on many levels of analysis regularly used by folklorists to examine what they agree is the legitimate stuff of their discipline—composition, performance, transmission, and meaning, among others—the products and processes of the folk revival fit or are substantially similar. My argument focuses on the texts of the two versions of "Barrett's Privateers" as a case study in analytical folk processes within the revival; Anne Lederman's piece, which follows, looks at their tunes and performance styles. I compare the two texts in terms of traditional compositional styles and examine their meanings for the cultures in which they were created.

Stan Rogers composed "Barrett's Privateers" in 1976 at the Northern Lights Folk Festival in Sudbury, Ontario. As he tells it, this is the song's background:

> I was hanging out with the Friends of Fiddlers Green [a primarily British group of performers who ran and were the house band at the folk club of the same name]. . . . And they were hanging out in their own rooms, all into singing sea shanties. I loved the parts, it was great fun, but I wanted to sing lead and have them sing the harmonies for a change. But I didn't know any of these songs, because I was a total neophyte in traditional music . . . so I went back to my room and I thought over a story a poet friend of mine had told me about Nova Scotian privateering in the time of the American Revolutionary War. I got this little bit of a tune running through my head, and twenty minutes later I had "Barrett's Privateers" written down.[2]

A few years later, Alan Reid and Brian McNeill recorded a version of it on their album *Sidetracks*. They describe it as "a song which came to Brian from Sandy Colquoun one night in the Burn's Bar in Falkirk, and which has undergone a little folk process of its own. The words here are quite different from the original ones written by Stan Rogers in Toronto."[3]

Brian McNeill, who was mainly responsible for this—in his terms— "folk-processed" version, says of "Barrett's Privateers": "At first I thought it was a traditional song. And then I thought, 'Oh no. . . . Somebody's put a hand on this at some point.' I thought it was one of these fragment things that somebody had cleaned up."[4] Apparently, the friend from whom McNeill learned "Barrett's Privateers" shared this misconception:

> Sandy Colquoun sang this song and we noticed nothing but the chorus; we noticed it was a sea song and it had a chorus. And we all got pretty drunk and we went away and we didn't think any more about it. And at the time Alan and I were recording an album and I kept thinking, "I don't have a song to sing for this album. That's a really good song." So I went and tracked Sandy down about two weeks later and I said, "What's that song?" He said, "It's called 'Barrett's Priva-

teers.' " And I said, "Who wrote it?" He says, well, "I don't know." And then I said, "Is it traditional?" He said, "I think so."

What interests me is not only that McNeill and Colquoun, like so many other performers who mistake Rogers's songs for traditional ones, didn't know that "Barrett's Privateers" was a recent composition by a Nova Scotian expatriate living in Ontario, but also that their version is distinctly different from his, though the basic tune contour and the first four verses are similar. The changes are particularly notable because Rogers's own version of the song is so well known in North America among folksong enthusiasts, and because they occurred a mere five years after the first recording of the song. Under circumstances of familiarity and popularity, one might expect to find only such aspects of performance style as tempo or instrumentation varying, and in this relatively short time span, very gradual textual change. In fact, all the other performers—British and North American—whose versions of "Barrett's Privateers" I have heard reproduced accurately the Rogers tune and text; even stylistic changes of this very popular song tend to be minimal. Thus the pervasive and significant textual alterations of the Reid-McNeill piece are all the more striking.

Folklorists are, of course, quite accustomed to discovering transformed versions of traditional folksongs. G. Malcolm Laws comments, "One sure method of distinguishing traditional songs from those learned directly from print is by the textual variations which inevitably occur in folksong."[5] The evident assumptions are that traditional songs won't be learned from print, and that other songs won't be learned orally. The first point has been contended by folklorists,[6] but neither notion has been totally abandoned by those working in the field. However, I have seen no evidence that when performers learn songs orally—from a recording or in person—they are any less inclined to change it than when they learn songs from written sources. And as I'll discuss later, Brian McNeill's sources were both oral and written.

Apart from such stylistic attributes as sentimentality, expression of community values, and conventional expression,[7] textual change remains one of the standard definitional hallmarks of folksongs, distinguishing them from popular or art songs. Folksongs exhibit not only continuity and selection, but also variation; that is, a folksong's versions share certain aspects of plot and wording and are relatively widely dispersed through time and space, but they also differ from each other in significant ways,[8] reflecting the cultures, times, and personalities of their singers. "Barrett's Privateers" appears, then, to be the kind of apparent anomaly that deserves further attention: a recently composed, original, "popular" song that acts like a traditional folksong in the sense that performers other than its author have molded and transformed it.

The Folksong Revival

In what is arguably the most important introductory textbook on the discipline of folklore, Barre Toelken describes a folk group as "people who share some basis for informal communal contacts, some factor in common that makes it possible, or rewarding or meaningful, for them to exchange informal materials in a culturally significant way."[9] Toelken comments that "we would expect to find that the group will have maintained itself through its dynamics for a considerable time and that the expressive communications have thus become the educative matrix in which children of the group—or newcomers to it—are brought up."[10] In considering a folk group's dynamic, one should investigate performers, audiences, situations of presentation, and sociocultural contexts in addition to folklore items or texts.

Thus, the contexts in which "Barrett's Privateers" was written (the Friends of Fiddlers' Green party) and then diffused to its Reid-McNeill version (learned at a British folk club)—as well as the actual textual variations—are significant. A shared aspect of its process of creation and subsequent transmission lies in the folksong revival begun in the late 1950s and continuing with various degrees of vigor to the present time. The revival took different forms in each culture, but in their respective countries—Canada and Britain—both Stan Rogers and the Battlefield Band were active participants in this historical[11] movement.

Jan Brunvand defines the folksong revival as "the widespread popularizing in recent decades . . . through professional singers and groups, concerts, and the mass media, of music that was or purported to be folk music."[12] Though to many folklorists the revival epitomizes what Richard Dorson called "fakelore,"[13] this evaluation is not common to all. It is not clear whether Brunvand and Dorson exclude the revival for textual or contextual reasons. However, this volume is not the first to address the folk revival as a folkloric context. For example, Joan Kosby looked at the folksong revival club at St. Albans, England, examining the club's face-to-face communication, its role in bringing together a group of individuals with shared ideas, residence, and interests, and its history as a dynamic element in the transmission of folk traditions.[14] Michael Pickering and Tony Green's collection *Everyday Culture: Popular Song and the Vernacular Milieu* states the argument in terms of historical processes rather than static definitions, but clearly places the folk revival among other aspects of vernacular culture.[15] While my task here is not to argue the relative merits of the folksong revival as a stimulus for the formation of what folklorists consider folk groups, evidently it brought people together into cultural groups that functioned with distinctive dynamics, and these were the circumstances under which the two versions of "Barrett's Privateers" were created and used. Further, I will argue that the "movement culture"[16] of the revival partly shaped the variations between them.

The Original

"Barrett's Privateers," though one of his most successful songs, was not one of Stan Rogers's favorites. His mother, Valerie, commented: "Stan said to me that he hoped he would never write another song that would haunt him like 'Barrett's Privateers' because they got so totally sick of it. . . . I asked him in the spring of '83 of all the songs he'd written which was he most proud of, he named them in this order: 'Make and Break Harbour,' 'The Jeanie C,' and 'The Last Watch.' Those were his three favorites, that he was proudest of having written." In an interview published in the revival publication *The Folk Life* in 1978, Stan stated:

> I [wanted] to write stuff that [sounded] like what the people in the Maritimes play—when they're not playing Country and Western. . . . I wanted to try to write the kind of songs that more closely reflected the Maritimes themselves than stuff I'd heard before. There are fine Maritimes writers, but they tend to write in a very uptown style—they write pop songs about the Maritimes. I wanted to write some songs that would sound like anything from thirty to two hundred years old. . . .[17]
>
> I'm very much interested in traditional music, and I hear more and more of it all the time. I've written a new song, "The Flowers of Bermuda," which sounds like another of those "traditional" sea songs.[18]

Valerie Rogers told us that British revival performer Steve Turner's recorded version of "The Flowers of Bermuda" was Stan's favorite because, he said, " 'It sounds like it's four hundred years old.' " Clearly, then, Stan wanted his songs to appear traditional, and associated this with their sounding old. Set during the American Revolutionary War, "Barrett's Privateers" reflects this aesthetic:

> Oh the year was 1778
> (How I wish I was in Sherbrooke now!)
> A letter of Marque came from the King
> To the scummiest vessel I've ever seen
> (God damn them all!)
>
> [chorus:]
>
> I was told we'd cruise the seas for American gold
> We'd fire no guns! Shed no tears!

> But I'm a broken man on a Halifax pier
> The last of Barrett's Privateers
>
> O, Elcid Barrett cried the town
> [(How I wish . . .)]
> For twenty brave men, all fishermen, who
> Would make for him the "Antelope" 's crew
> [(God . . .)]
>
> [chorus]
>
> The "Antelope" sloop was a sickening sight
> She'd a list to the port and her sails in rags
> And the cook in the scuppers with the staggers and jags
>
> On the King's birthday we put to sea
> We were ninety-one days to Montego Bay
> Pumping like madmen all the way
>
> On the ninety-sixth day we sailed again
> When a bloody great Yankee hove in sight
> With our cracked four-pounders we made to fight
>
> Now the Yankee lay low down with gold
> She was broad and fat and loose in stays
> But to catch her took the "Antelope" two whole days
>
> Then at length we stood two cables away
> Our cracked four-pounders made an awful din
> But with one fat ball the Yank stove us in
>
> The "Antelope" shook and pitched on her side
> Barrett was smashed like a bowl of eggs
> And the main-truck carried off both me legs
>
> So here I lay in my twenty-third year
> It's been six years since we sailed away
> And I just made Halifax yesterday.[19]

"Barrett's Privateers" shares with the traditional call-response sea shanties that inspired it a distinctive structure: two internal lines of chorus within each verse as well as a full chorus. "Rio Grande" is an example of this form:

> Oh, a ship went a-sailing out over the bar
> ('Way for Rio!)
> They've pointed her bow to the Southern Star
> (And we're bound for the Rio Grande!)

[chorus]

Then away, bullies, away!
Away for Rio!
Sing fare ye well, me Liverpool gels,
And we're bound for the Rio Grande!

Oh, say was ye never down Rio Grande
[('Way . . .)]
Them smart senoritas, they sure beats the band
[(And . . .)] [chorus], etc.[20]

It is very common for shanties to have the form A (line) A (line) with
or without a chorus, but the A (line) B B (line) (chorus) of "Barrett's
Privateers" is apparently anomalous. The shanty is not the only model for
this song; in terms of its narrative, "Barrett's Privateers" closely resembles
the traditional ballad: "Ballads are organized by focusing on an action. The
action is generally one in which a dramatic transformation occurs, leading
to someone's death or marriage or some other cataclysmic event."[21]

"Barrett's Privateers" centers on a single episode, relies on narrative,
and concentrates on the story's action. There is an emphasis upon cause
(Barrett recruits local fisherman) and effect (the narrator is maimed). The
events are arranged chronologically, but only one—the battle—receives
much attention. And also like the ballad, the characters are limited to two—
the narrator and Barrett. Further, like the Child-type ballad more than the
broadside, the song avoids moralizing. The listener might suspect that
Captain Barrett was to blame for the loss of the battle, the ship, and the
narrator's legs, but the song never explicitly says so. Finally, the narrative
is told by "leaping and lingering," as Francis Barton Gummere called the
ballad's characteristic movement from one action highlight to another, with
little or no intervening description.[22]

However, there are some differences between "Barrett's Privateers"
and traditional ballads, some of which parallel differences between Child-
type and broadside ballads. Rogers tells his tale in narrative form alone,
without dialogue from the characters. The listener might have difficulty
reconciling the notion that ballads are "impersonal" with "Barrett's Privateers" refrain of "God damn them all." Rogers presents the scene more
than is usual in Child-type ballads; he devotes an entire verse, for instance,
to describing the "Antelope." There is little formulaic repetition in the
verses, and the openings and closings are quite abrupt. Finally, of course,
the rhyme scheme, ABB, is not ballad form's usual ABCB.

Yet Rogers was quite successful in his attempt to create an old-sounding
piece. He took elements of traditional forms and crafted a design that does

not exactly match them structurally or stylistically, containing a number of unconventional features, but which nevertheless maintains sufficient echoes to leave the impression that his song is historically founded, not only historically motivated.

The Variant

I was unable to trace precisely what happened to "Barrett's Privateers" between Stan Rogers's version and Brian McNeill's. McNeill says that the words he got from Sandy Colquoun

> were extremely fragmented and didn't make sense in themselves, so I cleaned it up a little bit.... I don't know exactly how I did that at all, now.... The original tape that we had, there were bits where Sandy would just stop singing it and say, "I can't remember the rest of this verse." He'd made a tape ... and he let me hear it and then for some reason I couldn't keep the tape and I had to actually go away. I had two shots at the song. He sang it that night, I tracked him down, he gave me a tape, and he was actually there while I listened to the tape, and he took the tape away again, and then he sent me a copy of the words. And the copy of the words, ... there would be half a verse or something, maybe about two or three verses.... [Then] I had to go off on tour to Brittany and I sort of rehearsed the song on that solo tour and I'm sure the actual words changed again a little bit on that.

It's interesting, given Laws's assumption about how traditional songs would be learned, that McNeill acquired "Barrett's Privateers" from both oral and written sources. His version is in many senses quite different from the original. Though its first four verses are quite close to the Rogers song, the resemblance breaks down considerably in the final four, and there is one verse fewer.

> In 1812 in the month of May
> (How I wish I was in Sherbrooke now!)
> When a letter of Marque came from the King
> To the scummiest vessel I've ever seen
> (God damn them all!)
>
> [chorus:]
>
> I was told we'd sail the seas for American gold
> We'd fire no guns! Shed no tears!
> But I'm a broken man on a Halifax pier
> The last of Baratt's Privateers

"Ah well" says Baratt through the town
[(How I wish . . .)]
"With twenty good men, all fishermen, who
Would make for me the 'Antelope''s crew"
[(God . . .)]

[chorus]

On the King's birthday we put to sea
Went ninety-one days to Montego Bay
Pumping like madmen all the way

The "Antelope" sloop was a sickening sight
With a list to the port and her sails in rags
And the cook in the scuppers had the staggers and the jags

Baratt he worked us to the bone
We'd maggoty meat and weevily bread
And watery rum. We'd be better off dead

On Christmas Eve in the afternoon
An American sloop came into view
And Baratt cries to her "Heave to" [no intervening line or chorus]

They came alongside to get on board
And the Yankee ship opened up broadside
And I lost one leg and most of my hide
God damn them all [no chorus]

When they brought me home from sea
"No work for one-legged Jack" they'd say
And I cursed Baratt to my dying day
[(God . . .)] [chorus]
God damn them all.[23]

There are a number of superficial textual differences between this and
the Rogers version of "Barrett's Privateers." In the first four verses, note
the spelling of "Baratt" in the McNeill version (from the album cover);
the relocation of the period in question from the American Revolutionary
War to 1812; the change from a "cruise" in Rogers's chorus to a "sail" in
McNeill's, and the rationalization of the name "Elcid Barrett" to " 'Ah
well,' says Baratt." The final four verses include the addition of a verse-
long portrayal of Baratt's personal style as a captain, and a slight change
in the description of the American vessel. Though it more or less follows
the story line of the original, its deviations are significant. In some ways,
it more closely resembles a traditional text. For example, several lines and

phrases in the "new" final four verses are commonplace and familiar formulae in traditional texts, such as the triad of "maggoty meat and weevily bread and watery rum."

Variation

Both versions of "Barrett's Privateers" manifest some of the structures found in oral composition.[24] Valerie Rogers commented that "Stan would write songs in his head, because he didn't have time to sit down and write, then when the deadline was there, he would sit down and get it all down on paper." This method is evident from the arrangement of Rogers's version into three sets of three verses. The first set provides the scene with respect to the "Antelope" and its crew; the second takes the vessel to the place and time of its decisive battle; and the third details that battle and its consequences. However, such structures do not appear exclusively in oral texts, as my own research on Ontario poetry,[25] among others, indicates.

McNeill's version is differently arranged (hence the reversal of verses three and four in the original) again into three sets but with the first comprising only two, not three verses. This text marks and displays its structural pattern more clearly than does Rogers's. Note, for example, that each of the three sets of verses is introduced with a time indicator: "In 1812 in the month of May"; "On the King's birthday we went to sea"; and "On Christmas Eve in the afternoon." Such time indicators do not appear elsewhere in this version, though similar ones serve in other capacities in Rogers's text.

In the McNeill version, the chorus serves markedly as part of the scene setting. McNeill works more freely with the chorus than does Rogers, for example omitting it completely from the second and third last verses. As a result, he reaches the action more quickly than Rogers does. McNeill's first set of verses serves the same function as Rogers's—setting the scene of Barrett's recruitment for the "Antelope." The second set differs from the original in that it shows qualities of the "Antelope"'s crew (hardworking "madmen"), the sloop itself (sickening), and Captain Barrett (stingy and cruel) respectively. Like Rogers, in his final set of verses McNeill outlines the battle and its consequences. The main differences in the semantic deployment of structural elements, then, are found in the middle sections of the versions.

These changes are not simply arbitrary rearrangements of textual raw material; they result from and effect different meanings for the two versions. These are based within the national cultures of the creators of the versions, as well as within the movement culture of the revival. Rogers's version is distinctly a Canadian song, concerning the results of Canadian-American conflict. Canadians are notorious for their concern with distinctive national identity, having been culturally dominated throughout their history by larger imperialist nations: first Britain, and more recently the United States. Economic historian Harold Adams Innis argued that Canada's resource-based economy has determined its role as a hinterland, and others have detailed the effects of outside domination on Canadian society and culture. Though social class is not unimportant, many Canadians see conflict primarily in regional terms.[26]

It is difficult, perhaps impossible, for a country as large and diverse as Canada to maintain a single perspective. Frequently, as in the recent debates over free trade with the United States, regional interests come into direct conflict with one another. Northern, western, and eastern Canadians often argue that the concerns of the largest, most populous, economically powerful region of southern Ontario tend to dominate federal politics. Though "Barrett's Privateers" is set in the eastern province of Nova Scotia, the conflict or competition with the United States that is its subject is probably of greatest interest to southern Ontarians. The song's examination of American-Canadian conflict is expressed in terms acceptable to the region in which Rogers was brought up—urban Ontario—though his personal loyalty was to the Maritimes. Ontario (which sees itself as "central Canada" or even more inclusively "Canada" writ large) perceives the threat to its identity as originating in the United States. This is the topic of "Barrett's Privateers."

The setting is the period of the American Revolutionary War, a major conflict between Americans and the British Loyalists who eventually formed Canada. Fully four of the nine verses of Rogers's version concentrate upon the meeting and subsequent battle between the Canadian and American vessels. The American ship is never so called; it is referred to as "a bloody great Yankee," "the Yankee," and finally "the Yank." This trope personifies the ship in terms of its nationality, and underscores the narrator's identification of his true adversaries—Americans in general rather than that ship in particular. It is also significant that the Canadians do not win the conflict; the wealth and power of the Yankee ship, overblown and "fat" though it is, are too much for its adversary. Barrett, as the representative of Canada, is seen to be as fragile as an egg, overwhelmed by the again "fat" and obviously solid Yankee ball.

The Maritimers who are the victims of the incident, promised a voyage without any military conflict, get its very opposite—a battle in which they are the losers. Blame for the outcome does not lie solely with Barrett, who promised them a "cruise"; their expectations that privateering would be without guns or tears and that the Americans would simply hand over the money were unreasonable. Further, the fellow Maritimer who made that promise to them, Captain Barrett, is explicitly a victim himself. The listener might not blame him much more than his privateers for what happened, or at the very least could feel that if he had knowingly led the others into this impossible situation he was certainly punished as severely as possible for it. The fault lies with those Yankees, who didn't take the same light-hearted attitude as did the privateers, and with the Canadians, who were not prepared for the seriousness of the acts they endeavored.

McNeill's song, in contrast, is clearly British and its main concern is with relations of economic class rather than those of region or political nationality. The differences between the two are as pervasive as their actual locations in time and space. For example, McNeill at first thought the song's setting was English: "With the original set of words, it took me a long time to work out that it was meant to be a [North] American song, that the actual base of the ship was in ... Halifax, Nova Scotia, 'cause there's no mention of that. I thought it was Halifax, England—at first, anyway." His understood context for the song, then, is nineteenth-century Britain in a period of historical class struggle discussed in E. P. Thompson's *The Making of the English Working Class:* "Class happens when some men, as a result of common experiences (inherited or shared), feel and articulate the identity of their interests as between themselves, and as against other men whose interests are different from (and usually opposed to) theirs. The class experience is largely determined by the productive relations into which men are born—or enter involuntarily."[27]

Recognition of class conflict entered the British folk revival through diverse sources, such as the writings of A. L. Lloyd and the songs of Ewan MacColl. The revival developed during a historical period in which class was recognized as a cultural issue. For example, the early plays of John Osborne expressed the frustration of newly educated working-class people in the 1950s and 1960s with their inability to rise within a political economic hierarchy based upon class.[28] The position of the working class and the anomalous place of the bourgeoisie are concerns of "Baratt's Privateers."

In the McNeill version, the ship is "an American sloop," and "the Yankee ship." No personification is employed; this is not a conflict of nationalities: "It's not an antiwar song. . . . No, the whole point of the song, the whole point of the story, is about a guy who went out to risk everything, and was a privateer. And the fact that one nationality was there and another nationality wasn't is very much incidental, you know. . . . It's not about nationalities and war and big ethics like that, it's about some poor bastard getting his legs shot off." Though McNeill resisted my notion that "Baratt's Privateers" is about class conflict, I still feel that his song is about exploitation, and about personal gain and individual loss. This helps to explain why there is a verse-long description, completely original to this version, of Captain Baratt's character and the conditions on board his ship, and why the battle itself receives attention in only two verses, half the number in the prototype. The song makes it clear that Baratt will not cut into the profits he expects from the voyage by treating his workers well. The final verse's reference to work, or lack of it—"'No work for one-legged Jack' they'd say"—as well as the narrator's "And I cursed Baratt to my dying day" underscore who is to blame for the story's outcome: Baratt himself, not the Americans. In the McNeill version, Baratt and the "Antelope" do not explicitly lose their battle, and when I told McNeill that Barrett dies in the end of Rogers's song, he said, "This is all fascinating to me." The final outcome for the narrator is thus even worse: he definitely loses out, and Baratt certainly does not end up with the just desserts he gets in Rogers's version.

There is no presentation of the voyage on the "Antelope" as a cruise—it is hard work, a realistic sail. The best the sailors can expect is reasonable and fair treatment, and the justification for the song is that they do not receive it while the voyage is underway, or in the aftermath of the battle. Stan Rogers's Canadian nationalist parable that unprepared, poorly equipped Canadians should not try to take on Americans in battle is transformed in the McNeill version to a story of exploitation for personal gain.[29]

McNeill learned the identity of the composer of "Barrett's Privateers" before the album was published: "I'd never heard of Stan Rogers. . . . I can't remember where I heard the original song, but you know that live recording that Stan did of it? I heard that, and I thought 'Oh Jesus, the words that I've got are just totally different from that. Also, we've changed the tune around quite a lot.' " McNeill could not detail how his version varied from Stan's, but he clearly did not share my interpretation that the two versions had substantively different stories: "There are verses, obviously, that we missed out, and bits of logic that seem to be missed out in ours. . . . I think you get a better sense of the story out of [Stan's]. . . . I see it as being a more complete story, that's all."

Traditions

Anyone familiar with the Anglo-American folksong tradition, especially that of Atlantic Canada, would immediately notice that both versions of "Barrett's Privateers" resemble the war ballads and ballads of sailors and the sea that comprise the first and second sections of G. Malcolm Laws's *American Balladry from British Broadsides.*[30] They are particularly close to Laws J2, "Waterloo I," as shown by the following fragmentary text, collected in 1929 by Elisabeth Bristol Greenleaf and Grace Yarrow Mansfield, and published in their *Ballads and Sea Songs of Newfoundland:*

> It happened on a Wednesday in the lovely month of June.
> I went for to convince my love, all in her youthful bloom,
> Where the press gang lay in ambush and up to me they drew,
> And the very next day we marched away to fight at Waterloo.
>
> It happened on a Wednesday, the day I put on my dress,
>
> ———
>
> My waistcoat of the scarlet, my hat and feather too,
> And that very day we marched away to fight at Waterloo.
>
> The day we fought at Waterloo it was a bitter blast,
> It was by our honorable captain, we was ordered to Belfast,
> And when we got to Belfast town, those words, I heard him say:
> "I'm very much in doubt, my boys, that we won't gain the day."
>
> ———
>
> Our captain cries, "My heroes brave, come keep your courage true,
> And I hope to God we gain the day we fights at Waterloo."
>
> At four o'clock in the afternoon we was ordered on the plains;
> At eight o'clock that evening the bloody fight began.
> The first shot took my arm from me, so loudly I did bawl,
> And the very next shot took my leg from me; then I was forced to
>   fall.
>
> I laid down on those weary plains to rest my aching bones,
>
> ———
>
> ———
>
> Where ofttimes I cried and wished I'd died that night in Waterloo.
> It was when my comrades' day's work was done, 'twas up to me they
>   drew.
> Out of eighteen hundred heroes brave we only lost but two,
>
> ———
>
> Where we made them yell and quit the field that night at Waterloo.
>
> It was by our honorable captain we was ordered on the cars;
> We had to go on horses' backs the distance been so far.
> I thought you were strong-limbed when first you leaved your dear,
> But now you deserves a pension of thirty pound a year.[31]

In some ways, "Barrett's Privateers" repeats "Waterloo." Its tripartite structure is similar: a young man is recruited; he engages in battle; he loses limbs in it. Yet the historic events to which the songs refer are different,

and they vary symbolically as well. There is a "captain" in "Waterloo,"
but unlike Baratt, he is a good officer, and unlike Barrett, he survives. The
battle of Waterloo is a victory for the speaker, who is rewarded with a
pension for the rest of his life. The "Antelope" loses its battle, and the
protagonist of "Barrett's Privateers" faces an uncertain (in the McNeill
version, explicitly gloomy) future. As a prototype or source for "Barrett's
Privateers," "Waterloo" is an unlikely candidate. It is by no means a well-
known song. The only text from oral tradition to which Laws refers is
the above version from Newfoundland. Yet it does indicate some shared
underlying structures and values in Canadian songs of this type.

A more familiar song, both in the Atlantic provinces of Canada and in
the folksong revival, is "The Flying Cloud." Horace P. Beck describes it
as "Perhaps one of the most popular of the longer ballads found in
America."[32] Stan Rogers had probably heard this song before he composed
"Barrett's Privateers," or perhaps he had read it in Edith Fowke's popular
and generally well-known *Penguin Book of Canadian Folk Songs*.[33] The
following version is from W. Roy MacKenzie's *Ballads and Sea Songs from
Nova Scotia*, from the singing and recitation of Harry Sutherland, River
John, Pictou County:

> My name it is Robert Anderson, I'll have you understand;
> I belong to the city of Waterford, near Erin's happy land.
> When I was young and in my prime and health did on me smile,
> My parents doted on me, I being their only child.
>
> My father bound me to a trade in Waterford's own town;
> He bound me to a cooper there by the name of William Brown.
> I served my master faithfully for eighteen months or more,
> Till I shipped on board the *Ocean Queen* bound for Valparaiso's shore.
>
> But when I reach Valparaiso's shore, I fell in with Captain Moore,
> Commander of the *Flying Cloud*, belonging to Trimore.
> Most kindly he invited me on a slaving voyage to go,
> To the burning shores of Africa where the sugar-cane doth grow.
>
> The *Flying Cloud* was a Spanish ship, twelve hundred tons or more.
> She could easily sail round anything bound down from Baltimore.
> I've often seen that gallant ship with the wind on her afterbeam,
> With royals and to'ga'n's'ls set, running nineteen off the reel.
>
> The *Flying Cloud* was as fine a ship as ever swam the sea,
> Wherever spread a main topsail before a lively breeze.
> The sails were as white as the driven snow, and upon them were no
>   stains.
> She had eighteen brass nine-pounder guns she carried by after main.

In the course of a few weeks after we arrived on the African shore,
With eighteen hundred of those poor slaves from their native isle we
    tore.
We marched them down upon our decks, we stowed them in below.
'Twas fourteen inches to a man was all they had to go.

And the very next day we put to sea with our cargo of slaves;
It would have been better for those poor souls had they been in their
    graves.
For the plague and fever came on board, swept half of them away;
We dragged their dead bodies on deck, and threw them in the sea.

In the course of a few weeks after we arrived on the Cuban shore.
We sold them to the planters there to be slaves for ever more,
For to hoe in the rice and the cotton fields beneath the burning sun,
Or to lead a sad and lonely life till their career was run.

But soon our money it was all spent, we put to sea again.
And Captain Moore he came on deck, and said to us his men,
"There's gold and silver to be had if you with me remain.
We'll hoist the lofty pirate flag and scour the Spanish Main."

To this of course we all agreed, excepting five young men;
And two of them were Boston chaps, and two from Newfoundland.
The other was an Irishman belonging to Trimore.
I wish to God I had joined those men and went with them on shore.

We robbed and plundered manys a ship down on the Spanish Main,
Caused manys a widow and orphan child in sorrow to remain.
Their crews we made them walk the plank, caused them a watery
    grave;
For the saying of our captain was that a dead man tells no tales.

Pursued we were by manys a ship, by liners and frigates too,
And manys a time astern of us their burning shells they threw.
It's manys a time astern of us their cannons loud did roar,
But 'twas all in vain down on the main to catch the *Flying Cloud;*

Till a man o' war, a Spanish ship, the *Dungeon,* hove in view.
She fired a shot across our bows, a signal to heave to.
To this of course we paid no heed, but flew before the wind;
When a chain-shot took our mizzen down, 'twas then we fell behind.

We cleared our decks for action soon, as the *Dungeon* hove alongside;
And soon across our quarter-decks there ran a crimson tide.
We fought till Captain Moore was killed, and seventy of his men,

When a bombshell set our ship on fire; we were forced to surrender
then.

It's next to Newgate we were brought, bound down in iron chains,
For murdering and plundering of ships at sea down on the Spanish
Main.
'Tis drinking and bad company that made a wretch of me.
Come all young men, think of my downfall, and curse to the pirate
sea.

And it's fare you well, you shady bowers, and the girl that I adore;
Her voice like music soft and sweet shall never charm me more.
No more I'll kiss her ruby lips, or press her lily-white hand,
For I must die a scornful death, all in a foreign land.[34]

One might consider "Barrett's Privateers" a version of "The Flying
Cloud" minus the biographical opening, the slaving voyage, the initial successes, and the gallows farewell. The tripartite narrative structural elements
of "Barrett's Privateers" are shared with "The Flying Cloud": scene-setting
with respect to ship and crew recruitment; taking the ship to the scene of
its decisive battle; and the battle and its consequences. Both "The Flying
Cloud" and "Barrett's Privateers" have lengthy descriptions of the ships
themselves, though the "Antelope" is described in disparaging terms and
the "Flying Cloud" in glowing ones. In both it is the captain, not "Waterloo"'s press gang, who is responsible for the narrator's presence on board,
and ultimately for his downfall. In Rogers's "Barrett's Privateers" and in
"The Flying Cloud," the battle is lost and the captain killed; the warning
is explicitly against "drinking and bad company" rather than against allowing
oneself to be exploited by the unscrupulous, though such an interpretation
could be implicit. It is clear, then, that Stan Rogers's "Barrett's Privateers"
is consistent with existing traditions of Canadian folksong. The McNeill
version's relation to Rogers's "Barrett's Privateers" is likewise familiar in
traditional culture. These issues are detailed below.

Folk Processes

When I asked McNeill to expand on his idea of the folk process,
referred to in his notes for "Baratt's Privateers," he described it as "not
learning [a song] properly, I guess. Learning it by accident. Learning it
with no thought to learning it." His other comments were equally telling.
I asked him whether in learning traditional songs he would consciously
or unconsciously change them, and he said, "We change them any way
we feel like it." But for songs with known writers, he said,

You are under legal limitations. . . . Mostly if we're going to pick a modern songwriter and do a song from them, we would stick very faithfully to the words. . . . If the rights are still alive then there's somebody who's written that song for a purpose, whether it's to make money or whether it's to be a good song, and you've got to respect that. If I'd known that Stan Rogers had written that song on the day when I got it, I would have made sure that I got the right version before I did it. . . . I wouldn't be happy with someone changing one of mine, because at that point, let's face it, there is a financial element in it, and we're professional performers, and if somebody changes mine then they can challenge the copyright on it, who gets paid for it. And I certainly wouldn't be happy with that.

As long as they are not copyrighted and their creators remain "anonymous," traditional folksongs are not seen as exchange-value commodities by revival performers. Clearly, McNeill's sense of the inviolability of nontraditional songs is based more on his respect for a creator's rights and feelings and on the fact that commerce is involved than on style. Ownership or copyright in Western, materialistic, professionalized culture is the right of the person who originated the piece. Songs are a commodity, and they have monetary exchange value. Ownership of cultural expressions, however, has different bases in traditional communities. The right to perform a song can be passed through families, or can belong to a particular group.[35] Songs cannot be expressed in terms of capitalist use value or exchange value, but in terms of reciprocity and the creation and maintenance of social ties. In traditional communities, songs are not commodified.

Under such circumstances, performers can authentically appropriate the materials available to them, not only in the sense of making them their own, but also by transforming them so that they become apposite to their contexts. For example, in Ontario there are individuals considered by their communities to be poets who, in the local newspaper, put their names to popular verse that they did not author, in the sense that the piece is not fully original to them. These presenters of poetry take responsibility for its presence in the newspaper and thus for its relevance to their neighbors. By putting their name to a piece, they are acknowledging their accountability for it, not suggesting that they are responsible for the text's origin, or for its originality, though in many cases they may change words, lines, even whole verses in order to increase the appositeness of a particular piece.[36] The same thing can happen to traditional songs within the revival.

This folk process may superficially resemble plagiarism, but it is not the same thing. As Michel Foucault[37] points out, plagiarism is a historically derived concept based more on the notion of ownership than on the location and identity of the original creator. Clearly, the academic concepts of authorship and plagiarism don't apply readily to traditional culture. Though the situation is rather different, Stan Rogers's "Barrett's Privateers" (accidentally) underwent a form of appropriation that is not dissimilar to what happens to popular verse in Ontario, or to other forms of traditional culture in process.

One could characterize these versions of "Barrett's Privateers," and their variations, in terms of their creators' intentions and styles. Eleanor Long suggests that "there are four basic types of folk artistry; ... it does not matter in the least whether the artists concerned are literate or illiterate, amateur or commercial, addressing an isolated homogeneous community or a sophisticated mass public."[38]

The performer who may make the fewest changes in the received text Long calls the perseverator, her first type of folk artisan. Often described as "conservative, 'weak,' 'uninspired,' 'timid,' 'insensitive,' "[39] this individual is actually motivated instead by a great respect for the integrity of a traditional text, and insists that it be faithfully reproduced. This is but one legitimate and culturally recognized approach to tradition. As Roger Abrahams points out, perseverators are valuable to the folklorist precisely because they do not consciously select or alter their songs.[40]

Long's second type, the confabulator, generally makes changes in the text that he or she feels would make it a better artistic performance. Creativity is expressed primarily "in style rather than content, drama rather than coherence, and fancy (in the Coleridgean sense) rather than imagination."[41] Of confabulators, Long suggests: "They stand in no particular awe of received tradition; they may *add* narrative themes...; they may *revise* the text to conform to a tentative notion of 'better sense' or greater appropriateness...; or they may simply *improvise* for the sheer love of improvising...."[42] Long's third type of folk artist, the rationalizer, makes "the text conform to a previously-adopted, extra-textual system of values that is of significance to the singer.... [The rationalizer] differs from the perseverator in *feeling free to manipulate his material;* but he differs from the confabulator in that his manipulations are *governed by an independent principle.*"[43] That is, a principle independent of the rationalizer's feelings for the artistic quality of the song, such as a concept of morality in the widest sense, figures in his or her decision to make a song part of an active performed repertoire, or to make changes in it. The differences between the rationalizer and confabulator may be difficult to determine in many cases.

Finally, Long's fourth type, the integrator, "is as aware of tradition as the perseverator, as innovative as the confabulator, and as conscious of the need for organization and consistency as the rationalizer. He goes beyond all three, however, by *creating* texts that are unique."[44] An integrator's original texts bear a close relationship to the local song tradition; some indeed may enter that tradition. Long points out that in an integrator's work, "what appears from a synchronic point of view to be a manifestly non-traditional and idiosyncratic text invariably turns out to be, from a diachronic point of view, an amalgam of very traditional materials drawn from a number of linguistic and historical sources and merely given an 'original' verbal embodiment."[45] That is, a song that might immediately appear to be nontraditional in the sense that its text has not undergone the processes of continuity, selection, and change, actually has a manifest and demonstrable link with the folksong tradition in its larger sense. Such songs are not simply reproductions of a tradition, but as Edward D. Ives suggests of songmaker Joe Scott, "if . . . we limit ourselves to looking for [his] artistry in his skillful adaptation of a rather broad range of traditional elements to new yet equally traditional subjects, we can nonetheless still speak of him not only as a good workman, but also as a creative and original artist."[46]

Perhaps it is better to see these four types as kinds of processes rather than as kinds of personalities. I would suggest, however, that the changes from the Rogers to the Reid-McNeill version of "Barrett's Privateers" display the work of confabulation. McNeill, in any case, saw his effect on the version of the song that he heard in those kinds of terms: "a set of words that were extremely fragmented and didn't make sense in themselves, so I cleaned it up a little bit." He clearly did not see his changes as affecting the meaning of the original song. Yet the result is the transformation of a nationalistic Canadian song into a rather different piece. Despite the fact that its adaptor belongs to the revival, then, the McNeill version of "Barrett's Privateers" fits readily into traditional forms of folksong transmission.

This is also true of the original "Barrett's Privateers." By indirectly basing it on the Anglo-American broadside war and sea ballad tradition, yet composing an entirely new work, Stan Rogers's ballad making is integrative. Obviously, not all the songs of an integrator, whether a Stan Rogers or a Joe Scott, enter tradition, but Edith Fowke has called Rogers "the only Canadian currently writing songs she felt might 'live'; that is, which had that particular quality to ensure their being sung and recorded for years to come."[47] This comment highlights national as opposed to regional interests, and raises the eternal question of when fleeting popularity can be considered to have transformed into tradition, but Fowke's stamp of approval may be something of a self-fulfilling prophecy; she has become a national legitimator or validator of folkloric materials.

These two "Barrett's Privateers," one directly a version of the other and both standing in an indirect yet clear relationship to an existing tradition and even to two Laws text-types within that tradition, show that mechanisms and processes identified by folklorists in nonrevival contexts also operate within the revival. There is no doubt that this song is exceptional. Most new compositions of the folksong revival, like the vast majority of songs composed in any community, will not be selected to continue into tradition; nor will they undergo the kinds of transformations seen in the McNeill version of "Barrett's Privateers." However, as the present work shows, the processes of selection, continuity, and variation so often identified as defining aspects of folklore are maintained, if only because in this case the song's recreator thought it was traditional.

What has happened to "Barrett's Privateers" is worthy of attention because it can so easily be related, despite its revival context, to a scholarly tradition of examining traditional folksong texts. The original and its variant can be analyzed as folksongs, not because of some special or unique essence they share with such pieces, or even because they and their prototypes were partly transmitted in oral form. "Barrett's Privateers" and "Baratt's Privateers" appear to follow the patterns of folksongs because the commodification of traditional songs has not proceeded to the extent it has for other kinds of songs, even within the context of the folk revival. Thus, the culture deems it legitimate and appropriate for Stan Rogers to draw upon traditional structures and models, rather than trying to be totally "original," in his performance context. And because nobody "owns" folksongs, as they do popular or art songs, Brian McNeill considered it legitimate and appropriate that he fix up what he got of "Barrett's Privateers" because he thought it was a traditional song. The processes of selection, continuity, and variation are not limited to traditional societies or their performance contexts, but can take place in other kinds of folk groups.

NOTES

I am grateful for the friendly cooperation and assistance of Valerie Rogers and Brian McNeill in answering my questions, and for permission to quote them. I also thank Brian McNeill, and D. Ariel Rogers of Fogarty's Cove Music for permission to quote song texts.

1. Edward D. Ives, *Larry Gorman; Lawrence Doyle;* and *Joe Scott.*
2. "An Interview," p. 4.
3. Reid and McNeill, *Sidetracks.*
4. This and all subsequent uncited quotations come either from my interview with Brian McNeill in Ottawa, Ontario, 4 May 1988, or from my interview with Valerie Rogers in Hannon, Ontario, 2 January 1987.

5. Laws, *American Balladry*, p. 94.

6. See for example Casey et al., "Repertoire Categorization," which discusses the place of the Doyle songbooks in Newfoundland tradition, and Rosenberg's "It Was a Kind of a Hobby."

7. Abrahams and Foss, *Anglo-American Folksong Style*, pp. 5–6.

8. Halpert, "Vitality of Tradition and Local Songs."

9. Toelken, *The Dynamics of Folklore*, p. 33.

10. Ibid., p. 51.

11. I am using the term historical in a sense similar to that of Wright in *On Living in an Old Country:* existing meaningfully in the present and informing current ideology.

12. Brunvand, *Folklore*, p. 138.

13. Dorson, "Folklore and Fakelore."

14. Kosby, "An Ethnography of the St. Albans Folk Music Club."

15. Pickering and Green, *Everyday Culture.*

16. Lieberman, *"My Song Is My Weapon."*

17. "An Interview," p. 4.

18. Ibid., p. 5.

19. Rogers, *Fogarty's Cove.* Copyright Fogarty's Cove Music, 1976, used by permission.

20. Hugill, *Shanties and Sailors' Songs*, p. 146.

21. Abrahams and Foss, *Anglo-American Folksong Style*, p. 78.

22. Gummere, *The Popular Ballad.*

23. Reid and McNeill, *Sidetracks.*

24. Buchan, *The Ballad and the Folk.*

25. Greenhill, *True Poetry.*

26. Innis, *The Fur Trade in Canada;* Clement, *The Canadian Corporate Elite.* A basic introduction to regional issues in the resource-based Canadian political economy can be found in McCann, *Heartland and Hinterland.*

27. E. P. Thompson, *The Making of the English Working Class*, pp. 9–10.

28. See for example Lloyd, *Folk Song in England,* and Osborne, *Look Back in Anger.*

29. See Lederman's comments on the changes in the music, and on the Reid-McNeill version's structure. Note that the verse and musical structure counterpoint one another, but each highlights the significance of the final three verses.

30. Laws, *American Balladry*, pp. 128–63.

31. Greenleaf and Mansfield, *Ballads and Sea Songs of Newfoundland*, p. 165.

32. Beck, "The Riddle of 'The Flying Cloud,' " p. 123.

33. Fowke, *The Penguin Book of Canadian Folk Songs*, pp. 34–36.

34. Mackenzie, *Ballads and Sea Songs from Nova Scotia*, pp. 283–85.

35. See for example Pocius, " 'The First Day That I Thought of It.' "

36. See Greenhill, *True Poetry.*

37. Foucault, "What Is an Author?"

38. Long, "Ballad Singers, Ballad Makers, and Ballad Etiology," p. 231.

39. Ibid., p. 232.

40. Abrahams, "Creativity, Individuality, and the Traditional Singer."

41. Long, "Ballad Singers, Ballad Makers, and Ballad Etiology," p. 233.
42. Ibid., pp. 232–33.
43. Ibid.
44. Ibid.
45. Ibid., p. 234.
46. Edward D. Ives, *Joe Scott,* p. 408.
47. Taylor, "Folk Music Is What Folks Sing."

"Barrett's Privateers": Performance and Participation in the Folk Revival

Anne Lederman

Introduction

According to his own account, Stan Rogers wrote "Barrett's Privateers" initially as an attempt to participate in certain aspects of a traditional singing experience—that of a small group of people gathering over a few brews and, solely for their own pleasure, indulging in some rousing choruses of adventure on the high seas.[1] When he reproduced the song on stage, Rogers found that, for the most part, his audiences were equally enthusiastic about participating in a simulation of this experience. They delighted in joining in, keeping a vigorous rhythm and shouting out the chorus. In spite of the fact that none of them could possibly have ever had any personal experience of the kind described in the song, Stan's audiences made "Barrett's" the most popular and most requested song he ever wrote.

Other performers in Canada and the United States began to sing and record "Barrett's Privateers." In my own experience,[2] it became a kind of standard at many folk revival events in North America,[3] such as song circles, folk clubs, backroom sessions, and concerts. That it was spread at least as much by ear as through recordings is indicated by the fact that within just a couple of years, many people who knew the song seemed unaware that it had a known composer, and indeed, thought it was much older than it was. Ariel Rogers, Stan's wife, says, "I have heard of at least, I would say, twenty groups or individuals who thought it was traditional."[4] A folk "hit" had been created. What is so interesting is that, in contrast to a pop hit, which is spread largely by radio and recordings, "Barrett's" became known mostly through participation in live situations. Everyone joined in, strangers or friends, those who knew the song was Stan's and those who did not. Indeed, revival events became the cultural context of the song; that is, just as a traditional song has a home in a certain "folk group," a group of people united by some commonly held factor,[5] participants in the folk revival formed a kind of folk group for "Barrett's Privateers."

Within a few years, the song spread to the British Isles, through the medium of Rogers's recording,[6] through musicians who went back and forth between Britain and North America, or through both. I could not establish the exact chronology of events through this process, but within five years we end up with a recorded version by two members of Scotland's Battlefield Band, Alan Reid and Brian McNeill.[7] In their version, not only is the story rather different from the original, but, equally significant, the entire nature of the song's musical presentation has changed. Theirs is a highly arranged version in which participation would have been difficult or impossible, as we shall see. According to McNeill, he and Reid learned a fragmented version of the song from a fellow Briton, Sandy Colquoun, added words themselves, and came up with a musical arrangement, all under the assumption that the song was "traditional . . . one of these fragment things that somebody cleaned up."[8] McNeill also said that he and Reid performed the song on stage much as it appears on their recording.[9]

Thus, we have a song that began as a personal and self-conscious attempt to recreate a traditional participatory musical experience in a nontraditional context, that of the folk revival. Within this nontraditional milieu, however, the song followed a time-worn path of oral transmission, loss of known authorship, and alteration, bringing it truly into the realm of anonymous tradition, not just an imitation of such. From there it followed another standard revival path. That is, as a "traditional" song, it was arranged for concert performance and copyrighted again (the Reid-McNeill version) in a form quite different than the original. Ironically, the Reid-McNeill version of "Barrett's Privateers" is precisely the kind of song Stan Rogers usually performed but was deliberately trying to get away from in the case of "Barrett's."

Therefore, the experience of "Barrett's Privateers"—a song born and nurtured within the folk revival—is a wonderful vehicle for examining and illuminating the paradoxical values at work within the revival phenomenon: those of active participation versus passive consumption of music; those of accessible, repetitive musical structures that encourage participation versus complex through-composed ones that do not; and those of informal, noncommercial "folk" communication—mutable transmission by oral means—versus professional and commercial "art" communication, in which authors or composers are known, copyrights must be respected, borrowings must be done with permission, and the integrity of the original must be maintained. In short, the revival attempts to incorporate the values of traditional folk cultures as well as those of formal art traditions and of popular music. Unfortunately, these values are frequently in conflict. "Barrett's Privateers" demonstrates some of these conflicts. Further, it demonstrates both how the folk revival functions as a modern folk community, and, at the same time, how this "folk group" differs from older, traditional societies.

Form and Performance

Stan Rogers, Alan Reid, and Brian McNeill were all professional stage performers when their versions of "Barrett's Privateers" were recorded. Each used a combination of original and traditional material in their performances. Each arranged their songs, borrowing from "art" music traditions in which musicians insert instrumental sections, add counterpoints and harmonies, and orchestrate their selections with various instruments that come in or out at prearranged points in the piece. Thus, in the hands of performers such as these, traditional folk songs and original songs alike are frequently rendered as formal performance pieces, presented to the audience for listening and appreciation.

In contrast, the techniques just discussed are all largely antithetical to older Anglo-Irish folk music in a more traditional, nonprofessional North American context. First of all, in a nonstage setting, the separation between performer and audience is not nearly so marked, and most participants are generally much more actively involved in the music. This involvement may include singing choruses, improvising harmonies, playing along on an instrument, dancing, clapping, or interjecting comments and encouragement. Musicians, for their part, do not generally work out exact harmonies or complex instrumental accompaniments to songs. Also, in informal settings, musical dynamics change little from one verse to the next. Listeners are left to react in their own ways merely to the facts of the story themselves, without musical-dramatic cues.

There are exceptions to these tendencies, as there has been mutual influence between stage performance values and those of more informal settings from the beginning of their interaction. Singers and musicians in traditional communities are generally respected for their abilities, and performance values come into play to a greater or lesser extent even in such casual settings as house parties. But, in my observation, a traditional musician in a nonstage setting rarely, if ever, feels a need for the kind of deliberately dramatic, arranged presentation we frequently see in stage performance of the same material. The opposite is not true, however. Stage performers frequently do try to recreate in concert situations the more traditional, more participatory kinds of audience involvement. Rogers's performance of "Barrett's" was an example of this.

Stan translated "Barrett's Privateers" directly from his backroom experience to the stage. He always sang it *a capella*. The chorus was consistent musically and came in at the same time after each verse so that it was easy for an audience to learn and join in. The verse has internal refrains, a pattern typical of both British and Afro-American folksong, and one that encourages participation. As Greenhill has pointed out, all versions of "Barrett's" that we have found, other than Reid and McNeill's, are exceedingly true to Rogers's: they maintain the choruses intact and, with one exception, are all *a capella*. In my experience, this fidelity is atypical of revival performers, who, although usually respecting the text of a copyrighted song, generally put some individual stamp on the music by altering the arrangement, mood, style, or instrumentation in some way.[10] It is likely that these other musicians who recorded "Barrett's" were involved in a live performance of the song at some time, and that this active participation is largely responsible for the unusual "perseverance"[11] of the song.

I would hypothesize that musicians, in general, will maintain a piece more accurately if they have direct personal contact with its source. Likewise, the further removed one is emotionally, physically, or culturally from a human source, the more likely one is to alter the materials at hand. Learning music from recordings, radio, and other mass media is an example of the extreme of dissociation, while participation in live situations is the closest kind of association. Many participants in the folk revival, at least in Canada, have had little direct experience with older folk traditions—those community-based activities in which music is passed on orally over generations. Rogers seemed to offer this kind of a "folk" (live, participatory) experience for these revival participants, urbanites who were starving on a diet of music from electronic boxes. Other musicians paid tribute to the experience by maintaining the song in its original form.

The structure of "Barrett's Privateers" is atypical for a traditional ballad (see transcription, fig. 1). For example, while traditional ballads are usually set in two- or four-line stanzas with four stresses in each line, Barrett's has a five-phrase verse plus chorus (counting the "God damn them all" as the fifth phrase of the verse). Also, the relative lengths of the phrases are unusually asymmetric. The first line of the verse is four beats, followed by phrases of 5, 4, 4, and 2 beats respectively. The phrases of the chorus are 6, 5, 4, and 6 beats (except the final phrase of the first verse in which the last note is held longer). The fact that so many revival people have mistaken "Barrett's" for a traditional sea song in spite of its unusual form indicates, to some extent, their unfamiliarity with that tradition.

Verse 1

① All other verses one beat shorter.

Figure 1. Stan Rogers, "Barrett's Privateers," *Fogarty's Cove,* Fogarty's Cove Records, FCM 1001. © Fogarty's Cove Music, transcribed by Anne Lederman with permission. Original key: C#. First verse sung solo by Stan Rogers. All subsequent verses have harmonies on the refrain lines and choruses.

McNeill himself was not so easily fooled. He says, "At first I thought it was a traditional song. And then I thought, oh no ... somebody's put a hand on this at some point." However, he still took it to be based on an older song, perhaps because it did not occur to him that someone might write a first-person song about piracy in 1975. (That he and so many others did so is certainly a tribute to Rogers's sense of traditional language and melodic line.) This assumption, and the fact that he heard only a fragmented version, led McNeill to change and/or add some words. His melody, too, is slightly different than Rogers's (see fig. 2), although we do not know whether he and Reid altered it or it was altered by others before it reached him. In addition to having new words and bits of melody, however, the

Figure 2. Alan Reid and Brian McNeill, "Baratt's Privateers," *Sidetracks,* Topic Records 12TS 417. Transcribed by Anne Lederman. Original key: D. Verses 2–7: M.M. 96; verse 8: M.M. 88; chorus 8: M.M. 92–96.

Reid-McNeill version is also a complex instrumental structure, full of dramatic changes in tempo and texture. This is in stark contrast to the other recorded versions of the song.

Further, in spite of their initial experience of the song in a pub setting where, by McNeill's admission, "what caught me in the song was the chorus," their arrangement does not greatly encourage participation. In the Reid-McNeill version, the first two "God damn them all" refrain lines begin in different places relative to the verse; they are timed differently and are at different tempos. There are three tempo changes during the course of the song. The chorus is omitted after two of the verses. The internal timing of the chorus is inconsistent and it is sung in equal two-part harmony, making it hard for the listener to know what the melody is. Although it is possible to join in fairly easily on the refrain lines and the chorus from verses two to six, all of the above-mentioned practices discourage one from doing so because of the sense of unpredictability that is established right at the beginning and the difficulty in finding the melody. We must conclude, therefore, that active audience involvement was not a major concern for Reid and McNeill.

Reid and McNeill have made liberal use of formal compositional techniques in their arrangement. Figure 3 charts the dramatic structure implied by their use of changes in tempo and instrumentation, which effectively subdivide the song into the six sections indicated. They start off at a slow tempo, a way of setting a mood and catching the ear of the audience for the words. Accompaniment is simple off the top—just the concertina sound[12]—creating the illusion of a solo storyteller accompanying himself. There is a shift of gears into a faster tempo at the tag before the second verse, marked by the entrance of a new instrument, the cittern. The song moves ahead fairly straightforwardly until the end of the third chorus, where an instrumental tag and another change in instrumentation occur, back to the concertina. Fiddle is added for verse five, building up the texture again into a major instrumental section, the first climax. This climax ends with a dramatic drop to *a capella* for the sixth verse. Another build begins with the addition of concertina and mandolin on verse seven but the final verse drops back to the solo concertina and slower tempo of the beginning. The song concludes with a final chorus that pulls out all the stops, picks up the tempo again, and uses all the instruments introduced over the course of the song. An extra "God damn them all" is added at the very end. In summary, instrumental bridges set off the first four sections, and tempo changes plus changes in instrumentation mark the last two. There are two climaxes, the first after verse five—the long instrumental followed by a dynamic change to *a capella*—and the second at the final chorus.

Dramatic changes from solo voice or voice plus one instrument to thickly textured instrumental and vocal sections, such as those in Reid and McNeill's arrangement, are compositional techniques typical of concert music (including some pop music) or music for drama rather than of folk tradition. A further use of formal technique is demonstrated by the first climax, after verse five. This instrumental section, followed by a sudden shift to *a capella*, occurs at what is sometimes termed the "golden section" in music: a point approximately two-thirds of the way through a piece that is often marked by some significant musical event.[13]

How does Reid and McNeill's musical arrangement complement their words? Looking at the six sections in turn yields the following: an introductory verse that sets the scene; two verses that give us more background; two middle verses that describe the conditions on ship; a climactic section that signals the beginning of the battle itself; a final verse that describes the aftermath of the experience, bringing home its personal effect on our narrator by returning to the atmosphere of the lone storyteller and his concertina; and a last climactic section, the final chorus, which is both a musical recapitulation and a reminder of the most important statement the narrator wishes to make, the bitter epitaph, "God damn them all." The instrumental bridge after verse five, the first climactic section, separates prior events from the battle itself. This use of music to set off events in time is typical of music in a dramatic context.

The Reid-McNeill musical structure also corresponds well with Greenhill's analysis of the words, subdividing them into three groups of three verses each. The tag after the first three verses, while short, introduces two new instruments, fiddle and bass, whose recurrence characterizes the middle section. The major instrumental separates the middle three verses from the last three, at the golden section.

One of the distinguishing features of the Battlefield Band among revival performers is the complexity and skill of its arrangements. Personally, I find the Reid-McNeill version of "Barrett's" quite moving as a listening experience. In any case, what is noteworthy is the very different relationship their version establishes between performer and audience compared with the original. It is a much more formal relationship, and it is a clear example of the kind of sophisticated dramatic performance valued by revival performers and audiences in general.

Even musicians from traditional cultures often feel they must adjust their style and presentation to suit the stage, frequently adopting more dramatic techniques and more complex instrumentation. For example, prairie fiddlers often insist on adding drums and bass when recording or playing for large dances away from home, even though they rarely use them in their own communities. Therefore it is misleading to write off revival

Section:	1		2				
	Verse 1	chorus	tag	V 2	ch.	V 3	ch.
Tempo:	slow (M.M.=76)		faster (M.M.=92-96)				
Instru-mentation:	concertina		cittern	cittern mandolin			

Figure 3. "Baratt's Privateers," Reid-McNeill arrangement.

	3					4		5	6 CLIMAX II	
tag	V 4	ch.	V 5	ch.	CLIMAX I instrumental	V 6	V 7	V 8	ch.	tag line
cittern mandolin fiddle concertina bass	con.	con. bass	con. fiddle	con. fiddle cittern bass	con. fiddle cittern mand.	a cap.	cittern con.	slow (M.M.=88) con.	fast (M.M.=92-96) con. cittern fiddle bass	

Figure 3, continued.

performers as not being true folk musicians because they have been influenced by professional performance values. By emphasizing the separation between performer and audience, the stage seems to encourage performers of any background to introduce more variety and drama into their performances in direct proportion to audience passivity. The revival celebrates both the personal, active participation of folk tradition and the power, gloss, and drama of stage traditions, and is caught in continual dynamic tension between the two. This tension can not only inspire the creation of such a participatory, old-fashioned song as "Barrett's Privateers" but can just as easily lead to the transformation of such a song back into a carefully worked-out dramatic performance, as we see here.

Folk Groups

The designation "folk group" has usually been reserved in the past for people united by such factors as "ethnicity, religion, region, occupation, age, and kinship affiliation."[14] However, the dissemination of recorded music has created many groupings of listeners who may be widely separated geographically, and who may or may not share cultural background, common interests, values or experiences. Should these groups, united around a particular musical style, be considered folk cultures the way older societies are? Participants in the folk revival, for example, seem to have no obvious geographic-historic cultural base, although they tend to be urban and middle class. The performers are usually paid, which is a symbol of the fact that they are expected to be professional entertainers, capable of holding an audience in thrall—an audience that has also paid to see them. This may have an effect on what and how they choose to perform. The size and composition of the audience for any particular performer may have a lot to do with the promotional ability of his or her record company or manager, or with the whim of a radio programmer. Overall, the revival differs from the kind of folk community defined above in two major ways: its tendency toward professional performance and all that that entails—stage concerts, light and sound technology, mass-media, money and marketing—and the absence of shared life experience on a daily level among its participants. In the minds of many, these factors make the folk revival a spurious kind of "folk" activity and its artistic expressions a similarly dubious kind of folklore. Let us look at these two factors in turn.

"Barrett's Privateers" demonstrates both the professionalism of the revival and its opposite—the casual exchange of musical expressions. Stan Rogers and all others who have recorded the song are paid performers. The song was spread through commercial recordings and through large, paid concert events. However, it was also spread through backroom sessions and the kind of informal personal contacts by which any song traveled in the past. As "Barrett's" shows us, this latter process of personal exchange has the same potential to engender change in the words and tune of a modern song as it did in the past, and for similar reasons, including incomplete exchange, memory gaps, and changes of cultural context. This similarity of process within the revival and within older folk groups is sufficient for us to consider the revival a kind of folk culture, albeit one having significant differences from traditional societies.

These differences should not be minimized. First of all, the involvement of mass media freezes a song in a particular form, offering a counterforce to the changes resulting from oral transmission. Further, mass media and the resulting larger numbers of listeners help to create "stars," thus encouraging large performance events rather than smaller community gatherings. And again, the fact that performers are paid in the revival brings in business and copyright concerns that may affect how a song is spread and/or altered.

With regard to our second principle, that of shared life experience, the recent work of scholars such as Jackson,[15] Joan Kosby,[16] and Edith Fowke[17] emphasizes some similarities between mass-media–influenced groups (such as the folk revival) and traditional folk communities. Fowke's "Filksongs as Modern Folksongs" discusses science fiction conventions at which songs inspired by science fiction literature are sung. These groups meet regularly and have developed certain behaviors, attitudes, and language that they hold in common. Other such special-interest groups might include those who frequent a certain folk club over several years, as is the subject of Joan Kosby's work, or the audience at a certain regularly held music festival. These groups may develop their own mythologies, their own heroes, and their own sense of group history, complete with reminiscences of past gatherings and attempts to preserve certain behaviors or attitudes, just as in older folk groups. On a larger scale, one might argue that people, usually young people, from widely separated places have created several musical cultures over the past forty years or so, each with its own associated behavior and lifestyle. Some of these people are in close proximity on a daily basis, but they also share a similar culture with groups in other places. In these cases, the mass media, in the form of recordings, radio, and television have been important means of communication. This situation could be compared to a cultural diaspora, in which one ethnic group has established several communities in widely separated areas, all of whom hold many cultural expressions in common.

However, most of the human interaction centered around mass-media forms of culture is much more impermanent than that of traditional societies. The culture of a traditional society is shaped by years of interdependence, often over several generations. The effects of such ongoing personal contact on culture, often heightened by shared geography, working conditions, economic status, and ethnicity, are undoubtedly profound. In contrast, mass media have the potential to create a common popular culture for very large groups of people over vast distances but, curiously, only for relatively short periods of time. Is this, perhaps, because the impersonal communications of the mass media cannot create the strong human relationships needed to sustain cultural expression over time?

The transitory nature of popular culture as compared to older cultures seems especially surprising when one considers the mass media's ability to freeze songs in recorded form. In fact, however, this material permanence may be directly responsible for the impermanence of the song as a relevant cultural expression. Recorded material is no longer flexible, no longer adaptable to changes in context. In the past, the music in a given culture continually evolved along with the culture's values and behavior patterns, thus remaining current, whereas a song that cannot change at all becomes quickly dated.

However significant these differences between older cultures and modern groups may be, it is not productive to describe the cultural expressions of older societies as "authentic," implying that more commercial forms are somehow "inauthentic" or "fake." What is important is the recognition that traditional musical cultures and modern performance-oriented ones are separate. That is, the folk revival is a new culture, not an extension of older ones. It looks to older folk cultures for its inspiration, but ultimately it translates old music into its own context and its own aesthetic values, largely those of pop and art music.

That the revival should be considered a separate folk culture and not merely an expansion of traditional music to a wider audience is supported by the fact that, for the most part, neither revival audiences nor members of traditional societies appreciate the music of the other. Members of many traditional cultures dislike the versions of their music performed by "professional" musicians from outside the original culture,[18] but it is just as true that revival audiences often cannot appreciate the performances of musicians from traditional societies. Revival audiences, schooled as they are in pop culture, generally prefer the performances delivered by musicians who are similarly schooled, either younger players from the traditional cultures or, more often, musicians from outside the original cultures entirely. In many cases this has the unfortunate effect of giving far more fame and fortune to revival musicians than to the musicians from whom they learned. It also means that, rather than helping to increase understanding of older folk traditions, the revival often has the opposite effect. It further marginalizes these traditions by encouraging people to expect flashy performances of folk music, enhanced by a skilled use of technology. Revival audiences, as people exposed to commercial music everywhere, are less and less able to enjoy the participatory musical experiences and straightforward delivery of most older traditions.

Conclusion

The branching pathway followed by "Barrett's Privateers" demonstrates that the folk revival, in spite of the separation of its participants and its use of mass media, functions in many ways like an older folk group united by geographic, ethnic, or historical factors. It has a certain aesthetic sensibility of its own and, most important, feels itself to be a kind of community, united around a certain style of artistic expression. Within it, there is a fair amount of exchange of musical materials, mostly but not exclusively among performers.[19]

Moreover, as "Barrett's" also shows us, the values of the revival often differ dramatically from those of older groups that were the source of much of its musical inspiration. Some of these differing values are: the separation of performer and audience marked by a tendency toward passive consumption of music rather than active involvement by the audience; the corresponding tendency to dramatic and highly arranged performance styles as opposed to informal, participatory ones; the blending of sounds and techniques from many different traditions learned impersonally, as opposed to the evolution of a particular musical tradition in the hands of those who are almost exclusively involved in that one tradition. All of these oppositions create conflicts within the revival, especially for musicians from older cultures or for those who have had intensive personal contact with the older cultures.

Revival events have grown larger and more staged in Canada over the past fifteen years, and there have been correspondingly fewer performers from traditional cultures, whose simpler style of presentation is often not suited to the expectations of audiences at these events. However, although the context is not always suitable, people at these large events are often interested in the idea of traditional music—its verbal themes, its melodies, and its participatory nature. "Barrett's Privateers" is tailor-made to fit this paradoxical situation. It has all of the aesthetic sensibilities of the revival. It is original but suggests age by its sound and its story. Its form is unusual and catchy. It has sophisticated phrasing but is easy to learn. It can be either an exhilarating call-and-response or an intense listening experience. It works around the fire or on stage in front of ten thousand people.

"Barrett's Privateers," as a true product of the folk revival, leads us to the inevitable conclusion that success in this modern musical culture, the folk revival, comes from making old music sound new and new music sound old.

NOTES

1. See the companion paper in this volume by Pauline Greenhill, " 'The Folk Process' in the Revival: 'Barrett's Privateers' and 'Baratt's Privateers.' "

2. I participate in the folk revival in Canada as a performer, mainly as a fiddler and singer in various styles of traditional music. I am also an ethnomusicologist. My own fieldwork has been largely on Métis music and dance traditions of Manitoba, and I have arranged for some of the Métis performers to appear at folk festivals in Canada. Analyzing the revival with the same tools one applies to older cultures has been an interesting venture.

3. I use the term "folk revival" to refer to the phenomenon of the past twenty years or so in which it has become popular to perform traditional music and original material inspired by tradition to audiences outside of the communities from which the music comes. It also includes the dissemination of this music through the mass media. Performers in the folk revival may be from within or outside of the traditions involved. They may or may not consider themselves "folk" musicians. Within the revival as a whole, as in general North American society, the term "folk music" is used in many different ways.

4. Phone conversation with Ariel Rogers, 10 August 1989.

5. Such commonly held factors include ethnic background, location, age, religion, and so on. For further discussion of this principle, see Bauman, "Differential Identity."

6. Stan Rogers, *Fogarty's Cove.*

7. *Sidetracks.*

8. This and all other quotations from Brian McNeill come from Greenhill's interview with McNeill in Ottawa, Ontario, 4 May 1988.

9. McNeill stated that their live version "would be based on the recorded version" in terms of the arrangement of choruses and the timing but "was much simpler" in instrumentation, as he and Reid overdubbed several instruments on the recording.

10. McNeill said that, although he would respect the words of a song with a known composer, he does not mind altering the melody slightly.

11. For Eleanor Long's term "perseverator," as discussed in Greenhill's companion paper, see Long, "Ballad Singers, Ballad Makers, and Ballad Etiology."

12. The concertina and bass sounds were done on a synthesizer. However, for clarity I will use the names of the instruments the synthesizer imitates.

13. The theory of the "golden section" is based on the Greek principle of visual proportion, in which a whole is divided into two parts, so that the ratio of the smaller to the larger part is the same as that of the larger part to the whole. This ratio is also created by the Fibonacci series, in which every integer is the sum of the preceding two, beginning 0, 1, 1, 2, 3, 5, 8, 13, 21, and so on. As the series progresses, the ratio of each number to the succeeding number more nearly ap-

proaches the ideal golden section ratio, usually taken as .618 to 1. Ernö Lendvai developed the theory in relation to Bartok's works in "Bartok und die Zahl." Others, such as Sam Dolin of the Royal Conservatory of Music in Toronto, have since theorized that it applies to much western "art" music.

14. Bauman, "Differential Identity."

15. Jackson, "The Folksong Revival."

16. Kosby, "An Ethnography of the St. Albans Folk Music Club."

17. Fowke, "Filksongs as Modern Folksongs."

18. Instances of this abound in my own experience as well as in that of other researchers. For example, many prairie fiddlers of my acquaintance feel that their traditional tunes are played wrongly by well-known recording artists. Further, during a conversation I overheard at the Miramichi traditional song festival in northern New Brunswick, regarding the performance of the one hired singer from Saint John (the largest city in the province), a woman said rather disapprovingly to her companion: "It was all right, but she's more of a professional."

19. This raises the idea that folk revival performers might be considered a kind of folk group separate from the rest of the revival. As they share some rather specialized experiences, such as the backroom sessions, this approach could prove fruitful.

PART 3

Named-Systems Revivals

Lederman's description of the paradoxes in the "new aesthetic" aspect of folk music revivalism suggests that while it may be seen as a separate social milieu in which authenticity is, in Posen's words, "a 'flavor,'" connections persist between it and the "traditional" musics on which it is founded. In this section we turn to another aspect and outgrowth of the great boom in which such connections are much more central, "named-systems" revivals.

Why this term? As we have seen, the conventional approach to folk music begins with text—combinations of words and music—and moves next to style. As Stekert suggested, many in the boom (and since) have found this perspective sufficient. "Utilizers" took texts and, to a lesser extent, the styles associated with them, for commercial purposes. Those involved in the "new aesthetic" built their own artistic tradition upon folk texts and styles. But those involved in the great boom whom Stekert called "imitators" often followed a quite different path, one involving not just text and style but immersion in music-cultures: aggregates of shared repertoire, instrumentation, and performance style generally perceived as being historically and culturally bounded by such factors as class, ethnicity, race, religion, region, commerce, and art. These contextual aggregates—which I call systems—are, characteristically, named. Hence the pedestrian but, I hope, straightforward title of this section.

The seven essays in this section deal with the revival process in such named systems as blues, bluegrass, and old-time fiddling. All explore questions of acculturation and social change. The very act of naming requires, for those to whom the name is new and unexplained, some kind of definition process. The result, it appears, always changes the system. Sometimes revivalists become part of the system; and it appears that often the system is gentrified when this happens. Such changes suggest that while there may be considerable cultural differences between the revivalists and nonrevivalists who share involvement in the system, integration and transformation can take place because of agreement about the cultural values that the system is thought to embody.

Such systems may also serve as didactic vehicles for the teaching of music. Following the lead of Mantle Hood, ethnomusicologists have treated apprentice music performance in such music-cultures as a way of learning music in its widest cultural contexts.[1] In 1968 D. K. Wilgus pointed out that the New Lost City Ramblers, mentioned in several earlier articles and discussed by Feintuch in the first article in this section, were "basically the kind of performance group essential in any well-run school of ethnomusicology. They have," he said, "learned the music from the inside, by imitation and by tutoring from folk musicians." Wilgus lamented that "they have not been integrated into academic study—and both sides are poorer for the separation."[2] Recently Carol Silverman, writing about "The Folklorist as Performer," discussed her own experiences as a performer and researcher of Balkan dance and song. She sees "all performers as implicit educators and the folklorist/performer as a particularly effective educational combination." Unfortunately, as she notes, many folklorists continue to view this kind of performance with ambivalence, perhaps because of a need felt by academic folklorists to be perceived as "scientific" and "objective." Silverman points out that contemporary theorists are now reexamining assertions of objectivity and are now aware of "the reflexive interactive nature of all fieldwork." Consequently, performing folklorists "are often in a unique position to investigate the issue of reflexivity."[3]

Silverman, like those writing in this section, first became involved as an "imitator" (her term) in the music-culture she later came to study. Whenever people make the choice to become involved in a named system we must consider the question Stekert raises in her discussion of "imitators"— why has such a choice of expression not been possible within the individual's "native" culture or environment? What, indeed, prompts people to seek other roots, to become specialists in named-systems revivals? These essays address that question and provide a number of suggestions about how individuals in modern society work to find musical answers to cultural dilemmas.

In "Musical Revival as Musical Transformation" Burt Feintuch draws upon his experiences as musician and scholar in two historically and geographically separate named-system revivals. Articulating a view of the revival as an allied grouping of musicians, scholars, and other would-be conservationists to save "the tradition," he raises issues of consciousness and unselfconsciousness, individual and community, and insider and outsider. Using examples from his recent field research in Northumbrian pipe music and from the old-time music revival of the 1970s, he shows how perceptions of style constitute the agenda for authenticity as tradition is constructed or reconstructed. He argues that revivals of this kind create their own canons of repertoire, style, and authenticity. They are, therefore, in his terms, transformations. Feintuch, whose awareness of the current depth of involvement by folklorists in public sector folklore is reflected in his editorship of *The Conservation of Culture*, advocates the inclusion of such folk revivals among the types of emergent tradition studied by folklorists.

"Starvation, Serendipity, and the Ambivalence of Bluegrass Revivalism," my study of bluegrass revivalism, deals with another transformation, the one that took place in bluegrass music during the period between 1965 and 1970. Building upon terminology suggested by the ethnomusicologist Mark Slobin to describe the roles available to revival participants, it presents examples of two such individuals. Both argued in print for canons of transformation that were paradoxical because (1) they were based upon an invented past, and (2) invented or not, a past tradition can never be regained. An important feature of this example of named-system revival is the tendency for revivalists to tie authenticity of experience to a perceived lack of self-consciousness of tradition. When the transformation came—bringing with it consciousness of tradition, as evidenced in the widespread currency of the term "traditional bluegrass" after 1970—these revivalists had two choices: they could become activists in transformed tradition, leaving their theoretical canons in favor of a more pragmatic approach; or they could abandon their involvement in the system altogether.

In the last two decades many folklorists have developed new approaches based upon the idea of folklore as behavioral process. Following this performance-oriented line of thought Philip Nusbaum approaches expressive behavior relating to two music systems as an "experiential domain." In "Bluegrass and the Folk Revival: Structural Similarities and Experienced Differences," he draws from the work of Dell Hymes and builds on his own research on conversations analysis in considering the resultant process of expressive consensus about music as "traditionalization." Nusbaum depicts two music-cultures—from his perspective, the revival is another named system—in terms of what other scholars have called ethnographic reality, showing how the two resemble each other and yet are different. This approach is typical of many behavioral approaches to folklore in that it restates the question of contextual authenticity in new terms that focus upon the freedom of individuals to select from their experiences those elements with which they may construct their own sense of tradition.

Jeff Todd Titon's "Reconstructing the Blues: Reflections on the 1960s Blues Revival" illustrates well the way in which named-system revivals grew out of the great boom, and once again emphasizes the central place of phonograph recordings in revival processes. Titon examines "the interpreters' hegemony over the artists," with particular attention to a key writer on the topic, Samuel Charters. He cautions us that it is not just revivalists who play roles but also researchers, and that ultimately "no one is free from constituting domains through interpretive acts." Like Lederman and Rosenberg, Titon finds paradox in revival: it is "an imaginative act" that can only happen if the revivalists think there is something to be revived—what Feintuch would call the canon.

While Titon focuses on the blues revival's vital discovery period of the fifties and sixties, in "*Living Blues* Journal: The Paradoxical Aesthetics of the Blues Revival" Peter Narváez moves toward the present, examining the ways in which thinking from the earlier era continues to shape images of the music. He does this by analyzing a specialist publication, *Living Blues*, as an expression of the social relations of the revival.

Discussing revivalism in terms of Wallace's concept of revitalization movements, he offers a four-point model of the processes involved in the seeking of cultural alternatives—a model that helps to explain the motivations behind the transformations described in the first two articles in this section. He then turns to the major focus of the article, a discussion of the editorial policy promulgated by the "folk revival elite" who created *Living Blues*. This policy stresses that blues is a black music, and denies the possibility of white participation in the making of the music itself. Narváez indicates that in this and other ways the contents of the magazine foster a picture of the blues that is not consonant with what Nusbaum would call blues's experiential domain—not only are blueswomen slighted, but the widespread contemporary phenomenon of racially mixed blues bands goes unacknowledged in the magazine. In part this reflects the stereotype of the blues performer as a black working-class male of rural background. It also touches upon a major issue in named-systems revivalism: if the system is conceived of in cultural terms, then how can it be authentically preserved and promoted outside the compass of those cultural terms? Is John Hammond, Jr., really a case of "defying the ear with the eye," as Stekert put it? This is the same question discussed by Nusbaum, and it is raised again in different ways by Blaustein and Mitsui in following essays.

Richard Blaustein's experiences as a musician in and student of the contemporary old-time fiddling revival provide the starting point for "Rethinking Folk Revivalism: Grassroots Preservationism and Folk Romanticism," his survey of issues surrounding outsider participation in grass-roots revivals. Noting that revivals are not always started by outsiders, he argues that ultimately the question of the origins of the participants is not as important as the question of how they come together to create a satisfying system.

Blaustein is debating a perspective toward folk revivalists that has dominated the thinking of public-sector folklorists in the administration of folk festivals. This perspective is articulated in Wilson and Udall's *Folk Festivals,* an organization and management handbook "prepared for those who wish to present the carriers of folk traditions in festivals that are accurate and respectful in depicting folk culture."[4] By *"carriers of tradition"* [their emphasis] they mean "those artists who grew up in the tradition in which they perform or create and learned their art in family or in community as a part of daily life" (p. v). By contrast, Wilson and Udall state: "the terms *urban folksong revival performer* and *folk revival performer* eventually came into use to describe the performance of urban imitators of rural folk styles. These misleading terms are still used to refer to artists who have adopted or imitate a folk style rather than reviving an art which previously existed in their own families or communities" (p. 8). Later, in a section called "A Confusion Regarding Folk Culture," they suggest that "an authentic folk artist seldom uses such a term in describing himself," and set forth a series of categories of "the major types of performers who describe themselves or are described by others as folk performers," distinguishing between those who are "reared" and those "not reared" "in the culture" (pp. 18–22). Blaustein disagrees with this stance, which accepts the importance of named systems but denies the significance of participation in them by outsiders except in the roles of researcher, advocate, or presenter.

Blaustein's scholarly position with regard to grassroots musical movements has been paralleled by similar arguments from grassroots intellectuals in a heated debate about revivalists in old-time music. Beginning in 1989 the *Old-Time Herald* published a series of articles and letters on the topic in its column "Issues in Old-Time Music." Outsider performer Mac Benford initiated the series with an article that argued in favor of what Nusbaum would call the reality of old-time music. A year later Joe Wilson offered a lively defense of his position, and the debate continues.[5]

The issue of who speaks for "the folk" can be debated only with great difficulty when the scholars disagree about who are and who are not the folk. What appears as unbiased advocacy can, in this situation, actually be a case of aesthetic selection by one elite in competition with another. Blaustein suggests new ways to approach this tangled situation by drawing from the experiences of scholars in other fields working with other cultures.

The central role of phonograph recordings in what Blaustein calls "cross-cultural transfusions" is nowhere more evident than in the phenomenon of Japanese involvement in hillbilly, old-time, country, and bluegrass music. As Toru Mitsui explains in "Reception of the Music of American

Southern Whites in Japan," the primary—for many the only—context for this exotic music was phonograph records. Similarly, most people outside of Japan first became aware of Japanese interest in this sector of North American music when they discovered the many fine Japanese reissue albums of it in the late 1960s.[6]

By presenting a perspective from outside North America, Mitsui offers a measure of the extent of the diffusion and influence of North American culture on other parts of the world.[7] He reiterates a point noted by Goldstein, that the revival of American folk music had as a spin-off the stimulation of other revivals in Britain and elsewhere in Europe, and explores the reasons why this did not happen in Japan.[8]

NOTES

1. Hood, *The Ethnomusicologist.*
2. Wilgus, "From the Record Review Editor: Revival and Traditional," p. 173.
3. Silverman, "The Folklorist as Performer," p. 35.
4. Wilson and Udall, *Folk Festivals,* p. v. Subsequent citations to this work will be made parenthetically in the text.
5. Benford, "Folklorists and Us." A storm of correspondence in the *Herald* followed Benford's letter, and Wilson published a reply there, "Confessions Of A Folklorist." For over a year every issue of the magazine following the appearance of Benford's piece carried letters about the topic, and Wilson's piece prompted a fresh flood; the debate continues as this is written. An independent expression of ideas similar to those of Blaustein is Bradley's *Counterfeiting,* which articulates the viewpoint of a cultural outsider who has become an accepted figure in a named system, old-time fiddling.
6. See Kahn, "Folksong on Records," and Rosenberg, "Nine Reasons," an article that deals in part with the editor's first meeting with Mitsui in 1966.
7. For another study of the diffusion of southern American music abroad, see Hale, "A Comparison of Bluegrass Music Diffusion."
8. In 1990 a considerably abridged, earlier version of this paper was read at the Fourth Symposium of the International Musicological Society in Osaka, and that version subsequently appeared in the proceedings of the symposium as "Reception of the Music from the American South in Japan," in Tokumaru et al., *Tradition and Its Future in Music,* pp. 457–64.

Musical Revival as Musical Transformation

Burt Feintuch

Since 1984 I've been studying a regional musical revival in Northumberland, England's northeasternmost county, exploring the revival's historical underpinnings and its contemporary embodiment.[1] The Northumbrian revival centers on a musical instrument called the Northumbrian smallpipes, a small, quiet, mellow bagpipe, blown by a bellows rather than by mouth. The smallpipes nearly became extinct in the years following World War II, with perhaps no more than fifty people in the world playing the instrument. But in the last couple of decades there has been an enormous growth of interest in the Northumbrian pipes. These days perhaps as many as two thousand people play, the majority of them in Northumberland and vicinity. Describing the efforts of revivalists there, a professional musician who makes his living as a revivalist performer of music from the region told me, "We are repairing the tradition, and [it] is gathering momentum again."[2]

Studying a musical revival hits fairly close to home for me, because like many other folklorists of my generation, I was influenced in my choice of a career by folk music revivals in the United States and Great Britain. In fact, an earlier set of experiences with Northumbrian music helped point me toward a career in folklore.

In 1969, I spent a semester as an exchange student at the University of Durham, just south of the Northumbrian border. My enthusiasm for what I then thought of as folk music, but would now describe with other qualifiers, including the term *revivalist,* led me to what was at the time the center of the Northumbrian revival—the Folk Song and Ballad Club at Newcastle's Bridge Hotel. Most Thursday nights, I took the train from Durham to Newcastle and walked from Central Station in the direction of the High Level Bridge, a nineteenth-century engineering masterpiece. In the bridge's shadow, I sat in a pub and listened to song and music the likes of which I'd never heard. The connection between musical expression and locality was palpable. This came as a revelation; for me, *folk music* had symbolized distance from my suburban, middle-class life. But at the Bridge Hotel, the music linked art and place, joining history and the contemporary city. At closing, I'd make my way back to the train station, the walk complicated by brown ale but memorable nonetheless because it took me down streets named in the songs and tune titles. I wanted to know more about those connections between aesthetic expression and place; in the study of folklore, I found that to be possible. Sixteen years after that semester in England, I went back for the first of a number of field trips, scholarly questions, nostalgia, and an enduring enthusiasm for the music motivating my return. Inevitably, my work in Northumberland has made me reflect on largely avocational interests and experiences.

My enthusiasm for regional musics continued to grow after that first visit to Northumberland helped me see how deeply planted music can be. As a graduate student in the early and mid-1970s, in the days when interest in older southeastern United States fiddle and banjo music was burgeoning, I began learning to play that music, commencing with fiddle lessons from a native New Jerseyan who later moved to West Virginia to be closer to the music that inspired him. My first academic job, in Kentucky, gave me the opportunity to experience much of that music firsthand. Not long ago, talking about his impending fortieth birthday, another friend of mine, a native New Yorker I had met in Kentucky, whose passion is playing old-time southeastern banjo tunes, said to me, "You know, some day I'm going to be one of those old farts you folklorists like to visit."

What strikes me about that remark and the one I quoted earlier, about repairing the tradition, is that each revivalist musician identifies a *tradition,* one directly, one by implication. Having done so, each locates himself in relationship to it, placing himself inside it. One prerequisite, it seems to me, for a folk revival is a shared sense of *the tradition* as well as a notion of how participants are related to that tradition. There's an irony in this. The term *revival* implies resuscitation, reactivation, and rekindling, and many revivalist musicians assert that they're bolstering a declining musical tradition. But rather than encourage continuity, musical revivals recast the music—and culture—they refer to. They are actually musical transformations, a kind of reinvention. And in reality, each revival achieves its own momentum with its own standard repertoire and styles and its own selective view of the past. In this essay, I want to assay the semantic irony that revivals are transformations. I'll focus on aspects of both revivals—developing an idea of *the tradition,* codifying a repertoire, sanctioning style, and using models, along with the significant involvement of scholars and other conservers in shaping the revival. Because I know the Northumbrian revival better, I'll give it more attention, adding anecdotal parallels from the old-time music revival as I experienced it.

History reveals that the idea of a distinctive Northumbrian musical tradition is more a reflection of the concerns of the music's chroniclers than an inventory of the region's music. From Bishop Thomas Percy and Joseph Ritson through mid-nineteenth-century antiquarian efforts and the 1960s work of A. L. Lloyd, as well as in the long history of popular song publication, it is possible to trace the development of an idea of a distinctively Northumbrian music. These days, that idea focuses primarily on the notion of a peculiarly Northumbrian body of song and music, generally thought to be the property of shepherds.[3] Many smallpipes revivalists believe themselves to be continuing a tradition that comes from the beautiful Northumbrian countryside, resurrecting a music that once belonged primarily to shepherds. Many would say it is a music that embodies a kind of Northumbrianess. For instance, the president of the Northumbrian Pipers' Society, a revivalist organization founded in 1928, wrote in the early 1980s that the piping revival is part of "the cause of traditional Northumbrianess."[4]

When the revivalist pipers speak of *the piping tradition* the phrase carries a distinctive set of connotations, and every time pipers strap on a set of pipes they wrap themselves in a set of associations linking their music to an idealized view of a bucolic past populated by musical shepherds who were proprietors of a uniquely Northumbrian body of tunes. The historical and ethnographic evidence suggests something considerably different from that view. Nothing indicates that the smallpipes have ever been primarily a rural instrument. Over the instrument's approximately 250 years of reasonably well documented history, the pipes have largely been an urban instrument, played primarily by gentlemen in the region's largest cities and market towns. In fact, for the past two hundred years the pipes' continuing existence can be attributed to the desire of urban people to see the instrument revived. Believing that they were resurrecting a shepherds' instrument, acting in the cause of "true Northumbrianess," the urban gentlemen were actually the primary community of pipers. They invented a tradition in order to revive it. It turns out that the current revival is at least the fourth major revitalization movement directed at the Northumbrian smallpipes.

Scholars have played a considerable role in the Northumbrian revival. They were, for the most part, antiquarians, but calling them that is not to belittle their efforts. In the 1850s the Society of Antiquaries in Newcastle-upon-Tyne, the region's major city, appointed an Ancient Melodies Committee, charged with documenting and thereby preserving the region's music. Thirty years later, the publication of *Northumbrian Minstrelsy* was the result.[5] The *Minstrelsy* has been described as the first modern folk music collection, largely, I think, because its editors were forward-thinking enough to include song melodies and a set of instrumental tunes in addition to song texts. About a third of the *Minstrelsy*'s pages are devoted to pipe tunes. Until more modern tune books supplanted it, the *Minstrelsy* helped shape the core repertoire of the piping revival. As recently as the 1960s, one rare-book shop in Newcastle sold photocopies of the long-out-of-print *Northumbrian Minstrelsy*, primarily, it appears, to pipers. A. L. Lloyd, the late scholar and revivalist singer, author of what is generally regarded as the most authoritative modern book on English folksong, also played a significant role in shaping the piping revival.[6] I'll return to him a bit later. The point here is that scholars and other conservers shaped the idea of Northumbrian music and made a corpus of melodies available to the revivalist musicians.

Thinking back to the early and mid-1970s when I was more closely involved in the old-time music revival, I realize that the community of musicians I knew then also predicated their music on a distinctive notion of *the tradition* they were reviving, tending, in many cases, to view themselves as insiders. As in Northumberland, the notion combined a romanticized view of rural life with an accrual of information from influential, although not necessarily authoritative, sources. Also as in Northumberland, scholarly and revivalist networks commingled. The old-time music revival is linked historically to the wider American folksong revival. Of course, American scholars and collectors played a vital role in that broad revival, making repertoire available, serving as advocates, presenting performers, and themselves performing. In a 1981 essay, Ray Allen maintains that what distinguished the old-time music revival from the larger revival, at least in the 1970s, was a purist strain, the revivalists' belief that in style and repertoire they were largely indistinguishable from the older community-based musicians from whom the revival music derived.[7]

Both Ray Allen and Norm Cohen suggest that the 1952 Folkways set of LPs entitled *Anthology of American Folk Music*, which reissued golden-age hillbilly recordings (along with period recordings of other musical genres such as Cajun music and country blues), sparked the revival and that the 1958 founding of the New Lost City Ramblers, a revivalist band dedicated to recreating the sound of those old records, marks the actual beginning of the old-time music revival. Mike Seeger, a founding member of the New Lost City Ramblers and a widely respected solo performer is, of course, a member of a family that profoundly inspired the direction of the American folk revival. Seeger family members generally attribute their interest to their patriarch, Charles Seeger, whose academic work brought the sounds of Library of Congress field recordings into the family household.[8]

By the early 1970s, two more recent LPs had defined old-time music, at least for the people I knew. One, a 1967 record by the Hollow Rock String Band, featured the fiddling of Alan Jabbour, now the director of the American Folklife Center at the Library of Congress. The other, the first LP by a Chapel Hill group called the Fuzzy Mountain String Band, emphasized tunes learned directly from older musicians or from field recordings.[9] Alan Jabbour was the conduit for a number of the Fuzzy Mountain band's tunes, and in his later scholarly work on documentary LPs he has continued to infuse the revival with new repertoire. Blanton Owen, recently the Nevada state folklorist, was a member of the Fuzzy Mountain band. Liner notes thank Richard Blaustein and Tom Carter, both of whom are now folklorists. Although Jan Brunvand has written that "[revivalists] are largely irrelevant to the study of folklore," it is easy enough to make a case for folklorists being very relevant *in* the study of revivalists.[10] It is virtually impossible for folklorists to study folk music revivals in the United States and Britain unreflexively.

Perhaps unintentionally, the Hollow Rock and Fuzzy Mountain bands helped shape the repertoire and point of view of the revivalist players of that moment. Shunning music derived from 1920s and 1930s commercial hillbilly recordings, they implied the existence of a purer strain of music, a stream of tradition separate from the forces of commerce, a set of styles rooted in something other than the confluence of locality and the mass-mediated marketplace. And in so doing, they provided a substantial portion of the core repertoire for the revivalist fiddlers and banjo players I knew, helped define appropriate performance style, and pointed to a set of traditional performers as models of the pure strain.

A series of publications established the core repertoire of the Northumbrian piping revival, with the 1970 *Northumbrian Pipers' Tune Book,* published by the Northumbrian Pipers' Society, at the center. The first known pipers' tune book, published sometime between 1800 and 1805 by John Peacock, was connected to efforts to save the pipes from oblivion, and it documents a repertoire of which only a small portion is played today, although some of the *Northumbrian Minstrelsy,* published about eighty years later, bears a striking resemblance to Peacock's tunes.[11] In 1936, the Northumbrian Pipers' Society published its first tune book, with the goal of providing a repertoire. That publication was expanded considerably, yielding the 1970 Northumbrian Pipers' Society book.[12] Today, at music sessions, at competitions, at piping classes, and across the spectrum of piping events, tunes from the Pipers' Society book are inevitably what is played, and many pipers carry the book in their pipe cases. One tune book has had the effect of centering the revival's repertoire. I should also note that perhaps because so many pipers are musically literate, it is commonly held that tunes in the book must be played as written. Questions of intention aside, the editors of the 1936 and 1970 editions of the tune book have played a major role in defining what is played in what the pipers describe as a folk or traditional music.

A. L. Lloyd, one of the driving forces behind the post-1950 burgeoning revivalist interest in English folksong, was convinced, primarily on the basis of his familiarity with the *Northumbrian Minstrelsy* and a number of unpublished tune manuscripts, that the Northumbrian piping repertoire was the most distinctive of England's regional musics. He is said to have believed that the pipe tunes bore a resemblance to some of the eastern European musics that also fascinated him. Certainly, Lloyd desired to see a genuinely British—as opposed to American-derived—revival, and as artistic director of Topic Records, the mainstay record label of the British revival, he was able to translate that conviction into action.

Colin Ross, the contemporary revival's leading pipemaker and an untiring missionary for the pipes, says that Lloyd was determined to see a Northumbrian repertoire made available to a new generation of pipers.[13] A pet project was an LP based on an unpublished manuscript dating from the 1770s and the Peacock tune book of about 1800. The record presented a repertoire of tunes that had not been played for perhaps 150 years, infusing them, to some extent, back into the revival. Like the Pipers' Society tune book, this LP, entitled *Cut and Dry Dolly*, presented a set of tunes that were, to all intents and purposes, new to those who were playing the pipes, and those tunes caught on because they came from authoritative sources.[14] Reviving the pipes created the instrument's present-day repertoire.

Both revivals have seized upon musical models who serve to authenticate and traditionalize those revivals, especially in regard to playing style and repertoire. A sense of authenticity seems contingent upon how a person makes music and how a person is located socially—a model manages the contradictory tasks of typifying and serving as an example of what is exceptional, the best. Ruth Finnegan has written about what she terms the *folk music world* in an English community, Milton Keynes, considerably to the south of Northumberland. She points out that for many of the enthusiasts the scholarly work of Cecil Sharp and other late-eighteenth and early-nineteenth-century English folksong scholars established the criteria for "folkness" or authenticity.

Although the Northumbrian and old-time music revivalists don't quote Sharp, they tend to act in accordance with Finnegan's description of the way in which the early—and now considerably criticized—paradigm operates in the revival. She says that in this view, "folk tradition was handed down over the ages, primarily by little-educated country dwellers. The lore of this 'folk' was held to be simple and spontaneous, owing more to 'nature' than conscious art, more to communally held tradition than individual innovation, with each nation and, to an extent, each region having its own 'folklore' implanted deep in the soil and soul of its people."[15] Finnegan goes on to say that folk music is seen by the Milton Keynes enthusiasts as growing over time from national or regional roots, that it is remembered primarily by older people, and that it comes largely from unlettered rural people.[16]

Whether they've read Sharp notwithstanding, the revivalists I know tend to see models as representing grass-roots communities of musicians. Idiosyncrasy wouldn't work; models are representations of an idealized view of musical sound, technique, and social setting as they exist in a romanticized organic community. But in many cases, those models are not the embodiments people believe them to be.

For example, in the 1920s the gentlemen pipers of the Northumbrian Pipers' Society were very taken with the piping of a man named Tom Clough. A coal miner, Clough was an almost incredibly proficient player, evidently much better than any known piper of the day. His music came to him from his family; it is difficult to demonstrate that he represented any sort of active and local community of pipers beyond his father and grandfather. Nearly an anomaly, Tom Clough was an exception rather than the rule, but he became the first twentieth-century icon of the music, a living embodiment of what the gentlemen believed piping should be— exquisite music played by a man of the earth, a true Northumbrian. As a consequence, a man who was essentially unique in his music came to be considered the best model of the tradition.[17]

Moreover, a new generation of mostly middle-class pipers, beginning in the mid-1960s and early 1970s, acted very much in the spirit of the antiquarians who had preceded them, looking to the countryside for shepherds and others to model their piping on. They did find a few. But because what we might call the "normal" state of affairs in the piping world is either ongoing or attempted revival based in urban areas, the stereotypical pipe-playing shepherds were hard to find. In fact, only two pipers—neither of them shepherds—were in the public eye in those years. One, Jack Armstrong, was the leader of the region's best-known country dance band, a frequent guest on regional radio broadcasts who was very much aware of the symbolic weight of his performing. Not a rural man, he affected a rural image strongly evocative of what the public wanted the piping tradition to be. His playing was legato, measured. In the modern revival, he occupies one end of the continuum of styles deemed traditional, although in reality he was a self-taught piper who learned outside of the region, having only his memory and his own creativity on which to base his playing. History shows that he had no connection to a community of musicians, at least until later in life when he formed his band, the Barnstormers (with whom he played the fiddle), and began seeking out rural musicians from whom he learned tunes. Yet many say that Jack Armstrong exemplifies the Northumbrian piping tradition.[18]

The other end of the continuum is occupied by Billy Pigg. A much less self-conscious symbol, Pigg was the stuff of which legends are made. Born in 1902 in the urban part of the county, he eventually became a farmer. By 1928 he was barred from competing in piping contests, because he had won them all. A much more lyrical and adventurous piper than Jack Armstrong, much more willing to take musical chances, Billy Pigg was like Tom Clough, who had first inspired his playing, in that his dexterity and musicality were close to astonishing, especially to the fledgling revivalist players who began visiting him. Like Clough, he was an exception. Not part of any "natural" community of pipers, he was, and continues to be, seen as the "real thing," an embodiment of Northumbrianess.[19]

Armstrong and Pigg became the revival's polarities, fixing its limits, authenticating and traditionalizing the music for its new audience. A decade and a half after they had both died, their proponents are vociferous. To Armstrong's followers—many of them older fans who grew up with his radio broadcasts—Billy Pigg was a wildman, imprecise and eccentric in his playing. According to Billy Pigg's followers, many of whom came to piping from the broader folksong revival, Jack Armstrong made "Northumbrian muzak," dull and unimaginative.

These days, the revival has created a new icon in the person of Joe Hutton. A gentle and genial man and a virtuoso musician, Hutton has the additional virtue of being a retired shepherd. Ironically, he believes that the pipes are a coal miners' instrument. This may be because he was the only piper in his part of the county. As a young man he had to travel a full day to get to piping lessons in one of the county's market towns. He saw other pipers once or twice a year at the major musical competitions, a number of which were established by urban revivalists. Although he formed his music in isolation from other pipers, he is frequently introduced as a "true Northumbrian," the last of the real pipers. He is widely emulated by young pipers. With two other retired shepherds, a fiddler and a harmonica player, playing in an ensemble style the three created with the encouragement of a well-known professional performer, he has become something of a national emblem, featured on television and radio, and performing all over Britain. Joe Hutton is an unusually accomplished piper, and his motivations are sincere. He is held in great esteem by almost all the revivalist musicians who know him, buy his recordings, and in some cases emulate his playing style. For a new generation of pipers and enthusiasts, Joe Hutton was a dream come true.[20]

In the old-time music revival, there has also been the tendency to take what is largely unique as typical. As the revival gained momentum, young players searched for the most archaic tunes, the most striking performance styles, the musicians deemed least tainted by mass-mediated music. For example, what seems to have been scores of northern revivalist musicians flocked to Surrey County, North Carolina, to see the late fiddler Tommy Jarrell for those reasons. For many of those revivalists, Jarrell became the means by which style could be evaluated, a touchstone, a standard of comparison. It seems that learning directly from a model is one way to locate oneself inside the tradition. A young fiddler I knew some time ago, a New Jersey native who spent much time when he was in his twenties visiting and learning from old fiddlers in Kentucky, is described in a recent revivalist magazine as "one of the only people left to embody an entire musical tradition."[21]

Clearly, both revivals have tended to shape their models. The Kentucky fiddler J. P. Fraley, whose Rounder LP influenced quite a number of revivalist musicians when it was issued in the late seventies, told me once that he doesn't like the record.[22] Fraley claims that the producers had him play an old-fashioned repertoire he knows but neither enjoys playing nor believes represents his music. Writing on the relationship of bluegrass music to the broad folk revival, Neil Rosenberg has shown something similar in pointing out that the very influential group led by Lester Flatt and Earl Scruggs developed two different performance repertoires, one for their familiar audiences, one for their newer folk revival audiences.[23] Models authenticate, but they may represent a very selective view of a scene that is either more diverse, as in the case of old-time music, or essentially nonexistent, as in the case of Northumbrian piping.

It is this selective view that causes revivals to reinvent, to be transformations. Musical revivals, at least the two I know reasonably well, create their own canons of repertoire, of style, of authenticity. This is a sort of creative editing, a paring away of those characteristics and features deemed inappropriate and a reorganization of what is left. Raymond Williams labels the result of this kind of process a *selective tradition,* and he notes that a selective tradition is really a rejection of much of what was once a living culture, thanks to this editing mechanism.[24] Returning to the first quote I cited, the one about repairing the piping tradition and adding new momentum to it, I would suggest an alternative formulation. Although the piping revivalists make constant reference to "the piping tradition," what they have actually done is create their own historically conditioned and socially maintained "artistic paradigm," a transformation of the music—and culture—they think they have revived.[25] Each of the revivals I've discussed makes constant reference to the music it derives from, yet neither is really *of* that music. Each of the revivals achieved its own momentum, with its own preferred repertoire, its own sanctioned styles, and its own selective view of the past.

Although that observation may sound disparaging, I don't mean to be deprecatory. In a body of scholarship that is closely related to the subject of folk revivals, the anthropological study of revitalization movements, it is a truism that revitalization transforms the subject of its efforts.[26] As our own view of tradition evolves, we realize that *tradition* is a social and academic construct standing for and resulting from an ongoing process of interpreting and reinterpreting the past.[27] Rather than castigate folk music revivalists as if they had somehow corrupted what does not belong to them, as some folklorists have tended to do, it seems to me that we should understand folk music revivals as transformations, much in the same way we have come to accept explorations of other species of artistic uses and reinterpretations of folklife, as in the example of the study of folklore and literature. Such a view could help us locate folk music revivals where they belong, among the many emergent aspects of culture that also carry the banner of tradition.

NOTES

This essay is a revised version of a paper I presented as part of a panel on revivalism that Jeff Titon and I organized for the 1987 American Folklore Society conference. Thanks to Jeff for his reading of this paper and many good conversations on the notion of revivals.

1. The National Endowment for the Humanities, the American Council of Learned Societies, Western Kentucky University, and the University of New Hampshire have been generous in support of this research. I also owe gratitude to the University of Durham's Department of Anthropology for hosting me as a visiting scholar during two of my five field visits to Northumberland. Most important of all, I am grateful to the many people in Northumberland who welcomed me into their lives.

2. Interview with Alistair Anderson, 5 October 1984, Louisville, Kentucky. My field tape NP-1984-01.

3. Until recently, many regional songs (not the instrumental music of the pipes) were strongly identified with coal mining, but this association seems to be fading, as is the mining itself.

4. Bibby in his unpaginated introduction to *The Northumbrian Pipers' Second Tune Book*.

5. Bruce and Stokoe, *Northumbrian Minstrelsy*.

6. Lloyd, *Folk Song in England.* A current generation of scholars is reevaluating Lloyd, frequently uncharitably. See, for example, Harker's very important critique *Fakesong* and essays by Leslie Shephard, Roy Palmer, Vic Gammon, and David Arthur in Russell's *Singer, Song and Scholar.*

7. Allen, "Old Time Music."

8. Norm Cohen, "Record Reviews: The Revival."

9. Hollow Rock String Band, *Traditional Dance Tunes; The Fuzzy Mountain String Band.*

10. Brunvand, *Folklore,* p. 23.

11. Peacock, *A Favourite Collection.*

12. *The Northumbrian Pipers' Tune Book.*

13. Interview, 25 June 1985, Monkseaton, England. My field tapes NP-1985-14/15.

14. *Cut and Dry Dolly.*

15. Finnegan, *The Hidden Musicians,* p. 66. It's worth pointing out that this is a model that lingers in academic settings, too, and that something quite like it is evident in much public-sector folklore work. In that regard, the enthusiasts and the scholars are in many cases not far apart.

16. Ibid., pp. 66–67.

17. The only widely available recording of Clough's playing is on the 1976 anthology of historical recordings, *Holey Ha'Penny.*

18. Armstrong recorded widely, beginning in the 1940s, with records being issued into the early 1970s. Perhaps the best introduction to his work as a piper and country dance band leader is *Jack Armstrong, Celebrated Minstrel.*

19. Pigg's involvement with the revival is too complex to chronicle here. However, it's worth pointing out that he seems to have doggedly sought out other musicians—pipers, fiddlers, and piano players—for company, even when it meant difficult travel. And at a time when travel from the city—Newcastle—to the country was also difficult, urban revivalists began visiting him, casting him in the role of model. Like Armstrong, he also played on the radio and was known to a wide range of people because of the mass mediation of his music. He was not, however, a country musician in the sense that the revival presents—an unsophisticated member of an agrarian community in which music figured prominently and "naturally."

The best introduction to Pigg's music is the LP of amateur recordings, *The Border Minstrel.*

20. Hutton has recorded one solo LP, *Joe Hutton of Coquetdale.*

21. Dirlam, "Bruce Greene," p. 19.

22. J. B. and Annadeene Fraley, *Wild Rose of the Mountain.*

23. Rosenberg, *Bluegrass: A History,* p. 169.

24. Williams, *The Long Revolution,* pp. 50–51.

25. For the notion of *artistic paradigm,* see Clignet, *The Structure of Artistic Revolutions.*

26. The classic works in this scholarship are Linton's "Nativistic Movements" and Wallace's "Revitalization Movements."

27. Handler and Linnekin, "Tradition, Genuine or Spurious."

Starvation, Serendipity, and the Ambivalence of Bluegrass Revivalism

Neil V. Rosenberg

We need to study folklore revivals because they tell us about our own unexamined assumptions concerning the other things we study. Recently Bruce Jackson chronicled the American folksong revival in terms that identify it as the historical precedent for our discipline's current involvement in the public sector.[1] Ironically, in this activity we shun revivalists in favor of those whom we consider legitimate tradition-bearers. Yet many in the discipline were revivalists before becoming folklorists. Elsewhere I argue that folklorists have never been free from revival influences.[2] Revivals are artistic movements, and art characteristically leads science in the generation of new ideas, giving free rein to intuition, while science is compelled to test its intuitions. As social scientists we folklorists who were revivalists have tended to ignore the meaning of our own past and to disagree with the ideas of our peers who remain engaged as revivalists.[3] We do this even though our worldview was shaped and continues to be shaped by the revival experience. We must examine the morphology of revival in order to understand ourselves.

The study of revivals in folklore begins with the question of the appropriateness of using the word "revival." Some have argued against using it because they find it denotatively inaccurate. It is true that when we look carefully at revivals we often find that the things being revived (1) haven't completely died out—that is, however moribund they may be they don't necessarily require revival—and (2) are made into something different by the revival process; that is, revival kills, maims, or mutates them. Moreover, frequently many of the people involved in revivals are outsiders who are reviving things novel to them.[4] I would argue that, granting the accuracy of these observations, we are still dealing with people for whom, and events in which, revival is the predominant motive, the underlying reason for action. And the word's connotation of religious fervor captures an essential aspect of the phenomenon: the verve, zeal, energy, and fervor of revivalist involvement.

In 1979 David Evans presented a four-stage historical framework for the folk music revival in America. All stages are important and can, I suspect, be seen in other revivals as well. But in this study I focus on the last two, the striving for authenticity in recreating folk styles, which leads to increasing competence and authenticity, and to conscious specialization and regionalism or ethnicity. Evans views the final result positively, arguing that "ethnic and regional traditions . . . have taken on a new life at a time when some . . . were showing signs of becoming moribund." The resulting new compositions and development and experimentation of old styles are, he suggests, "processes that have always taken place in healthy folk traditions."[5]

Mark Slobin's discussion of the revival of American ethnic music offers insights into these processes. In considering two recent revivals, the klezmer music revival of the 1970s and the great American "folk revival" of the 1940s to 1960s, Slobin points out that "it is usually a very small number of key individuals who set the pace and/or serve as a source for an entire ethnic community."[6] He divides the roles played by activists in these movements into three categories: historian/researchers, elder statesmen/repositories, and performance acolytes/band creators.

Without these activists, says Slobin, revivals don't happen. But, he adds, there must be an answer to the question of *why* the activists' activities are accepted by the community to which they are addressed. To answer this question we must first consider the word "community." For example, among those who have enthusiastically embraced revived klezmer music are people who are either not Jewish or consider themselves Jewish but are considered by some other Jews to be Jewish in name only, or to be lapsed or marginal Jews. In this case, and, I would argue, in all others, the "community" refers to a culturally heterogeneous group of people for whom the thing being revived has some essential cultural (and therefore communal) meaning. Here, I realize, we are skating close to tautology: it can be argued that revival defines or redefines a community. Indeed, both Jackson and Posen argue that the folk revival itself constitutes a real community.[7] I will return to this point at the end of my essay.

There is another way of defining community with regard to music that may help us to arrive at a general answer to Slobin's *why*. This is to follow the perspective of Edward D. Ives, who has said that folksong traditions are "not carried on by a group but by individuals within that group who . . . take a special interest in songs."[8] I think that Ives is not very far here from von Sydow's idea of active bearers of tradition, except for the different meaning the word "tradition" holds for him.[9] But for the purposes of this discussion I move on to reformulate Ives's statement, and, implicitly, von Sydow's, as follows: folksong and music traditions consist of musical systems perpetuated by communities consisting of specialized performers and knowledgeable audiences. But then the question arises, How do we distinguish between these specialists and the revival activists?

Slobin offers another set of role descriptions that helps answer this question. Two of his students attended an old-time music workshop in West Virginia and developed terminology to describe the participants. They called the outsiders who came to absorb the local music "tourists." The exponents and teachers of the older traditions were called "old masters." And those individuals who were the driving force behind the workshop were "immigrants." These people had taken on the local lifestyle, gotten close to the "old masters," and served as mediators of the tradition, standing between them and the tourists.[10]

Why not combine these roles with Slobin's earlier set? The role of elder statesman/repository can be equated with that of old master. The roles of historian/researcher, performance acoylte/band creator, and immigrant are overlapping spheres of activism for which the word "revivalist" is most appropriate. Tourists are best viewed as musicians in transition. They are apprentices who are being taught by the revivalists and the old masters to become specialists. Now, to the *why*. Revivalists perceive the music system as threatened, moribund, or unappreciated—usually for ideological and aesthetic reasons. They believe it to be morally and artistically worth preserving. This is the source of their vision of the system, the fuel for their zeal. They initiate apprentices into a tradition that is being transformed by their vision.

This transformation, the key element in revival, is difficult to perceive and understand clearly because the rhetoric of revivalists is reactionary. Although in their activities as historians, researchers, and musical acolytes revivalists are keenly interested in authenticity, they characteristically create new perspectives. This is because the issue of authenticity usually does not arise until a revival begins. Of course specialists are always concerned about being musically "right" and "good," but these are terms that are usually shaped much more by an experienced sense of the nuts and bolts of tradition than by abstract criteria about text, texture, or context, or by openly ideological concerns. Revivalists become revisionist historians when they attempt to establish standards of authenticity. They view the tradition's past not only from an ideological viewpoint but also from a new temporal and experiential viewpoint, and almost always also from the viewpoint of a different class.

If revivalists are like immigrants in some ways, they differ from most immigrants—except, perhaps, colonists—in that they are from a dominant class and therefore have the power to choose the terms on which they will assimilate. This aspect of the process is never a smooth one. Often revivalists disagree among themselves about their visions of authenticity. Revivalists may also disagree with specialists who, like Almeda Riddle, are prompted through contact with revivalists to develop and articulate their sense of what is right and good into a personal theory of authenticity.[11] From such debates emerges a reinterpretation of the tradition. In Ben-Amos's terms, tradition becomes "canon."[12] Handler and Linnekin hold that this is always the case, stating that "tradition is a model of the past and is inseparable from the interpretation of tradition in the present."[13] But, I would argue, this only happens when something is expressly *identified* as tradition. This process can occur in a specialist community without the intrusion of revivalists, for tradition-bearers are not necessarily unselfconscious about their own traditions, and changes of many kinds, including reinterpretation, take place in all traditions. But the presence of revivalists seems to lead to certain *kinds* of reinterpretation.

There may be a tendency toward romantic purism, in which revivalists will not countenance certain types of repertoire, style, performer, or performance context; not being "pure," they cannot be "authentic." Alternatively, a gentrified musical form may develop, in which working-class music is recast for middle-class audiences, often in the interest of artistic or commercial "viability" or "progress." Debates over reinterpretation in revivalist-influenced traditions involve a dialectical struggle between these two positions.

Whatever happens, we can be certain that once a revival begins, the tradition is affected. Revisionist perspectives are communicated to specialists who previously took their system for granted and may even have expected it to become moribund. Those specialists who accept the revivalists help them transform the community's vision of the tradition. New specialists, whether they are tourists or the children of old masters, begin to include aspects of the revival perspective in their perception of the tradition. Eventually the revivalists who remain involved become specialists, and ultimately some may be accepted as old masters. Those specialists and revivalists who remain are the new activists. They combine a revival zeal with the specialists' sense of community.

But many revivalists abandon the revival when they recognize the inherent conflict between reaction and revision. In the remainder of this paper I illustrate this aspect of the revival process using examples from bluegrass. For a musical form that, by the most generous estimate, has existed for little more than half a century, bluegrass has become associated with the word "tradition" to a surprising extent. The association began when bluegrass was discovered in the 1950s by folk revivalists who equated "tradition" with authenticity. Although the revivalists who first wrote about this music recognized that it was a new variety of commercial country music, they emphasized its role in the revival of earlier traditions. Ralph Rinzler wrote in 1956 that "the banjo, along with many of the 'old-time' songs, had been revived" and stressed the idea that the bluegrass repertoire was closer to the tradition of folk or 'old-time' songs than to "the modern tradition of popular Tin Pan Alley or hillbilly songs."[14] Thus bluegrass was seen by the revivalists as an authentic folk revival already in progress when they arrived. Its name provided them with a ready-made organic metaphor that helped to verify its traditionality.[15]

In the next decade this argument was embraced and refined by folklorists. The 1965 *Journal of American Folklore* article by Mayne Smith stressed that while bluegrass is a commercial concert music, it "shares more stylistic traits with folk tradition than any other well defined category of hillbilly music now produced in quantity." He also argued that bluegrass "is closely related to folk tradition on an extra-musical level" and that "bluegrass musicians are in constant contact with folk tradition."[16] Smith's article was widely read by bluegrass revivalists and specialists because it was reprinted in 1965 by the JEMF and serialized in the first widely distributed fan magazine, *Bluegrass Unlimited,* in 1966–67.

The terminology of folkloric identity, with its connotations of revival and preservation, was quickly assimilated by the bluegrass community. The invention of bluegrass festivals in the mid-1960s fueled the bluegrass revival. Only after this, when the revival movement was well underway, did the coinage "traditional bluegrass" become common.[17] In articles and letters in the new fan magazines, revivalists and specialists debated the future of the music. This was a political debate about the means by which authenticity was to be maintained while the music was culturally preserved and commercially promoted. Frequently it was fought on progressive versus traditional lines, but people of all viewpoints regularly invoked the past in order to validate their interpretation of the present. Two articles written during that period illustrate one vein of bluegrass revivalist thinking with regard to the meaning of the past. They convey feelings of considerable ambivalence about the revival process.

I begin with an article titled "Starvin' to Death" written by Pete Kuykendall, published in the February 1967 issue of *Bluegrass Unlimited.* Kuykendall certainly is one of those "activists" described by Slobin, perhaps the original bluegrass revivalist. By 1967 he had established his credentials as a bluegrass musician, arranger, composer, publisher, producer, disc jockey, historian, and discographer. He was a moving force behind the establishment of *Bluegrass Unlimited* and eventually became its publisher and editor, a post he still holds.

Kuykendall's brief essay is an editorial about, in his words, "the 'state of the art' in bluegrass music today." Structurally, it resembles a sermon. It begins with a quote from a recognized "old master," Washington DJ Don Owens, who once told him, "You know, the best music that bluegrass musicians ever played or recorded seems to have been when they were starvin' to death."[18] Kuykendall identifies this period as the years between 1947 and 1955, and says the music by "the bluegrass greats" from that era forms the repertoire now performed by most bands, rather than the present repertoire of the same "greats." This is because the early musicians were more aware of total band togetherness; their singing was more closely felt, they placed less emphasis on individual musical prowess and were more involved in the group sound, listening to each other more closely. They expressed themselves more honestly since they were not quite so aware of the monetary gains to be derived from their efforts. This was a proper kind of individualism: expression of emotion through music. The "starving to death" music was spontaneous and musically sincere. The musicians simply gave it their best. There were no "session men" on their records, and what they recorded was the real thing, with no horns, drums, or electric guitars. The dominant attitude was "say something musically, and if it sells all the better," not "is it on the charts yet?"

Turning to the then-current state of the music, Kuykendall finds that there are not many creative individuals or groups recording in 1967, and that with a few exceptions most new records lack the fire and drive of those from ten to fifteen years earlier. He sees mostly unsuccessful experimentation in instrumentation and in repertoire, which is not perfected in terms of total band sound. This sad situation is, he says, the result of undue emphasis on individual technical accomplishment. More band unity is needed, particularly in the attention paid to singing the proper parts. Another problem is that many of the established greats don't seem to care about the quality of their current product as long as it is a commercial success. There is, as well, a lack of original material. He gives several contemporary examples of imaginative uses of new material, but complains that too many groups sound lazy or careless. He concludes by alluding to the great bands of the past, saying that "even if they were hungry they put heart and soul into what they were playing."

Kuykendall, the music producer, set forth a romantic view of the music in which there was a golden era when classic music was produced because the musicians were purely and communally involved in the product. Now there are inferior standards of music production because of self-centered musical individualism, commercialism, and carelessness. Though he pointed to ways of improving the music, he ended on a classically religious revival note, by again stressing the connection between purity and poverty.

The second article is my own "Bluegrass and Serendipity," which appeared in the November 1967 issue of *Bluegrass Unlimited*. Although earlier that year I had published an article on bluegrass history in the *Journal of American Folklore*,[19] this one was written not as a scholarly piece but as a communication from a revivalist with experience as a musician, promoter, manager, and teacher. My argument, illustrated with three personal experience narratives, was that the impact of bluegrass was greatest when encountered unexpectedly, that is to say, "serendipitously." While wishing bluegrass musicians prosperity and greater exposure, I held that greater exposure meant "forced obsolescence ... change for change's sake ... saturation." I spoke of fans who wished that recordings of classic performances, like those Kuykendall had written about, could "make number one on the country charts and miraculously convert the whole world to bluegrass," and suggested that they would discover that "success of that sort would merely serve to saturate the market and wipe out the interest in bluegrass altogether." I concluded that "most bluegrass fans secretly or subconsciously or subliminally enjoy the relative obscurity of the music, enjoy the challenge of seeking it out instead of having it shoved at them, and, like me, enjoy hearing it when they least expect it."[20] Although it didn't mention festivals, I now see the article as an oblique comment about their predictability. This article speaks of music consumption in terms that parallel Kuykendall's discussion of music production. It too romanticizes past contexts, placing a value on obscurity similar to Kuykendall's valuing of hunger. Its stance is one that Jackson would consider "purist": I argue that real revival would be the death of the tradition.[21]

What are we to conclude from these articles? First, we can note that their particular revisionist rhetoric argues for authenticity of text and texture in terms of context, a rather progressive stance for the folkloristics of 1967. But we can also see that their revisionist history is inaccurate. For example, neither mentions Bill Monroe, the central figure in the early years of the bluegrass revival. Monroe's best music was made not when he was starving to death but when he was at his height as a money-maker. And he was necessarily, not serendipitously, present at all bluegrass festivals. In part, these articles are position statements in an important revisionist debate about the relative importance of Monroe vis-à-vis younger musicians, particularly Flatt and Scruggs.

They also testify to these two revivalists' doubts about the process in which they were involved, by making authenticity unobtainable in the present. Both articles associate authenticity with a period prior to bluegrass musicians' consciousness of the expanding commercial viability of the music as a traditional form, a new viability that the revival offered them through festivals and the accompanying consumer movement. Tacitly, these articles link authenticity of experience with a lack of self-consciousness of tradition, which is consistent with Redfield's view of folk culture.

Ultimately, though, these are arguments by revivalists against their own self-consciousness. Their expression of skepticism about solving the problems of authenticity represents the first step away from a revivalist perspective toward a specialist point of view. As such they are documents of a rite of passage in which an impossible revisionist past is safely buried, and the revivalist is integrated into the specialist community as an activist. They could have very well been the last thing about bluegrass that either Kuykendall or I wrote had we decided not to join the reinterpreted community. Other bluegrass revivalists, like Mayne Smith and Ralph Rinzler, did make some kind of final statement and then moved on.[22] Kuykendall and I chose to stay; our writings after that became more pragmatic as we expressed our continuing activist involvement in the music as editor and historian.

All revivals have this effect: through work with specialists to reinterpret the tradition they fashion a new musical system that is more satisfying to some specialists and revivalists and less satisfying to others. Those who are satisfied remain to become activists within the community. While the revivalists may constitute a community it is a temporary camp with transient traditions. Some move from it into the permanent community, while others move on to become revivalists elsewhere or, perhaps, to become folklorists.

NOTES

My thanks for reading and criticizing the manuscript for this essay go to Pat Byrne, Melissa Ladenheim, Colleen Lynch, James Moreira, Peter Narváez, and Mayne Smith.

1. Jackson, "The Folksong Revival."
2. Rosenberg, " 'An Icy Mountain Brook.' "
3. Stekert, "Cents and Nonsense."
4. Slobin, "Rethinking 'Revival,' " p. 42; Jackson, "The Folksong Revival," p. 195; and Goldstein, "Robert 'Fiddler' Beers," pp. 47–48.
5. Evans, "Record Reviews: Folk Revival Music," p. 109.
6. Slobin, "Rethinking 'Revival,' " p. 39.
7. Jackson, "The Folksong Revival," p. 202; Posen, "On Folk Festivals and Kitchens," p. 11.
8. Edward D. Ives, *Lawrence Doyle*, p. 251.
9. Ben-Amos, "The Seven Strands of Tradition," pp. 106, 118–19.
10. Slobin, "Rethinking 'Revival,' " pp. 42–43.

11. Abrahams, *A Singer and Her Songs.*

12. Ben-Amos, "The Seven Strands of Tradition," pp. 114–16.

13. Handler and Linnekin, "Tradition, Genuine or Spurious," p. 276.

14. Rinzler, brochure notes, p. 1.

15. Handler and Linnekin, "Tradition, Genuine or Spurious," p. 275.

16. L. Mayne Smith, "An Introduction to Bluegrass," pp. 250, 251. Smith's article was reprinted elsewhere three times between 1965 and 1969.

17. The earliest appearance of "traditional bluegrass" in print that I have found came in a letter to *Billboard* from a young DJ, Bill Knowlton, who, in announcing the move of his show "Bluegrass Breakdown" from the Fordham University station in New York to a station in Connecticut, urged "traditional bluegrassers" to send records. See *Billboard,* 27 March 1961, p. 40.

18. Kuykendall, " 'Starvin' to Death,' " p. 4.

19. Rosenberg, "From Sound to Style." This article had a reprint history similar to that of L. Mayne Smith's "An Introduction to Bluegrass."

20. Rosenberg, "Bluegrass and Serendipity," p. 3.

21. Jackson, "The Folksong Revival," p. 195.

22. Rinzler, "Bill Monroe"; L. Mayne Smith, "First Bluegrass Festival."

Bluegrass and the Folk Revival: Structural Similarities and Experienced Differences

Philip Nusbaum

Introduction

Those of us who take part in Bluegrass know that it is more than a collection of song texts. Bluegrass includes playing the music, listening to it, socializing, collecting records, preparing for Bluegrass events, reading Bluegrass literature, and numerous other planned and improvised activities. Participation in Bluegrass is voluntary. It is an interest in Bluegrass, not necessarily the sharing of a regional, occupational, ethnic, or family background, that stimulates this participation. Those who take part traditionalize their experiences through Bluegrass by their continued participation in the many repeatable types of activity within Bluegrass and through the repeated personal contacts made within it.[1] This report begins with a discussion of some of the organizing impulses behind the enactment of what I call the Bluegrass experiential domain. Following that, I contrast features of the Bluegrass and Revival experiential domains.[2] The two domains are similar because they share *types* of activities and expression. However, they do not share specific points of reference within these shared types.

Experiential Domains

My use of "Bluegrass" (with a capital "B") herein refers to the Bluegrass experiential domains. When I use "bluegrass" (with a lowercase "b"), I refer to bluegrass music. Similarly, "the Revival" refers to the experiential domain of the folk Revival while "the revival" refers to revival music.

Although most people first become involved in Bluegrass because of bluegrass music, it is not the only reason they remain involved. Bluegrass includes social settings that they experience as being connected, such as bluegrass jam sessions, meetings of bluegrass organizations, bluegrass concerts, and sociability with other Bluegrass participants.

Use of the term "experiential domain" moves analysis away from the idea that there are bodies of "society," "culture," "folk," or "lore" to discover. Within each experiential domain, there are activities and behaviors perceived by the participants as typical. However, individual activities and behaviors are not usually experienced by participants to be exactly the same as those created in other enactments. For example, many Bluegrass occasions may include the sharing of meals. Each meal might be experienced as a typical Bluegrass event but its content may be idiosyncratic.[3]

An experiential domain also includes the activities that seem new to participants. For example, at a bluegrass festival, Bluegrass buddies might converse about subject matter that they previously had not discussed. However, some other aspect of the encounter might be familiar—they may have been old friends, or perhaps the conversation took place within a familiar setting.

In general, within an experiential domain based on friendship relations, such as Bluegrass, participants predicate their action on familiarity with at least one aspect of the setting. Familiarity might be centered on the overall shape of an activity, such as a jam session, the friends one is interacting with at a given moment, the old songs being played, or some other slice of experience. In addition, in a setting where having a good time is at the foreground of experience, experiences that are familiar make the entire occasion seem comfortable, including aspects that might otherwise seem unfamiliar.

Whether old or new, everything seems to belong to a setting if the setting itself is comfortable. When an activity takes place in a comfortable setting, participants are more likely to attend other enactments of the same type of activity. They are also more likely to seek out the same types of people, the same specific people, and the same types of conversational subject matter. The type of activities experienced, the type of people as well as the specific people encountered, and the specific subject matter of conversations all become means for participants to traditionalize their relationships with each other, within a specific experiential domain, at subsequent occasions.

From this perspective, the interest is less in cataloging the individual components of an experiential domain and more in accounting for the sensibility to participants of activities within an experiential domain. For example, I am interested in the coherence of individual Bluegrass conversations as well as the continuities between types of Bluegrass settings or activities that enable participants to traditionalize their behaviors across multiple settings.

Recognizing that taking part and gaining fluency in a experiential domain such as Bluegrass helps people further their interests, both locally and more broadly, is important to folklorists because it allows the tying of micro situations to macro ones on an ethnographic basis. Individual situations are seen as having connections and discontinuities with other situations within a given experiential domain.

Bluegrass: The Model of Sociability

There is a tendency, when discussing a musical idiom, to cast discussion in terms of the stars of the idiom. However, in Bluegrass, most of those who play and sing (or, "pick and sing") bluegrass play in jam sessions, or in short-lived bands whose performing careers are limited to a few public appearances. In addition, those who play bluegrass represent but a fraction of those who participate in Bluegrass. The shared interest in bluegrass music is the basis of Bluegrass participation, both by players and by those who do not play. Participants attend Bluegrass events not only to play and listen to bluegrass music, but to participate in activities associated with it.

While there are typical occasions at which bluegrass music is played and Bluegrass participants converse, specific activities within many of these events are to a great extent improvised. For example, at a festival, jam session,[4] or party, Bluegrass participants come and go as they please, engage in conversation with many other participants, play instruments, decide to have a bite to eat, and spontaneously move from location to location within a setting.

The casual attitude participants bring to most Bluegrass events and the improvised nature of activities indicate one of the threads connecting Bluegrass settings: sociability. In sociability, conversation is its own object.[5] At a typical Bluegrass event, participants have access to many of their friends, with whom they improvise conversations and activities.

At Bluegrass events, those taking part assume that other participants share their love for Bluegrass and thus are available for companionship. Once companionship is established between participants, they can include interests other than Bluegrass in their conversations.

The following transcript shows how, through sociability, two participants enacted and validated their common interests, in Bluegrass and each other. It was recorded at a Bluegrass outdoor event in Albert Lea, Minnesota, on 30 September 1989. The conversation is one I had with a woman named Pam, whom I met through Bluegrass. We have encountered each other occasionally at Bluegrass events in Minnesota. We were talking about Peter Wernick, a star of bluegrass, who plays the banjo for the group Hot Rize. News about the stars sometimes becomes the subject matter of Bluegrass conversations. However, in socializing, it frequently happens that conversation leads away from its original focus.[6] In the following, once the name "Pete Wernick" entered into the conversation, "Pete Wernick" was used as a resource by the conversationalists to introduce other factors about their lives. Through such conversations, participants validate and traditionalize their common interest in bluegrass, their participation in Bluegrass, and the relationships they share.

Pam has a job in a medical field. She knew that our conversation was being recorded, and that I, a professional folklorist for the Minnesota State Arts Board, was "documenting folk culture" at the event. However, Pam also knew me as a fellow "picker," and our conversation seemed to me a typical one for us to share at a Bluegrass event. Between acts at the event, the public address system was playing an audio tape of Hot Rize, a nationally famous Bluegrass group. Pete Wernick and Tim O'Brien are stars of Bluegrass who perform in Hot Rize. Parentheses in the following transcript indicate instances of inaudible talk or enclose pertinent information regarding reading the transcript.

PN: What group is this? Pete Wernick and them? Tim O'Brien?

Pam: Hot Rize.

PN: Oh yeah.

Pam: Oh, you know about Pete Wernick being in the plane crash.

PN: Yeah.

Pam: Yeah. See, his picture was in *Life* magazine.

PN: No!

Pam: Yeah, uh huh. They had all these little captions of people (   ) the incident. How they felt about it.

PN: My wife's brother was, uh, lives near Sioux City and helped them clean up.

Pam: Yeah. (pause, 3 seconds) Fun.

PN: Weird.

Pam: Couldn't be any worse than my job. (pause, 3 seconds) (giggles)

PN: What is (   ) Why?

Pam: I work with parts.

PN: Oh, you do? (pause, 5 seconds) Well, that's about like your job then, I think. Only he saw something then decided not to look too hard anymore.

Pam: Um hmm.

When Pam and I spoke about Pete Wernick, we developed our common interest in Bluegrass. Simultaneously, we established our interpersonal connection within the setting to be one of sociability, where conversation is permitted to take its own course. As in this case, sociability can include the sharing of personal experiences. The repeated interaction of participants in Bluegrass settings could lead to conversation about similar subjects, cementing their bonds as buddies in Bluegrass.

While the sociability model predominates in many Bluegrass settings, the model is enacted differently at a festival when those taking part are afforded a freer range of movement than at a concert, where the audience faces the stage, which is not a posture conducive to conversation. Competent participants are able to take part in sociability in appropriate ways in each type of setting encountered.

Recurrent Subject Matter within the Bluegrass Experiential Domain: Authenticity

In Bluegrass sociability, while talk about "anything" might be formulated, talk relating to Bluegrass is impending.[7] While each conversation is unique, Bluegrass participants recognize recurrent conversational subject matter. Expressing recurrent themes such as the activities of "the stars" provides familiar grounds to which participants attach their developing points of view. It is comparable to playing bluegrass in a jam session, where "songs everybody knows" are played, but the performances are specific to the occasion, because pickers and singers, to a great extent, improvise their music.

Bluegrass music that is "the real thing" concerns Bluegrass participants. From time to time their conversation indicates the existence of an unwritten canon of Bluegrass "authenticity" regarding instrumentation, song types, and playing style suitable for bluegrass. Part of that concern is whether or not it is possible for a northerner to play bluegrass with the vitality attributed to southerners. In many conversational settings in the United States, including those in the North, Bluegrass music from the South is considered to be more hard-driving than northern bluegrass,[8] and the southern style is considered to be more authentic and the closer of the two to the spirit of the music as it evolved in the late 1940s and early 1950s.[9]

On the other hand, the "southern" model is not necessarily considered to be the only viable one, nor are northerners necessarily considered to be inauthentic players. Experienced participants in Bluegrass recognize many styles of bluegrass. They agree that bluegrass from Kentucky, Minnesota, or Japan is still bluegrass, and that participants may call any of those places, or others, home.[10]

"Authenticity" is one of many commonplace subjects discussed within Bluegrass. Subject matter can also concern the quality of a band's performance, the activities of Bluegrass stars, how one's own playing has been going, recent and future Bluegrass events, the ways in which the country music industry blocks the popularity of bluegrass, whether beer should be sold at bluegrass festivals, whether alcohol should be allowed in the stage area, and whether motorcycles should be permitted at bluegrass festivals. Conversations about authenticity provide a ground for enactment of relationships within the Bluegrass experiential domain. Even when subject matter is divisive, as is possible with the "authenticity" issue, the divisiveness traditionalizes relationships among participants by providing recurrent subject matter and recurrent roles (being "for" or "against" one style of bluegrass versus another).

Ethnographers interested in the experiential domain of Bluegrass should not determine what is and is not authentic bluegrass, or whether northerners or southerners can play in an authentic manner, but should describe the effect of commonplace subject matter such as "authenticity" within Bluegrass. Such subjects are explored idiosyncratically each time they are used.[11] However, the "authenticity" issue is so widespread that it and other recurrent Bluegrass subject matter are factors in making participants feel at home whether they find themselves in Kentucky, New York, or Minnesota.

Types of Events

Recurrent types of events and settings for events provide sets of familiar visual and aural cues, enabling participants to perceive given events and settings to be similar to others in Bluegrass. Such was the case with the Buckskinners' Rendezvous held at Albert Lea, Minnesota, on 30 September 1989, at which the transcript printed above was recorded. Rendezvous are a type of historical reenactment. In the upper Midwest, rendezvous are held over weekends during the warm-weather months. Rendezvousers (or buckskinners) create individualistic identities by dressing in old-fashioned clothing and setting up housekeeping in old-fashioned housing (frequently teepees). They evoke characters such as a fur trader, a hide tanner, or a cook, which loosely relate to the "frontier" but do not "document" the frontier with museum-style "accuracy." At rendezvous, they camp, sell "frontier" trinkets to tourists, and socialize with others in the encampment. By giving over a part of their event to Bluegrass, rendezvousers hope to increase attendance and revenue, enabling their annual event to grow. Because bluegrass music is considered old fashioned by rendezvous participants, members of the public, and Bluegrass participants, it "fits" the spirit of rendezvous.[12]

Although the rendezvous would not qualify as a bluegrass festival by strict definition, the setting was similar enough to that of most outdoor bluegrass festivals to enable enactment of Bluegrass. Many rendezvous contain a stage area for performances enjoyed by members of the public. During bluegrass performances, Bluegrass participants were sitting in the grass near the stage, talking to each other and listening to the music amplified by the public address system. Because the event was promoted through *Inside Bluegrass,* the publication of the Minnesota Bluegrass and Old-Time Music Association, and by word of mouth, many Bluegrass participants attended and met their friends there. Camping was available, there was plenty of space for jam sessions, and there were food stands, all of which are typically present at bluegrass festivals. Although some artists gave performances not of a bluegrass nature, the program and surroundings were generally similar enough to a "typical" bluegrass festival that participants were able to enact Bluegrass.

The model of sociability, the recurrence of conversational subject matter, and the holding of events in familiar surroundings are the factors that provide common grounds for enacting Bluegrass from place to place, and from time to time. They enable participants both to recognize a setting as a Bluegrass setting and to act effectively in multiple Bluegrass settings.

Folklorists and the Revival

Until recently, folklore research began not with behavior but with artifacts and the criteria for their "authenticity,"[13] or their adherence to a "canon" of folklore. Because the folk revival was not considered "authentic," many contemporary folklorists found themselves, during their graduate training, to some degree disconnected from it, even though it was the revival that attracted them to folklore in the first place. I was one of those folklorists.

Two years after receiving a B.A. in sociology from the City College of New York, after a year of substitute teaching in the south Bronx and another year driving a taxicab at night in New York City, I began to see graduate school as the road to a less dangerous career. In my teens, my first three record album purchases were Peter, Paul, and Mary releases. Later, in my freshman year of college, I was converted to Bluegrass. With this background, I was sure that I would find my future through attending the Folklore Institute at Indiana University.

However, since the revival was not considered to be "authentic," and because bluegrass was considered by some folklorists to be part of the revival, I was convinced that if I centered research on either one, I would jeopardize my chances of receiving my degree.[14] That I was correct is corroborated by the fact that only recently has Bluegrass received folkloristic book-length treatments,[15] and that twenty to thirty years after its greatest popularity, the Revival finally has been "rediscovered" by folklorists.[16]

The "revival" is important to us now because it represents an experiential domain. It no longer refers to folklorists' residual category for all that does not pass muster as a tradition, according to a folkloristic "artifact and authenticity" definitional scheme. Nor is "revival" the opposite of "tradition." Revival participants take part in activities that, for them, traditionalize both their activities and their interpersonal relationships.

Structural Similarities between the Revival and Bluegrass

Like Bluegrass participants, those involved in Revival choose to participate in their experiential domain. They enact their experiential domain at replicable types of events, through sociability. Similar to Bluegrass participants, Revival participants are concerned with issues such as "authenticity." However, there are differences between the experiential domains, too. The following discussion of event types, and of the importance of both a sense of history and musical aesthetics in each experiential domain, is not exhaustive. But I believe it offers enough description to account for the similarities and differences between Bluegrass and the Revival.

The Organization of Events
Anyone who has experienced Revival and Bluegrass events could not fail to notice that many of the same kinds of events are common to both: concerts, workshops, festivals, and other kinds of friendly get-togethers between participants. In addition, sociability pervades many Revival and Bluegrass settings. As in Bluegrass, the Revival is an experiential domain within which participants find and develop opportunities to traditionalize experiences with each other.

The History Impulse

Both Bluegrass and Revival ideologies hold that their music is disappearing and that quick action is necessary to prevent its extinction. In each case, "saving music" from extinction is self-validating expression. Participants idealistically believe themselves to be performing an important cultural service, while enjoying themselves. For example, one mandolin player of my acquaintance told me that it pleased him to have played a role in providing performing and recording opportunities for older musicians.

In all the years of my professional contact with music, the most frequently volunteered point of view offered to me by musicians and fans has been the concern for saving their music for future generations. The impulse to save a style of music is expressed by participants representing styles as diverse as bluegrass, African-American gospel music, and polka music. The concern for saving the music is voiced by those unconnected to the Revival, such as elderly Norwegian-American fiddlers in Minnesota, as well as by people well-connected with the Revival, such as singer-songwriters. Most likely, the impulse to preserve an experiential domain perceived to be "bigger" than any participating individuals is very old.

In addition to saving the music for future generations, in both Bluegrass and the Revival, learning about the history of the chosen music and sharing this knowledge are very highly regarded goals.

Aesthetics

As one would expect of musical experiential domains, Revival and Bluegrass musicians and audience members frequently have highly specialized tastes and attitudes[17] or ideologies[18] concerning music sound. According to David Evans, beginning with the 1970s, the Revival has been "characterized by an increasing competence and authenticity in the re-creation of folk style and a strong tendency toward conscious specialization and regionalism or ethnicity."[19] Similarly, bluegrass musicians characteristically strive to conform with what they consider to be Bluegrass tradition. When confronted about an intentional change made to the standard version of a song, in general, they refer to it as an innovation within the tradition, not a deviation from it. In 1990, and for at least the preceding decade, a range of styles considered traditional by Bluegrass or Revival participants was well known by players and other participants in each experiential domain.[20]

There are several structural similarities between Bluegrass and the Revival: the model of sociability is basic to both; senses of history and aesthetic criteria inform each; and there is overlap in the types of events featured by each. Other shared structural factors include (for American participants) using English as the means of spoken communication, and operating within the assumptions concerning everyday living shared by most Americans.[21]

These common reference points allow a participant in one experiential domain to take part easily in the other. For example, a Revival participant interested in "saving" folk music can readily identify with a similar impulse in Bluegrass. Likewise, participants in each experiential domain would recognize the sociability taking place at festivals in the other and might consider such instances as opportunities to have a good time.

Differences between the Revival and Bluegrass

Structural similarities may help participants move between the Revival and Bluegrass. However, differences in content between the Revival and Bluegrass exist and may strike discordant chords among participants.

Musical Content of Events

While Bluegrass and Revival experiential domains contain similar types of events, they differ because of the music played. Obviously, at Bluegrass events, bluegrass music is presented. At Revival events, other kinds of music are played. Knowing this, Bluegrass participants are less likely to attend Revival events, and those who do attend are less likely to meet their friends there.

The Historical Impulse

The impulse to save what is theirs is strong among participants in both Bluegrass and the Revival. However, participants in one domain do not believe they share a common history with those in the other. Those who have participated in Bluegrass for a number of years claim to be musical descendants of Bill Monroe, Flatt and Scruggs, and the Stanley Brothers. They may lament that younger converts to Bluegrass have never heard familiar bluegrass songs in their "original bluegrass versions" by these masters. Younger participants who champion groups playing "newgrass" music may disregard the advice of their elders that all the bluegrass they really need to listen to was recorded before they were born. While disagreements over the importance of bluegrass history versus the importance of innovation exist within Bluegrass, the foci of such discussions—who invented bluegrass, who have been its major stylists, how it has changed, and the relationship of Bluegrass to the country music industry—are recurring Bluegrass reference points.

On the other hand, Revival discussions of history refer to different events and different figures, and express different perspectives. Revival participants might refer to figures such as Pete Seeger and the Weavers, as well as Bill Monroe. Bluegrass participants would find only Monroe to be relevant. They either would make the connection between him and Seeger and the Weavers or wouldn't find it a compelling connection.

Aesthetics

While authenticity and quality of performance are important aesthetic criteria both to musicians and to active listeners within Bluegrass and the Revival, characteristics of musical style and performance conventions within each differ markedly.

A Bluegrass event is just that. If there are other styles of music presented, they are ones that participants perceive to be related to bluegrass. Typically these include older forms of American country music, such as the "old-time music" originating in the American South, or another form of "country music" that can be adapted to both the bluegrass instruments (fiddle, banjo, guitar, mandolin, resophonic guitar, guitar, bass) and the bluegrass style. At a Bluegrass event, bluegrass music performance always predominates over the performance of related music styles. Participants are interested in music historically or stylistically bound to bluegrass but are aware that bluegrass is their main interest.

On the other hand, performances during a Revival event could come from several areas of music. In addition, that which is presented at Revival events changes greatly over time. For example, in the late 1980s and early 1990s, in Minneapolis–Saint Paul, revivalists favor Cajun music. Revivalist Cajun dances are big social occasions at which Cajun food is sometimes served, and Cajun dances are taught to the local people by experts trained elsewhere. The current Cajun craze follows periods of elevated interest in British Isles music, singer-songwriters, and other forms.

While playing in an "authentic" style is now popular within the Revival, the political and multicultural perspectives of past Revival eras remain.[22] The percentage of "socially significant" songs is much greater in the Revival than in Bluegrass. In addition, Bluegrass songs bearing social messages deliver a different kind of message than those of the Revival that bear social messages. In Bluegrass, as in Anglo-American balladry, they are generally sung from the point of view of the singer.[23] For example, in the bluegrass song "Missing in Action" the singer comes home after being left for dead on the field of battle, only to see a picture of his wife, now married to another man.[24] The song's sentiment, and our sympathies, lie with the returnee, not with a political winner or loser. On the other hand, Revival songs are frequently *about* political troubles, centering not on the feelings of a protagonist but on the political situation.

The structural similarities between the Revival and Bluegrass allow Bluegrass and Revival participants to understand the logic of Revival events. However, to Bluegrass participants, lack of familiarity with Revival music, Revival subject matter, and participants in the Revival dulls the ring of familiarity with Revival events. Revival events present Bluegrass participants with music not completely to their liking. They also present a seemingly unconnected array of music styles, styles as disparate as Cajun dance music one year and Bulgarian singing the next. On the other hand, although Bluegrass participants recognize changes in bluegrass style over the years, it seems to them that most bluegrass being played today is recognizable as an updated version of the style originally heard about a half century ago.

Bluegrass Revivalism

Most Bluegrass participants have heard of the Revival. Some Bluegrass participants are former Revival participants or participate concurrently in the Revival and in Bluegrass. The ·Revival is sufficiently well known among those taking part in Bluegrass that an aspect of it, or the Revival itself, comes up as subject matter in Bluegrass conversations. In the previous article in this volume, "Starvation, Serendipity, and the Ambivalence of Bluegrass Revivalism," Neil Rosenberg describes how, at college age, some of his Bluegrass friends "discovered" they were revivalists, which caused them to become uneasy and leave Bluegrass. They considered themselves "different," not as "authentic" as others in bluegrass, and they thought that their participation in Bluegrass was inappropriate.

Some of my early experiences in Bluegrass paralleled the kind of experience Rosenberg documented. I became interested in bluegrass in the spring of 1966, when a coworker at the New York Public Library loaned me record albums by two bluegrass groups, the Greenbriar Boys and the Scottsville Squirrel Barkers. In the fall of that year, I started to learn to play the banjo. Later, when friends took me to Sunset Park in Pennsylvania, I was introduced to live bluegrass as it was played away from New York City. These experiences were very much like the Bluegrass experiences I would have in later years, living in Indiana, Iowa, and Minnesota. We gossiped about the stars of bluegrass; talked about the music, the records we heard, the shows we had been to; and attended Bluegrass events together. In addition, as Bluegrass fanatics at City College of New York, my friends and I sensed that the natural home of the music was far away from our campus. Sometimes the talk turned to Sunset Park, about the people there and how different from them we thought ourselves to be. We even questioned whether it was appropriate for us to attend events there. Like Rosenberg's friends, influenced by the folkloristic thought of the day, we too felt the dichotomy between traditionalist and revivalist. As a result, some of us left Bluegrass. Others found roles they felt acceptable within it.

Regardless of the relative importance to each of us of our self-questioning, in my twenty-plus years as a folklorist, bluegrass player, bluegrass fan, and bluegrass radio producer, I have never heard this anxiety discussed except privately by my friends in college and graduate school, and in the article by Rosenberg. I conclude that expressing anxiety over participating in bluegrass is not a commonly voiced concern among Bluegrassers.

I suspect that our self-questioning about our participation in Bluegrass had its source in being of college age and weighing the options of what we would do with the rest of our lives. Bluegrass was one of many beckoning worlds. Young people in rural Pennsylvania interested in Bluegrass and exposed to scholarly and popular writing about folk music that included notions about "authentic" and "revival" folk music may have been experiencing the same doubts as we urbanites.

However, to most people in Bluegrass, the participation of college-aged and college-associated people is considered to be normal.[25] While Bluegrass participants might note that another Bluegrass participant "comes from New York" or "has a Ph.D.," if the appearance of "obviously" college-aged people or New Yorkers at Bluegrass festivals is causing a crisis, it is a well-kept secret. While it may be true that such comments might not reach my ears because I could be perceived as someone linked to the college crowd, and from New York City originally, if being a native New Yorker or part of a "college crowd" were considered problematic to other Bluegrass participants, everyone in Bluegrass, including people like me, would have heard about it somehow. Most Bluegrass participants say they welcome all sorts of people, so long as they like bluegrass. While that could not possibly be true in all cases, acceptance is the prevailing norm of behavior. For the most part, if you say you like bluegrass, other Bluegrass participants will assume you desire and are available for sociability, unless proven otherwise.

In retrospect, it seems that the personal difficulty caused by perceiving oneself to be a revivalist within Bluegrass was not intentially brought about by other Bluegrass participants. It stemmed from the self-doubts of those afflicted with anxieties. Similar anxieties could also occur within the Revival.

However small the role of self-doubt in Bluegrass (or the Revival), it is no less significant than other impulses that participants share with each other. It is one expressed theme through which, in a variety of ways, participants can give meaning to their Bluegrass or Revival experiences. The strength of both Bluegrass and the Revival is that each accommodates so many interests and behaviors. They contain broad and expanding ranges of acceptable activities and ways of speaking.

Within the framework of Bluegrass sociability, there are acknowledged divisions one can observe in participants' behavior. These divisions are more profound than the distinction between "authentic" and "traditional." They can exist between the "stars" and everybody else, between jammers and listeners, between those who are in performing bands and those who are not, and between rival bands.

Formal and Informal Settings

While this essay has centered on relaxed, sociable settings, more formal types of settings exist within both Bluegrass and the Revival. For example, at board meetings of organizations supporting either pursuit, participants are expected to maintain businesslike decorum. When the organization selects bands to entertain at festivals and concerts, members must seriously consider the financial implications of their decisions, along with the artistic merits of the bands being considered. In addition, band rehearsals are often focused on learning songs and tunes, and devising appealing ways of presenting them. In these situations, nonserious interludes occur as brief interjections, not as part of sustained sociability.

Considerable differences exist between organizational settings and those featuring sustained sociability. However, these situations are not antithetical. Within each experiential domain they are experienced to be linked because Bluegrass or the Revival is discussed. In organizational settings, each is discussed in a more focused way than in social situations. The two types of situations provide opportunities for participants to develop different kinds of perspectives about Bluegrass or the Revival.

Caveat

The views of Bluegrass and the Revival expressed herein have stressed the mutual agreeability of participants. Of course, all is not always well. There are broken hearts, disenchanted band members, and participants who cannot get along together. However, these interpersonal disharmonies are exceptions proving the rule that Bluegrass and the Revival are marked by cohesion.

Conclusion

The motivating features in the Bluegrass and Revival experiential domains are musical. Motivated by an affinity for bluegrass or for a collection of styles termed "folk," Bluegrass and Revival participants begin and maintain interpersonal relationships. Not every conversation or activity within either experiential domain concerns only music. However, references to Bluegrass or the Revival, and the sociability base of each, are the glue holding participants together. Activities and subject matter referring to Bluegrass or the Revival are impending in participants' conversations.

The sociability base of both Bluegrass and the Revival encourages participants within each to develop activities and relationships in mutually satisfying ways, between settings within an event. For example, a bluegrass jam session where superficial politeness thinly masks the competition taking place, and Bluegrass buddies sharing a meal at a bluegrass festival are each understood by participants as typical Bluegrass situations, even though they are very different in nature.[26] The sociability base also encourages participation in Bluegrass or the Revival at multiple sites across a wide geographic area.

Both Bluegrass and the Revival are oriented toward similar kinds of events: festivals, parties, concerts, and other types of social occasion known to most Americans. In addition, the two experiential domains share types of subject matter. However, despite the features shared by the Revival and Bluegrass, participants experience the two to be different. Similarities such as sociability, affinity for a certain style or collection of styles of music, utilization of certain types of replicable events, and maintenance of concerns about music history and aesthetics are guides for expression. Bluegrass and the Revival have those impulses in common, but that which is relevant within each impulse differs. Participants in each experiential domain attend similar types of event and share similar types of interest, but the key reference points of each differ.

Not only are there replicable types of events and types of subject matter common to Bluegrass and the Revival. They also share other standard means of engaging contemporary Americans, including participants' organizations, professional associations, national and regional magazines, books, and television and radio programming. These are typical means used by a great many late-twentieth-century United States interest-based groups to get participants together, as well as to promote the interests they represent. In both the Revival and Bluegrass, activity takes place in ways that "everybody knows about."

In addition, the basis of participation does not depend upon living in a locale, working in a given occupation, or belonging to a certain ethnic group, but liking a music "anyone" could like. Participants "self-elect" membership. In effect, since the Revival and Bluegrass enact replicable events in many locations, they are mass movements, where participants can feel at home in many locations.

Far from eliminating the idiosyncracies of experience, the similarity of the structural elements of many experiential domains gives participants within one access to experiences within another.[27] It takes a certain amount of effort to gain access to Bluegrass or the Revival. Even though the structures of the movements are similar to each other, their content is not the same. However, to most Americans, the structure of both Bluegrass and the Revival contain relatively few impediments to those who wish to participate in either. Once new participants gain competence in the content of either Bluegrass or the Revival, they participate in what seems like a vast variety of experience.

NOTES

1. See Hymes, "Folklore's Nature and the Sun's Myth."

2. The conception of "experiential domain" is based loosely on that found in Berger and Luckmann, *The Social Construction of Reality*.

3. See Zimmerman and Power, "The Everyday World."

4. In this case, "jam sessions" refers to the impromptu sessions pickers and singers strike up casually, not to the contrived "jam sessions" programmed for the stages of bluegrass festivals.

5. See Simmel, "The Sociology of Sociability."

6. On methods of attaching an utterance to that of the previous speaker, see Sacks, "On the Analysability of Stories by Children," pp. 218ff., and idem, "Lecture Notes #4."

7. Similarly, for a group of former mental patients, having been a mental patient was shown to be impending subject matter. See Turner, "Words, Utterances, and Activities," pp. 203ff.

8. I have heard this point of view expressed in all four states in which I have lived: New York, Indiana, Iowa, and Minnesota.

9. In Minnesota, in summer 1987, Kevin Barnes, banjo player for the bluegrass group Stoney Lonesome, told me that the band we were listening to at the time, Southern Blend, really played like southerners. He said that in general, northerners played more complicated musical lines, while southerners played with a greater sense of drive and awareness of the total "band sound." On 30 September 1989, listening to the same band, Art Bjorngjeld, banjo player for the Bluegrass group Hardly Heard, volunteered to me that he thought the southern players had the music in their blood, and "I don't know why us northern boys even try."

10. One Minnesota picker, Ken Dugan, told me that he learned "Ice-Covered Birches" because it refers to the north country.

11. On the idiosyncratic nature of individual conversations, see Zimmerman and Power, "The Everyday World," pp. 80–103.

12. It would never occur to rendezvousers that they do not share the point of view of some, nor would it matter to them. Nor would it matter to most Bluegrass participants. They enjoy the opportunity to participate in Bluegrass.

13. This represents a change in folkloristic thinking since Dundes wrote about folklore research in his "The Study of Folklore in Literature and Culture."

14. Rosenberg documents the situation at Indiana University in *Bluegrass: A History*, pp. 4–5.

15. I am thinking of Rosenberg, *Bluegrass: A History*, and Cantwell, *Bluegrass Breakdown*.

16. See Jackson, "The Folksong Revival."

17. Riesman, "Listening to Popular Music," p. 408.

18. According to Rosenberg, revivalism has an ideological component. See his "Starvation, Serendipity, and the Ambivalence of Bluegrass Revivalism" in this volume.

19. Evans, "Record Reviews: Folk Revival Music," p. 109. He also writes that earlier revivals stressed artistic or political dogma of the revivalists, making the musical and social aspects of the revival very different than that which they were copying. It should also be mentioned that the movement of the 1970s has not obliterated earlier Revival trends. A glance at advertisements promoting touring "folk" acts indicates that the earlier phases are still with us.

20. That which is considered to be traditional Bluegrass changes over time. A striking example of such a change in perception concerns the Country Gentlemen. Through the 1960s and 1970s the Gentlemen were key figures in "progressive bluegrass." By the late 1980s, performing the same type of material they performed a decade earlier, they had become perceived as a middle-of-the-road bluegrass band.

21. For example, many Americans share concerns over such details such as how late can you call someone on a Sunday night, how long it should take to catch a city bus, how long it is appropriate to wait for others according to the type of occasion and the nature of the relationship, what to wear to an outdoor music event according to the weather, and so on.

22. Evans, "Record Reviews: Folk Revival Music," p. 108.

23. Gerould, *The Ballad of Tradition*, p. 38.

24. Available on LP by Jim Eanes on *Jim Eanes and the Shenandoah Valley Boys.*

25. In the 1960s and 1970s, the participation in Bluegrass of hippies and those who might express left-wing political stands drew the concern of some, as was true in many American situations.

26. On jam sessions, see Kisliuk, " 'A Special Kind of Courtesy' "; on competition, see Adler, "Dueling Banjos"; and on shared meals, see Adler, "Bluegrass Music and Meal-Fried Potatoes." I thank Neil Rosenberg for alerting me to these studies.

27. Many art forms, including polka music, quilting, and wood carving present themselves through an experiential domain structurally similar to Bluegrass and the Revival.

Reconstructing the Blues: Reflections on the 1960s Blues Revival

Jeff Todd Titon

The National Endowment for the Arts (NEA) grants money to artists and to organizations supporting artists. The NEA Folk Arts Program funds folk artists. One wintry March day in 1981 I was sitting in an office room in Washington, D.C., with a dozen anthropologists, arts administrators, museum workers, folklorists, and ethnomusicologists, and we were voting on grant proposals. I was beginning a three-year term on the Folk Arts Panel, an appointed group that recommends to the NEA which proposals should and should not be funded.

We had just had a lively discussion about a certain proposal. Everyone thought the idea was a good one, that the project was feasible, and that the proposing organization was sound. The problem was that the artists were a mixture of traditionalists and "revivalists." Folk arts did not fund revivalists. Some panel members felt that the presence of revivalists tainted the project and therefore we must not fund it. Others felt that because some of the presentations involved traditional artists exclusively, and because a respected professional folklorist was a consultant on the project, we should fund only that portion that presented traditional artists. The latter position carried the day and the project was recommended for funding at a lower figure with instructions to the presenting organization that Folk Arts money was to be used for traditional artists only.

At this point I remembered when I had first heard the term "revivalists." It was in the late 1950s when I was a teenager. Among the upscale suburban crowd and the bohemian college students and city dwellers, folk music was in vogue; it offered a meaningful musical alternative to rock and roll's vapid insistency. In the late 1950s most folksingers entertained their audiences with a mocking, ironic, "hip" or "beat" stance, a version of existentialism, the popular intellectual philosophy of the day, which viewed the world as populated with antiheroes. Singing folk songs—meaningful lyrics set to simple melodies with simple accompaniment on acoustic instruments—was one way of asserting humanity in an absurd universe. Feeling confined by the small world of our high school and the getting-and-spending of our parents, a few of us worked out our adolescent rebellion in terms of jazz, folk music, beat poetry, James Agee, Albert Camus, foreign films, and coffeehouses. My father was an amateur jazz guitarist and so I learned to make chords and accompany myself singing folk songs. In 1960 I bought my own guitar and began singing and playing in coffeehouses in my home city, Atlanta.

In the early 1960s many of us thought that this urban folk revival was dividing in two. In one camp were those who considered folksongs common property. Entertainers like Pete Seeger, the Weavers, Peter, Paul, and Mary, the Limelighters, and the Kingston Trio sang a mixture of traditional and newly composed material in "folk" style (using simple melodies, harmonies, and accompaniments) and encouraged audiences to sing along. In the second camp were singers like Joan Baez, the New Lost City Ramblers, Dave Ray, and John Koerner who tried to sing and play what they regarded as a traditional body of material (Child ballads, for example, or the music of Leadbelly) in a traditional way. These folksingers took on a burden of repertoire and technique that led to self-conscious artistry. My allegiance quickly passed from the first camp into the second, and as a college freshman in 1962 I spent several hours a day practicing guitar in the fingerpicking style of Etta Baker and Elizabeth Cotten. Among enthusiasts in the folk revival, debates were held about "authenticity" and "selling out." Who was "more ethnic" (as the saying went) than whom?

Folk music was democratic, acoustic, open to everyone; yet people tried to excel, to be recognized for skill and taste. Connoisseurship entered in: who was the best guitarist, who had the better record collection, who would make the next "discovery" of an obscure song or singer? Yet ego was held in check: one did not show off. Folksingers like Oscar Brand and Theodore Bikel were suspect: chatty and sophisticated actors on stage, they tried to entertain, sometimes at the expense of their material. But Joan Baez was praised for her self-effacing stage manner, which let the songs "speak for themselves." Among those who favored authenticity and tradition it was a short step to "reviving" traditions themselves, as by performing old-time string band music or blues or bluegrass, or by entering tradition, as Bob Dylan did when he became a singer-songwriter like Woody Guthrie and Pete Seeger. The folk revival was identified strongly with acoustic music, and when Dylan emerged at the Newport Folk Festival in 1965 playing electric guitar and backed by a rock band, many purists felt that Dylan had sold out and that the folk revival had been seriously weakened. This was the kind of analysis I remember going on in New England among college-student "folkies" in the first half of the 1960s.

I was reminded of these things while we were discussing the grant proposal. The NEA panel could identify revivalists easily enough: they had not grown up inside the family or community whose tradition they came later to practice; rather, to pick it up they had to cross ethnic, geographic, and class boundaries, or they learned it in some kind of institutional setting, and as often from other revivalists as from those with a birthright to the traditions they carried. Traditional folk artists carried tradition as inseparably as their native tongue.[1] But as I glanced around the panel an overwhelming irony struck me. I saw mostly lapsed revivalists. To be sure, still-performing Pete Seeger was on the panel, but many of the rest of us had once enjoyed professional if not spectacular careers in the folk arts. And we were voting to give money only to nonrevivalists. No conflict of interest here! (Or was a deep conflict being repressed?)

My epiphany was what Barbara Babcock and others would call a "reflexive" moment, a moment when one steps outside of oneself to look at oneself as someone acting in the world.[2] It is a moment of objectivity, a moment that philosopher Thomas Nagel would characterize as one in which our consciousness allows us to be aware of ourselves as subjects and objects simultaneously. And there lies a serious philosophical dilemma: "how to combine the perspective of a particular person inside the world with an objective view of that same world, the person and his viewpoint included."[3]

In this essay I turn a reflexive eye on the blues revival of the 1960s, a movement in which I participated as collector, performer, promoter, record producer, guitar teacher and music school cofounder, biographer, fieldworker, historian, and interpreter. Although I will review some of my own activity, I will concentrate on an exemplary early work by Samuel Charters that ushered in and set the tone for the revival that followed. I will look also at Charters's second thoughts in his preface to a 1975 reprint of his pioneering book. The larger question is the relationship of revivalist activity to blues itself. The governing metaphor at the time for what we were doing was "discovery" and "rediscovery," as if what we were doing was finding something that was unknown or had been lost. But the notion of discovery is complex, as anyone knows who has thought about the grade-school "fact" that Columbus discovered America. Our discoveries, like those of the European explorers, were mixtures of invention and interpretation, and in a way instead of finding our object, blues, we constituted it.

Hindsight, a climate encouraging reflexivity, and my reading of recent work in literary and anthropological theory lead me to conclude that those of us who participated in the revival thought we had discovered an object called blues, which we then set out to think about, document, analyze, and, in some cases, perform. Instead, by our interpretive acts, we constructed the very thing we thought we had found. This is not to say there was nothing "out there" called blues. I am not defending a position of philosophical idealism here. Rather, I am saying that the various activities of the blues revivalists constituted a commodity called "blues" that came to be consumed as a popular music and a symbol of stylized revolt against conservative politics and middle-class propriety.

Prior to this revival blues had been a music by and chiefly for black Americans; the revival turned it into a music by black and white Americans primarily for white Americans and Europeans. To be sure, some black folksingers had been a part of the folk music revival that was centered in New York City since the 1930s and directed largely at whites; in fact the revival began with the black songster Leadbelly, and during the 1940s and 1950s other black folksingers (Josh White, Brownie McGhee and Sonny Terry, and Big Bill Broonzy) became part of a nightclub and concert folk music circuit extending to Europe. With the exception of Leadbelly, each of these performers had a prior commercial career singing blues to black audiences. Yet when presented as folksingers for urban white audiences, they performed ballads like "John Henry," folksongs, and spirituals as well as some blues.[4]

The blues revival was fueled by the folk revival, especially at first, but it might not have touched so many city and suburban whites had they not already been weaned on rock and roll, a music heavily rooted in blues and rhythm and blues. Folkies rejected rock; blues fans disliking rock preferred prewar, acoustic blues, but rockers embraced the postwar blues with its electric guitars, electric basses, and drum sets—the rock instrumentation. Jazz also helped bring about the blues revival.[5] The Beat movement in literature, with its interest in the black American jazz artist as existential role model, prepared an intellectual path for people like me who, in looking for something that would mark them as nonconformist, came upon the blues.

The blues revival brought commercially recorded blues music and black musicians before the white public. White, middle-class, city and suburban men (and a far smaller proportion of women) initiated the revival. In the United States, the revival was launched in 1959 with the publication of Samuel Charters's *The Country Blues,* along with an accompanying record album of the same name, as well as a Charters-recorded album of Lightnin' Hopkins, the singer with whom he framed his book.[6] The revival did not end suddenly, but the scale of activity declined dramatically after the 1970 Ann Arbor Blues Festival, where most major blues artists performed before an audience of ten thousand. I date the major phase of the revival from 1959 to 1970, and note that, as I write, in the late 1980s, a new one is in full swing.

The blues revival documented, presented, and interpreted. Charters's work was preceded by that of record collectors who explored country blues and also the "classic blues" of the women blues "queens" like Bessie Smith and Ma Rainey.[7] Collectors canvassed the United States for 78 rpm records in factory warehouses, goodwill stores, junk shops, and the homes of people who might have bought them. They pored over these records, puzzling about singers with nicknames—"Blind Lemon Jefferson," "King Solomon Hill," "Bo-Weavil Jackson"—what romance in these names! Hobbyists, their pastime was buying, selling, listening, and imagining. Record magazines published early blues discographies and tantalized their readers with life-sized photos of rare labels. Jazz magazines such as the English *Jazz Monthly* ran notes-and-queries columns. In the early 1960s *Blues Unlimited* and other magazines devoted entirely to blues arose; they printed record reviews, discographical notes and queries, interviews with blues singers, news and itineraries, obituaries, and an occasional interpretive article. Eventually blues fans moved from thinking about blues as a kind of folk music (the "folk-blues") to blues as a music unto itself.

It was a short step from collecting 78s to reissuing them on long-playing albums. When Folkways published the companion album for Charters's book, *The Country Blues,* a group of record collectors in the New York area issued a counter-album, *Really! The Country Blues.*[8] This was the beginning of Origin Jazz Library (OJL). The New York "mafia," as it later came to be known, felt Charters had underrated the Mississippi Delta, where the most outstanding blues had originated; their first album was devoted entirely to the "father" of Delta blues, Charley Patton, and *Really!* included several Mississippi recordings and sought to upstage Charters's efforts. I am sure my love for Delta blues dates from my listening to the early OJL reissues and reading about the collectors' quests to locate singers who might still be alive. Many other reissue albums followed in the early and mid-1960s, particularly from OJL and Folkways in the United States, and from several English companies. As the decade progressed and the revival received increasing public attention, collectors worried about copyright infringements, but the flow of reissues increased, and by 1970 most of the material of interest to collectors could be found in long-playing record albums issued by companies such as Yazoo (approximately fifty albums), Roots (forty albums; an Austrian company), Blues Classics (twenty-five albums), and OJL (twenty-three albums).

In 1963 and 1964 the blues revival gained strength from the "rediscovery" of Mississippi John Hurt, Skip James, Son House, and Bukka White (to name the four most prominent), once only exotic names on record labels. Collectors turned promoters and encouraged the rediscoveries to record anew; the singers practiced (although usually they were recorded soon after the first meeting, lest the treasure slip away), made albums, and began playing their acoustic music, often sounding uncannily like their recordings decades earlier, at clubs, coffeehouses, and festivals. Some went on tour to Europe and Japan. Their appearances at the Newport Folk Festival in 1963 and 1964 turned them into a media event, and they were written up in the weekly news magazines while they secured record contracts with major labels: Son House and Booker White on Columbia, and Skip James and John Hurt on Vanguard. Folk music still was big business; singers like Joan Baez and groups like Peter, Paul, and Mary continued to inspire young imaginations throughout the United States, and when folk festivals featured the rediscovered singers along with the revivalists, they were making a statement about roots that the media, reporting about the civil rights movement and looking for heroes, could not ignore. More field research resulted and new favorites like Mance Lipscomb and Fred McDowell emerged. Traditional artists were documented; many more albums were released featuring field recordings. Post–World War II blues with electric guitar, particularly the Chicago-styled version, moved into the revival in the middle of the decade when people realized that the British Invasion (particularly the music of the Rolling Stones) was blues-based. The Stones, after all, had taken their name from one of Muddy Waters's blues songs. And a white blues harmonica player from Chicago put together the Paul Butterfield Blues Band and had a blues single high on the pop charts: "Born in Chicago." Soon other blues band leaders had major record contracts: James Cotton, James Montgomery, and Charlie Musselwhite, to name a few. Some were revivalists, and some were traditional artists enjoying second careers in the revival, but in a sense all were revivalists because they were reviving a music that had fallen in popularity.

The 1960s blues revival grew out of the earlier urban folk revival and it had two strains, two sides. First, it was a romantic movement among idealists of all ages, involving a love for blues as a stylized revolt against bourgeois values. So it appealed to people who came out of the intellectual wasteland of the Eisenhower era, the age of the "organization man," the other-directed conformists who made up the "lonely crowd."[9] Rejecting conformity to middle-class values, blues revivalists embraced the music of people who seemed unbound by conventions of work, family, sexual propriety, worship, and so forth. The blues revival was a white, middle-class love affair with the music and lifestyle of marginal blacks. The romantic strain projected a kind of primitivism on the blues singer and located him in a culture of natural license. On the other hand, the blues revival was remarkably oriented to records and the record-listening experience. It was begun by collectors for whom 78s were exotic mysteries engendering endless theorizing. The collector strain in the revival was scientific in method if not spirit: blues music was objectified on recorded artifacts that seemed real (after all, they could break) and, unlike most living beings, held still when one tried to analyze them. A dialectical energy involving acquisitiveness and fantasy fueled the revival.

First and most important were the collectors' efforts at gaining discographical control over the vast number of recordings. Listing blues records by artist, sidemen, title, date, record company name, release number, and matrix number culminated in the massive Dixon-Godrich prewar blues discography.[10] Most collectors used discographies innocently enough. If you liked Blind Blake, for example, Dixon-Godrich would tell you which records you needed for a complete collection. Discographers aimed at scientific objectivity; their compilers strove to print accurate information about records while refraining from evaluation. No discography would tell you which Blind Blake records were best.

But the discographers' work embodied a paradox. Choosing which records to include and which to exclude was not always easy. The discographers used collectors' criteria rather than the criteria of the general public (who probably would have included white artists) or the criteria of the general African-American public (who did not make rigid distinctions between blues, rhythm and blues, and jazz, for example). The paradox is that while the collectors assumed they were merely providing information about something that already existed in the world, their discographies came to define the blues canon. If a record was listed, it was blues; if not, it wasn't.[11]

Collecting is an act of appropriation. As James Clifford reminds us, collections are efforts "to make the world one's own, to gather things around oneself tastefully, appropriately. . . . The self that must possess but cannot have it all learns to select, order, classify in hierarchies—to make 'good' collections."[12] As museums appropriate objects for preservation and display, these objects come to be authentic and authenticating cultural representations, to "stand for" a "school" of painting, say, or an extinct species, or a human group's former way of life. And just as museums order their artifacts into an authoritative reconstruction, so record collectors arrange their discs into something that represents "blues."

In that representation, process becomes artifact and engenders new cultural activities: collectors listening and talking about "blues" on the record. Paul Oliver, the most highly regarded English blues writer of the past thirty-five years, recognized that for most Europeans, the experience of blues is an experience of recordings: "Though there's nothing quite like listening to a blues singer in person, in a club or on his house porch especially, for me as for most enthusiasts, those records have been the raw material of our experience."[13] This fascination with the recorded artifact produced a distancing that the "real thing" (hearing the music live) couldn't quite dislodge. So, for example, when Muddy Waters toured England in the 1950s, Oliver noted that "his rocking blues and electric guitar were meat that proved too strong for many stomachs" that had been expecting something closer to "folk music" than rock and roll.[14] Waters, unlike Big Bill Broonzy, did not know or did not care that the European audience had a preconception of blues that fixed it in an earlier, acoustic era.

Nor is it clear that Waters would have drawn a sharp distinction between blues, rhythm and blues, and rock and roll, or classified himself then as a blues singer only. When he toured England he was at a stage in his career when he was aiming at the teenage record market. "I'm a Man," "Mannish Boy," and other such songs penned for Waters by Willie Dixon sought to capitalize on the newly discovered record buying power of teenagers, the market that Waters's Chess stablemate, Chuck Berry, had exploited. Only when his career faltered in this arena in the early 1960s and he found a second career in the blues revival did he return primarily to blues. The fascination with the recorded artifact and the desire to have singers recreate those artifacts and conform to *a priori* images is a collector's fixation. As Charles Keil points out, many of those images were racist stereotypes: "The worst white ideas about blacks are accepted a second time and worked through with a vengeance in the personae of Muddy Waters, a natural force like the Mississippi, a rolling stone with mojo powers; Howlin' Wolf, a raging beast, the tail dragger humping around on all fours; Sonny Boy Williamson, pushing 60 when he first records for Chess but still just a 'boy' whose smiling face can sell King Biscuit Flour."[15] And Oliver's phrase, "on his house porch especially," reveals the collector's desire to put the singer in his place: the country porch was a more "natural" (i.e., close-to-nature) context, but in 1984 it was terribly anachronistic.

"Natural" context suggests something of the underlying romantic imagination that reconstructed "blues" in the act of interpretation, and this brings me to second aspect of the revival, romanticism, and to Oliver's counterpart in the United States, Samuel B. Charters, whose popular 1959 book and reissue album both introduced and delimited the field of commercially recorded "country blues." In most of his writing Oliver shows the collector's fascination with facts: names, dates, places, and so on. Charters cared less for fact and wrote evocatively, using the resources of fiction as he wrought his subject into being. Later writers took Charters to task for conceptual sloppiness and bad history. For example, Charters had devoted a chapter in *The Country Blues* to Leroy Carr, whom later writers regarded as the most important early *city* blues singer.

Charters's definitive book reveals romantic enthusiasm born of existential commitment, and a conflict between his personal taste and the aesthetic criteria he inferred from the black record audience. In his preface,
he wrote that he would devote space to the blues singers in proportion to
their popularity (as shown by record sales in the black communities) rather
than impose his personal preferences. This, he felt, would guarantee objectivity. Immediately contradicting himself, he offered a justification for
a chapter on Robert Johnson, whose records did not sell very well:

> It has seemed to me artificial to discuss the music on any other level
> than that of its relationship with its own audience. This has resulted in
> an extensive study of the marketing and sales of blues records in order
> to achieve as high a degree of objectivity as possible. It would be rel-
> atively simple to select groups of recordings and develop a thesis on
> either a musical or a sociological basis, but the truth has been that the
> blues audience is capricious and not in the least concerned with musical
> or sociological concepts. Two singers, Rabbit Brown and Robert John-
> son, have been discussed at length, despite their minor roles in the story
> of the blues. Brown was discussed in a contemporary review and some
> further comment seemed important, and the music of Robert Johnson
> was of considerable interest to the study of blues styles. (pp. xvii-xviii)

Johnson, most writers now believe, played a major role in blues history
because his innovations and repertory passed orally to so many other artists
in the Mississippi-Memphis-Chicago blues tradition; sales of his records
are beside the point. But Charters could not avoid selecting a group of
recordings and then developing a thesis. He railed against the Bluebird
recordings of the 1930s that featured Bill Broonzy, Washboard Sam, and
Sonny Boy Williamson:

> In the years before the second World War, Bluebird exploited the
> blues with a persistence and thoroughness that made its blues releases
> almost as popular as the standard vocal releases on Victor. The country
> blues were a commercial success. In the 1930s, they became as repetitious
> as the city blues had been in the 1920s. The personal vocal styles and
> the intense, personal styles were almost eliminated. Instead of individual
> accompaniments, there were small groups. . . . To make individuality
> even less noticeable, Bluebird used a group of house musicians who
> accompanied everybody. The singers were not even singing their own
> blues most of the time. (p. 183)

Charters had a simple thesis: blues was a traditional art form whose
chief value lay in its "intensely personal expression." Intensely personal
expressions sounded defiance in an age of conformity. Robert Johnson is

important in *The Country Blues* because he epitomized the kind of romantic, even existential, artist-hero that Charters envisioned as "bluesman." Johnson is mysterious: "Almost nothing is known of his life" (p. 207) except that he was murdered and died young. Charters reports a rumor that would make any record collector shudder: "There is a story that his first recordings were done in a billiard parlor and a drunken fight broke out after he recorded. Someone threw a billiard ball at one of the engineers and smashed several of the masters" (p. 208). But above all Charters views Johnson as a tortured, driven poet. He is "superbly creative" (p. 207); his lyrics have a "superb imagery" (p. 209); and "the finest of Robert Johnson's blues have a brooding sense of torment and despair" (p. 209). Fair enough; evaluate Johnson's blues as poetry. But Charters goes on to say that "his singing becomes so disturbed it is almost impossible to understand the words" (p. 210). Here, he confuses the singer with the person and fails to realize that Johnson's intensity is calculated art. Different "takes" of the same song from these sessions, perhaps unavailable to Charters, show little change and indicate that Johnson was not incoherent or "disturbed," but an artist and a perfectionist.

Charters's portrait of Lightnin' Hopkins frames the book and, not surprisingly, yields more information about revivalist romanticism than about Hopkins. Supposedly a description of the way Hopkins turns a worksong into a blues, it reveals instead Charters's construction of Hopkins and the moment. "In a poor, shabby room in the colored section of Houston, a thin, worn man sat holding a guitar, playing a little on the strings, looking out of the window. It was a dull winter day, a heavy wind swirling the dust across the yard. There was a railroad behind the houses, and a few children were playing on the rails, shivering in their thin coats. . . " (p. 15). Hopkins sings a few verses of what Charters thinks is a work song, "Ain't No More Cane on this Brazos," and then Charters divines Hopkins's thoughts: "He sat a moment, thinking of the hot, dusty summers on the flat cotton lands along the Brazos River, thinking of the convict gangs singing as they worked, the guards circling them slowly, a shotgun across the saddle" (p. 16). Hopkins sings a couple of lines more, and then "He stopped to drink some gin out of a bottle under the chair. He drank nearly a half pint of raw gin, using the metal cap of the bottle for a glass" (p. 16). After the long drink he sings what seems a complete performance. Charters concludes: "The man was named 'Lightnin'' Hopkins, from outside of Centerville, Texas. 'Ain't No More Cane on this Brazos' was a song he had heard when he was a young man, working in the fields. His own song ['Penitentiary Blues'] was a reshaping and reworking of the old work song into something intensely personal and expressive. He had changed it into a blues" (p. 17).

Charters's depiction sends up warning signals. The clichéd phrases ("poor, shabby room," "thin, worn man," "dull winter day," "hot, dusty summers") suggest an observer who sees in predetermined categories. The stereotyping continues when Hopkins downs the most "raw" drink imaginable (straight gin) as if to provide a metaphor for the transformation of the "raw" verses of the worksong into the finished blues. I do not doubt that he drank the gin; what concerns me is why this detail is selected and others omitted. But the most telling aspect of Charters's portrait of the artist is that by constructing in accordance with his already formed expectations, he misunderstood what he heard. I think that instead of changing a worksong into an "intensely personal" blues song, as Charters would have it, Hopkins was merely hesitating as he recalled and refashioned a blues song he had recorded a dozen years earlier as "Grosebeck Blues."[16] I came to this conclusion after listening to the versions of "Penitentiary Blues" ["Grosebeck Blues"] that Hopkins recorded commercially prior to his meeting Charters, and after considering the lyrics of these versions with the lyrics Charters prints. The earlier "Grosebeck Blues" is in quatrain-refrain form; the resulting "Penitentiary Blues" attaches Hopkins's earlier quatrains to a new improvisatory refrain.[17] He makes a new blues song from an old one, not from a worksong.

Because Charters "knew" that blues songs developed from worksongs, he was predisposed to interpret what he heard as Hopkins turning a worksong into a blues, an instance of blues ontogeny recapitulating phylogeny. But in the light of information he did not consider, the account seems wrong and, because he was careful enough to record Hopkins's music and generous enough to make it available, we can read through his construction to what probably took place. And, of course, this incident reveals strikingly how the blues revival, thinking it was performing acts of interpretation on something "out there" called blues, constituted blues through its interpretive acts. I don't mean that Charters was making blues in the sense that he was singing them, of course; but he was making them in the sense that he was constituting a domain he called blues, and he was arbitrating and divining meaning within that domain, just as I did when I suggested a different interpretation.

In this light it is interesting to follow Lightnin' Hopkins's and John Lee Hooker's careers through the revival decade as they progressed from blues singers to folksingers to blues singers once again. Hopkins and Hooker were discovered and recorded in the late 1950s for folk and blues revival audiences. Both were presented as folksingers who made up their own lyrics and accompanied themselves on acoustic guitar. Both Hopkins and Hooker made many 78 rpm records in the late 1940s and early 1950s, and prior to their discovery in the late 1950s they were singing before audiences in the black communities, fronting small bands and playing electric guitar. The producers of folk music concerts and albums must have asked them to change to acoustic guitars and sing without a band backup. Their current music must have sounded too much like rock and roll. Acoustic music—folk music—was thought unadulterated. Ironically, then, Charters and other folk music promoters unplugged the electric guitars, assuming the authority to alter Hopkins's and Hooker's music to sell it to the folk revival audience. In so doing, they probably felt they were removing the "electric" taint. But a few years later, after the Stones, the Butterfield Band, and Bob Dylan's appearance with an electric guitar at the 1965 Newport Folk Festival, Hopkins and Hooker were promoted as blues singers and when they recorded for the blues revival, they were plugged in once again.

To complete the interpreter's hegemony over the artist, he must deny "authority" to the artist, leaving the interpretive field to himself. Charters moves in this direction when writing [above] that "the blues audience is capricious and not in the least concerned with musical or sociological concepts." Harold Courlander, whose *Negro Folk Music U.S.A.* was the period's standard treatment of its subject, goes the rest of the distance. I quote from the beginning of his chapter on blues: "Too often, in recent times, folk song performers, innocent bystanders, and casual rustic acquaintances have been called upon to provide definitions, the history, and the philosophy of folk songs.... The value of this 'personal interview' approach to problems of analysis and definition is limited if not altogether precarious. Nevertheless, we might take a look at what some folk and blues singers have had to say about blues."[18]

Here Courlander sets the stage with his tone. "Casual rustic acquaintances," for example, and several other condescending phrases not only deny interpretive authority to folksingers but tell the reader that he and the writer belong to a more highly educated class. Courlander's tone may have been an extension of the sophisticated patter one could hear on the urban folk stage. And so he reviews some native theories:

> Huddie Ledbetter, Sonny Terry, and Bill Broonzy, among others, have tended to identify blues with melancholy or miserable feelings of one kind or another. As Ledbetter put it—in a pat, theatrical way: "When you lay down at night, turning from one side of the bed all night to the other and can't sleep, what's the matter? Blues got you.... When you get up in the morning and sit on the side of your bed, may have father and mother, sister and brother, boyfriend or girlfriend or husband or wife around you, you don't want no talk out of 'em. They ain't done you nothing, you ain't done them nothing, but what's the matter? Blues got you."

Broonzy may have come a bit closer to talking about the blues song rather than "the blues" when he said: "Blues is a natural fact, something that a fellow lives. If you don't live it, you don't have it." What he meant, I think, is that a real blues song grows out of real life, unlike many other kinds of popular songs. However, blues singers are not likely to be able to tell us much more than this about the blues form or its development. Their role is to sing, not explain how it all came to be, or why it is as it is. (pp. 123–24)

Leadbelly was not trying to define blues songs but to connect the emotion to universal experience. Courlander dismisses Leadbelly's view, not by refuting it, but by attacking its sincerity: if it is "theatrical," then it must be false, an act. Broonzy is allowed to speak for himself, but Courlander must translate his meaning: "What he meant, I think, is . . . ." If the blues singers do not know what they are talking about, or if they are insincere and apt to be lying, we should not trust their interpretations. Instead, here is Courlander's educated, "objective" voice telling us what the blues "are":

As a form of expression, blues are certainly much more than a statement of personal misery. At its base, the blues song is a sort of exalted or transmuted expression of criticism or complaint, the very creation or singing of which serves as a balm or antidote. The finer the singing or the creative effort, the more effective is the song as a catharsis. A singer in a Louisiana prison declared, "Whenever you sing the blues just right, why you feel like a million, when you may not have a dime. . . . That's the best part of my life, is blues." (p. 124)

Courlander's interpretation turns on the notion of catharsis, but I think he has Aristotelian tragedy in mind, not blues. "Exalted" is a strange word to describe the lowdown imagery of blues lyrics. "Creation or singing" is a willful evasion; I want to ask him whether the catharsis comes with the creation or the performance (why not both?), and I am sure he has no clue; he has not thought it through. "Balm or antidote" cleverly takes the weight from the comparison to tragedy; blues is a lesser thing. And his conclusion is rampant with irony; having denied interpretive authority to blues singers, he quotes one to "prove" his point about catharsis. His interpretation does not hold; ideas war against each other, they spin and cancel each other out. Yet his strategy is clear: quote the native point of view if you must, but discount it and substitute your own, reporting occasional native viewpoints when they support your views. In that way he constructs the domain he calls "blues."

I continue with other writing from this period, including my own Ph.D. thesis. Most of us were satisfied to seek out blues singers' ideas and present them in their own words as "folk evaluation."[19] In my thesis, later published and honored as the outstanding book on "nonclassical" music of its year, I took pains to represent many blues singers speaking what they actually had said in conversations and interviews, but always organized in categories that I learned from ethnomusicologists or took from my interest in history, music, and poetry: what was the social status of the blues singer; how were blues songs composed and transmitted; was blues a protest music; were blues songs autobiographical; and so on.[20] In other words, my portrait proceeded by my analytical categories; I sought their information but not their way of thinking about it. I was impatient with questions such as "What is the blues?" and in my own fieldwork seldom asked it. Thinking I was presenting their view, I was presenting my construction of it. Again, that is not to say I made it up; but I did fashion the raw material of interviews into a chapter on "The Singers' Perspective" that cohered on the basis of my experience, not theirs.

My reaction to Lazy Bill Lucas's repertoire and record collection reveals how different were our views. Bill was the first blues singer I got to know as a friend. We lived in the same city; we played music together; I spent time at his apartment; and in 1969 I joined his blues band as a guitarist. I knew him for a few years before I heard the word *ethnomusicology* or understood what fieldwork was. Bill's performing repertoire seemed to me to be a mix of blues and lesser material. I liked his blues songs but did not care as much for his rhythm and blues pieces. His record collection reflected his repertoire and included what I thought of as rare Chicago blues alongside common rock and roll (e.g., Fats Domino). One of his favorite songs was Domino's version of "Blueberry Hill," a big rock hit from the mid-1950s. Bill, of course, did not sort the music out in the same categories I did. My difficulty, as I view it with hindsight, stemmed from a "pure" conception of blues deriving from collectors' criteria. A rare record on the Blue Lake label in Bill's collection got me excited. Finding a home recording of Bill and Snooky Pryor and Homesick James in Bill's basement was a monumental discovery. To Bill, the Blue Lake record was just another of Sunnyland Slim's performances; he had heard him so often. And for Bill the home recording was just a performance that had not resulted in a record contract, not a unique document of a historical moment.

Nor was I fully aware how much of what they told me was a product of previous interactions between folklorists, record producers, fans, and historians on the one hand, and blues singers on the other. To be sure, I knew that some singers' views had been influenced by their dealings with well-meaning promoters; who could think that Leadbelly had composed "Bourgeois Blues" without exposure to leftist ideas, or that Big Bill Broonzy's autobiography, written at the end of his life for a European blues fan, was not partly the result of his second career on the revivalist circuit?[21] Anecdotes (later proven untrue) circulated about Alan Lomax and Son House, or more recently about John Fahey and Booker White. But somehow, I thought, my purposes were pure—after all, research, not exploitation, was my aim—and I felt the singers would recognize that and respond thoughtfully and honestly to my questions, giving me the answers in the 1960s that they would have given in the 1920s and 1930s, before all the revival hoopla. Barry Pearson has shown how naive that notion was, and how, confronted with revivalists, blues singers fashioned stories to satisfy their new audience.[22] By the late 1970s I had come around to the position that what we take to be oral history is often better understood as fiction.[23]

My notion of what anthropologists call "native point of view" or "folk evaluation" rested on two incorrect assumptions: that there existed a dominant or definitive viewpoint that could be reified into "what blues singers (in general) believe," and that there existed a more or less unsullied viewpoint that could be extracted from what the singers said in conversation with me and other researchers. The concept of "folk evaluation" turned too much on the wishful thought of a pristine "folk" and a separation between them and us. While on the one hand I tried to bridge that gap, playing guitar in Bill's band, I also played my role as researcher, and when I wrote my book I thought of myself fully in the latter role.

As Berger and Luckmann have shown, all of us are socialized into an ongoing construction of reality.[24] After childhood we do not come wholly innocent to any situation. All revivalists acquired preconceived notions of blues. Charters went looking for blues as folk music, and of course he discovered what he was looking for. Charters got his expectations about blues from his activities in the interpretive community of jazz buffs and folk music aficionados. When in the mid-1960s I began doing blues research in earnest I scrutinized every blues fan magazine, read every blues book and article (there weren't many) and every record jacket liner note I could get my hands on, and was thus brought into the blues research interpretive community. As a result I began to see and hear the things that were commonly discussed: the differences between "Delta blues" and "East Coast blues," for example. I acquired an attitude, developed prejudices, became something of a connoisseur. I knew, or thought I knew, what was authentic. In short, I became part of the blues revivalist interpretive community, and I can best understand my activities then within this matrix. Blues singers were socialized into the world of the blues revival as well. They learned that certain kinds of performances were better received than others, and they adjusted their shows accordingly. They learned that they would have to deal with a myriad of questions from interviewers. They, too, acquired attitudes. Some did research of their own; John Jackson, for example, a

Virginia blues singer, has built an outstanding collection of reissued blues recordings and has incorporated some of these songs into his repertoire while incorporating the liner notes into his reflections on the history of blues. But if our social theories were naive, it would be hard to find a word to describe our political ideas. What was at stake for those who participated in the blues revival?

Revivalism is peculiar politics; is it reactionary or revolutionary? Charters, reviewing *The Country Blues* in the retrospective preface he wrote for the 1975 reprint, claimed, "We were trying to turn what we did with our lives into a political act, and what I did, in part, was write this book" (p. ix). And it is his retrospective on the blues revival and his part in it that I want to take up here, if only to suggest that readers be cautious about anyone's hindsight, mine included. Charters saw himself to be anticipating the 1960s counterculture in conjuring an alternative to mainstream America. He wrote:

> I could have shouted, and I could have criticized—but instead I tried to present an alternative. If my books from this time seem romantic it's because I tried to make them romantic. . . . *The Country Blues* was two things. It was a romanticization of certain aspects of black life in an effort to force the white society to reconsider some of its racial attitudes, and on the other hand it was a cry for help. I wanted hundreds of people to go out and interview the surviving blues artists. I wanted people to record them and document their lives, their environment, and their music—not only so that their story would be preserved but also so they'd get a little money and a little recognition in their last years. So there was another kind of romanticism in the book. I was trying to make the journey to find the artists as glamorous as possible, by describing the roadsides, the farms, and the shacks, and the musicians themselves. What I was doing wasn't academic, and it wasn't scholarly, but it was effective. (p. xii)

Was Charters really aware of political choices (shouting, criticizing, presenting an alternative, or working for change) or was he, rather, swept up for a time in the very romanticism he says he chose to employ? A good test would seem to be his portrait of the black culture he said he felt was direct, open, and honest. "I found that the awareness of the real sources of power in the society, the consciousness of social inequalities, and the direct expression of sexuality in the black culture was so much closer to the American reality that I felt I somehow had to make people conscious of what these other voices were saying" (p. x), he wrote, but his phrase "the American reality" is odd in this context. What can it mean? In the sentence just quoted it suggests "reality" in contrast to "appearance." But for Charters both the appearance and reality of 1950s bourgeois American culture was stifling. "At the same time I believed that if I could make people hear the voices of black Americans they might begin to see them as human beings, and not as stereotypes" (ibid.). And yet his portraits are romantic stereotypes. We've seen how he conjured up Lightnin' Hopkins at the book's beginning. We predict the book will end with Hopkins walking slowly down the street into the gathering darkness while Charters laments the impending death of the blues. Not quite, but almost: "Lightnin', in his way, is a magnificent figure. He is one of the last of his kind, a lonely, bitter man who brings to the blues the intensity and pain of the hours in the hot sun, scraping at the earth, singing to make the hours pass. The blues will go on, but the country blues, and the great singers who created from the raw singing of the work songs and the field cries the richness and variety of the country blues, will pass with men like this thin, intense singer from Centerville, Texas" (p. 266).

The blues will go on, diminished. This is Charters's romantic lament, leavened by a false existential toughness. Hopkins lonely and bitter? How can Charters presume to know? The blues has continued for almost a century, despite sixty years of predictions of its impending demise. Cultures and music-cultures ebb and flow, diminish and strengthen. Some die, but the blues continues dynamic and emergent; the current interest in blues has resulted in a surge of new reissues, new blues artists such as Robert Cray, and surely will result in new writing about it. Already the new revival is under way, attempting another interpretation.

As a gloss on this theme, I quote a few lines from Wallace Stevens's poem, "The Man with the Blue Guitar":

> The man bent over his guitar,
> A shearsman of sorts. The day was green.
>
> They said, "You have a blue guitar,
> You do not play things as they are."
>
> The man replied, "Things as they are
> Are changed upon the blue guitar."
>
> And they said then, "But play, you must,
> A tune beyond us, yet ourselves,
>
> A tune upon the blue guitar
> Of things exactly as they are."
>
> II
>
> I cannot bring a world quite round,
> Although I patch it as I can.

• • •

>Here I inhale profounder strength
>And as I am, I speak and move
>
>And things are as I think they are
>And say they are on the blue guitar.[25]

Stevens was not known as a connoisseur of blues music. These lines might be taken as a brief for Courlander's view that blues singing is cathartic: that is, by changing "things as they are," the singer or artist purges sorrow. Instead, the poem turns on its relation to Picasso's painting *Man with a Guitar*, in which everything *but* the guitar is blue. The poem suggests that the guitar, a figure for the imagination, turns the green day blue. My point has been the same: the blues revival, like all revivals, including the folklore and folklife movement itself, is an imaginative act owing its ongoing activity to a paradox. That paradox is this: for activity to take place, people must think there is something stable "out there" called blues (or called folklore, for that matter), which the revival then does things to; it celebrates artists and songs, reissues records, rediscovers artists and makes new records, promotes concerts, writes discographies and histories, and in general interprets the activity called blues music. Rather than telling what blues is, the revival makes it what it is, just as in Stevens's poem the guitar makes the day blue. But for the revival to proceed, the revivalists must believe otherwise, that they are merely finding (discovering) something rather than constructing (constituting) it.

The period of the blues revival, after all, was also the era of civil rights and black power, when interpretive voices from the black community spoke loudly on racism and exploitation in music as in all aspects of American life. One black history revue I performed in then had Lazy Bill Lucas singing blues in a slave hut.[26] For the revue's purposes, blues was a music of complaint, and therefore the slave setting was appropriate. I told the show's director that scholars thought blues began no earlier than the 1890s; the show, I thought, was committing an anachronism. I had my say but the show went on as planned. Four years later as I was listening to thousands of blues lyrics in preparation for an anthology of transcriptions, I decided that complaint wasn't the "real" theme of the blues; freedom from mistreatment was.[27] The blues, I felt, was an important and positive part of the black heritage. Meanwhile, though, some voices in the black community concerned with developing a distinct black "aesthetic" devalued the blues as a music of resignation and the past.[28] Nowadays, on the contrary, black writers such as Houston Baker and Henry Louis Gates see blues as proof of a historically rooted, distinctly black attitude toward life, an attitude that is alive to the complexities of living and thinking and feeling, and an attitude that turns life into art.[29]

To the musicians, the blues revival of the 1960s was a way to earn money, prolong their careers, achieve prestige from recognition, and remain artists. The promoters enjoyed bringing this music to a popular audience but they were not entirely altruistic: they exercised power and made money for themselves. Collectors satisfied desires for acquisition and control. Academics found intellectual and other pleasures and wound up furthering their careers.[30] The interpreters viewed blues within the matrix of their ideas of black music and culture. For many fans, blues represented a lifestyle and a stylized, artistic revolt against confining bourgeois values. Writers concerned with the black experience constructed blues as a historical expression and fit it into a contemporary agenda. The folklorists on the NEA panel viewed blues as a cultural treasure, threatened and in need of support. No one, then, is free from constituting domains through interpretive acts. Instead, various interpretive communities—whether blues scholars, musicians, black historians, or folk arts programs—engage each other in a negotiation over meaning that finally is political and implicates us all.

NOTES

This is a revised version of a paper read at a panel on Revivalism at the 1987 annual meeting of the American Folklore Society, in Albuquerque. The panel was co-chaired by this writer and Burt Feintuch, and it included Neil Rosenberg and Edward D. Ives. I am grateful to Steve Feld, Barry O'Connell, Burt Feintuch, and Neil Rosenberg for their comments and suggestions on an earlier draft. Excerpts from "The Man with the Blue Guitar" are taken from *Collected Poems* by Wallace Stevens. Copyright 1936 by Wallace Stevens and renewed 1964 by Holly Stevens. Reprinted by permission of Alfred A. Knopf, Inc.

1. See Hobsbawm and Ranger, *The Invention of Tradition.*

2. Babcock, "Reflexivity: Definitions and Discriminations." See also Ruby, *A Crack in the Mirror.*

3. Nagel, *The View from Nowhere,* p. 3.

4. Mention must be made of Kenneth Goldstein, Alan Lomax, Harry Oster, and Chris Strachwitz who located and recorded several black folk and blues singers at the height of the folk revival during the latter 1950s and early 1960s; the recordings appeared mainly on Atlantic, Prestige, and Arhoolie. Prestige had one album series called Prestige/Folklore and another called Prestige/Bluesville. Most of these albums appealed to the folk revival audience rather than to hard-core blues fans, however.

5. In the 1950s jazz was popular on college campuses, particularly when played by small combos like Dave Brubeck's and big bands like Stan Kenton's. Record

companies capitalized on this craze with albums such as Brubeck's *Jazz Goes to College.* Many colleges began their own jazz bands at this time.

6. Charters, *The Country Blues.* All page references that follow in the text are to the 1975 edition. The albums are *The Country Blues* and *Lightnin' Hopkins.*

7. David Evans and I preferred the term "vaudeville blues" because most of these women had backgrounds in stage shows before recording blues songs. I also objected to the judgment implied by "classic" attached to a genre that I didn't value as highly as country (or as I came to prefer, "downhome") blues.

8. See the data for *Really! The Country Blues* in the discography for this volume.

9. Whyte, *The Organization Man,* and Riesman, Denny, and Glazer, *The Lonely Crowd* were two best-selling interpretations of middle-class American behavior in the 1950s.

10. Dixon and Godrich, *Blues and Gospel Records.* (London: Storyville Publications, 1964). A second edition was published in 1969 and a third, revised, edition in 1982.

11. This became a serious issue with the post–World War II discography, *Blues Records* by Leadbitter and Slaven, because they overlooked many blues records. Their discography was not, therefore, regarded as "authoritative." An "authoritative" second edition is awaiting full publication; the first volume (A–K) appeared and is already being amended in the blues magazines.

12. Clifford, *The Predicament of Culture,* p. 218.

13. Oliver, *Blues Off The Record,* p. 274.

14. Ibid., p. 266.

15. Keil, "People's Music Comparatively," p. 121.

16. Hopkins recorded four takes of "Grosebeck Blues" in 1947 for Gold Star in Houston. Takes 2 and 3 were reissued on *Early Recordings Vol.* 2; take 4 may be found on *Fast Life Woman.* The correct spelling of the place is Groesbeck.

17. That is, a quatrain followed by a refrain comprises each verse.

18. Courlander, *Negro Folk Music U.S.A.,* p. 123. Other citations from this work are given parenthetically in the text.

19. The term "folk evaluation" is anthropologist Paul Bohannon's; it means the informant's own ideas. See Merriam, *The Anthropology of Music,* p. 31.

20. Titon, *Early Downhome Blues.*

21. Ledbetter, "Bourgeois Blues"; Broonzy, *Big Bill Blues.*

22. Pearson, *"Sounds So Good To Me."*

23. Titon, "The Life Story."

24. Berger and Luckmann, *The Social Construction of Reality.*

25. Wallace Stevens, "The Man with the Blue Guitar," from *Collected Poems* (New York: Alfred A. Knopf, 1964).

26. *Dat Feelin',* presented at the Tyrone Guthrie Theatre, Minneapolis, in the fall of 1970.

27. I completed the anthology in 1974 but for several years could not find a publisher. The trade houses told me that most of the books they had published in black studies in the past five years had not met sales expectations. (Their implication was that black people did not read.) The first edition of Titon, *Downhome Blues Lyrics,* appeared in 1981; the second in 1990.

28. Gayle, *The Black Aesthetic.*

29. Baker, *Blues, Ideology, and Afro-American Literature;* Gates, *The Signifying Monkey.*

30. Between 1965 and 1971 I was a graduate student in American studies. When I said to my adviser that I wanted to write my Ph.D. thesis on blues, I was told that I should think carefully about the academic consequences of scholarly research into a music that had never been given such serious treatment. I was told that it would hurt my chances of getting a job teaching in a university. I was advised to obtain an additional degree in order to improve my chances on the market. For that reason I got the M.A. in English in addition to the Ph.D. in American studies. I got a job in an English department. Many of my classmates did not get jobs; the market was tight and grew tighter. Having my dissertation published did not merely further my career; it probably kept me in the profession.

Living Blues Journal: The Paradoxical Aesthetics of the Blues Revival

Peter Narváez

Although it was typically "tasteless" and imbued with painful cari-cature, one of the recorded satirical sketches created and performed by Cheech and Chong (Cheech Marin, Tommy Chong) in the early 1970s embodied a fundamental paradox of the blues revival that will be one of the foci of this analysis of *Living Blues* journal, namely, that of a group of European-Americans appreciating and abetting African-American folk per-formers and their music, while simultaneously attempting to influence the aesthetics of those performers and their audiences and thus possessively determine the course of their art.[1] Entitled "Blind Melon Chittlin'," the recording lampoons the major personae of the blues revival—blues artists, producers of blues consumer goods, and finally their target markets—blues audiences. The setting for the piece is a blues recording session in which an aggressive, mercenary, and exploitive producer, appropriately named "J. R." from the infamous TV character on "Dallas," records an "old" blues artist that he "signed the other day," "Blind Melon Chittlin'."[2] The old blues singer, whose name is obviously a pun on Blind Lemon Jefferson, receives payment for the session in the alleged form of his namesake[3]—"ten dollars," "a bottle of booze," and "a hooker." Ironically, J. R.'s plans for going "gold" with a young white audience entail directives to Chittlin' that are not unlike John Lomax's insistent demands on Blind Willie McTell while recording for the Library of Congress in 1940,[4] that is, J. R. wants the singer to sing a protest blues that chronicles past social injustices perpetrated by whites against blacks. Thus, J. R. appeals to "Blind Baby" to sing "not just [another] blues ... but ... an epic document depicting the struggle of the black people against the white devil slavemasters." Far from achieving this objective, however, J. R. is forced to record many takes and deal with serious, unforeseen difficulties posed by the black artist: first, the old singer appears incapable of understanding or following orders and tends to fall asleep; second, his musicianship is inadequate (e.g., he fails to play his harmonica properly because he forgets to hold it in his hand; the thumping of the artist's feet, although indicative of that "old natural rhythm," creates a disturbing noise); third, the singer does not enunciate his words clearly enough to meet the demands of "kids today" who are "hung up on the lyrics," and even when Chittlin' does articulate his lyrics clearly, J. R. cannot comprehend the meaning of his black dialect. For the finale, "Blind" educates and covertly insults J. R. by physically demonstrating the content of his dialect code through unzipping his fly and showing J. R. his huge "ding dong." At that moment musical and racial stereotypes unexpectedly merge-emerge as a phallic signifier. A simultaneous overlay of bathos, the serious intentions of the project, and the ridiculous results compounds the producer-artist conflict into humor. Thus, an ambitious white producer spends the majority of his time attempting to manipulate the aesthetics of a black performer who is difficult to deal with and full of surprises. In addition, the conclusion of the sketch implies that it is the know-it-all white producer who is ultimately educated in the ways of the blues, and that through an arduous struggle between producer and artist a mutually acceptable, albeit unforeseen, blues product is attained. The Cheech and Chong piece, therefore, not only demonstrates the aforementioned paradox, but it also depicts blues products as being *discursive accidents.* As this essay will explain, the blues as discursive accident recapitulates the dialectic "flow and ebb pattern" of folk revival in general and *Living Blues* journal in particular.

The peculiar strains of social relations depicted in the foregoing scenario have also played themselves out in other cultural scenes and forums of the blues revival including *Living Blues* journal. Like Blind Melon's song, the original producers of *Living Blues* never foresaw the maturing of their offspring in quite the way that it has occurred. As longtime *Living Blues* editor Jim O'Neal has stated, the originators of the publication "didn't really anticipate that it would grow into what it did."[5] The birth of *Living Blues* in the spring of 1970 was an American response to the earlier and by then well-developed British blues magazines, *Blues World* and *Blues Unlimited.* At that time a group of white blues fans who worked and congregated at the hub of blues activity in Chicago, Bob Koester's Jazz Record Mart, "felt that it was insane to have to read British blues magazines to find out about music in Chicago," and so, with "seed money" from Koester, published the first issue.[6] The group knew that in comparison to their British counterparts, their location gave them a strategic advantage and they wanted to exploit it. *Living Blues* editor Amy van Singel explains:

"We were trying to beat [the British blues magazines] at their own game. We felt a bit superior to them because we could study the music live, first-hand, and talk to the artists with more immediacy. We wanted to be complimentary, not necessarily like rivals. We didn't want to cut them out of the market or anything. We just felt there was room for our view-point as well."[7]

The venture was also a well-meaning, educational, and altruistic en-deavor by a group of people who loved blues and who were steeped in the ideals of the civil rights movement of the sixties. They were keenly aware that the American public was generally ignorant of the significance of black musical culture and they wanted to set the record straight. In a recent farewell editorial Jim O'Neal has recalled that *Living Blues* "began in the wake of the civil rights era and the late '60s blues-rock boom as a blues fans' magazine produced by a committee of aficionados, most of us neophytes, who simply believed that there should be a publication in the United States to give credit to the black artists who created the music and sustained it as a living tradition."[8]

Published as a quarterly in Chicago, the blues capital of the world, *Living Blues* initially was typed, inexpensively printed, thirty-seven pages long, cost fifty cents, billed itself as "America's first blues magazine," and had seven editors.[9] Even though it took "at least five years to get a thousand people on the subscription list," five thousand copies of each issue were usually printed, several thousand being left over "to sell as back issues."[10] In the spring of 1974 Jim O'Neal and Amy van Singel became the sole managing editors, the whole operation being housed in their basement. Van Singel observes, "it was very much a Mom and Pop magazine."[11] The couple were assisted by two associate editors and various regional con-tributing editors. By that time each issue was approximately fifty pages in length, sported a glossy cover, was for the most part typeset in three columns, and generally had a much more polished look than the earlier magazines. Although the price slowly escalated to two dollars, this look was generally maintained through the spring of 1983 (# 56). The next issue brought dramatic changes: a color cover and glossy paper throughout; a slightly larger format (from 8³⁄₈" × 10⁵⁄₈" to 8¹⁄₂" × 11"); a different logo; larger typeface; a more spacious layout; and an increase in retail price to three dollars. In an unusually lengthy editorial, coeditor Jim O'Neal ex-plained the "facelift" as a result of *Living Blues* having received "academic credentials," that is, organizational and publishing support, from the Center for the Study of Southern Culture at the University of Mississippi.[12] The move to Mississippi, which "created a storm of controversy among some longtime blues supporters who felt the magazine had gone too slick, shifted its goals, or just lost the flavor of the old Chicago LB,"[13] was completed in 1986 with the move of the editors to Mississippi (issue #69) and in 1987 with the closing of the Chicago *Living Blues* office (#73).

The paradoxical strains of social relations evidenced by *Living Blues* during its seventeen-year history are better understood if the writers for the journal are viewed in the journal's early years as having been active agents of a rather unique folk revival in which they functioned as a by-stander audience, folk revival elite who communicated through narrowcast codes.[14] Through the years, as this group actively negotiated with ever increasing numbers of performers and growing audiences, some members of the group assumed, sometimes grudgingly, new participatory business roles in the production of a variety of blues consumer commodities and mass entertainments. Out of what appeared to be practical necessity, there-fore, *Living Blues* made greater use of broadcast codes. One result of these negotiated accidents, that is, this ideological shift from folk revival to more mainstream popular culture and from narrowcasting to broadcasting, was that a segment of earlier participants felt betrayed and withdrew their active support. To follow the strands of this argument, it is first appropriate to review the ideal prerequisites of folk revivals.[15] These are:

1. A perceived need for cultural alternatives.
2. The availability and authentication of a defined body of culture in the past, which is judged to be more aesthetically pleasing and beneficial than a comparative portion of contemporary culture.
3. A means whereby to revivify and reify such elements of past culture.
4. And finally, if a given folk revival is more than an exercise in nostalgia, that is, a bittersweet experience of reliving a remembered past, then folk revival requires a faith that in the future, new and equally vibrant forms will emerge from the selected past forms that have been rekindled in the present.[16]

Like many other forms of sociocultural change, folk revival arises out of a restless or vehement dissatisfaction with one's own contemporary culture. Unlike other social movements that dwell on the creation of al-together new alternatives (e.g., futuristic utopianism) folk revivalists are inclined to search for viable cultural alternatives in folk cultures of the past, oftentimes folk cultures that are conceived as being in some way connected to their own history.[17] When they are discovered, revitalizing elements of culture are then authenticated. For the sophisticated revivalist the process of authentication involves not only defining a specific cultural form in terms of its physical characteristics, that is, denoting a form as genre or signifier, but it also may entail the development of signifieds, that is, some understanding of the social context of the form (who? why?), a sense of the origin, growth, and establishment of such creations (when and how?), a view of the geographical locus of their enactment (where?), and finally, a clear perception of their relevance to the social present. Thus, in their quest for viable alternatives, folk revivalists may develop a complex multidimensional vision of social and cultural history.

One area of potential understanding that the folk revivalist is usually hesitant to pursue, however, is the territory of other-society aesthetics, i.e., the aesthetics of the historic culture-producer group that exhibited the vibrant forms currently revitalized. This is because revivalists have been enamored with the forms they zealously propagate from their first contact with them and they possess a deep esoteric, in-group commitment to their own culture-bound aesthetic values. All committed revivalists, therefore, think of themselves as having a degree of aesthetic expertise— they know what they like.[18] The realm of aesthetics, therefore, is the existential, emotional side of folk revival, and because the previously-cited characteristics of folk revival are ideals that are rarely matched by realities, the aesthetic experience of folk revival exhibits a chronological "flow and ebb" structure of: (1) ecstatic revelation of previously unknown or unappreciated aesthetic codes (e.g., discovering and listening to early recordings of a traditional music); (2) exciting anticipation and preparation for similar, renewal experiences (e.g., a search for similar recordings and the artists who performed on them, or seeking out artists who perform in similar styles); (3) reification of such renewal experiences through negotiated performance events (e.g., attending live performances at clubs, festivals); and finally, (4) accommodation to new, unanticipated aesthetic codes that have developed through negotiated performances (e.g., the appreciation, acceptance, or resignation to new forms that derive from older models). The revelatory event, an initiatory moment when one ecstatically experiences a cultural alternative, is pivotal to all folk revival commitment for it energizes and motivates the potential revivalist to social action. When Peter Guralnick first discovered the long-playing record *Robert Johnson: King of the Delta Blues Singers* he listened to it "half a dozen times that day." He says:

> Sometimes I can evoke the breathless rush of feeling that I experienced the first time that I ever really heard Robert Johnson's music. Sometimes a note will suggest just a hint of the realms of emotion that opened up to me in that moment, the sense of utter wonder, the shattering revelation. I don't know if it's possible to recreate this kind of feeling today—not because music of similar excitement doesn't exist but because the discovery can no longer take place in such a void . . . with the same sense of innocent expectation that caused my friends and me to hold our breath, all unknowing, when we first played Robert Johnson's songs on the record player.[19]

Through time and experience, initial aesthetic revelations eventuate in accommodations to new aesthetic realities. Thus, Carl Boggs, writing in 1975, judged that the creative spark, evident in early blues recordings, was lacking as the blues revival became a mass phenomenon: "While the creative forces that inspired blues during its heyday of the thirties, forties, and fifties are clearly gone, there is ironically now a greater *awareness* of the music in the society as a whole, as measured by the number of blues record albums being released, the proliferation of blues clubs and festivals, and the broadening circulation of books and magazines devoted at least in part to blues."[20]

In addition to the cultural prerequisites of folk revivals and the flow-and-ebb pattern of folk revivalist involvement in aesthetic codes, it should be understood that folk revivals are integral parts of larger sociopolitical movements, e.g., ethnic, regional, nationalist, neonationalist, subcultural. Within these larger contexts, a specialized "folk revival elite" takes on the responsibility of creatively identifying, authenticating, and popularizing edited portions of the past, and in general for recreating a new past as an intellectual crystal ball that, it is hoped, will be intently gazed at by those who are attempting to refurbish or establish alternative identities through ascertaining viable cultural "roots." With regard to the revival of the culture of black America as part of the black civil rights movement, the quasi-foreign, exoteric variable of race has sometimes effectively prevented or encumbered Caucasian Europeans and European-Americans from consciously adopting traditional forms of African-American culture as expressive behaviors of their own. Whites who have become participating, active bearers of black cultural traits have assumed one or more of the following revival postures: (1) ignoring or not acknowledging issues of race and culture; (2) dismissing racial differences as a secondary matter and concentrating on culture as "style";[21] (3) accepting the black past as part of an "American" or "Southern" heritage;[22] (4) viewing traditional black expressions as vital aspects of the human drama of which they are a part.[23]

Still other white revivalists of black culture have adopted a halfway strategy, accepting the unity of racial and cultural distinctions—thus distancing themselves from the original producer-culture, black America—while still assuming the role of "bystander audience."[24] As far as the blues revival is concerned, this bystander audience has consisted of highly enthusiastic, aesthetically critical, financially supportive, seemingly passive bearers[25] of African-American blues tradition.[26] Historically, this bystander role has been facilitated by the advent of phonograph recordings and radio, media that provide enjoyment in a variety of private and public contexts and allow for the close scrutiny of redundant, almost identical-sounding performances, by persons spatially, temporally, and socially distant from original performance contexts.[27] In particular, the programmability of phonograph records has enabled white revivalists to cultivate their own aesthetic standards while actively programming the performances of their favorite artists, often in domestic presentational social contexts, e.g., playing and displaying one's favorite records during an informal friendship gathering. Beginning in 1959 with Samuel B. Charters's exciting seminal work *The Country Blues,* through the works of David Evans, Bill Ferris, Peter Guralnick, Mike Leadbitter, Paul Oliver, Mike Rowe, Jeff Titon, and others, major blues authenticator-writer-critics have been initially drawn to the blues as record-loving members of a bystander audience.[28] By virtue of their authenticating writings, these members of a bystander audience also became elites of the blues revival. The writers for *Living Blues* have formed a part of this elite group as well.

The editors and writers who launched *Living Blues* were enthusiastic bystanders who certainly did not think of themselves as a folk revival elite. As a coterie of white blues fans who were primarily record collectors, they wanted to educate themselves and others about an esoteric subject—blues, an historically definable genre of black music. They initially viewed *Living Blues,* therefore, as a forum for a certain kind of education. They did not want to interfere with musical culture. They simply wanted to find out more about it and inform their peers. Such a project would not necessarily take a long time. Jim O'Neal's reflections reveal an early sense of the finite nature of the venture: "We thought it was just a magazine for other fans. I remember Bruce [Iglauer] saying at one of the early meetings that he thought that after five years or so, and everybody would have read the magazine, that nobody would need to read the magazine anymore and there wouldn't be anymore need for it because all the blues fans would know everything by then."[29]

The bystander role also meant giving black artists a forum. Amy van Singel has stressed, "We were trying very hard to figure out what black people listened to in addition to what we liked."[30] Thus, some of the most prominent *Living Blues* features, such as artist interviews, or first-person, "black voice" articles, which read like edited transcriptions of oral life history interviews with black artists,[31] appeared to communicate black experience and attitudes directly to white audiences. Perhaps the bystander role was made most evident to the *Living Blues* readership through photographs and blues-event reviews, which continually reiterated the journal's encoded message that whites should assist a living black blues tradition but they should not actively interact with it in performance except as an audience. With very rare exceptions,[32] when white musicians appeared in photos with black artists they inevitably were accompanists and as such were shown in the background. Similarly, whites sometimes appeared as music students of black blues performers who were portrayed in instructional roles at festival workshops. Except for some early examples, however, technical "how to play blues" articles have been strenuously avoided, since such pursuits would lead to an understanding of blues as performance rather than black culture. An official *Living Blues* editorial policy maintaining the unity of culture and race—blues performance therefore being the exclusive domain of blacks—was explicitly articulated by one of the editors, Paul Garon, in 1973.[33] At that time two editorials were prompted by a number of letters, several of which were printed, that criticized editor Amy van Singel's *Living Blues* review of the 1972 Ann Arbor Blues and Jazz Festival. In that review van Singel generally ignored the white blues performers who appeared on the program (Dr. John, the Siegel-Schwall Blues Band, among others), all of whom she summarily dismissed with "I still get my kicks from black bluesmen."[34] Garon's editorials supported van Singel's position by asserting that blues cannot be understood through an acoustic definition, i.e., as aurally perceived music, but rather blues is a "black American working-class music" "with its own historical, cultural, economic, psychological and political determinants." Thus, "it was [blacks] and [blacks] alone, who produced the blues." Garon said further "that deprived of its historical base ... the blues as purveyed by whites, is no longer the blues, and thus is not the concern of *Living Blues*."[35]

These editorials were appropriately followed in the subsequent issue (#14, 1973) by an academic-sounding subtitle for the publication—"A Journal of the Black American Blues Tradition." For many readers these pronouncements came as no particular surprise since from the onset of the magazine, the editors' and authors' dominant status as a knowledgeable folk revival elite teaching a readership was made clear. Thus, on the first page of the first issue the editors announced that "blues speaks for itself," and while they did "not intend to explain, define, or confine the blues" (bystander role), they hoped "to present some insights into this tradition" (folk revival elite). The expertise that "insights" alluded to was in keeping with the kind of medium that *Living Blues* was—a form of *narrowcasting*. As is the case with all narrowcast codes, *Living Blues* was aimed at a specific homogeneous audience. Amy van Singel describes the *Living Blues* audience as "a very, very limited market. I think it's limited for a couple of reasons, namely a lot of people who like blues can't read or they don't read. And it's hard to market a magazine. It's much easier to sell a blues record in fact, or to go out and hear live blues in a bar, but people don't look beyond their noses to want to really study it very often. It has to be a certain kind of personality."[36] Moreover, a narrowcast code resists conventionalization (e.g., current musical fashions); it is elaborated, exhibiting specialist jargon (e.g., kinds of blues, artists, labels, aesthetic terminology); and in narrow-casting, an audience anticipates enrichment from knowledgeable communicators. A successful narrowcast code, therefore, not only teaches but it also cultivates elitism, in the dichotomous, insider-outsider, esoteric-exoteric sense of "we" know more than "they." Writers for *Living Blues* directly taught through a question-and-answer department,[37] feature essays on individual artists, articles that discussed regional fieldwork,[38] and also through reviews of blues consumer goods: records, books, and events.

Successful folk revival, however, also depends on the resuscitation of past expressive forms through enactment, that is, the living experience of performance. From its inception in the spring of 1970 to the present day, *Living Blues* magazine has served this function *par excellence*. As its title indicates, *Living Blues* has sought to breathe vitality into historical forms through a vision that has emphasized their relevance to contemporary music. The signifier "living" also connotes the contrasting perception, that much vernacular culture in the latter twentieth century is experienced as "dead," canned, prepackaged, synthetic, and removed from the pulse of actual life.[39] In keeping with this dynamic view, *Living Blues* has promoted blues performers who provide continuity with a relevant and usable past. The editors initially proclaimed, "we believe that the blues is a living tradition,"[40] and as indicated above, the knowledgeable communicator, authenticator role of *Living Blues* writers certainly fulfilled the ideational, historical dimension of the blues tradition. But a living tradition means more than excavating the past through historical interviews, writing lengthy obituaries, and reviewing reissue recordings. First, it meant reviving the careers of older artists, and unless the permanent encoded message of *Living Blues* was going to be "blues is a moribund musical form performed by old blacks for young whites," it also meant promoting active blues performers through recordings and revival engagements. The process of altering one's status from being a member of a folk revival elite who communicated, through narrowcast codes, to being an engaged participant in the business of producing blues entertainment commodities, through broadcast codes, is well articulated by Jim O'Neal:

> This was a gradual thing. I started out just as a writer and collector and I wasn't involved in any business with the musicians really at all. From the early issues on an escalating basis it got to where I was doing more and more with the musicians—trying to book them and later getting into the recording business and working on festivals and tours and just doing more for them than just writing about them. I ran into that real early. I would interview one of the artists and they would immediately start talking to me about why don't I book them or why don't I record

them? I realized that there was more I could be doing but I couldn't do it all. I couldn't do the magazine and record them and try to coordinate some of the other activities. I was just trying to do too many things there for a few years. I decided I'd rather be an active participant right now than an observer and writer, so that is one reason why I made the change [move to Mississippi and resignation from the editorship of *Living Blues* journal].[41]

Like all magazines, *Living Blues* is a form of impression management that provides a framed world, one that espouses a particular set of values through a series of encoded messages. As a vehicle of communication, perhaps the greatest paradox of today's *Living Blues* journal is that it is attempting to appeal to a heterogeneous audience through two contradictory codes. From its inception *Living Blues* journal was aimed at a well-defined group rather than a mass audience, and thus tended to communicate through a narrowcast code. Yet, because of economic pressures as well as the popular and marketable nature of its object, an historic popular music, the journal has slowly drifted from a narrowcast code toward a broadcast code. Like the publishers of any fanzine, the original editors of *Living Blues* wanted their publication to be viable and popular among blues enthusiasts, and so it may be argued that elements of a broadcast code have been observable since the early issues. Thus, its structure rapidly became highly "formulaic," i.e., *Living Blues* readers could anticipate variations of content within the boundaries of familiar and well-established conventional structures (e.g., identical editorial fields; reports of blues events; at least one interview per issue; classifieds; record reviews and advertisements). In keeping with a broadcast code then, the cultural experience of the *Living Blues* audience has long been an important source of the journal's redundant messages. But it must be emphasized that, although the relatively small circulation of the journal has generally been maintained,[42] this audience-experience source has become more and more significant in recent years. Thus the encoded message that has been transmitted with ever-increasing volume through blues news, notices of tours, events reviews, and events programs is "great blues performances are happening everywhere; why aren't you there?" or "why aren't you attending more of these events and getting in on more of the action?" Blues radio guides and hit parade charts based on radio play signify a further, electronic extension of this same other-directed message, a message that clearly moves the blues further away from its stylistically multifarious traditional folk origins toward what might be viewed as a standardized, mass-mediated product featuring star celebrities and glitz.[43] Jim O'Neal reveals that the ennui brought on by these kinds of monotonous, simplistic, redundant messages played a large part in his decision to resign as editor. "I had just gotten tired of trying to keep all the blues news about the touring acts and the high energy blues bands knocking everybody's socks off in this town and that town. You know it just got boring to me after awhile. It had grown to the point where a lot of people were sending in the news and it was kind of self-sufficient in that respect. It didn't need me and I just wasn't that interested in what they were writing about."[44]

Adherents of an original, unconventional, narrowcast code protest when the messages of those codes are conventionalized and adopted by a mass audience through broadcast codes. Their criticism, of course, is always that the newer broadcast versions of the older narrowcast messages are degraded and inferior forms of the originals. They may feel betrayed, therefore, and withdraw their support. Given a relatively steady circulation, a 1987 *Living Blues* journal survey, indicating that over 50 percent of the readership has been reading the publication for less than five years, reveals that, indeed, many longtime readers have dropped out recently.[45] In the case of *Living Blues* and its readership, then, the movement from narrowcast to broadcast codes has coincided with the chronological, dialectic flow-and-ebb pattern of folk revival aesthetic experience cited earlier. Thus the withdrawal of a certain portion of older blues revival enthusiasts should not necessarily be lamented, for as indicated earlier the ebb portion of such aesthetic experience involves accommodation to new, unanticipated aesthetic codes, and withdrawal from the subscription lists of a journal is a form of accommodation.

The shift of codes and audiences, however, is also indicative that the blues itself has changed and to a certain extent *Living Blues* journal has changed with it. Atavistic features remain, however, and these should be cited. To begin with, the historical basis for male chauvinism in the blues is less relevant than ever, and it certainly should not be reflected in developmental blues criticism. Blues sung by women, particularly vaudeville-style singers, has always been slighted in *Living Blues* journal. Out of seventy-eight issues, women have been featured on only five covers, and it may be added that greats like Memphis Minnie, Sippie Wallace, or Alberta Hunter, although alive during the journal's tenure, were not among them. Another point of view that might better be thought of as a survival is the blues-as-a-single-performer. While historically many forms of down-home blues were played by soloists, and urban blues have always featured individual entertainers, the recent *Living Blues* survey indicates that blues fans today recognize blues as a collective activity, that is, a music played by groups who interact among themselves and with audiences.[46] This recognition is not reflected in *Living Blues* journal accounts that continue to focus on individual performers while neglecting musical and performance contexts.[47]

In addition to these neglected aspects of content, however, it is the bankrupt "blacks only" policy, a legacy of Paul Garon, that remains the greatest historical anomaly in *Living Blues* today. Through this policy *Living Blues* journal continues to cling to its former exclusivistic, narrowcast code with a dogmatic fervor that is slowly eroding its credibility as a contemporary journal. In his second and final editorial on the "blacks only" policy, Paul Garon used an intriguing, although highly inaccurate analogy to illustrate his point, noting that "a magazine dealing with Eskimo art would hardly be tempted to devote space to reproductions of Eskimo sculpture turned out by white suburbanites, regardless of the *quality* of the suburbanite product."[48]

In American culture there is no basis for comparing the relatively moderate cultural impact of Inuit visual iconic signs to the massive acculturations and syncretisms of African-American and European-American aural symbolic sign systems. Neither blacks nor whites have been resistant to borrowing each other's aggressive sonic signs.[49] Perhaps one of the most powerful images conveying the forceful entry of black music and black life into white culture was made in the 1950s by Norman Mailer. While his focus is jazz, the experience he cites is equally true for blues. He notes that "it is no accident that the source for Hip is the Negro for he has been living on the margin between totalitarianism and democracy for two centuries. But the presence of Hip as a working philosophy in the sub-worlds of American life is probably due to jazz and its *knifelike entrance into culture* [my emphasis]. . . ."[50] The refusal of *Living Blues* to accept any aspect of an acoustic definition of blues is absurd. Music is a primary medium of communication that invades our senses, and as Roland Barthes has perceived, music has an immediate "definitive substance"; it is "an organism which scrupulously contains its own message within itself."[51] Whatever the rationale for the *Living Blues* "blacks only" policy, until relatively recently when some younger blacks, largely in interracial groups, have begun to develop the genre in new directions, this policy has tended to delimit blues to historical forms, thus placing severe restrictions on any potential for further generic growth. Thus most writers for *Living Blues* have been exclusively concerned with recognizable traditional black musical forms to the neglect of contemporary black culture or a disparagement of its modern musical manifestations. Interestingly, the racial-cultural policy of *Living Blues* has placed the journal recently in the paradoxical position of having to give support to a highly creative modern blues performer, Robert Cray, who though being black and appreciating blues roots, is the first to admit that his own childhood reflects the same kind of middle-class existence that children of all descents from other American career military families have experienced. Cray first learned blues not in juke joints or from records by Robert Johnson and Blind Blake, but rather from recordings by Eric Clapton of the Cream and Jimi Hendrix. As he explained in *Living Blues*, his personal life history makes it difficult to sing the songs of older blues singers: "I can't sing the songs with the same kind of emotion, or the same kind of stories as those guys that lived in the South and picked cotton . . . that moved to Chicago could sing. . . . Those are my blues songs that I sing about."[52]

It should be clear, therefore, that the most important reason for curtailing the "blacks only" policy is that it is demeaning to contemporary black blues artists. The historic roots of the music must always be acknowledged and viewed in terms of black cultural tradition. Older blacks have appreciated and still welcome being the well-deserved recipients of deference, plaudits, monetary rewards, honorary recognition, as well as other "affirmative actions" that not only publicly display the great musical accomplishments of these artists but also symbolically assist in rectifying the inequities of the past. However, it is important to emphasize that younger blacks want their skills to compete among all blues performers, and as musicians with increasingly similar backgrounds to their white contemporaries, their understanding of blues, like that of whites, has become more acoustic, intellectual, and less derived from actual Jim Crow experience. Therefore, they see no reason to be judged separately from whites who play music in the blues tradition. One might cite the analogy of Quincy Jones, the jazz great and music producer, who was recently asked how it felt to be one of America's top black producers. His response was that he did not want to be thought of as one of America's top *black* producers, rather, he wanted to be recognized as one of *America's* top producers. In other words, he wanted his achievements to be judged against everyone else's, regardless of race. In the case of contemporary blues, whites and blacks have often learned from the same recorded sources and have interchanged musical ideas amongst themselves. They jam with each other and/or are in the same bands together, and there is no need here to list even the most prominent of the many, many interracial bands that currently exist worldwide. As Boggs has observed, "there are many talented [white] musicians who have made their own contributions to blues and who, consequently, have the support of the black blues community itself."[53] Blues, like jazz before it, has become a music of all races and ethnicities, in large part because internationally so many people can relate to the black experience as expressed in music. These same persons find it especially reprehensible when *Living Blues* fails to publish understanding appreciations of fallen blues artists such as Mike Bloomfield and Paul Butterfield.

It may be argued that the deaths of these white musicians were covered in mass magazines like *Rolling Stone,* but in fact blues fans should have expected a more sensitive, knowledgeable, and in-depth treatment of their careers and contributions from *Living Blues* than from any popular music source. They instead had to deal with an inexplicable silence. I would like to close by quoting from Mike Bloomfield's remarkably honest little book about his relationship with Big Joe Williams, *Big Joe and Me,* for he articulates better than I ever could, the cross-cultural triumph of the blues tradition: "Joe's world wasn't my world, but his music was. It was my life; it would be my life. So playing on was all I could do, and I did it the best that I was able. And the music I played, I knew where it came from; and there was not any way I'd forget."[54]

NOTES

I initially presented this article as a paper in March 1988 on a "Blues People and Blues Cultures" panel of a conference held by the Popular Culture Association in New Orleans. The panel was chaired by William Ferris, director of the Center for the Study of Southern Culture at the University of Mississippi, publisher of *Living Blues.* At the time he mentioned that my criticisms and concerns were appreciated and that they were shared by others; he asked me for a copy of the presentation. I am pleased to report that since then, for whatever reasons, *Living Blues* has altered its content and is addressing criticisms regarding race and blueswomen. *Living Blues* has improved.

1. Cheech Marin and Tommy Chong, *Cheech and Chong.* Special thanks to Michael Kolonel for first bringing this record to my attention and for providing me with discographical information. *Living Blues* journal first appeared in the spring of 1970 and has continued publication to the present day. The most extensive blues-revival accounts are popular histories of the blues revival in Britain, and that is appropriate since organized British interest in blues preceded and became a model for similar activities in the United States and elsewhere. The standard general account is Groom, *The Blues Revival.* The activities of British blues musicians have been traced more recently by participant Brunning in his *Blues.*

2. On the worldwide impact of "Dallas," see Katz and Liebes, "Decoding *Dallas.*"

3. It is interesting to compare Charters's account of Mayo Williams's alleged payment to Jefferson for Paramount recording sessions: "At the end of a recording session, Williams would have a few dollars for him, a bottle and a prostitute" (*The Country Blues,* p. 64).

4. Hear the remarkable interview of Blind Willie McTell by John A. Lomax, "Monologue on Accidents," *Blind Willie McTell: 1940.*

5. Interview with Jim O'Neal, 18 March 1988.

6. Interview with Amy van Singel, 18 March 1988.

7. Van Singel interview. For more comments on complimentary coverage see her editorial for the tenth anniversary issue, "No Special Writer Here."

8. O'Neal, "Leaving Blues," p. 2.

9. The editors were Diane Allmen, Paul Garon, Bruce Iglauer, Jim O'Neal, Andre Souffront, Amy van Singel, and Tim Zorn. There was an interim period during which *Living Blues* journal was a bimonthly, as it is now.

10. Van Singel interview.

11. Ibid.

12. O'Neal, "Editorial."

13. O'Neal, "Leaving Blues," p. 2.

14. On narrowcast and broadcast codes see Fiske, *Introduction to Communication Studies,* pp. 78–81.

15. Like most discussions of folk revival, these prerequisites have been influenced by Wallace's classic discussion of "revitalization movements." While his model is still useful, parts of it, portraying the social organism under stress and the supernatural qualities of political movements, appear quite dated. See "Revitalization Movements."

16. On nostalgia and folklore see Narváez, " 'The Newfie Bullet.' " The best work on nostalgia and popular culture is Fred Davis, *Yearning for Yesterday.*

17. Some revitalization movements, such as the cargo cults, embrace cultural forms that are perceived as being foreign. See Wallace, "Revitalization Movements," p. 267. This is not usually apparent in folk revivals, although perceived racial boundaries have made the foreign element a factor in the blues revival.

18. Hence the dismay of contemporary revivalists who "discover" older performers who made commercial disc recordings in the past only to find their informants' contemporary performances lacking because of changes of repertoire, content, style, or differences of instrumentation (e.g., acoustic to electric). At this point, the revivalist may maintain that the performer "peaked" in her early years, thus viewing the artist's "new" aesthetic preferences as being attributable to incompetence due to age, alcoholism, or disease.

19. Guralnick, "Searching for Robert Johnson," p. 27.

20. Boggs, "The Blues Tradition," p. 116.

21. Keil, *Urban Blues;* Mailer, "The White Negro."

22. Malone, *Southern Music, American Music.*

23. See the introductory remarks in Sackheim, *The Blues Line.* This also is the position expressed in the *Toronto Blues Society Newsletter.*

24. Toelken notes that bystander audiences "may in fact be the most enthusiastic about those aspects of performance style that match their own stereotypical expectations. These people may also affect the nature of the performance, but the influence may lie along the lines of outsiders' taste." See *The Dynamics of Folklore,* p. 108.

25. On active and passive bearers of tradition see von Sydow, "On the Spread of Tradition." The advent of audiovisual technology has muddled the clarity of von Sydow's passive and active bearer categories, performance categories that were used to describe the workings of folklore diffusion via the sensory media of "oral tradition."

26. Sometimes such bystanders have been active performing participants but have managed to ideologically maintain their cultural distance, thus achieving a

passive posture of sorts. For example, Paul Garon, an author, former *Living Blues* editor, and musician, acknowledges that he will "never forget" publicly performing with the late Big Joe Williams; see Garon, "Big Joe Williams." But Garon believes that because he is white, whatever he himself plays, I would assume even as an accompanist, despite its black cultural source, is *not* blues; see Garon, "Editorial" [1].

27. I say "almost identical" because the wearing factor of analogue discs creates more and more noise with repeated playings, thus seriously altering original fidelity. Interestingly enough, the sounds of "scratchy" records have often been appealing to blues enthusiasts who experience such noise as a sign of age and legendary value, a distorted but engaging window to the past. The frozen, immutable quality of performances on records has also contributed to dogmatic and static musical aesthetics that are based on "favorite," repeatable moments, moments that performers in person are expected to replicate; almost inevitably their living re-creations fall short of the mark.

28. Charters, *The Country Blues;* Evans, *Big Road Blues;* Ferris, *Blues from the Delta;* Guralnick, *Feel Like Going Home;* Leadbitter, *Nothing But the Blues;* Oliver, *The Meaning of the Blues;* Rowe, *Chicago Breakdown;* and Titon, *Early Downhome Blues.*

29. O'Neal interview.

30. Van Singel interview.

31. For example see: "Eddy Clear Water"; Welding, "Gambler's Blues"; and O'Neal, "Joe Willie Wilkins." Also in the "black voice" category one would have to include Willie Dixon's sporadic question-and-answer column, "I Am the Blues," which commenced in 1976.

32. Exceptions include O'Neal, "[Harmonica Frank Floyd]," and the inclusion of white groups in supplemental festival programs, e.g., Sandmel, "The Nighthawks."

33. Garon, "Editorial" [1]; Garon, "Editorial" [2].

34. Van Singel, "Ann Arbor Blues and Jazz Festival 1972."

35. Garon, "Editorial" [1].

36. Van Singel interview.

37. "Blues Questions and Answers" first appeared in issue #6 and sporadically continued through issue #39.

38. E.g., the fieldwork articles in issues #5, 6, 11, 12, 13, 32, and 63.

39. Hence the thirst for and enthusiasm that greets "real" things that hold the possibility of immediate success or failure such as live sporting events and the comic TV variety show *Saturday Night Live.*

40. Allmen et al., "[Editorial]."

41. O'Neal interview.

42. The circulation today is approximately six thousand (special thanks to Brett Bonner of the *Living Blues* staff for this information). According to Jim O'Neal that is generally what it was before the move to Mississippi.

43. For an update of Adorno's argument that popular music is standardized by industrial capitalism in the same manner that material commodities are, see Gendron, "Theodor Adorno Meets the Cadillacs."

44. O'Neal interview.

45. Peter Lee, "Living Blues Survey," unpublished photocopied results of survey conducted in the fall of 1987. The same sense of betrayal is reflected by the reaction of an older guard of knowledgeable *Living Blues* journal readers to the directions that the "W. C. Handy Awards" have taken in recent years. See "Handy Awards Forum."

46. Peter Lee, "Living Blues Survey." The top seven types of blues that interest *Living Blues* readers the most are group forms.

47. An excellent article that portrays a blues group (Lonnie Brooks) on the road is Freedman, "Blues Breaker."

48. Garon, "Editorial" [2]. Garon goes much further in condemning the "damage" that whites have inflicted on the blues in his *Blues and the Poetic Spirit*, pp. 40–61.

49. For example, see Narváez, "Afro-American and Mexican Street Singers," and O'Neal, "Interview: Lillian McMurry."

50. Mailer, "The White Negro," p. 313.

51. Barthes, *The Eiffel Tower*, p. 121.

52. Varner, "Robert Cray," p. 19. Brunning, *Blues*, p. 10, cites an even stronger statement by Cray: "Anybody can sing the blues, you don't have to be black. I wasn't born in the South and picked cotton; I like to sing this music because it's about real life situations." The most perceptive piece on Cray is Gilmore, "Blues with a Bullet."

53. Boggs, "The Blues Tradition," p. 132.

54. Bloomfield, *Me and Big Joe*, p. 39.

Rethinking Folk Revivalism: Grass-roots Preservationism and Folk Romanticism

Richard Blaustein

My active interest in folk music bloomed in the summer of 1959 after attending a Pete Seeger concert in western Massachusetts. I returned to Abraham Lincoln High School in Brooklyn, New York, that fall to find that many of my classmates were similarly smitten. Lincoln High was located in the Brighton Beach section, a hotbed of progressive politics and thus an early center of urban folk music activity. Woody Guthrie had lived only a few blocks away from our school; hootenannies and folk concerts were regularly held in the neighborhood's union halls and cultural centers. Izzy Young's Folklore Center and the now legendary Sunday picking sessions in Greenwich Village's Washington Square were only a short subway ride away.

After studying the rudiments of old-time and bluegrass banjo with Roger Sprung, one of New York City's first Scruggs-style pickers, I took up the fiddle, largely because of infatuation with the sound and style of the New Lost City Ramblers. By 1961, I was a member of a hybrid bluegrass–old-time band at Brooklyn College that performed extensively at concerts and coffeehouses in New York and New England; in 1963, we transformed ourselves into a jug band during a shortlived fad that evaporated the very next year with the arrival of folk rock and the British invasion. Suddenly I found myself part of a small but fervent group of diehard citybillies who kept on playing old-time music and bluegrass regardless of the shifting currents of musical fashion.

Even then, I was distressed by pronouncements by kingpins of the urban folk music revival declaring that a performer had to be born and nurtured in a traditional community to be considered an authentic folk musician. The country fiddlers I had begun to visit and record up in western New

England seemed perfectly happy to teach me what they knew regardless of my New York Jewish background. Unencumbered by purist preconceptions, they considered anyone who enjoyed and played old-time music to be one of their own kind. In fact, they were especially pleased to see a big-city kid showing so much enthusiasm for old-time country music.

After I become a card-carrying member of the Vermont-based Northeast Fiddlers Association in 1966, I realized that I had bridged the gap between something that was being called a revival (but which was really more like a crosscultural transfusion) and a genuine grass-roots folk revival of fiddle music that was spreading across the United States and Canada without any apparent attention from professional folklorists.[1] Having established credibility in this movement as a successful contest fiddler and certified fiddle contest judge, I began to reconstruct the history of these grass-roots organizations devoted to the preservation and perpetuation of old-time fiddling as a living art. The realization that the growth of the old-time fiddlers associations could be studied as a contemporary cultural revitalization movement gave me the impetus to pursue a career in folklore and write a doctoral dissertation on the subject.[2]

At least two major revivals of traditional fiddle music occurred in the United States during this century. The first took place in the early 1920s. The country had just shifted from a war economy to a domestic consumer economy; the nation's population for the first time in American history had become predominantly urban rather than rural; and a revolutionary new African-American style, jazz, was driving all competitors out of the mainstream of popular culture. Several folklorists including Simon Bronner, Paul Wells, and I have written about the role of Henry Ford in promoting the revival of old-time fiddling and dancing during this period;[3] apart from Wayne Daniel's research on the Atlanta fiddle contests and their sponsor, the Georgia Fiddlers' Association, little is known about the formation of fiddling organizations in other sections of the United States during the twenties.[4]

A second revival of old-time fiddling, which continues today, took shape in the late fifties and early sixties. Once again, the United States had experienced the transition from wartime austerity to a burgeoning domestic consumer economy; the farming population of the country continued to plummet, accelerated by advances in agricultural technology and applied chemistry; and yet another innovative African-American–based style, rock and roll, was capturing the imagination of an increasingly youthful popular entertainment audience. Nashville record producers were abandoning instruments with distinctively rural connotations like the fiddle and steel guitar in order to penetrate broader urban and youth markets. Though the urban folk music revival undoubtedly played a positive role in redefining the value and worth of older forms of country music like old-time fiddling, this second revival of fiddle music was not a direct product of that revival. It appears to be a genuine grass-roots preservationist movement. Between 1963, when the Idaho Old-Time Fiddlers Association was officially chartered, and 1974, no less than twenty-four regional, state, and national old-time fiddlers associations had been established throughout most of the United States.[5] The results of a mail survey that I conducted in 1984–85 with the invaluable cooperation of Charlie Walden of the Missouri State Old-Time Fiddlers Association showed that the number of active fiddlers organizations had doubled in ten years; while some of the older associations had fissioned or collapsed, new ones had arisen to take their place, some located in areas that had no fiddling organizations ten years previously.

How can we explain the rise of the old-time fiddlers association movement in post–World II America? Basically, these organizations can be demonstrated to be part of an ongoing cultural revitalization movement, defined by Anthony F. C. Wallace as "any deliberate, conscious, organized attempt by members of a society to create a more satisfying culture."[6] These grass-roots preservationist organizations have emerged because they fulfill enduring expressive needs and desires that mainstream popular entertainment and mass media cannot satisfy. As the British sociologist Anthony D. Smith remarks in *Theories of Nationalism,* "Given the dislocations of industrialisation and urbanisation, what can be more natural than that men should wish to replace the sense of lost community by creating new groups more adapted to the new conditions?"[7] According to Robert T. Anderson, an American anthropologist, the formation of such organizations is a typical response to rapid social change. Voluntary associations like the old-time fiddlers associations provide traditionalists with enclaves of cultural stability in nontraditional environments. Such organizations reorganize older social institutions and give them a new legal-rational structure more in accord with the corporate and bureaucratic patterns of modern social life.[8]

Old-time fiddlers associations encourage the active preservation of the fiddling tradition in various ways. They sponsor fiddle contests and noncompetitive jam sessions. They publish newsletters and foster tape-swapping networks and the production of custom recordings of fiddle music. By these and other means they bring together people who play, enjoy, and identify with this music. All of these activities contribute to a revitalized fiddling tradition in modern America, but perhaps the most significant of them is the old-time fiddlers contest.

Though the fiddle contest tradition in America dates back to colonial times and continues to provide an institutional focus for vital, uninterrupted regional fiddling traditions in the southern Appalachians and the

Southwest, in most other sections of the United States the promotion of fiddle contests has been a major feature of the old-time fiddling revival only since the early 1960s. Currently there are hundreds of contests held under the auspices of old-time fiddlers associations throughout the country.

The proliferation of these events can be attributed to many causes. An important one is increased disposable income and leisure time among the middle-aged and elderly skilled blue-collar and self-employed business people of rural background who form the bulk of the membership of the old-time fiddlers associations. Another is the development of the interstate highway system and the attendant growth of the recreational vehicle industry, which has encouraged the emergence of various types of temporary mobile communities and also the willingness of chambers of commerce and civic organizations to support events that attract tourist dollars. Along with the urbanization of mainstream country music, which has reversed somewhat in the wake of the commercial success of new traditionalists like Emmy Lou Harris and Ricky Skaggs, and the continuing deterioration of the traditional rural social institutions that once provided outlets for fiddlers, these factors have contributed to the emergence of the fiddlers contest as perhaps the most significant context of grass-roots fiddling in the United States today. Younger fiddling buffs pack their families into campers and spend their vacations at contests; some retired people take up fiddling as a full-time avocation and spend their time following the regional and national contest circuits that have sprung up across the continent.

There are good reasons for claiming that, whatever other functions they may serve, modern American fiddle contests are actually secular rites of cultural intensification. Fiddling-contest participants periodically shed the social and economic roles that define them in the outer world to regain a sense of solidarity with others sharing their identification with old-time fiddle music. Though some hardbitten contenders at fiddle contests have been known to closet themselves with their accompanists until they have honed their contest tunes to razor sharpness, most participants are in a relaxed and playful frame of mind. Musicians and spectators assemble in parking lots and campgrounds where they visit back and forth, freely exchanging food and drink.[9] While most contestants will take time out to work up their competition pieces, informal music-making goes on constantly, often from sunset to daybreak.

In contrast to the highly structured and controlled quality of contest performance, the music at these parking-lot picking sessions is typically exuberant and occasionally inspired. New tunes and licks are learned and swapped during these sessions; when top contenders are involved, the result may be pyrotechnic displays of improvisatory virtuosity reminiscent of the "cutting contests" of jazz musicians in which each participant attempts to outdo the others with novel and intricate variations on the old tunes. Nonperformers hover on the fringes, not only step dancing or just soaking in the music but frequently recording it on portable tape recorders; expert amateur recordists with high-quality equipment are also commonly found at the formal competitions as well. When they are not actually jamming or competing, the musicians and their friends and families spend their time discussing the merits and weighing the chances of the various contestants, comparing instruments and exchanging instrument lore, listening to tapes, telling stories and jokes, and otherwise behaving like a modern folk group. Old friends who have met through fiddling associations and contests will generally try to camp together; these events not only serve to bolster the musical tradition itself but they also recreate the atmosphere of the family reunions, communal labor events, and the other traditional rural social institutions at which old-time fiddling played such an important role in the past.

A contemporary fiddle contest is not, however, a literal return to the past. As Anthony F. C. Wallace maintains: "Once cultural transformation has been accomplished and the new cultural system has proven itself viable, and once the movement has solved its problems of routinization, a new steady state may be said to exist. The culture of this state will probably be different in pattern, organization and *Gestalt* as well as traits from the earlier steady state; it will be different from that of the period of cultural distortion."[10]

Musically speaking, the pressures of competition have resulted in the dominance of a highly polished, deliberate, complicated style of contest fiddling, strongly based in the longbow techniques of Oklahoma and Texas. This has led many ambitious competitors to abandon local styles and tunes in favor of Southwest-based contest fiddling, a development that upsets some fiddler association members but seems perfectly natural to others. Given the overall tendency in modern societies toward increasing technical complexity and specialization, the development of sophisticated, cosmopolitan competition styles like contemporary American contest fiddling really should come as no surprise, however disturbing this might be to people who are emotionally attached to the older forms.

Indeed, the emergence of these redefined and reconstructed cultural patterns and social institutions obliges the folklorist to reflect upon the validity of basic assumptions that have shaped the profession's philosophy and practice. Presently many folklorists on both sides of the Atlantic are reconsidering basic definitions of folklore. Regina Bendix has observed that a growing number of European folklorists have rejected purist, antiquarian concepts of folk society and culture and have accepted the notion that folklorismus, or the folk romantic movement, is a legitimate and perhaps even central folkloristic concern in a rapidly changing modern world.[11] Herman Bausinger has decided that folklore and folklorismus are ultimately inseparable; Ulrike Bodemann and Konrad Köstlin have independently concluded that folk revivalism, one of the most common expressions of folklorism, is a compensatory response to social and cultural displacement: folk revivals can actually be explained as a recurrent type of cultural revitalization movement.[12]

Some North American folklorists have also begun to take folk revivalism seriously; in general, though, the subject of folk revivalism still arouses confusion and controversy among professional folklorists on this side of the Atlantic. As Bruce Jackson comments in his article "The Folksong Revival," most American folklorists who entered the profession during the late fifties through mid-seventies, when the "folklore vs. fakelore" controversy was still a live issue, found it expedient to enhance their scholarly credibility by disassociating themselves from the so-called urban folk music revival.[13]

Only quite recently have American folklorists recognized the limitations of traditional concepts of folklore that ultimately derive from the ideology and rhetoric of romantic nationalism. Barbara Kirshenblatt-Gimblett has recently challenged the elitist, exclusionary implications of these organic romantic notions, particularly the idea that an individual must be born into a given social or cultural group to be a legitimate participant in its expressive traditions. She suggests that concepts of voluntary or intentional ethnicity espoused by American social theorists such as Anya Royce and Werner Sollors and antihegemonic theories of cultural revivalism developed by Eric Hobsbawm and other British sociologists and anthropologists influenced by the Italian Marxist philosopher Antonio Gramsci can help lead American folklorists toward a more realistic understanding of folk culture in contemporary societies.[14]

The shift in American folkloristics from a textual focus toward a contextual focus has led the profession in a progressively sociological direction. Simon Bronner has noted growing interest among folklorists in studying the expressive culture of formal organizations.[15] I would submit that the profession has even more to gain by focusing upon the history of the development of voluntary organizations expressly established to preserve and promote various forms of folk culture. The emergence of associations and institutions fostering the revival of ethnic, regional, and national folk traditions, especially music and dance, has accompanied the rise of the bureaucratic, industrial nation-state and in many ways appears to be a universal form of compensation for displacement and alienation arising from social change. The establishment of voluntary associations centering around folk arts helps to give immigrants and other displaced people a sense of stability that compensates for the anomie resulting from rapid social change.[16] The challenge to folklorists is to adequately account for the complex dialectics of:

1. modernization and traditionalization;
2. hegemony and separatism;
3. grass-roots preservationism and transethnic folk romanticism;
4. localized efforts to preserve distinctive cultural identity and the transmutation of kinship-based traditions into the collective property of affinity or special interest groups.

One source of folk revivalism is alienation from an unsatisfactory cultural identity, leading to folk romanticism; a second source is a subjective sense of deteriorating tradition, resulting in grass-roots preservationism. Historically, these two types of folk revival movements are equally prevalent and rarely separable; instead, they tend to reinforce one another in a symbiotic fashion.

This is certainly true of folk music revivals. As Philip V. Bohlman suggests in *The Study of Folk Music in the Modern World*, "the concept 'folk music' is in need of considerable overhaul and . . . we need to wrench its moorings from a cultural setting which no longer exists, if it ever did."[17] Indeed, Bohlman says we need to reassess how we think about folk music. The quest for the archaic and authentic distorts and restricts our capacity to envision the full range of modern musical cultures: "Exceptional has been the perspective that did not turn toward the past, idealizing and revering a community of folk music that was just out of reach and then fretting over the best ways to rescue folk music before it disappeared."[18]

Bohlman recognizes the positive significance of folk revivals as forms of adaptation to changing social conditions: "new groups form as societies become more complex, creating in the place of overall collectivity sublevels in which these groups spawn new forms of expressive behavior."[19] Bohlman challenges the assumption that the development of mass media and popular culture inevitably results in cultural homogenization, or to use Alan Lomax's pet term, "cultural grey-out": "modernization encourages new ways of looking at old styles and different repertoires and thereby sets the stage for revivals and revitalization."[20]

Like his student Philip Bohlman, the ethnomusicologist Bruno Nettl accepts adaptation and synthesis as normal features of evolving, changing traditions. Instead of dismissing transcultural and interethnic manifestations of folk revivalism from serious consideration, Nettl seeks to understand their meaning and value to all of the various kinds of people who become involved in them. Nettl also questions the validity of the concept of cultural grey-out, predicated in the romantic assumption of a pure, organic community, and proposes instead an adaptive and pluralistic model of musical acculturation that allows for change and choice: "Once, a people had its own music; more recently, it might 'have' or participate in many musics, but perhaps only one with which it truly identifies itself. And from this also stems the strong interest of ethnomusicologists in the emblematic function of music, the emphasis on music as closely related to ethnicity, its immediately recognizable sound one of the most powerful symbols of the group."[21]

Nettl is philosophically in accord with theorists like Anya Royce and Werner Sollors concerning the active role of individuals in defining their personal and collective identities. Royce proposes that people manipulate their identities in varying contexts to attain optimum personal satisfaction; identity is not merely a matter of external ascription and pedigree but is subject to the conscious decisions of individuals concerning how they present themselves to others. It is not enough to say that modern people live in multicultural societies; rather, Royce insists, we must recognize that individuals as well as societies can be multicultural and transethnic: "An 'ethnic group' is a reference group invoked by people who share a common historical style (which may only be assumed), based on overt features and values, and who, through the process of interaction with others, identify themselves as sharing that style."[22]

Werner Sollors is also highly conscious of the limitations of traditional concepts of ethnicity: "we have to develop a terminology that goes beyond the organicist imagery of roots and can come to terms with the pervasiveness and inventiveness of syncretism."[23] Like Royce, Sollors sees modern ethnicity not as the simple extension of long-standing cultural traditions but rather as a countervalent creative response toward assimilation through which individuals and groups reassert distinctive identity by adopting and espousing particular styles of expression: "Modern ethnicization is a form of symbolic boundary constructing which increases cultural vitality."[24]

One of the most influential recent scholarly works to deal with these questions is Hobsbawm and Ranger's *The Invention of Tradition*. Hobsbawm sees the invention of tradition as a recurrent process of substantiating the distinctive identity of a group by imputing antiquity (and hence authenticity and legitimacy) to forms of cultural expression that may actually be very new. Romantic nationalist and ethnic separatist movements, typically led by alienated middle-class individuals (here we see the influence of Gramsci), are attempts to offset hegemony; that is, acceptance of the cultural dominance of a ruling elite. However, Hobsbawm notes that such cultural movements are not restricted to disaffected intellectuals who develop romantic identification with other, presumably more colorful and soulful social strata; they also occur on the grass-roots level as reactions to physical and psychological displacements caused by modernization, urbanization, and industrialization.[25] Whether such attempts at cultural revitalization stem from ideological alienation or actual socioeconomic displacement, they share a common goal: the restoration of an idealized communal culture believed to be in danger of disintegration.

Many folklorists tend to characterize folk revivalists as disaffected middle-class intellectuals who have developed romantic identification with some idealized exotic group. However, when devoted tradition-bearers believe cherished forms of cultural expression to be in danger of dying out, they too will actively attempt to establish voluntary organizations devoted to their revival. Organized efforts to preserve folk music date back to the beginning of the eighteenth century in the British Isles; these early revivals of Welsh, Scottish, and Irish folk music were promoted by nostalgic immigrants, a pattern still very much alive today. Many illuminating parallels can be drawn between revivals of traditional instrumental music in the United States and the British Isles.

Peter Cooke, in *The Fiddle Tradition of the Shetland Isles*, recognizes the significance of organizations devoted to the active preservation and perpetuation of traditional music.[26] There are several such organizations in the Shetlands that promote traditional fiddling. These include the Shetland Folk Society, established in 1946; the Shetland Fiddlers Society, which includes the famous fiddle band Da Forty Fiddlers, founded in 1960 by the noted fiddler and revival promoter Tom Anderson; and also several local groups including the Lerwick Accordion and Fiddle Club (no date given) and the Unst Fiddle Society (1967). These organizations all provide regular opportunities for performers and enthusiasts to play and enjoy traditional music. Cooke stresses that the style of music that comes out of these clubs is not necessarily "da aald Shetland fiddling"; as in North America, fiddling has been heavily affected by classical violin tone and technique; in the particular case of the Shetlands, contemporary mainland Scottish fiddling has also been very influential.

An interesting development in Shetland has been the incorporation of fiddling into the local educational curriculum. Upon his retirement from business in 1971, Tom Anderson devoted himself entirely to teaching fiddle to Shetland children, most of them girls, in the public schools. Peter Cooke and Pamela Swing, an American folklorist and fiddle music scholar who worked with Anderson as a fiddling teacher in the Shetland schools, independently report that this project has encouraged the emergence of a syncretic "New Shetland" style with clearly transregional elements rather than the antiquarian resurrection of older Shetland fiddling styles. Comparable developments can be found in Ireland and the United States, where we observe elaborate, standardized contest or exhibition styles seemingly submerging older, more localized repertories and performance techniques. Here the institutionalization of traditional music through formal organizations and competitive events, and also the development of specialized media networks diffusing custom albums and cassettes of currently fashionable fiddle stylists, replaces the premodern "classic folk" patterns of performance and communication based on oral transmission and direct face-to-face contact. These changes in Shetland fiddling can be considered a clear-cut example of the selective reconstruction of tradition.

On the mainland of Scotland, active attempts to collect, publish, and promote traditional music date back at least two hundred years. George Emmerson states that devotion to Scottish national music by members of all social classes continued through the course of the eighteenth century.[27] Published collections of Scottish songs and dance tunes compiled by amateur and professional musicians appeared in print as early as 1726 in Edinburgh. The Highland Society, established in 1776 by Scottish gentlemen residing in London, sponsored a piping contest at the 1781 Falkirk Tryst, a yearly cattle market.[28] Fiddle contests were also part of Scottish musical culture; an article in the *Scots Magazine* in 1809 describes the young Niel Gow (1727–1807), Robert Burns's favorite fiddler, winning a contest that included the finest players in all of Scotland. Gow's victory resulted in his patronage by the Duke of Atholl and later the Countess of Gordon.[29] George Emmerson records that J. Scott Skinner (1843–1927) won a similar competition that included the major fiddlers of his day in Inverness in 1863, and that fiddling contests had been common for over a century.[30]

Another wave of Scottish grass-roots preservationism expressed itself in the formation of strathspey and reel societies. The Edinburgh Strathspey and Reel Society was established in 1881. "Interest in fiddle music then seemed to be in decline," noted the organization's first president, James Stewart Robertson, in the society's minutes, and hence it was "very desirable that this class of music not be allowed to fall back as undoubtedly it was doing for the past few years."[31] The outcome was the establishment of a voluntary association for "upholding and developing the taste for our old national highland strathspey and reel music on the fiddle."[32] The idea of the strathspey and reel society spread only gradually; a Highland Reel and Strathspey Society was founded in 1903, a similar group was organized in Aberdeen in 1928, and the Elgin Strathspey and Reel Society began in 1937. There was also an Orkney Reel and Strathspey Society as well.[33] These groups, which feature large numbers of fiddlers playing written arrangements of fiddle tunes under the direction of conductors, are still quite popular in Scotland; similar groups can also be found in Canada's Cape Breton and Prince Edward Island.

A more recent development in the revitalization of Scottish traditional music has been the advent of accordion and fiddle clubs since the early 1970s. There are now over fifty such clubs in various parts of Scotland. Like American old-time fiddlers associations, these groups meet monthly or bimonthly and provide their members with opportunities to meet and play with other amateurs of traditional music; occasionally the clubs also sponsor concerts by outstanding professional fiddlers and accordionists.[34] A coordinating organization, the National Association of Accordion and Fiddle Clubs, which corresponds to the National Old-Time Fiddlers Association in the United States, also exists.[35]

Fiddle contests are still important in Scotland. Some major contemporary contests include the National Fiddle Competition initiated by the BBC in 1969, the Golden Fiddle Award contest organized by the *Daily Mail* in 1977, and the National Fiddle Championship, sponsored by the Lothian District Council, which also was begun in 1977.[36]

Like Scotland, Ireland also has a long, continuous history of folk music revivalism. Captain Francis O'Neill (1849–1936), himself one of the greatest of Ireland's migrant folk revivalists, noted that the revival of the Irish harp was initiated by James Dungan, an Irish merchant in Copenhagen, who organized and subsidized three gatherings of Irish harpers in Granard, County Longford, in 1781, 1782, and 1783.[37] In 1791, a group of "patriotic gentlemen" organized a harp festival in Belfast; in 1807 they formed the Belfast Harp Society, which sponsored an annual harping festival that lasted through the 1830s. A Dublin Harp Society was formed in 1807, and a later revival of Irish harping was led by Father T. V. Burke, who founded a new harp society in Drogheda in 1842, which only lasted a few years.[38] The formation of the Society for the Preservation and Publication of the Melodies of Ireland by the collector-revivalist George Petrie resulted in the publication of *The Petrie Collection of the Ancient Music of Ireland* in 1855. The Gaelic League, founded in 1893, was very active in promoting Irish traditional music and dance around the turn of the century.

Comhaltas Ceoltoiri Eireann is the most substantial modern organization devoted to the preservation of Irish traditional music. Founded in 1951 as an offshoot and extension of the Piper's Club of Dublin, which dates back to 1908, the CCE presently has four hundred branch societies in Ireland and ten other countries that meet regularly to offer instruction in Irish music and dance; it sponsors a series of contests that culminates in an annual international Irish folk arts festival, the *Fleadh Cheoil,* and also maintains a paid professional staff through membership fees and government grants.[39] Current membership of the organization is approximately thirty-five thousand, with thousands of competitors and hundreds of thousands of spectators taking part in its events.

Like the old-time fiddlers' contest in the United States, the *fleadh cheoil* is perhaps the most important context of performance for modern performers of Irish traditional music. These competitions are organized in hierarchical order, ranging from county and regional to provincial and national. Forty-three *fleadhs* were held in 1981; forty-five in 1984. The national competition, the *Fleadh Cheoil na hEireann*, attracts participants from all over Ireland, with substantial contingents from Britain and the United States.

Edwin O. Henry, who has studied this centralized organization, notes its effects on Irish traditional music, which parallel modern contest-oriented instrumental styles in Scotland and North America. While certain instruments and genres are encouraged, others are not. Players of the uilleann pipes are welcomed; musicians playing Irish tunes on the bouzouki are excluded. To simplify the task of judging, only the jig, reel, hornpipe, and slow air are permitted in competition; other more restricted tune types such as the polka and the slide are banned from competition. As Henry says, this policy validates certain aspects of the ongoing tradition while delegitimating others. Parallels to this situation can be found in arguments among American contest fiddlers concerning, for example, the age of tunes and the use of tunings other than standard GDAE. In Ireland as elsewhere, competition accelerates stylistic change and standardization. It is only natural that competitors should emulate the performances of winning contestants, but the unintended result is the restriction of the full range of styles and tunes to suit the criteria of the judges.

According to Henry, one of the obvious effects of competition is the increasing technical refinement of fiddling and the assimilation of classical violin technique—which Peter Cooke refers to as "the Westernization of Western music." As in the United States, tape recorders and custom albums have made the music of outstanding competitors easily accessible to aspiring contestants.[40] Clearly not a purist or antiquarian, Henry feels that revivalist organizations like the CCE can only preserve the traditions they espouse in a selective, syncretic fashion, and that their major role in modern societies is to provide new contexts of performance for evolving cultural traditions.

Like Henry, Bruno Nettl believes that revivals of traditional music enable modern people to offset disorientation and displacement by enabling them to periodically regenerate an idealized primordial community that is evoked through particular historical musical styles: "As other means of identification become less effective, music is increasingly stressed. I would agree this is why world music of the twentieth century has retained its diversity."[41]

Displacement can be symbolic as well as literal; alienation, the more abstract form of displacement, accounts for transcultural folk romantic movements like the urban folk music revival in the United States and Britain. Historically, the alienation of middle-class intellectuals from urban, industrial, commercial, bureaucratic values has characteristically led to romantic identification with idealized folk communities that have seemingly preserved their primal integrity, uncorrupted by the metropolis.[42] Disaffected people reacting against perceived strictures and constraints of an oppressive social order will often attempt to create more satisfying identities for themselves by taking on selected aspects of the cultural symbology of romanticized exotics. As the cultural anthropologist George De Vos observes: "the ethnic identity of a group of people consists of their subjective symbolic or emblematic use of any aspect of culture, in order to differentiate themselves from other groups. These emblems can be imposed from outside or embraced from within."[43]

The folklorist R. Raymond Allen addresses the challenging question of adaptive cultural identity in his article "Old-Time Music and the Urban Folk Revival."[44] Noting that academic discussion of the urban folk revival movement dates back at least to 1963, when the *New York Folklore Quarterly* published the proceedings of a symposium devoted to the controversial subject, Allen views Jan Brunvand's dismissal of urban folk revivalism as "irrelevant to the study of folklore" as a reflection of "historical short-sightedness and failure to recognize the cultural significance of the phenomenon."[45] Allen considers the recent urban folk revival a specific manifestation of a continuing history of at least two hundred years of romantic folk revivalism in the Western world rather than an isolated event.[46] He postulates that old-time music "revivalists," that is, musicians who have adopted traditional rural American styles of instrumental folk music not part of their immediate ethnic or geographic backgrounds, have nonetheless developed an authentic sense of community based upon shared affinity. Like other folk romantic movements, the old-time music revival entails the rejection of what is perceived to be a dehumanizing, hegemonic social order and the quest for an idealized primordial community. This particular movement has strong elements of antimodernism, anticommercialism, and antiurbanism: "This romanticizing of rural living through old-time music suggests that what is actually being revived is not only a genre of folk music but cultural elements of a bygone era that symbolize a better way of life."[47]

Allen is one of very few American folklorists who has attempted to relate the development of folk music revivals to the theories of nativism and revitalization propounded by the cultural anthropologists Ralph Linton and Anthony F. C. Wallace:

Strong parallels can be drawn between the revitalistic movements described by Wallace and Linton and the old-time music revival. During the past two decades, many young Americans have felt a disillusionment with their cultural *Gestalt*. Rapid modernization and technological advancements caused psychological stress, which, for a small group, has been eased by the revival of an old folk form symbolic of a happier past when people lived closer to nature. Whether or not rural culture is, in reality, an idyllic garden of Eden, is inconsequential. The point is that old-time music represents the mythos of simpler existence, and playing it brings revivalist musicians spiritually closer to that way of life.[48]

Of course, very much the same thing could be said of nostalgic immigrants who selectively reconstruct their traditional cultures, which highlights the inadequacy of the term "revivalist" as used by most American folklorists. The ethnomusicologist Mark Slobin, in his essay "Rethinking 'Revival' of American Ethnic Music," suggests that folklorists misapply the term "revival" in most cases.[49] In Slobin's opinion, traditions do not usually totally die out; what is actually happening is the reinterpretation or reinvention of traditions rather than their literal rebirth. The term "revival" is widely used because cultural forms are subjectively perceived to decay, even disappear, and then reemerge in revitalized forms.[50] Why do these movements take hold? Slobin suggests that they stem from the recurrent need of individuals to reconsider and reconstruct their social and cultural identities.[51]

Regarding transethnic folk revivalism, Slobin notes: "A great deal of contemporary revivalism is not done by people who claim a direct lineage to the expressive culture involved ... a group of people more or less arbitrarily decides that a certain self-defined tradition means so much to them that they will not only become engrossed in it themselves, but will try to teach it to others, even going so far as returning to the putative homeland of the tradition to do so."[52]

Slobin's students have studied this type of transethnic adaptive folk revivalism in Ireland and Appalachia. In both cases, we find "tourists," who are occasionally and marginally involved in soaking up an exotic tradition, and also "immigrants," who attempt to adopt what they perceive to be the traditional life style of a given culture and who develop apprentice-acolyte relationships with "old masters," people who have bona fide organic connections with the communal tradition in question. These "immigrants" typically serve in mediating and interpretive roles between the "tourists" and the "old masters."[53] Here again, we can see that transethnic cultural relationships based upon affinity, on shared common interest, can often supplement and even come to replace classical communal relationships grounded in kinship and territoriality. The interaction of grass-roots preservationists and folk romantics leads to the creation of new social institutions that focus upon the selective reconstruction of an idealized cultural past. As such, both forms of folk revivalism have a great deal to tell us about the meaning, function, and value of folk traditions in the lives of modern people. To quote Mark Slobin, "They come close to the heart of folklore studies in complex societies whose patterns of affinity-grouping, taste-making and self-conceptualization are extremely fluid and highly stimulating."[54]

The folk romantic movement, or folklorismus, has been a continuously vital aspect of modern life since the eighteenth century. The rejection of the hegemony of urban-industrial-commercial-bureaucratic values and the return (symbolic, periodic, or actual) to an idealized rural-pastoral-spiritual-organic community have appeared in various forms, including the development of academic folklore itself. As Anthony D. Smith observes: "To regenerate the community, and endow it with an original personality, writers and artists institute periodic folk revivals; they go out among the peasants and farmers, commune with nature, record the rhythms of the countryside, and bring them back to the anonymous city, so that rising urban strata may be 'reborn' and possess a clear and unmistakable identity."[55]

Modernization does not inevitably lead toward cultural homogeneity; instead, pressures toward hegemony generate regional, ethnic, and nationalistic separatism. The emergence of voluntary associations devoted to the active preservation and perpetuation of traditional cultures is a commonplace in the modern world. Similarly, the advent of new communications media does not necessarily result in "cultural grey-out," marginal cultures being eclipsed by the mainstream. Instead, we see a multiplicity of special interest groups actively producing their own media networks in response to the sensed inadequacy of mass culture.

Classical models of folk society and culture don't describe what is actually going on in the real world; as long as we permit these mistaken dichotomies to shape the ways in which we serve as partisans, advocates, or presenters of folklife, we will continue to celebrate the cultural legitimacy of some groups of people while delegitimating others, except in passive, predetermined consumer roles.[56] If organically authentic bearers of folk tradition are willing to accept newcomers and outsiders who have come to appreciate and identify with their traditions of expressive culture, then folklorists ought to follow suit and accept the validity and legitimacy of these affinity-based relationships. If folklorists are concerned with being good ethnographers, or social and cultural historians, or something other than proponents of a particularly convoluted form of elitism that perceives itself as populism, then they need to abandon their historic quest for the authentic and concern themselves with the actual.

In conclusion, to do justice to the complex realities of modern social and cultural life, folklorists must examine both forms of folk revivalism, grass-roots preservationism and folk romanticism, in a serious and objective manner. This will entail the abandonment of inaccurate terms and mistaken dichotomies that have resulted in the confusion and controversy still surrounding this subject. A careful reconsideration of the histories of various types of folk revival movements in comparative perspective can revitalize folklore scholarship itself.

NOTES

1. Toelken, "Traditional Fiddling in Idaho," describing the Weiser contest, is a rare exception.

2. Blaustein, "Traditional Music and Social Change."

3. One folklorist was aware of Ford's work at the time: Robert W. Gordon. See Kodish, *Good Friends and Bad Enemies*, p. 59.

4. See Daniel, "Old-Time Georgians Recall." Cauthen, *The Fiddle and Well-Rosined Bow*, provides additional references to state and regional fiddling associations in the South during the twenties.

5. See Blaustein, "Traditional Music and Social Change."

6. Wallace, "Revitalization Movements," p. 279.

7. Anthony D. Smith, *Theories of Nationalism*, p. 28.

8. Anderson, "Voluntary Associations in History," p. 217.

9. See Adler, "Bluegrass Music and Meal-Fried Potatoes."

10. Wallace, "Revitalization Movements," p. 275.

11. Bendix, "Folklorism."

12. Ibid., p. 8.

13. Jackson, "The Folksong Revival," p. 203.

14. Kirshenblatt-Gimblett, "Mistaken Dichotomies."

15. Bronner, *American Folklore Studies*, pp. 125–28.

16. See Anderson, "Voluntary Associations in History."

17. Bohlman, *The Study of Folk Music*, p. xvi.

18. Ibid., p. xix.

19. Ibid., p. 95.

20. Ibid., p. 124; also see Lomax, *Folk Song Style and Culture* pp. 4–6.

21. Nettl, *The Western Impact on World Music*, p. 19.

22. Royce, *Ethnic Identity*, p. 19.

23. Sollors, *Beyond Ethnicity*, p. 15.

24. Ibid., p. 247.

25. Hobsbawm, "Introduction: Inventing Tradition."

26. Cooke, *The Fiddle Tradition of the Shetland Isles*, pp. 127–28.

27. Emmerson, *Rantin' Pipe and Tremblin' String*, p. 39.

28. Alburger, *Scottish Fiddlers and Their Music*, p. 160.

29. Ibid., p. 94.

30. Emmerson, *Rantin' Pipe and Tremblin' String*, p. 102.

31. Alburger, *Scottish Fiddlers and Their Music*, p. 195.

32. Ibid.

33. See Emmerson, *Rantin' Pipe and Tremblin' String*, p. 106.

34. Alburger, *Scottish Fiddlers and Their Music*, p. 197.

35. Munro, *The Folk Music Revival in Scotland*, p. 20.

36. Alburger, *Scottish Fiddlers and Their Music*, p. 203.

37. O'Neill, *Irish Minstrels and Musicians*, p. 474.

38. Ibid., p. 475.

39. Henry, "Institutions."

40. Ibid., p. 92.

41. Nettl, *The Western Impact on World Music*, p. 165.

42. See Anthony D. Smith, *The Ethnic Revival*, pp. xi–xii.

43. De Vos, "Ethnic Pluralism," pp. 16–17.

44. Allen, "Old-Time Music."

45. Ibid., p. 66.

46. Ibid., p. 71.

47. Ibid., p. 78.

48. Ibid., p. 79.

49. Slobin, "Rethinking 'Revival.' "

50. Ibid., pp. 38–39.

51. Ibid., p. 40.

52. Ibid., p. 42.

53. Ibid., p. 43.

54. Ibid.

55. Anthony D. Smith, *The Ethnic Revival*, p. 106.

56. See Kirshenblatt-Gimblett, "Mistaken Dichotomies," p. 151.

The Reception of the Music of American Southern Whites in Japan

Toru Mitsui

In April 1988 I saw for the first time a certain young girls' group, the Nakajima Family Band, playing bluegrass music. The band, which consisted of four sisters ranging from eight to twelve years of age, had been discussed—although not widely—among bluegrass enthusiasts in Japan. The girls are, of course, Japanese by nationality, and speak only the Japanese language.

The band astonished me with several songs, especially "Raw Hide," a fast instrumental number that requires advanced technique. If one listened to the musicians carefully, one could hear that they were inexperienced and rough-edged, because it had been only a year since they had begun to learn how to play the banjo, fiddle, mandolin, and guitar, respectively. The vocals, led by the youngest with a guitar that looked enormous because of her small size, were also unstable, and to me their English pronunciation had an embarrassingly thick Japanese accent. The exception was "Turkey in the Straw," a tune so familiar even in Japan that it has Japanese lyrics. This enabled the girls to deliver much more easily, although there is always a certain strangeness even to me, a Japanese, in hearing the Japanese language accompanied by a typical bluegrass sound. The feeling one got from the whole performance was, however, very pleasant, and it was reinforced by their costumes, complete with cowboy hats, bright-colored checkered shirts, and blue jeans (the youngest in a pair of overalls).

They were the most attractive and most applauded band at a bluegrass concert given in Fukuoka. The band was formed and rigorously trained by the proud father of its members, who had been playing bluegrass and old-time music in Japan since his college days in the late sixties and early seventies. The girls were usually supported as an ensemble by a bassist, their mother, who has been playing since her junior-college days.

After their own performance the girls were joined by a gentleman, Tsuyoshi Hashimoto, who sang a couple of songs such as "Cindy" backed by them and accompanied by his own banjo. The age contrast was visually conspicuous because the banjo-picker, a managing director of a newly formed company in Fukuoka, is even older than the girls' parents and his performing activities date back to his college days in the late 1950s and early 1960s. His interest extended back even further, to the days when, as a high school student, he was first charmed by bluegrass music after being a fan of Tommy Collins, Hank Williams, and other mainstream country and western favorites of the time. It is an interesting coincidence that, at around the time when a handful of teenagers in Berkeley, California, including Neil Rosenberg, got interested in bluegrass music,[1] a few Japanese teenagers across the Pacific Ocean were attracted to the same music. Tsuyoshi Hashimoto was an old college classmate of mine. In the early 1960s we were fellow members of a college country and western band that played rockabilly, Hawaiian, Tin Pan Alley, and Japanese popular songs as well. It was through him that I was invited to speak at a forum about the music of American southern whites that preceded the concert.

That afternoon we reunited as a duet, and as the eldest group performing on the occasion, we sang a couple of old-time songs accompanying ourselves with guitar and Appalachian dulcimer. It was our first public performance in twenty-six years, the last one being in early 1962, with banjo and guitar, at a New Year's party of the Japan-America Society of Fukuoka. That party was held in an officers' club on one of the two U.S. military bases then located in the suburbs of Fukuoka.[2] There were several other entertainers at the gathering, including a female group doing Japanese traditional music. It was backstage there that I first realized how the sound of a banjo string, when it is being tuned up, resembles that of a shamisen, which uses a head made of catskin instead of calfskin, and twine instead of steel strings. The time we spent backstage was also memorable in that, when we were practicing in the dark outside the backstage door to avoid having the sound of our instruments mingle with the wailing of the shamisen music, a smiling old American in a checkered shirt came up, possibly drawn by our music, and flattered us by saying something to the effect that we sounded like we were from Kentucky.

The other groups in the 1988 concert in Fukuoka belonged to the generation between ourselves, in our late forties, and the girls described above.[3] The span of generations of the performers there covered roughly the entire range of the Japanese people who have come to love American bluegrass

music and old-time music or hillbilly music—though such a young performing female group as the Nakajimas is exceptional.

In the late 1950s there were a few other people who got interested in
bluegrass music, at least in the Tokyo area and in the Osaka area, and an
article on bluegrass along with a photograph of Bill Monroe appeared in
a popular music monthly as early as March 1958.[4] The writer of that article
and other persons who showed an interest in bluegrass at that time were
obviously several or even many years older than I, and they had been
listening to country and western music in general and had hit upon bluegrass music among newly imported records, as was the case with my friend
mentioned above. As to the bluegrass records pressed and released in Japan,
by 1958 there already existed "Kentucky Waltz"/"The Prisoner's Song"
by Bill Monroe and His Blue Grass Boys, the only 78 rpm Japanese single
of bluegrass music, and in January 1958 "Jimmie Brown, the Newsboy"/
"Cabin on the Hill" by Flatt and Scruggs was released. It was not until
December 1959, almost two years later, that the Flatt and Scruggs 45 rpm
single was followed by another bluegrass single, "Dixie Breakdown"/
"Your Tears Are Just Interest on the Loan" by Reno and Smiley.[5]

The interest some people had in this kind of American music, which
was later to be called country and western, could have originated in late
1945 or in 1946, that is, soon after World War II, when Japan was under
occupation and the American forces brought their exotic cultures with
them to the country. But even before the war, after around 1934, there
were quite a few hillbilly records pressed in Japan. Even the present-day
Japanese followers of this music would be surprised to know that it was
actually possible to hear at that time in Japan, through Japanese labels,
Vernon Dalhart, Carson Robison, the Hill Billies, Jimmie Rodgers, Ted
Hawkins and Riley Puckett, Gene Autry, the Shelton Brothers, Elton Britt,
W. E. O'Daniel and His Hillbilly Boys, the Prairie Ramblers, and others.[6]

Therefore, it could be argued that the Japanese interest in what is called
old-time music or in country music in general had sprung up not very
many years after it became available in the form of phonograph records
for Americans. It is very likely, however, that the interest was sporadic
and quite limited because of the scarcity of published material. A book
titled *Keiongaku to sono record* (Light music and its records), published in
1938,[7] includes "Hilly[*sic*]-Billy Songs" as a section under "Swing Music."
However, only three pages are allotted to it, with merely a dozen lines of
introductory notes—which present-day enthusiasts would find amusing and
almost hilarious—although they succinctly reflect how the music was accepted in prewar Japan. The notes are indeed followed by the names of
such artists as those listed above, but one wonders why Arthur Tracy

("The Street Singer") is listed as one of the most well-known "hilly-billy" singers. That would suggest that there was limited awareness of the genre, and there is little evidence of its being performed by Japanese, though further research is needed.

The postwar interest of some Japanese in contemporary hillbilly music was, in contrast, much more conspicuous. It was considerably stimulated by the U.S. military radio, the FEN (Far East Network), which played hillbilly records along with those of other musical genres. For example, the "Honshu Hayride," an early-afternoon show alliteratively titled after the name of the largest of the Japanese islands, was easily heard, if you were interested enough to tune in, in the Japanese homes in the vicinity of the U.S. military bases scattered all over Japan. The broadcasts continued for quite a long time after the war. When I was a college student, I soon became familiar with "The Devil's Dream," the show's instrumental theme.

Some listeners were so enthusiastic that they formed their own bands to play the contemporary hillbilly music, and a couple of them, converted tango bands, even recorded songs for Japanese labels as early as 1948.[8] Interestingly enough, quite a few of these musicians came from aristocratic families. The titled-nobility system was abolished in late 1946 when the new constitution of Japan was promulgated, in English and Japanese, with a statement, "Peers and peerage shall not be recognized," in Chapter III, Article 14. Nevertheless, the college students who performed hillbilly music semiprofessionally in Tokyo unmistakably grew up as the sons of dukes, viscounts, or barons. For instance, Atsutaka Torio, the bassist of the Chuck Wagon Boys, was a son of Viscount Koyata Torio. He published his memoirs, which included an account of a mischievous nursery-school-days episode with the present emperor, just six weeks after the emperor's accession to the throne in early 1989. The sons of peers were enjoying a comparatively rich life when most other people were generally suffering from hunger as a consequence of Japan's defeat in World War II. It must have been their relative affluence that enabled them to purchase musical instruments and pseudo-cowboy costumes, and to have enough time to enjoy listening to the music and to practice performing it. They were also educated enough to have a liking for a foreign musical culture in the first place, and to get interested in something that requires a somewhat advanced knowledge of the language used.

What, then, attracted the bluebloods of Japan to the blue-collar music from the American South? It was presumably the very exoticism of the music, the feeling of openness and liberation it yielded along with a touch of rusticity, and the romanticism of the West with its images and ideas of the Wild West, prairies, adventures, and mobility. And the attraction might well have had much to do with the idea of American democracy that was suddenly advocated by the new Japanese authorities; this concept was awkwardly grafted onto the Japanese way of thinking immediately after Japan was defeated in World War II and the United States occupied the country. Democracy gives one the idea of liberation with its implication of social equality, and liberation involves openness and freeness, which is suggested by the image of the West in "Western" music.

In any event, the term "Western" music was adopted apparently soon after American country music of the mid-1940s was willingly accepted by the first generation of enthusiasts. It was associated with the popularity of the "Western," a genre of films newly imported from the United States in postwar Japan, though Western films were not known as "Westerns," but as *seibugeki,* the term's Japanese translation. "Western," designating country and western music, prevailed for an unusually long time in Japan considering the fact that the term has never been fully established in the United States as an appellation for country music in general. Even the gradual replacement of "hillbilly" by "country and western" in America since the late 1940s did not much affect the Japanese tendency, as is shown by the title of a book published in 1963—*Western ongaku nyumon* (A guide to western music).[9] The title was obviously selected by the publisher to give the book a general appeal, even though the author states in the preface his awareness of the terminology in the United States and of the exceptional use in Japan.

A case could be made that it was not until the early 1970s that the general Japanese enthusiasts of the music became somewhat, if not sufficiently, conscious of the fact that it is from a cultural area called the South. The music, especially country music, came to Japan as a sound on disc without much of its cultural context; it was, above all, from the United States. The visual image on record sleeves, which was the only available clue to any cultural context, often had much to do with the West and cowboys, and included the Stetson hats, boots, and "Western" shirts the recording artists wore as stage costumes. The Japanese audience was not informed enough to know that it actually represented the "Western" aspiration of the southern rural people who preferred the romanticized image of cowboys to the derogatory one of the hillbillies. The liner notes by a handful of writers sometimes referred to the fact that the music was from the South, but this was usually used as a geographical term without much cultural implication, reflecting the writers' lack of interest in this aspect.

Bluegrass music was naturally taken as something that was from the South because it lacked the association with cowboys, except for the hats of the artists. In turn, mountaineers, who were supposed to be the performers of bluegrass music, were invariably romanticized as people who live, so to speak, in a rural heaven that can be anywhere in the United

States. To the limited Japanese audience, the white music from the American South was, in concept, simply something fascinating from "America," a land with richness, expansion, democracy, and possibilities. That image of the United States seemed to have been more appropriately reflected in rural "Western" music than in urban jazz and Tin Pan Alley songs whose popularity preceded it, in Japan as well as in the U.S., not only in time but in the size of the movement.

The reception and adoption of this fascinating music from America was an urban phenomenon, as is usual with any imported trend. It was considered fashionable to have a liking for the music, not to speak of performing it oneself. The pseudo-cowboy costumes of the performers helped to strengthen the effect, because every item of clothing was exotic, coming out of a completely different culture, although European clothes themselves had penetrated Japanese culture since they were first introduced some eighty years before. There was certainly an awareness of the relative rusticity of the music, and in that respect the enthusiasm was a kind of reverse snobbery. (It is no wonder that the followers of jazz often looked down on those of "Western" music because of their liking for less sophisticated, simplistic music, even though it is from America.)

Thus, younger Japanese who were so enthusiastic about "Western" music that they formed bands in the early 1950s, either following in the wake of their seniors or joining them, were also from well-to-do families in urban areas. They were also educated enough to be attending universities or colleges, mostly private. This was a time when the majority of young people of their age could not afford to enjoy the benefits of higher education, which would have helped to widen their view of the world, making them more inclined to get interested in things overseas. Besides being educated, the young enthusiasts were, thanks to their families, wealthy enough to buy not only records but musical instruments, and had enough leisure for practicing the instruments and singing.

Rockabilly performers in Japan, who tried to resemble American originals in the late 1950s as members of "Western" bands, were also largely from rich families who resided in metropolitan areas. As represented by the three top stars, one of whom was a singer of mixed British and Japanese parentage named Mickey Curtis, they were attracted to the music at an earlier age than their predecessors, and many gave up their studies and their access to a college education. The fact that the regular concert-hall show in Tokyo that featured their energetic performances was called "Western Carnival" indicates, among other things, that rockabilly was taken up by "Western" bands and was treated, if unintentionally, more as a derivation of or as an idiom within country music than it was in the United States.

Those who became interested in bluegrass music and tried to perform it themselves from the middle to late 1950s in Japan were, again, generally sons of prosperous families. My college classmate described above, for example, who was of the age of the rockabillies, lived in the largest city in southern Japan as a son of the vice president of one of a half dozen major electric power companies in Japan. That made it financially possible for him to develop his interest, through imported records, in such artists as Hank Thompson, Hank Williams, Bill Monroe, and Flatt and Scruggs, and also such "folksingers" as Burl Ives, Woody Guthrie, and Jean Ritchie.[10] In the late 1950s and early 1960s usually one had to place an order to get an LP record imported from the United States because few record stores stocked imported records. An LP cost more than 2,500 yen, which is now the price one pays for a CD. In the late 1950s this was equivalent to one-fifth of the beginning monthly income of the average college graduate.

Another, slightly younger friend of mine, Michio Higashi, grew up in Tokyo as a son of a prosperous couple born in Vancouver, Canada. As a nineteen-year-old student, he led a college band called the Ozark Mountaineers and was fortunate enough to have been funded by his father to tour around the United States. He traveled around America in the summer of 1961, staying with the late Mrs. Hank Williams for about a week in Nashville, when it was just a dream for most Japanese to go abroad. He learned a lot there, especially the playing techniques of bluegrass instruments. The Japanese pioneers had learned to play through listening to records, but without any visual models their technique and handling of the instruments was sometimes very imaginative. Higashi made a guest appearance on the Grand Ole Opry, singing "Will the Circle Be Unbroken" with a guitar for which he borrowed a capo from Earl Scruggs. (It was on 7 May 1960, that Yoshio Ono, a yodeler and a banjoist who debuted in Japan by signing with Japanese Columbia in 1957, performed on the Opry stage, with Flatt and Scruggs, as the first Japanese who had ever been given an opportunity to perform there.)[11] The story of Higashi's adventure was published in the second issue of *Moon Shiner*.[12] Since its founding in November 1983, this bluegrass monthly has periodically printed stories based on interviews with the older generation of Japanese performers of bluegrass music. The persons featured there, more than a dozen in number, also turn out to be urbanites who are middle class, if not very rich, and highly educated in the sense that they attended a college-level institution.

The American folk revival began to be imported in the early 1960s and became more popular in the mid-1960s, helping to stimulate further interest in music from the American South among young Japanese in the same social stratum, just as it did much more extensively among urban, middle-class college students in the United States. The popularity of American folk music in its various forms was enhanced particularly in the first stage by the visit of Pete Seeger, a middle-aged interpreter of traditional songs from the South and a left-wing protest singer-songwriter, who came to Japan for a concert tour in late 1963. It was a couple of weeks before the shooting of John F. Kennedy, whose fame was used in publicizing Seeger as "a former classmate of Kennedy at Harvard," though Seeger simply happened to have been enrolled there at around the same time as Kennedy, without getting acquainted with him and without graduating from the school.

During this period I was involved in the reception of the music of American southern whites in Japan, and backstage after one of Pete Seeger's shows I met an American GI who had been drafted while a college student in Seattle and was then stationed in Fukuoka. He soon became my good "pickin' and singin' " mate. I thus shared an interest in performing this kind of music substantially for the first time with an American, one who came from outside the southern culture and who enjoyed exchanging information about the whole range of music covered in the American folk revival.[13] On the other hand, Pete Seeger's visit prompted me to write a leaflet,[14] in both Japanese and English, criticizing the authenticity of performances by folk revivalists, which was handed out at the entrance of two concert halls in the area where I lived. It was handed to Seeger as well; he kindly responded to my possibly unskilled argument. I was armed only with what I had learned about traditional songs and ballads through the writings of Cecil Sharp, B. H. Bronson, William Entwistle, and other scholars, and with what I had heard through phonograph records, especially those collected in the *Anthology of American Folk Music,* compiled by Harry Smith, which I found in the library of the Fukuoka American Cultural Center, a U.S. governmental organization.

While pop-folk performers such as the Kingston Trio, the Brothers Four, and Peter, Paul, and Mary were enjoyed transitorily as something trendy, the imported American folk revival also produced, as in the United States, admirers of Bob Dylan. Dylan's songs were first introduced to the Japanese by Pete Seeger in his concerts mentioned above (although there were those who listened to Hugh Cherry's program of folk music syndicated on FEN carefully enough to catch the name of Dylan and to hear his singing, as GIs must have done). Dylan's perspective on the society and culture in which he lived and his way of expressing it through songs were so influential that quite a few Japanese youngsters not only listened to his recordings but tried to write and sing their own compositions with their own guitar accompaniment. This tendency later brought out, in turn, a current of new, more Westernized Japanese popular music, which to some extent rivals *kayokyoku*. (*Kayokyoku* is an older form of popular music that is characterized by musical features developed out of Japanese idioms. Culturally, *kayokyoku* could be compared to modern country music in America, though it does not have a particular regionalism.)

The interest in more traditional forms of the music from the American South, which was generated by the imported folk revival in Japan, was not so prominent because it was not directed toward new developments in Japanese popular music. But it was more persistent among a limited audience. As was the case in the United States, the folk revival attracted the Japanese to such tradition-oriented performers as Doc Watson and to the string band music from the 1920s and 1930s through the New Lost City Ramblers and LP reissues of the recordings from the period, drawing a new audience into bluegrass music. The members of the new audience whose interest in the music from the South was motivated by the folk revival—though they were usually as unaware of its southernness as their predecessors had been—were indifferent to and often disliked country and western music. Country and western was generally considered not to include bluegrass, again as in the United States, for its sound was characterized by newly composed lyrics, electric instruments, and unmistakably stylized nasal vocals, which were not compatible with the acousticity and the kind of argued authenticity of the revival.

The Japanese enthusiasts were educated urban young people, as was the case with enthusiasts in America, and what has been observed about the revival there can be applied literally to the Japanese enthusiasts: "it [the folksong revival that occurred in America in 1960] appealed primarily to individuals who celebrated traditions not their own. ... I think the revival can be fairly characterized as romantic, naive, nostalgic and idealistic."[15] The difference was, as can be easily understood, the depth of the cultural and social gulf in the case of Japan.

Some Americans who were not of Anglo-Saxon background were enthralled by typically Anglo-American folksongs, and more conspicuously, quite a few people showed a strong interest in the blues, an African-American musical form. But however great the racial, cultural, and social-class differences were in terms of tradition, both the educated urban young people and the older, not-so-well-educated rural people whose musical traditions attracted them lived in the same land, as one nation, and, perhaps more significantly, spoke the same language as that of the songs. On the other hand, to the educated urban young people in Japan, not only were these musical traditions something radically different from domestic ones, but also the country in which the musical traditions existed and were "revived" was located far across the ocean, and the language had no linguistic relation or resemblance to the one they used.

Then there again arises the question of why the Japanese were attracted to the rural music from the American South. Part of the reason was that, as mentioned above, America represented democratic ideals, although the image of the West was largely irrelevant to the newer enthusiasts. As was the case with the American educated urban young people, the newer Japanese interest was "romantic, naive, nostalgic"—a nostalgia for something that was lost by urbanization.

Other factors included American capitalistic power in internationally disseminating American musical products, as well as educational motives, which were shared by the preceding generation. First, the English language was familiar to most Japanese due to the fact that it was and remains the predominant foreign language taught in almost all educational institutions beyond elementary school, though written English has been overemphasized at the expense of oral English. Second, the Occidental characteristics of musical structures including melody, rhythm, and harmony were not at all foreign to Japanese ears. Since the late nineteenth century, music education at all levels in Japan has emphasized Western concepts and features of music, so much as to exclude from classrooms almost any music that is in Japanese indigenous idioms. Those Japanese compositions that are included are in Western idioms or are compromises with them. This has naturally fostered an almost irrevocable tendency among a majority of Japanese to look down on domestic music and its derivations. This tendency has been conspicuous among the well educated, and most of the enthusiasts for rural music from the American South were not exceptional in being indifferent to the music of older Japanese styles. It usually sounded antiquated and boring to the enthusiasts, and even if it didn't, the musical idioms of Japanese folk music were too different to prompt the enthusiasts of American folk music to look back on their own domestic musical traditions. Consequently, the imported folk "revival" had no visible influence on or relevance to Japanese folksongs, while the American folk revival noticeably led to revitalization of the domestic folk music in Britain and inadvertently contributed to the Celtic revival in Brittany. The performers and audience of Japanese folksongs were, on the other hand, not "hip" enough to have a liking for newly imported music.[16]

The extent and directions of the Japanese interest in the music of southern whites that has been surveyed above is reflected, to some degree, in the publication of a handful of more or less nationally circulated, nonprofessional specialist magazines. The most important one was *Country and Western*, which started in Tokyo in May 1963 with the subtitle "The Magazine for Bluegrass and Country." It was intended as an extension of the serial newsletter/program for regular record concerts in Tokyo that were organized by C&WMS (the Country and Western Music Society—interestingly, the name in Japanese was *seibu ongaku aiko kai* [Western Music Society]) and were held from mid-1950 to the early 1960s.[17] Later re-subtitled as "The Magazine for Country and Bluegrass," this bimonthly sold more than twenty-five hundred copies per issue in its heyday.[18] Then the main title was changed, in May 1978 (no. 86), to *Melody Ranch,* which was dubbed the "Country, Bluegrass and Folk Rock Magazine." This change was a symptom of the dispersal of interest in country music in Japan, alongside the growing tendency for country music to lose its stylistic identity, and the magazine was discontinued, with the May 1979 issue as the last edition.

Several years before the demise of *Melody Ranch,* there appeared *June Apple,* the first exclusively bluegrass magazine in Japan. This bimonthly, apparently named after the banjo instrumental by Wade Ward in *Claw-hammer Banjo* and launched in Tokyo in January 1974, obviously represented the inclination of the newly increased bluegrass audience to consider bluegrass music as incompatible with other forms of country music. With its heyday in the late 1970s, the magazine's title was changed in May 1981 (no. 44) to *Bluegrass Revival.* It ceased to exist after issue number 59 appeared in January 1983. However, ten months later, a new "bluegrass journal" came out in the Kansai area, the second-largest metropolitan area in Japan. This monthly, *Moon Shiner,* covers the overall bluegrass scene in Japan, and now enjoys a circulation of some fifteen hundred copies.[19] It is published by BOM Service (Bluegrass and Old Time Service). This import-record dealer is a Japanese version of County Sales in Floyd, Virginia, and has published a newsletter/catalog since March 1972.[20]

BOM Service has also been active as an organizer of a bluegrass festival, and its annual Takarazuka Bluegrass Festival, the largest and oldest among quite a few regional bluegrass festivals in Japan, enjoyed its eighteenth year in the summer of 1989 with an audience of about a thousand. As is the case with the devotees of other forms of country music, there are a large number of bluegrass listeners who love to hear the music performed by American recording musicians without much interest in what the Japanese musicians try to do with it, and so the number does not reflect the extent of the Japanese bluegrass scene in general. But, in any case, the festival has served as an annual reunion of some two dozen bluegrass circles scattered all over Japan. An affectionate observation on these regional circles, each of which has several performing bands, was given by Alan Senauke of Berkeley, California, who toured around Japan in October 1989, thanks to BOM Service, visiting and performing at various places:

> We [Senauke and his wife] had an unusual opportunity. Since I could work as a solo and play with local musicians, it was possible to visit

many towns, to see how the bluegrass scene is the same throughout the world, yet different in each place. Some shows were in small concert halls, some in "live spots," or smokey (sometimes, very smokey) bars. Some places had very elaborate, top of the line sound systems, some just the minimum that was necessary. Some audiences were entirely young, male students; some audiences were families and professionals nearer my own age. The music also varied greatly with each circle, some preferring traditional bluegrass, some leaning toward the more modern sounds. It occurs to me that this is all very like the noodles we ate (and we ate a lot of soba and udon, because we love it!). In each town, noodles were similar in appearance, but the preparation and taste was always subtly different. . . . And also I got an overview of Japanese bluegrass. Although the scene is not so large, and maybe there is not enough money to be bringing over all the favorite bands, each circle seemed to be very solid. There were many musicians and families deeply involved and loving the music, keeping it alive in their own area. I think this is a great strength.[21]

With the Takarazuka Bluegrass Festival as an annual rallying point (any band can perform there) and *Moon Shiner* as a monthly forum and information center, the regional circles of bluegrass can be said to visibly form a community, and it is, as Bruce Jackson reevaluated the folk revival community in America, "as legitimate as any other based on shared interest and knowledge."[22]

In contrast, the Japanese scene of other forms of modern country music is much less visible, with an apparent decrease of the number of enthusiasts and the disappearance of a country music section (which denotes modern country music other than bluegrass) from the majority of record stores. In terms of performance, there are a handful of live spots in Tokyo and the Kansai area, which often feature Japanese performers who have seen better days. The sensibility of the younger generation long since disregarded this kind of music and was oriented to more energetic and rhythmical forms of music—in which bluegrass music could be included,[23] though stylistically it is quite different from musical forms dominated by African-American elements.

On the other hand, there are a limited number of Japanese performers of early hillbilly or old-time music, and every autumn since 1984 the annual Old-Time Party, an all-night get-together, has been held in Kobe, an international seaport and one of the largest cities in the Kansai area. Again, there are those whose interest is in the music from the American South itself and not in what the Japanese musicians do á la J. E. Mainer's Mountaineers, Wade Ward, or Kenny Hall, and so the Old-Time Party does not give a full picture of how old-time music is received in Japan. It does, however, represent the performance scene of old-time music in Japan and the newer interest shown by the younger generation. Their interest in old-time music began sometime in the late 1970s, and some of them went straight to the homeland of the music to get lessons from native old-time fiddlers and banjoists, as was the case with Kosuke Takaki, who took a course in fiddle-playing at the Augusta Vintage Workshop in Elkins, West Virginia, in 1981, when he was twenty years old. Takaki then registered as a contestant at the Galax Old-Time Fiddlers' Convention in Virginia in the summer of the same year, and has since performed there many times, having won sixth place as a member of an old-time string band in 1984.[24]

According to a report by an American correspondent based in Hong Kong, a dozen bands, consisting of some thirty musicians, appeared at the Old-Time Party in 1987 with an audience that numbered about forty.[25] The background information about some of the performers, based on interviews by the correspondent, is interesting enough, as in the case with one of them who "started out playing guitar in the style of the Beatles and the Eagles, drifted into the music of David Bromberg and eventually met some Japanese musicians who played bluegrass and old-time." More interesting are the observations made by two American fiddling participants concerning the music-making itself. One of them, Valerie Mindel, a former member of Any Old Time, an old-time band in California, said to the reporter: "There I was at four in the morning, when we'd been playing more and more obscure tunes all night. I turned to say something to the fellow next to me and realized that for all the tunes we had in common, we couldn't talk to each other. He didn't speak English. I didn't speak Japanese. And somehow it didn't matter." And the other, Rob Craighurst from Virginia, made a musical comment: "The music was just like all the great music in American music—it's not a copy. It's like if someone says 'Your Japanese is very good,' that means it's not really very good. Well, we wouldn't tell them, 'Your old-time music is really good'—it's that good." One of the participants at the concert, Sumio Inoue, who started with the guitar style of the Beatles and the Eagles, was actually good enough to have won ninth place in the fiddle contest at the renowned Galax Old-Time Fiddlers' Convention, in Galax, Virginia, in the preceding year. Mike Miller, a Reuters correspondent, reported, "He has been playing old-time music for only seven years, and fiddle for just the past four."[26] And Inoue was not exceptional in winning in the convention, as Miller suggests. He was simply one of the dozen young Japanese winners there from 1979 to 1987.[27]

This now leads us to the question of tradition. Is what is excellently performed by a Japanese musician legitimately a part of the musical tradition of the American rural South? If not, what is it? Is it just a tasteful imitation or facsimile of something original? Is it form without content? In the field of bluegrass music, from which one is able to make a living by performing in the United States, there are at least three professional musicians who were born and raised in Japan, and have been active in the States for years. I was surprised when a part-time writer for a newspaper in Baton Rouge, Louisiana, told me, in the summer of 1983, that he was first attracted to bluegrass music when he was impressed by an exciting performance by a fiddler named Shoji Tabuchi, who now regularly performs at his own theater, built in 1989, in Branson, Missouri. The surprise could be compared with what I felt, nearly ten years before, when I found, in the library of the Country Music Foundation in Nashville, that the guitar a certain mountaineer musician was shown playing in the cover photograph of an album of the music from the Ozarks was a Yamaha model. Akira Otsuka, a former member of the Bluegrass 45, a disbanded Japanese group, has been with various bands in the Washington area, and plays "brilliant mandolin."[28] A banjo player, Hiro (an abridgment of Sumihiro) Arita, who resides in Boston, "knocked out" Alan Senauke by his musicianship when Senauke toured Europe with Arita and others in 1986,[29] and prompted a reviewer to describe his recorded performance as "hot, hot banjo playing."[30] Do these appraisals not have much to do with the traditional elements in the music?

It would perhaps be necessary, as is often said, to live the life that produced a musical tradition to get its real feeling. The late Merle Watson, the son of Doc Watson, said in the late 1970s: "There are a lot of good musicians coming up, but they aren't going into the old-time music, or at least playing it really well. I think one problem is they just don't feel the music. The old traditional folk-type tunes are really a music of the people, and if you didn't grow up with it and don't know the feeling of what you're playing, it's hard to play it."[31] This would be what makes "folk-type" music different from Western music, especially serious music or art music, which is, as Bruno Nettl says, conceived as "an internationally valid system, a set of techniques, which could be learned by anyone. . . . It is accepted that anyone, no matter where his original home or what his native culture, given enough talent, hard work, and experience, can learn to perform Western music."[32] That might be the reason why Seiji Ozawa can now be esteemed as one of the best conductors in the world and why there are quite a few Japanese violinists, pianists, and other instrumentalists who are active in some well-known orchestras in Europe. There are even a couple of important Japanese opera singers in Italy. And it might also explain the fact that the three Japanese bluegrass musicians mentioned above are successful as players of instruments that require sophisticated performing techniques.

Indeed, the Japanese have tried to master the musical techniques of the southern rural whites and to copy American models that have been available in the form of recordings. Frequently the closer to the models they are, the more highly they are esteemed in Japan. On the other hand, it is also true that many performers show in the music they perform that they have digested southern musical tradition in their own way. Their exposure to various performances by southern rural whites on record tracks and their own good experiences in performing in several substyles leads them more or less naturally to perform songs not necessarily in the fashion of some American performer, but in their version of a southern, rural, white musical style. They are much less "yellow skin, white masks," to modify a phrase by Franz Fanon.

What has made such a development possible is the length of time the Japanese have been studying and performing the music of the American South. More than thirty years have passed since the Japanese began performing bluegrass music, nearly thirty years since they first played more traditional music from the South, and more than forty years since the first hillbilly band was formed. There was a father-and-son group, much older than the Nakajima Family Band, that appeared on the stage of the Takarazuka Festival several years ago. Even though Sumio Inoue, who got ninth place at the Galax Old-Time Fiddler's Convention, only began performing old-time music in the early 1980s, it was a Japanese bluegrass group through which he was first exposed to music from American southern whites. And this bluegrass group, in turn, must have been motivated by another group, which again must have owed its existence to some senior group. That can easily be seen from the fact that many bluegrass bands were first formed as college bands who trained themselves as part of extracurricular activities.

Years have passed since an overseas musical tradition that was captured on record was first imported to Japan, with suggestions of its cultural background in the sound itself but without its tangible milieu. Couldn't it be argued that enough years have now passed for the Japanese to fashion unintentionally, out of that tradition, a tradition of their own, as it were, or at least a recognizable derivation? To make it legitimate, there is a country music community as described above, though it is limited to bluegrass devotees and to old-time music lovers who largely overlap with the bluegrass enthusiasts. Moreover, it is significantly characterized by lack of self-consciousness in terms of tradition.

R. Raymond Allen summed up an old-time music revivalist as "a musician of urban, suburban, or small town (non-agrarian) background who attempts to recreate traditional, rural, vocal and instrumental styles of folk music which were not present in the home or community in which he or she grew up."[33] In the case of the Japanese, however, the "attempts to recreate" have not been very conscious, whereas those of the American revivalists inevitably were. As we have seen, the American folk "revival" did not affect the revival of Japanese folk songs, so the "revival" has not been a revival to the Japanese, because it has been a phenomenon in a geographically and culturally far-off country. That culturally deep gulf naturally makes Japanese performances one step further removed from the performances of southern rural whites than are those of American revivalists such as Mike Seeger.

However, because the "revival" itself is insignificant to them, the Japanese have not worried much about the question of authenticity that is implied in revivalism, and thus are able to nurture their own version of an American tradition without constraint.

NOTES

Japanese personal names and book titles in this chapter are phonetically transcribed, for convenience, from the original spellings in Japanese and Chinese characters, which would be much more than Greek and Latin to the general readers of the present article. Exceptions are foreign words: it would be too confusing to give a transcription as, say, "bulugruasu" or "burugurasu" when the spelling in Japanese is manifestly designed to signify "bluegrass."

1. Rosenberg, liner notes.

2. "New Year's Program" by the Japan-American Society of Fukuoka, on 13 January 1962, at Kasuga Officers' Club, Itazuke Air Base, Japan. The performances by four different groups of traditional Japanese musicians preceded "American Folk Songs" that consisted of "Home Sweet Home," "Bile 'Em Cabbage Down," and "She'll Be Comin' Round the Mountain."

3. The Nakajima Family Band later performed in the presence of Bill Monroe in Kumamoto. Kumamoto Prefecture held a large outdoor concert of some well-known country music performers from Nashville in October 1989, and Mr. and Mrs. Nakajima took their daughters backstage to jam with Bill Monroe. Though the dream was not realized, the girls surprised and excited Monroe so much, by suddenly starting to play when he came out of the dressing room upon request, that he clogged to their music. It was all filmed on video by the crew from the Kumamoto Office of NHK (Japanese Broadcasting Corporation) and was broadcast later on its satellite channel. The Nakajimas' meeting with Bill Monroe is reported by Hashimoto in ["Meeting with Bill Monroe"], in a newsletter published in Fukuoka.

4. Fumio Suzuki, "Mountain music."

5. Nagai, "Nihonban bluegrass record ichiran."

6. Katsuhiko Suzuki, "A List of C and W 78 RPM Records."

7. Karahata et al., *Keiongaku to sono record.* Preceding the book by four years there appeared a small collection of cowboy songs—*Cowboy aisho kashu.* The cover obviously duplicates, with small modifications, that for *The Lonesome Cowboys Songs of the Plains and Hills* compiled by John White and George Shackley, the reproduction of which can be found in White, *Git Along, Little Dogies,* p. 6.

8. The group named the Western Ramblers was the most prolific. See Katsuhiko Suzuki, "A List of C and W 78 RPM Records," pp. 33–34.

9. Takayama, *Western ongaku nyumon.* The book consists of a short historical survey, biographies of 150 artists/groups, comments on 100 songs, and an annotated list of 100 albums released in Japan. In *Jazz,* a book on American popular music that was published ten years earlier, the word "South" does not appear at all in the four-page section on "Western Music," though it briefly refers to "hill-billy songs" after spending many words on "cow-boy songs"; see pp. 257–60.

10. LP records of "Folk Music" from the United States listed in the July 1959 issue of *Schwann* (Long Playing Record Catalog), which Hashimoto perused in 1959 and 1960, were more than twice as many as those listed under "Cowboy and Hillbilly," a subdivision of "Popular Music"—pp. 158–60 and 168–70 respectively.

11. Isaji, "Nihon no Western kashutachi."

12. Inaya, "Bokurawa Mandolin."

13. Thane Mitchell, after having been discharged from military service, graduated from the University of Washington in Seattle, and has been active in the folk scene there as a performer and organizer.

14. Mitsui, "Folksong and Folk-Singer." The "purist" argument was repeated, in a way, in my letter to the editor of *Sing Out!;* see Mitsui, "Correspondence."

15. Jackson, "The Folksong Revival," p. 195.

16. It was not until the mid-1970s that young Japanese showed an interest in traditional Japanese music serious enough to perform it themselves. The first were the Champloos, from Okinawa, led by Schokichi Kina, who combined rock music with the traditional Okinawa idioms. The Champloos were then followed many years later by the Takio Band, led by Takio Ito, who revitalized Japanese folksongs with contemporary interpretations. An appraisal of Ito by a Japanese writer, in English, was recently published in a British monthly; see Mogi, "Singing the Fishing." It should also be noted than an obscure bluegrass trio, Anges Blanc, formed by Japanese female junior-college students in 1989, features a vocalist who used to sing Japanese folksongs in her childhood. Her powerful voice trained by singing them is quite suitable to bluegrass vocalization.

17. Telephone interview with Takashi Shimbo, who was the editor-in-chief of *Country and Western,* 9 February 1990.

18. Telephone interview with Masaaki Yoshimura, who assisted Shimbo as an editor, 9 February 1990.

19. Telephone interview with Saburo Watanabe, the publisher of *Moon Shiner,* 1 February 1990.

20. The somewhat quantitative overview, above, of the Japanese interest in southern white music could be supplemented with the amount of the sales of my books on the music published in the 1960s and 1970s. *Bluegrass ongaku* (Bluegrass music), the publication of which by the Traditional-Song Society was partly sub-

sidized in 1967 by the college where I taught, sold the five hundred copies printed within several years. Its revised and enlarged edition was published in 1975 by a commercial publisher in Tokyo, Bronze-sha, and sold five thousand copies before the 1979 reprinting of a thousand copies. *Eikei America minzoku ongaku no gakki* (The instruments of Anglo-American folk music), another book published, in 1970, by the Traditional-Song Society, sold its edition of three hundred copies in several years. *Country ongaku no rekishi* (A history of country music), which owes much to Bill Malone's *Country Music U.S.A.*, was published by the largest Japanese publisher of books on music in 1971, Ongaku-no-tomo-sha. It started with five thousand copies and had two reprintings, in 1974 and 1976, two thousand copies each.

21. Senauke, "Alan kara no message." The quote is from the original version in English titled "A Letter to Japanese Bluegrass Lovers." Courtesy of Saburo Watanabe, the publisher, and Goro Tani, the editor, of *Moon Shiner*.

22. Jackson, "The Folksong Revival," p. 66.

23. It should be noted that a new generation of collegiate bluegrass performers are often not well-off. According to Saburo Watanabe, the owner of BOM Service, the music that is left now for less-well-off students to play is bluegrass; if one plays bluegrass, one can do without expensive electric and electronic instruments and equipment, although many students with money opt for this equipment.

24. Interview with Kosuke Takaki in Kyoto, 22 March 1990.

25. Mike Miller, "Old-Time Music in Japan." Note that this is a report of the Old-Time Party in 1987, not the one in 1988. This is a slightly enlarged version of what was originally written, with the title "American Fiddle and Banjo Music Alive and Well in Japan," for *Asahi Evening News*, a Japanese English-language newspaper, in November 1987. Miller is a Reuters correspondent, who, according to Takaki, came all the way from Hong Kong to cover the concert, because he is an old-time music enthusiast himself, playing the old-time guitar, and is now the husband of Valerie Mindel, a former member of Any Old Time, a women's old-time band in California, who is quoted in the report. The photostat copy of the report was printed in the liner notes to *Galax International*. Miller published the longer version of the report a year later in *Old Time Herald* with a different title and picture, without referring to the fact that it was originally a newspaper report written in 1987.

26. Miller, "Old-Time Music in Japan," p. 11.

27. See Fenton's "Chronological List of Overseas Ribbon Winners at the Galax Old-Time Fiddlers' Convention 1935–87" in his "Descriptive Introductory Notes." As to Japanese winners at other contests, as far as I know, Kosuke Takaki, as a member of a string band, won fourth place at a fiddlers' convention in Deer Creek Maryland in 1981 (see Fenton, "Descriptive Introductory Notes," p. 13), and much earlier, in the summer of 1973, Noboru Morishige, who became a member of the Stonemans, a bluegrass band, won third place in the fiddle contest at Mac Wiseman's festival in Renfro Valley. See Green, "Noboru Morishige," p. 27.

28. Rosenberg, *Bluegrass: A History*, p. 367.

29. "Alan Senauke Interview," p. 16. This interview is particularly interesting because it is illustrated with a photograph that shows Senauke, while training in a temple in Shizuoka Prefecture in May 1989, enjoying a bluegrass jam with a

Japanese band from a neighboring city in the temple building, wearing his zen monk's uniform, and with his head shaven as a zen monk.

30. Blech, "Review."

31. Stambler and Landon, *The Encyclopedia of Folk, Country and Western Music,* p. 779.

32. Nettl, *The Western Impact on World Music,* chapter 29. The "Suzuki Method," a training method in the playing of classical violin devised by a Japanese, Shin'ichi Suzuki, has been so highly regarded as to draw people from Western countries to his school in Matsumoto.

33. Allen, "Old-Time Music," p. 66.

Bibliography

Abrahams, Roger. "Creativity, Individuality, and the Traditional Singer." *Studies in the Literary Imagination* 3 (1970): 5–36.

———. "Folk Songs and the Top 40—A Symposium." *Sing Out!* 16.1 (1966): 12–21.

———, ed. *A Singer and Her Songs: Almeda Riddle's Book of Ballads.* Baton Rouge: Louisiana State University Press, 1970.

Abrahams, Roger, and George Foss. *Anglo-American Folksong Style.* Englewood Cliffs, N.J.: Prentice-Hall, 1968.

Adler, Thomas A. "Bluegrass Music and Meal-Fried Potatoes: Food, Festival, Community." In *"We Gather Together": Food and Festival in American Life,* ed. Theodore C. Humphrey and Lin T. Humphrey, pp. 195–204. Ann Arbor: UMI Research Press, 1988.

———. "Dueling Banjos: Overt and Covert Competition in Amateur Bluegrass Performance." *JEMF Quarterly* 21 (1985 [1989]): 9–16.

"Alan Senauke Interview." *Moon Shiner* 6.10 (1989): 15–17.

Alburger, Mary Ellen. *Scottish Fiddlers and Their Music.* London: Gollancz, 1986.

Allen, R. Raymond. "Old-Time Music and the Urban Folk Revival." *New York Folklore* 7 (1981): 65–81.

Allmen, Diane, et al. [Editorial]. *Living Blues* 1 (1970): 1.

Anderson, Robert T. "Voluntary Associations in History." *American Anthropologist* 73 (1971): 209–22.

Armstrong, Frankie, and Brian Pearson. "Some Reflections on the English Folk Revival." *History Workshop Journal* 7 (1979): 95–100.

Babcock, Barbara. "Reflexivity: Definitions and Discriminations." *Semiotica* 30 (1980): 1–14.

Baker, Houston A., Jr. *Blues, Ideology, and Afro-American Literature: A Vernacular Theory.* Philadelphia: University of Pennsylvania Press, 1984.

Barrow, John. "Folk Now." In *The People's Past,* ed. Edward J. Cowan, pp. 206–18. Edinburgh: Polygon, 1980.

Barry, Phillips. "What Is Tradition?" *Bulletin of the Folk-Song Society of the Northeast* 1 (1930): 2–3.

Barthes, Roland. *The Eiffel Tower and Other Mythologies.* New York: Hill, 1979.

Bauman, Richard. "Differential Identity and the Social Base of Folklore." *Journal of American Folklore* 84 (1971): 31–41.

Bausinger, Herman. *Folk Culture in a World of Technology.* Bloomington: Indiana University Press, 1990.

Bayard, Samuel Press. "Decline and 'Revival' of Anglo-American Folk Music." *Midwest Folklore* 5 (1955): 69–77.

Beck, Horace Press. "The Riddle of 'The Flying Cloud.' " *Journal of American Folklore* 66 (1953): 123–34.

Becker, Howard S. *Art Worlds.* Berkeley: University of California Press, 1982.

Becker, Jane S. "Revealing Traditions: The Politics of Culture and Community in America, 1888–1988." In *Folk Roots, New Roots: Folklore in American Life,* ed. Jane S. Becker and Barbara Franco, pp. 19–60. Lexington, Mass.: Museum of Our National Heritage, 1988.

Becker, Jane S., and Barbara Franco, eds. *Folk Roots, New Roots: Folklore in American Life.* Lexington, Mass.: Museum of Our National Heritage, 1988.

Ben-Amos, Dan. "The Seven Strands of Tradition." *Journal of Folklore Research* 21 (1984): 106–31.

Bendix, Regina. "Folklorism: The Challenge of a Concept." *International Folklore Review* 6 (1988): 5–15.

Benford, Mac. "Folklorists and Us: An Account of Our Curious and Changing Relationship (with More Personal Reminiscences)." *Old-Time Herald* 1.7 (Feb.-Apr. 1989): 22–27.

Berger, Peter L., and Thomas Luckmann. *The Social Construction of Reality: A Treatise in the Sociology of Knowledge.* Garden City, N.Y.: Anchor, 1967.

Best, Richard L., and Beth A. Best. *New Song Fest.* 1948. Rpt. New York: Crown, 1955.

Bibby, Roland. *The Northumbrian Pipers' Second Tune Book.* Newcastle-upon-Tyne, England: Northumbrian Pipers' Society, 1981.

Blaustein, Richard. "Traditional Music and Social Change: The Old Time Fiddlers Association Movement in the United States." Ph.D. diss., Indiana University, 1975.

Blech, Kerry. "Review: Galax International." *Old-Time Herald* 1.8 (May-July 1989): 31.

Bloomfield, Michael. *Me and Big Joe.* San Francisco: Re/Search Productions, 1980.

Bluestein, Gene. *The Voice of the Folk: Folklore and American Literary Theory.* Amherst: University of Massachusetts Press, 1972.

Boggs, Carl. "The Blues Tradition: From Poetic Revolt to Cultural Impasse." *Socialist Review* 8.2 (1978): 115–34.

Bohlman, Philip V. *The Study of Folk Music in the Modern World.* Bloomington: Indiana University Press, 1988.

Botkin, B. A. "Applied Folklore: Creating Understanding through Folklore." *Southern Folklore Quarterly* 17 (1953): 199–206.

———. "The Folksong Revival: Cult or Culture?" In *The American Folk Scene,* ed. David A. DeTurk and A. Poulin, Jr., pp. 95–100. New York: Dell, 1967.

Reprinted from *Folk Music and Dance* (Newsletter of the U.S. National Committee, IFMC) 4 (April 1964): 1–4.

———. "The Folksong Revival: A Symposium." *New York Folklore Quarterly* 19 (1963): 83–142.

———. "Little Magazines of the Folk Revival." *New York Folklore Quarterly* 19 (1963): 62–66.

———. "Notes." *Journal of American Folklore* 57 (1944): 215.

Boyes, Georgina. "Performance and Context: An Examination of the Effects of the English Folksong Revival on Song Repertoire and Style." In *The Ballad Today*, ed. Georgina Boyes, pp. 43–52. West Stockwith, Doncaster: January Books, 1985.

Bradley, Hank. *Counterfeiting, Stealing, and Cultural Plundering: A Manual for Applied Ethnomusicologists, with 12 Tunes for Fiddle, Composed by the Author.* Seattle: Mill Gulch Music, 1989.

Brand, Oscar. *The Ballad Mongers: Rise of the Modern Folk Song.* New York: Funk, 1962.

Brauner, Cheryl Anne. "A Study of the Newport Folk Festival and the Newport Folk Foundation." M.A. thesis, Memorial University of Newfoundland, 1983.

Bronner, Simon. *American Folklore Studies: An Intellectual History.* Lawrence: University Press of Kansas, 1986.

Broonzy, Bill. *Big Bill Blues.* New York: Oak, 1964.

Bruce, J. Collingwood, and John Stokoe. *Northumbrian Minstrelsy.* Newcastle-upon-Tyne, England: Society of Antiquaries, 1882.

Brunning, Bob. *Blues: The British Connection.* Poole, England: Blandford, 1986.

Brunnings, Florence E. *Folk Song Index: A Comprehensive Guide to the Florence E. Brunnings Collection.* New York: Garland, 1981.

Brunvand, Jan. *The Choking Doberman and Other "New" Urban Legends.* New York: Norton, 1984.

———. *Curses! Broiled Again! The Hottest Urban Legends Going.* New York: Norton, 1990.

———. *Folklore: A Study and Research Guide.* New York: St. Martin's, 1979.

———. *The Mexican Pet: More "New" Urban Legends and Some Old Favorites.* New York: Norton, 1986.

———. *The Study of American Folklore.* 3d ed. New York: Norton, 1986.

———. *The Vanishing Hitchhiker: American Urban Legends and Their Meanings.* New York: Norton, 1981.

Buchan, David. *The Ballad and the Folk.* London: Routledge, 1972.

Buchan, Norman. "Folk and Protest." In *The People's Past*, ed. Edward J. Cowan, pp. 165–90. Edinburgh: Polygon, 1980.

Bustin, Dillon. " 'The Morrow's Uprising': William Morris and the English Folk Revival." *Folklore Forum* 15 (1982): 17–38.

Caesar, Wendy. "Joan Baez: A Bibliography." *JEMF Quarterly* 12 (1976): 147–57.

Camp, Charles, and Timothy Lloyd. "Six Reasons Not to Produce Folklife Festivals." *Kentucky Folklore Record* 26 (1980): 67–74.

Cantwell, Robert. *Bluegrass Breakdown: The Making of the Old Southern Sound.* Urbana: University of Illinois Press, 1984.

————. "When We Were Good: The Folk Revival." In *Folk Roots, New Roots: Folklore in American Life,* ed. Jane C. Becker and Barbara Franco, pp. 167–93. Lexington, Mass: Museum of Our National Heritage, 1988.

Carpenter, Carole Henderson. *Many Voices: A Study of Folklore Activities in Canada and Their Role in Canadian Culture.* Ottawa: National Museums, 1979.

Casey, George J., Neil V. Rosenberg, and Wilfred W. Wareham. "Repertoire Categorization and Performer-Audience Relationships: Some Newfoundland Folksong Examples." *Ethnomusicology* 16 (1972): 397–403.

Cauthen, Joyce. *The Fiddle and Well-Rosined Bow.* Tuscaloosa: University of Alabama Press, 1989.

Charters, Samuel. *The Country Blues.* New York: Rinehart, 1959. Rpt. New York: DaCapo, 1975.

Check List of Recorded Songs in the English Language in the Library of Congress, Archive of American Folk Song, to July, 1940. Washington: Library of Congress, Archive of Folk Song, 1942. Rpt. New York: Arno, 1971.

Child, Francis James. *The English and Scottish Popular Ballads.* 1898. Rpt. New York: Folklore Press, 1956.

Clement, Wallace. *The Canadian Corporate Elite: An Analysis of Economic Power.* Toronto: McClelland, 1975.

Clifford, James. *The Predicament of Culture.* Cambridge, Mass.: Harvard University Press, 1988.

Clignet, Remi. *The Structure of Artistic Revolutions.* Philadelphia: University of Pennsylvania Press, 1985.

Coffin, Tristram Potter, and Roger deV. Renwick. *The British Traditional Ballad in North America.* Austin: University of Texas Press, 1977.

Cohen, John. "In Defense of City Folksingers." *Sing Out!* 9 (1959): 33–34.

————. "What Happened?" *Sing Out!* 20.4 (1971): 21.

Cohen, Norm. "Record Reviews: The Revival." *Journal of American Folklore* 100 (1987): 206–16.

Cooke, Peter. *The Fiddle Tradition of the Shetland Isles.* Cambridge: Cambridge University Press, 1986.

Coon, O. Wayne. "Some Problems with Musical Public-Domain Materials under United States Copyright Law as Illustrated Mainly by the Recent Folk-song Revival." In *Copyright Law Symposium, Number Nineteen,* pp. 189–218. New York: Columbia University Press, 1971.

Courlander, Harold. *Negro Folk Music U.S.A.* New York: Columbia University Press, 1963.

Cowboy aisho kashu. Tokyo: Shinko-gakufu, 1934.

Daniel, Wayne. "Old-Time Georgians Recall the Georgia Old-Time Fiddlers' Contest." *The Devil's Box* 15 (1981): 7–16.

Davis, Fred. *Yearning for Yesterday: A Sociology of Yesterday.* New York: Free Press, 1979.

Davis, Lloyd. "How Folk Music Got That Way." *Goldenseal* 17.3 (1991): 68–71.

Dégh, Linda. "Uses of Folklore as Expressions of Identity in the Old and New Country." *Journal of Folklore Research* 21 (1984): 187–200.

Denisoff, R. Serge. *Great Day Coming: Folk Music and the American Left.* Urbana: University of Illinois Press, 1971.
——— . "The Proletarian Renascence: The Folkness of the Ideological Folk." *Journal of American Folklore* 82 (1969): 51–65.
——— . "Reply to Haring." *Journal of American Folklore* 86 (1973): 60. (See Lund and Denisoff, below.)
——— . *Sing a Song of Social Significance.* Bowling Green, Ohio: Bowling Green University Popular Press, 1972.
DeTurk, David A., and A. Poulin, Jr., ed. *The American Folk Scene.* New York: Dell, 1967.
De Vos, George. "Ethnic Pluralism: Conflict and Accommodation." In *Ethnic Identity: Cultural Continuity and Change,* ed. George De Vos and Lola Romanucci-Ross, pp. 5–41. Chicago: University of Chicago Press, 1982.
Dirlam, Hilary. "Bruce Greene, Kentucky Fiddler." *Old-Time Herald* 1.1 (Fall 1987): 19–22.
Dixon, R. M. W., and John Godrich. *Blues and Gospel Records, 1902–1942.* London: Storyville, 1964.
Dixon, Willie. "I Am the Blues." *Living Blues* 29 (1976): 8.
Dorson, Richard M. *America in Legend.* New York: Pantheon, 1973.
——— . "Fakelore." *Zeitschrift für Volkskunde* 65 (1969): 56–64.
——— . "Folklore and Fakelore." *American Mercury* 70 (1950): 335–48.
Dugaw, Dianne. "The Popular Marketing of 'Old Ballads': The Ballad Revival and Eighteenth-Century Antiquarianism Reconsidered." *Eighteenth-Century Studies* 21 (1987): 71–90.
Dunaway, David K. "Charles Seeger and Carl Sands: The Composers' Collective Years." *Ethnomusicology* 24 (1980): 159–68.
——— . *How Can I Keep from Singing: Pete Seeger.* New York: Da Capo, 1981.
——— . "Unsung Songs of Protest: The Composers Collective of New York." *New York Folklore* 5 (1979): 1–19.
Dundes, Alan. "The Study of Folklore in Literature and Culture." *Journal of American Folklore* 78 (1965): 136–42.
——— . "Texture, Text and Context." *Southern Folklore Quarterly* 28 (1964): 251–65.
Dundes, Alan, et al. "Commentary." *Journal of Folklore Research* 21 (1984): 177–86.
Dunn, Ginette. *The Fellowship of Song: Popular Singing Traditions in East Suffolk.* London: Croom, 1980.
Dunson, Josh. *Freedom in the Air: Song Movements of the '60s.* New York: International, 1965.
Early, Gerald. "One Nation under a Groove." *The New Republic,* 15 and 22 July 1991, pp. 30–41.
"Eddy Clear Water." *Living Blues* 9 (1972): 10–13.
Eliot, Marc. *Death of a Rebel.* Garden City, N.Y.: Anchor, 1979.
Emmerson, George. *Rantin' Pipe and Tremblin' String.* Montreal: McGill-Queen's University Press, 1971.
Engle, David G. "A Sketch of the German Folk Revival Singer, Katzi Ritzel." *Lore and Language* 3 (1981): 67–79.

Evans, David. *Big Road Blues: Tradition and Creativity in the Folk Blues.* Berkeley: University of California Press, 1985.

———. "Record Reviews: American Folklore and Music: Bicentennial Series." *Journal of American Folklore* 91 (1978): 615–21.

———. "Record Reviews: Folk Revival Music." *Journal of American Folklore* 92 (1979): 108–15.

Feintuch, Burt, ed. *The Conservation of Culture.* Lexington: University Press of Kentucky, 1988.

Fenton, Mike. "Descriptive Introductory Notes." *Galax International.* Heritage HRC 067, 1988.

Ferris, William. *Blues from the Delta.* New York: Doubleday, 1978.

Ferris, William, and Mary L. Hart, eds. *Folk Music and Modern Sound.* Jackson, Miss.: University Press of Mississippi, 1982.

Finnegan, Ruth. *The Hidden Musicians: Music-Making in an English Town.* Cambridge: Cambridge University Press, 1989.

Fiske, John. *Introduction to Communication Studies.* London: Methuen, 1982.

Foucault, Michel. "What Is an Author?" *Partisan Review* 43 (1975): 603–14.

Fowke, Edith. "Filksongs as Modern Folksongs." *Canadian Folklore canadien* 7 (1985): 85–94.

———. *The Penguin Book of Canadian Folk Songs.* Harmondsworth, England: Penguin, 1973.

Freedman, Samuel G. "Blues Breaker." *Rolling Stone,* 24 Sept. 1987: 91–92, 95, 154, 157–58.

Friedman, Albert. *The Ballad Revival.* Chicago: University of Chicago Press, 1961.

Frisbie, Charlotte. "President's Report." *SEM* (Society for Ethnomusicology) *Newsletter* 24.2 (1990): 2.

Gahr, David, and Robert Shelton. *The Face of Folk Music.* New York: Citadel, 1968.

Garon, Paul. "Big Joe Williams (1903–1973)." *Living Blues* 57 (1983): 23.

———. *Blues and the Poetic Spirit.* New York: DaCapo, 1979.

———. "Editorial" [1]. *Living Blues* 12 (1973): 4.

———. "Editorial" [2]. *Living Blues* 13 (1973): 3.

Gates, Henry Louis, Jr. *The Signifying Monkey: A Theory of Afro-American Literary Criticism.* New York: Oxford University Press, 1988.

Gayle, Addison. *The Black Aesthetic.* Garden City, N.Y.: Doubleday, 1971.

Gendron, Bernard. "Theodor Adorno Meets the Cadillacs." In *Studies in Entertainment: Critical Approaches to Mass Culture,* ed. Tania Modleski, pp. 18–36. Bloomington: Indiana University Press, 1986.

Gentry, Linnell. *A History and Encyclopedia of Country, Western, and Gospel Music.* 2d rev. ed. Nashville: Clairmont, 1969.

Gerould, Gordon Hall. *The Ballad of Tradition.* Oxford: Clarendon, 1932.

Gilmore, Mikal. "Blues with a Bullet." *Rolling Stone,* 18 June 1987, pp. 40–42, 44, 88–90.

Glassie, Henry. *Passing the Time in Ballymenone.* Philadelphia: University of Pennsylvania Press, 1982.

———. "The Types of the Southern Mountain Cabin." In Jan Brunvand, *The Study of American Folklore,* pp. 338–70. New York: Norton, 1968.

Goldstein, Kenneth. *A Guide for Field Workers in Folklore.* Hatboro, Pa.: Folklore Associates, 1964.

———. "The Impact of Recording Technology on the British Folksong Revival." In *Folk Music and Modern Sound,* ed. William Ferris and Mary L. Hart, pp. 3–13. Jackson, Miss.: University Press of Mississippi, 1982.

———. "Robert 'Fiddler' Beers and His Songs: A Study of the Revival of a Family Tradition." In *Two Penny Ballads and Four Dollar Whiskey,* ed. Kenneth S. Goldstein and Robert H. Byington, pp. 33–50. Hatboro, Pa.: Folklore Associates, 1966.

Gonczy, Daniel J. "The Folk Music Movement of the 1960s: Its Rise and Fall." *Popular Music and Society* 10 (1985): 15–31.

Gottesman, Stephen N. "Tom Dooley's Children: An Overview of the Folk Music Revival, 1958–1965." *Popular Music and Society* 5 (1977): 61–78.

Green, Archie. "Hillbilly Music: Source and Symbol." *Journal of American Folklore* 78 (1965): 204–28.

———. "Interpreting Folklore Ideologically." In *Handbook of American Folklore,* ed. Richard M. Dorson, pp. 351–58. Bloomington: Indiana University Press, 1983.

———. *Only a Miner: Studies in Recorded Coal-Mining Songs.* Urbana: University of Illinois Press, 1971.

Green, Douglas. "Noboru Morishige: 'I Think This Is the Only Time I Can Do What I Want to Do.' " *Bluegrass Unlimited* 8.12 (1974): 12–28.

Greenhill, Pauline. *True Poetry: Traditional and Popular Verse in Ontario.* Montreal: McGill-Queens University Press, 1989.

Greenleaf, Elisabeth Bristol, and Grace Yarrow Mansfield. *Ballads and Sea Songs of Newfoundland.* Cambridge, Mass.: Harvard University Press, 1933.

Greenway, John. *American Folksongs of Protest.* Philadelphia: University of Pennsylvania Press, 1953.

Groom, Bob. *The Blues Revival.* London: Studio Vista, 1971.

Gummere, Francis Barton. *The Popular Ballad.* Boston: Houghton, 1907.

Guralnick, Peter. *Feel Like Going Home: Portraits in Blues and Rock 'n Roll.* New York: Outerbridge, 1971.

———. "Searching for Robert Johnson." *Living Blues* 53 (1982): 27–32, 34–37, 39–41.

Guthrie, Woody. *Born to Win.* Ed. Robert Shelton. New York: Macmillan, 1965.

———. *Bound for Glory.* New York: Dutton, 1968.

Hale, Antony. "A Comparison of Bluegrass Music Diffusion in the United States and New Zealand." M.A. thesis, Memphis State University, 1983.

Halpert, Herbert. "Vitality of Tradition and Local Songs." *Journal of the International Folk Music Council* 3 (1951): 35–40.

Handler, Richard, and Joyce Linnekin. "Tradition, Genuine or Spurious." *Journal of American Folklore* 97 (1984): 273–90.

"Handy Awards Forum." *Living Blues* 73 (1987): 14–15.

Haring, Lee. "The Folk Music Revival." *Journal of American Folklore* 86 (1973): 60. (See Lund and Denisoff, below.)

Harker, David. *Fakesong: The Manufacture of British 'Folksong' 1700 to the Present Day.* Milton Keynes, England: Open University Press, 1985.

———. "May Cecil Sharp Be Praised?" *History Workshop Journal* 14 (1982): 44–62.

——— . *One for the Money: Politics and Popular Song.* London: Hutchinson, 1980.

Hashimoto, Tsuyoshi. ("Meeting with Bill Monroe.") *Pubgrass* 33 (1989): 1–4.

Healy, Robert R. "American Folk Festivals: A Preliminary Survey." *Record Research* 42 (Mar.-Apr. 1962): 5–6, 19.

Henry, Edward O. "Institutions for the Promotion of Indigenous Music: The Case for Ireland's Comhaltas Ceoltoiri Eireann." *Ethnomusicology* 33 (1989): 67–95.

Hewison, Robert. *The Heritage Industry: Britain in a Climate of Decline.* London: Methuen, 1987.

Hirsch, Jerrold. "Cultural Pluralism and Applied Folklore: The New Deal Precedent." In *The Conservation of Culture,* ed. Burt Feintuch, pp. 46–67. Lexington: University Press of Kentucky, 1988.

Hobsbawm, Eric. "Introduction: Inventing Tradition." In *The Invention of Tradition,* ed. Eric Hobsbawm and Terence Ranger, pp. 1–14. Cambridge: Cambridge University Press, 1983.

Hobsbawm, Eric, and Terence Ranger, eds. *The Invention of Tradition.* Cambridge: Cambridge University Press, 1983.

Hood, Mantle. *The Ethnomusicologist.* Kent, Ohio: Kent State University Press, 1982.

Hugill, Stan. *Shanties and Sailors' Songs.* London: Jenkins, 1969.

Hymes, Dell. "Folklore's Nature and the Sun's Myth." *Journal of American Folklore* 88 (1975): 345–69.

Inaya, Shoichi. " 'Bokurawa mandolin no chogen sura shiranakatta': Bluegrass no daybreak in Tokyo" ("We didn't even know how to tune the mandolin": Bluegrass's daybreak in Tokyo). *Moon Shiner* 1.2 (1983): 15–19.

Innis, Harold Adams. *The Fur Trade in Canada: An Introduction to Canadian Economic History.* Toronto: University of Toronto Press, 1956. "An Interview with Stan Rogers." *The Folk Life* 3.1 (1978): 4–9.

Isaji, Rick. "Nihon no Western kashutachi, Part 1: Ono Yoshio" (Japanese western singers, Part 1: Yoshio Ono). *Rave On* 7 (1988): 77–79.

Ives, Burl. *Wayfaring Stranger.* London: Boardman, 1952.

Ives, Edward D. *Joe Scott, the Woodsman-Songmaker.* Urbana: University of Illinois Press, 1978.

——— . *Larry Gorman: The Man Who Made the Songs.* Bloomington: Indiana University Press, 1964.

——— . *Lawrence Doyle: The Farmer-Poet of Prince Edward Island.* Orono: University of Maine Press, 1971.

Jackson, Bruce. "The Folksong Revival." *New York Folklore* 11 (1985): 195–203. Reprinted in this volume.

——— . "Sanitary Signifying and Proliferating Ivy: Observations of the Citybilly at Work and Play." *Listen: A Musical Monthly* 2 (1964): 6; 3 (1964): 4–6.

——— , ed. *Folklore and Society: Essays in Honor of Benj. A. Botkin.* Hatboro, Pa.: Folklore Associates, 1966.

Jazz: hyakuman nin no ongaku (Jazz: The music for the millions). Tokyo: Kantosha, 1953.

"John Hammond, Critic and Discoverer of Pop Talent, Dies." *New York Times,* 11 July 1987.

Jones, Loyal. *Minstrel of the Appalachians.* Boone, N.C.: Appalachian Consortium, 1984.

Kahn, Ed. "Folksong on Records." *Western Folklore* 27 (1968): 224–28.

Kaplan, Arlene E. "A Study of Folksinging in Mass Society." *Sociologus* 5 (1955): 14–28.

Karahata, Masaru, Kobun Nogawa, and Tadashi Aoki. *Keiongaku to sono record.* Tokyo: Sansei-do, 1938.

Katz, Elihu, and Tamar Liebes. "Decoding *Dallas:* Notes from a Cross-Cultural Study." In *Inter Media,* 3d ed., ed. Gary Gumpert and Robert Cathcart, pp. 97–109. New York: Oxford University Press, 1986.

Katz, Ruth. "Mannerism and Culture Change: An Ethnomusicological Example." *Current Anthropology* 11 (1970): 465–75.

Keil, Charles. "People's Music Comparatively: Style and Stereotype, Class and Hegemony." *Dialectical Anthropology* 10 (1985): 119–30.

——— . *Urban Blues.* Chicago: University of Chicago Press, 1966.

Kirshenblatt-Gimblett, Barbara. "Authoring Lives." *Journal of Folklore Research* 26 (1989): 123–49.

——— . "Mistaken Dichotomies." *Journal of American Folklore* 101 (1988): 140–55.

Kisliuk, Michelle. " 'A Special Kind of Courtesy': Action at a Bluegrass Festival Jam Session." *TDR* 32 (1988): 141–55.

Klein, Joe. *Woody Guthrie.* New York: Knopf, 1980.

Knott, Sarah Gertrude. "The National Folk Festival after Twelve Years." *California Folklore Quarterly* 5 (1946): 83–93.

Kodish, Debora. *Good Friends and Bad Enemies: Robert Winslow Gordon and the Study of American Folksong.* Urbana: University of Illinois Press, 1986.

Koning, Jos. "The Fieldworker as Performer: Fieldwork Objectives and Social Roles in County Clare, Ireland." *Ethnomusicology* 24 (1980): 417–29.

Kosby, Joan. "An Ethnography of the St. Albans Folk Music Club." M.A. thesis, Memorial University of Newfoundland, 1978.

Kuykendall, Peter V. " 'Starvin' to Death.' " *Bluegrass Unlimited* 1.8 (1967): 4–5.

Laing, Dave, et al. *The Electric Muse: The Story of Folk into Rock.* London: Methuen, 1975.

Lawless, Ray M. *Folksingers and Folksongs in America.* New York: Duell, Sloan and Pearce, 1965.

Laws, G. Malcolm, Jr. *American Balladry from British Broadsides.* Philadelphia: American Folklore Society, 1957.

——— . *Native American Balladry.* Philadelphia: American Folklore Society, 1964.

Leadbitter, Mike. *Nothing But the Blues.* London: Hanover, 1971.

Leadbitter, Mike, and Neal Slaven. *Blues Records, 1946–1966.* London: Hanover, 1968.

Lee, Peter. "Living Blues Survey." Unpublished photocopied survey results, 1987.

Lendvai, Ernö. "Bartok und die Zahl." *Melos* 27 (1960): 327–31.

Levine, Lawrence W. "The Historian and the Icon: Photography and the History of the American People in the 1930s and 1940s." In *Documenting America, 1935–1943,* ed. Carl Fleischhauer and Beverly W. Brannan, pp. 15–42. Berkeley: University of California Press, 1988.

Lieberman, Robbie. *"My Song Is My Weapon": People's Songs, American Commu-nism, and the Politics of Culture, 1930–1950.* Urbana: University of Illinois Press, 1989.

Ling, Jan. "Folk Music Revival in Sweden: The Lilla Edet Fiddle Club." *Yearbook for Traditional Music* 18 (1986): 1–8.

Linton, Ralph. "Nativistic Movements." *American Anthropologist* 45 (1943): 230–40.

Lloyd, A. L. "Electric Folk Music in Britain." In *Folk Music and Modern Sound,* ed. William Ferris and Mary L. Hart, pp. 14–18. Jackson: University of Mis-sissippi Press, 1982.

———. *Folk Song in England.* London: Lawrence, 1967.

Lomax, Alan. "Bluegrass Background: Folk Music with Overdrive." *Esquire,* Oct. 1959, p. 108.

———. "The 'Folkniks'—and the Songs They Sing." *Sing Out!* 9 (1959): 30–31. Reprinted as liner notes to *Guy Carawan Sings, Volume 2.* Folkways FG 3548, 1959.

———. *Folk Song Style and Culture.* Washington: American Association for the Advancement of Science, 1968.

———. "List of American Folk Songs on Commercial Records." In *Report of the Committee of the Conference on Inter-American Relations in the Field of Music,* William Berrien, chairman, pp. 126–46. Washington, D.C.: Department of State, 1940.

———. "Preface." In *Folk Song U.S.A.,* ed. John A. Lomax and Alan Lomax, pp. vii–x. New York: Duell, 1947.

Lomax, John A. *Cowboy Songs and Other Frontier Ballads.* New York: Macmillan, 1910.

Lomax, John A., and Alan Lomax, eds. *Folk Song U.S.A.* New York: Duell, 1947.

Long, Eleanor. "Ballad Singers, Ballad Makers, and Ballad Etiology." *Western Folk-lore* 32 (1973): 225–36.

Lund, Jens. "Folklore and Politics Revisited, 1974: A Review Essay." *Folklore Forum* 7 (1974): 296–301.

Lund, Jens, and R. Serge Denisoff. "The Folk Musical Revival and the Counter Culture." *Journal of American Folklore* 84 (1971): 394–405. (See Haring and Den-isoff, above, for related notes.)

McCann, L. D. *Heartland and Hinterland: A Geography of Canada.* Scarborough, Ont.: Prentice, 1987.

McGregor, Craig, ed. *Bob Dylan: A Retrospective.* New York: Morrow, 1972.

Mackenzie, W. Roy. *Ballads and Sea Songs from Nova Scotia.* Cambridge, Mass.: Harvard University Press, 1928.

MacNaughton, Adam. "The Folksong Revival in Scotland." In *The People's Past,* ed. Edward J. Cowan, pp. 191–205. Edinburgh: Polygon, 1980.

McNaughton, Janet. "John Murray Gibbon and the Inter-War Folk Festivals." *Canadian Folklore canadien,* 3.1 (1981): 67–73.

Mailer, Norman. "The White Negro." In *Advertisements for Myself,* pp. 311–21. New York: Putnam, 1959.

Malone, Bill C. *Southern Music, American Music.* Lexington: University Press of Kentucky, 1979.

Marinus, A. "Differences in Style Between Unbroken and Revived Folk-Music Traditions." *International Folk Music Journal* 9 (1957): 28–29.

Meehan, Thomas. "Public Writer No. 1?" *New York Times Magazine*, 12 Dec. 1965, pp. 44–45, 130, 132–36.

Merriam, Alan. *The Anthropology of Music*. Evanston: Northwestern University Press, 1964.

Miller, Mike. "American Fiddle and Banjo Music Alive and Well in Japan." *Asahi Evening News*, Nov. 1987.

———. "Old-Time Music in Japan—A Small but Fanatic Following." *Old-Time Herald* 1.6 (Nov. 1988–Jan. 1989): 11–12.

Miller, Terry E. *Folk Music in America: A Reference Guide*. New York: Garland, 1986.

Mitsui, Toru. *Bluegrass ongaku* (Bluegrass music). 2d rev. ed. Tokyo: Bronze-sha, 1975.

———. "Correspondence." *Sing Out!* 15.2 (1965): 97.

———. *Country ongaku no rekishi* (A history of country music). Tokyo: Ongaku-no-tomo-sha, 1971.

———. *Eikei America minzoku ongaku no gakki* (The instruments of Anglo-American folk music). Toyohashi: Traditional-Song Society, 1970.

———. *Folksong and Folk-singer: On the Occasion of Pete Seeger's Coming*. Fukuoka: The author, 1963.

Mogi, Takeshi. "Singing the Fishing." *Folk Roots* 11.1 (1989): 35, 39.

Montgomery, Susan. "The Folk Furor." *Mademoiselle*, Dec. 1960, pp. 98–99, 118.

Moulin, Sven Eric. "Lead Belly, Burl Ives, and Sam Hinton." *Journal of American Folklore* 71 (1958): 58–65.

Munro, Ailie. *The Folk Music Revival in Scotland*. London: Kahn, 1984.

———. "The Role of the School of Scottish Studies in the Folk Music Revival." *Folk Music Journal* 6.2 (1991): 132–68.

Nagai, Hideo. "Nihonban bluegrass record ichiran" (Bluegrass records released in Japan: A listing). In *Bluegrass ongaku* (Bluegrass music), 2d rev. ed., ed. Toru Mitsui, pp. 196–222. Tokyo: Bronze-sha, 1975.

Nagel, Thomas. *The View from Nowhere*. New York: Oxford University Press, 1986.

Narváez, Peter. "Afro-American and Mexican Street Singers: An Ethnomusicological Hypothesis." *Southern Folklore Quarterly* 42 (1978): 73–84.

———. " 'The Newfie Bullet': The Nostalgic Use of Folklore." In *Media Sense: The Folklore–Popular Culture Continuum*, ed. Peter Narváez and Martin Laba, pp. 65–76. Bowling Green, Ohio: Bowling Green State University Press, 1987.

Narváez, Peter, and Martin Laba, eds. *Media Sense: The Folklore–Popular Culture Continuum*. Bowling Green, Ohio: Bowling Green State University Press, 1987.

Nelson, Paul. "Newport: Down There on a Visit." *Little Sandy Review* 30 (1965): 47–67.

Nettl, Bruno. *The Study of Ethnomusicology*. Urbana: University of Illinois Press, 1983.

———. *The Western Impact on World Music*. New York: Schirmer, 1985.

The Northumbrian Pipers' Tune Book. Newcastle-upon-Tyne, England: Northumbrian Pipers' Society, 1970.

Ohrlin, Glenn. *The Hell-Bound Train.* Urbana: University of Illinois Press, 1973.

Oliver, Paul. *Blues off the Record.* New York: Hippocrene, 1984.

———. *The Meaning of the Blues.* New York: Collier, 1963.

O'Neal, Jim. "Editorial." *Living Blues* 57 (1983): 3.

———. "[Harmonica Frank Floyd]." *Living Blues* 8 (1972): 2.

———. "Interview: Lillian McMurry of Trumpet Records." *Living Blues* 67 (1986): 15–28.

———. "Joe Carrie Wilkins." *Living Blues* 11 (1972–73): 13–17.

———. "Leaving Blues: Nothing Stays the Same Forever." *Living Blues* 75 (1987): 2–3.

O'Neill, Captain Francis. *Irish Minstrels and Musicians.* 1913. Rpt. Hatboro, Pa.: Norwood, 1973.

Orr, Jay. "Motion Picture Reviews." *Southern Folklore Quarterly* 47 (1990): 95–99.

Osborne, John. *Look Back in Anger: A Play in Three Acts.* London: Faber, 1957.

Patterson, John S. "The Folksong Revival and Some Sources of the Popular Image of the Folksinger: 1920–1963." M.A. thesis, Indiana University, 1963.

Peacock, John. *A Favourite Collection of Tunes with Variations Adapted for the Northumberland Small Pipes, Violin or Flute.* Newcastle-upon-Tyne, England: Wright, ca. 1800.

Pearson, Barry Lee. *"Sounds So Good to Me."* Philadelphia: University of Pennsylvania Press, 1984.

Peterson, Richard. "A Process Model of the Folk, Pop and Fine Art Phases of Jazz." In *American Music: From Storyville to Woodstock,* ed. Charles Nanry, pp. 135–51. New Brunswick, N.J.: Transaction, 1972.

Petrie, George, ed. *The Petrie Collection of the Ancient Music of Ireland.* 2 vols. Dublin: M. H. Gill, 1855.

Pichaske, David. *A Generation in Motion: Popular Music and Culture in the Sixties.* New York: Schirmer, 1979

Pickering, Michael, and Tony Green. *Everyday Culture: Popular Song and the Vernacular Milieu.* Milton Keynes, England: Open University Press, 1987.

Pocius, Gerald. " 'The First Day That I Thought of It Since I Got Wed': Role Expectations and Singer Status in a Newfoundland Outport." *Western Folklore* 35 (1978): 109–22.

———. "The Mummers Song in Newfoundland: Academics, Revivalists and Cultural Nativism." *Newfoundland Studies* 4 (1988): 57–85.

Porter, James. "Muddying the Crystal Spring: From Idealism to Realism and Marxism in the Study of English and American Folk Song." In *Comparative Musicology and Anthropology of Music: Essays on the History of Ethnomusicology,* ed. Bruno Nettl and Philip V. Bohlman, pp. 113–30. Chicago: University of Chicago Press, 1991.

Porter, Katherine Anne. "Flowering Judas." In *Short Story Masterpieces,* ed. Robert Penn Warren and Albert Erskine, pp. 384–97. New York: Dell, 1954.

Posen, I. Sheldon. *For Singing and Dancing and All Sorts of Fun.* Toronto: Deneau, 1988.

———. "On Folk Festivals and Kitchens: Questions of Authenticity in the Folksong Revival." *Canada Folk Bulletin* 2.3 (1979): 3–11. Reprinted in this volume.

Preston, Richard J. "C. Marius Barbeau and the History of Canadian Anthropology." In *Proceedings* of the Canadian Ethnology Society, 3, ed. Jim Freedman, pp. 122–35. [Ottawa: CES], 1976.

Randolph, Vance. *Ozark Folksongs*. 4 vols. 1946–50. Rpt. Columbia: University of Missouri Press, 1980.

Red Channels: Communist Influence on Radio and Television. New York: Counterattack, 1950.

Renwick, Roger deV. "Two Yorkshire Poets: A Comparative Study." *Southern Folklore Quarterly* 40 (1976): 239–81.

Reuss, Richard A. "American Folklore and Left-Wing Politics: 1927–57." Ph.D. diss., Indiana University, 1971.

———. "American Folksongs and Left-Wing Politics: 1935–56." *Journal of the Folklore Institute* 12 (1975): 89–111.

———. "Folk Music and Social Conscience: The Musical Odyssey of Charles Seeger." *Western Folklore* 38 (1979): 221–38.

———. "The Roots of American Left-Wing Interest in Folksong." *Labor History* 12 (1971): 259–79.

Rhodes, Willard. "Folk Music, Old and New." In *Folklore and Society: Essays in Honor of Benj. A. Botkin*, ed. Bruce Jackson, pp. 11–20. Hatboro, Pa.: Folklore Associates, 1966.

Riesman, David. "Listening to Popular Music." In *Mass Culture*, ed. Bernard Rosenberg and David Manning White, pp. 408–17. New York: Free Press, 1957.

Riesman, David, Reuel Denny, and Nathan Glazer. *The Lonely Crowd*. New Haven: Yale University Press, 1950.

Rinzler, Ralph. "Bill Monroe." In *Stars of Country Music*, ed. Bill C. Malone and Judith McCulloh, pp. 202–21. Urbana: University of Illinois Press, 1975.

———. Brochure notes. *American Banjo Scruggs Style*. Folkways FA 2314, 1957.

Ritchie, Jean. *Singing Family of the Cumberlands*. 1955. New York: Oak, 1963.

Robbin, Ed. *Woody Guthrie and Me: An Intimate Reminiscence*. Berkeley: Lancaster-Miller, 1980.

Rodnitzky, Jerome L. *Minstrels of the Dawn*. Chicago: Nelson-Hall, 1976.

Rosenberg, Neil V. *Bluegrass: A History*. Urbana: University of Illinois Press, 1985.

———. "Bluegrass and Serendipity." *Bluegrass Unlimited* 2.5 (1967): 2–3.

———. "Book Reviews." Review of *Baby, Let Me Follow You Down: The Illustrated Story of the Cambridge Folk Years*, by Eric von Schmidt and Jim Rooney. *Ethnomusicology* 24 (1980): 582–84.

———. "From Sound to Style: The Emergence of Bluegrass." *Journal of American Folklore* 80 (1967): 143–50. Reprinted by the John Edwards Memorial Foundation in 1967 as JEMF Reprint #11; in *Bluegrass Unlimited* 3.7 (1969): 6–12; and in Linnell Gentry, *A History and Encyclopedia of Country, Western, and Gospel Music*, 2d rev. ed. (Nashville: Clairmont, 1969), pp. 309–18.

———. " 'An Icy Mountain Brook': Revival, Aesthetics and the 'Coal Creek March.' " *Journal of Folklore Research* 28 (1991): 221–40.

———. " 'It Was a Kind of a Hobby': A Manuscript Song Book and Its Place in Tradition." In *Folklore Studies in Honour of Herbert Halpert: A Festschrift*, ed.

Kenneth S. Goldstein and Neil V. Rosenberg, pp. 315–33. St. John's: Memorial University of Newfoundland, 1980.

———. Liner notes. *Here Today.* Rounder 0169, 1983.

———. "Nine Reasons for Getting Acquainted with a Japanese Bluegrass Fan." *Bluegrass Unlimited* 2.4 (1967): 5–7.

Rowe, Mike. *Chicago Breakdown.* London: Eddison, 1973.

Royce, Anya. *Ethnic Identity: Strategies of Diversity.* Bloomington: Indiana University Press, 1982.

Ruby, Jay, ed. *A Crack in the Mirror.* Philadelphia: University of Pennsylvania Press, 1982.

Russell, Ian, ed. *Singer, Song and Scholar.* Sheffield, England: Sheffield Academic Press, 1986.

Ryan, W. P. *The Irish Literary Revival.* London, 1894.

Sackheim, Eric, comp. *The Blues Line: A Collection of Blues Lyrics.* New York: Grossman, 1969.

Sacks, Harvey. "On the Analysability of Stories by Children." In *Ethnomethodology,* ed. Roy Turner, pp. 216–32. Baltimore: Penguin, 1974.

———. "Lecture Notes #4." Unpublished, 1967.

Said, Edward. *Orientalism.* New York: Random, 1979.

Sandburg, Carl. *American Songbag.* New York: Harcourt, 1927.

Sanders, Clinton R. "Psyching Out the Crowd: Folk Performers and Their Audiences." *Urban Life and Culture* 3 (Oct. 1974): 264–82.

Sandmel, Ben. "The Nighthawks." *Living Blues* 57 (1983): 28.

Scaduto, Anthony. *Bob Dylan: An Intimate Biography.* New York: Grosset, 1971.

Seeger, Charles. "Folk Music in the Schools of a Highly Industrialized Society." *Sing Out!* 8 (1958): 26–29. Originally printed in the *Journal of the International Folk Music Council* 5 (1953): 40–44; reprinted in *The American Folk Scene,* ed. David A. DeTurk and A. Poulin, Jr. (New York: Dell, 1967), pp. 88–94, and in Charles Seeger, *Studies in Musicology* (Berkeley: University of California Press, 1977), pp. 330–34.

———. "The Folkness of the Non-Folk vs. the Non-Folkness of the Folk." In *Folklore and Society: Essays in Honor of Benj. A. Botkin,* ed. Bruce Jackson, pp. 1–10. Hatboro, Pa.: Folklore Associates, 1966.

———. "Prescriptive and Descriptive Music Writing." *Musical Quarterly* 44 (1958): 184–95.

———. "Professionalism and Amateurism in the Study of Folk Music." *Journal of American Folklore* 62 (1949): 107–13.

———. "Reviews." *Journal of American Folklore* 61 (1948): 215–18.

———. "Reviews." *Journal of American Folklore* 62 (1949): 68–70.

———. "Singing Style." *Western Folklore* 17 (1958): 3–11.

———. *Studies in Musicology.* Berkeley: University of California Press, 1977.

———. "Toward a Universal Music Sound-Writing for Musicology." *Journal of the International Folk Music Council* 9 (1957): 63–66.

Seeger, Pete. *How to Play the Five-String Banjo.* 3d rev. ed. Beacon, N.Y.: The author, 1962.

Senauke, Alan. "Alan Kara no message" (A message from Alan). *Moon Shiner* 7.4 (1990): 10–11.

Sharp, Cecil. *English Folk-Song: Some Conclusions.* London: Simpkin, 1907.

————. *Folk Songs.* 1920. Rpt. London: Novello, 1959.

Shelton, Robert. *No Direction Home: The Life and Music of Bob Dylan.* New York: Beech Tree, 1986.

Sherman, Ed. Liner notes. *Alan Lomax Presents Folk Song Festival at Carnegie Hall.* United Artists UAL 3050, 1959.

"Sibyl with Guitar." *Time,* 23 Nov. 1962, pp. 54–56, 59–60. Reprinted in *The American Folk Scene,* ed. David A. DeTurk and A. Poulin, Jr. (New York: Dell, 1967), pp. 216–30.

Silber, Irwin. "Peggy Seeger—The Voice of America in Folksong." *Sing Out!* 12.3 (1962): 4–8.

Silverman, Carol. "The Folklorist as Performer." In *Time and Temperature,* ed. Charles Camp, pp. 34–35. Washington: American Folklore Society, 1989.

Simmel, Georg. "The Sociology of Sociability." In *Theories of Society: Foundations of Modern Sociological Theory,* vol. 1, ed. Talcott Parsons, pp. 157–63. New York: Free Press, 1961.

Slobin, Mark. "The Neo-*Klezmer* Movement and Euro-American Musical Revivalism." *Journal of American Folklore* 97 (1984): 98–104.

————. "Rethinking 'Revival' of American Ethnic Music." *New York Folklore* 9 (1983): 37–44.

Slobin, Mark, and Jeff Todd Titon. "The Music-Culture as a World of Music." In *Worlds of Music,* ed. Jeff Todd Titon, pp. 1–11. New York: Schirmer, 1984.

Smith, Anthony D. *The Ethnic Revival.* Cambridge: Cambridge University Press, 1981.

————. *Theories of Nationalism.* New York: Harper, 1971.

Smith, Georgina. "Social Bases of Tradition: The Limitations and Implications of 'The Search for Origins.'" In *Language, Culture and Tradition,* ed. A. E. Green and J. D. A. Widdowson, pp. 77–87. Sheffield, England: CECTAL/University of Sheffield, 1981.

Smith, John L. "The Ethogenics of Music Performance: A Case Study of the Glebe Live Music Club." In *Everyday Culture: Popular Song and the Vernacular Milieu,* ed. Michael Pickering and Tony Green, pp. 150–72. Milton Keynes, England: Open University Press, 1987.

Smith, L. Mayne. "First Bluegrass Festival Honors Bill Monroe." *Sing Out!* 15 (1966): 65, 67, 69.

————. "An Introduction to Bluegrass." *Journal of American Folklore* 78 (1965): 245–56. Reprinted by the John Edwards Memorial Foundation in 1965 as JEMF Reprint #6; in *Bluegrass Unlimited* 1.3 (1966): 1–4; 1.4 (1966): 3–5; 1.5 (1966): 2–4; and 1.6 (1966):2–4; and in Linnell Gentry, *A History and Encyclopedia of Country, Western, and Gospel Music,* 2d rev. ed. (Nashville: Clairmont, 1969) pp. 206–7, 208–13, 216–23.

Sollors, Werner. *Beyond Ethnicity: Consent and Descent in American Culture.* New York: Oxford University Press, 1986.

Stambler, Irwin, and Grelun Landon. *The Encyclopedia of Folk, Country and Western Music.* New York: St. Martin's, 1987.

Stekert, Ellen. "Autobiography of a Woman Folklorist." *Journal of American Folklore* 100 (1987): 579–85.

————. "Benjamin Albert Botkin: 1901–1975." *Western Folklore* 34 (1975): 335–38.

————. "Cents and Nonsense in the Urban Folksong Movement 1930–1966." In *Folklore and Society: Essays in Honor of Benj. A. Botkin,* ed. Bruce Jackson, pp. 153–68. Hatboro, Pa.: Folklore Associates, 1966. Reprinted in this volume.

————. Review of *Born to Win,* by Woody Guthrie. *Western Folklore* 25 (1966): 274–76.

————. "Views and Reviews." *Tune Up: The Monthly Newsletter of the Philadelphia Folksong Society* 1.4 (Jan. 1963): 2–3.

Stephens, H. Page. "The Case of Missing Folk Music: A Study of Aspects of Musical Life in Stone County, Arkansas, from 1890–1980." *Mid-America Folklore* 10 (1982): 58–69.

Story of Yoshio Ono at the Grand Ole Opry. *Moon Shiner* 1.2 (1983): 15–19.

Suzuki, Fumio. "Mountain music no hanashi" (A story of mountain music). *Music Life* (Tokyo), Mar. 1958: 30–31.

Suzuki, Katsuhiko. "A List of C and W 78 RPM Records in Early [*sic*] Japan." Tokyo: Privately printed, 1972.

Takayama, Hiroyuki. *Western ongaku nyumon* (A guide to western music). Tokyo: Ongaku-no-tomo-sha, 1963.

Tamony, Peter. " 'Hootenanny': The Word, Its Content and Continuum." *Western Folklore* 22 (1963): 165–70.

Taylor, Gerry. "Folk Music Is What Folks Sing." *The [Saint John, N.B.] Telegraph-Journal and The Evening Times-Globe,* 28 Nov. 1978.

Thompson, E. P. *The Making of the English Working Class.* Harmondsworth, England: Penguin, 1968.

Thompson, Stith. "Folklore and Folk Festivals." *Midwest Folklore* 4 (1954): 5–12.

Titon, Jeff Todd. *Downhome Blues Lyrics: An Anthology from the Post-World War II Era.* 2d ed. Urbana: University of Illinois Press, 1990.

————. *Early Downhome Blues: A Musical and Cultural Analysis.* Urbana: University of Illinois Press, 1977.

————. "The Life Story." *Journal of American Folklore* 93 (1980): 276–92.

————. *Powerhouse for God.* Austin: University of Texas Press, 1988.

Toelken, Barre. *The Dynamics of Folklore.* Boston: Houghton, 1979.

————. "Traditional Fiddling in Idaho." *Western Folklore* 24 (1965): 259–62.

Tokumaru, Yoshihiko, et al., eds. *Tradition and Its Future in Music.* Tokyo: Mita, 1991.

Turner, Roy. "Words, Utterances, and Activities." In *Ethnomethodology,* ed. Roy Turner, pp. 197–215. Baltimore: Penguin, 1974.

Usher, Bill, and Linda Page-Harpa. *"For what time I am in this world."* Stories from Mariposa. Toronto: Peter Martin, 1977.

van Singel, Amy. "Ann Arbor Blues and Jazz Festival 1972." *Living Blues* 10 (1972): 6–9.

————. "No Special Writer Here." *Living Blues* 45–46 (1980): 4.

Varner, Ray. "Robert Cray, Part Two." *Living Blues* 74 (1987): 19–20.

Vennum, Thomas Jr., and Nicholas Spitzer. "Musical Performance at the Festival: Developing Criteria." In *1986 Festival of American Folklife Program Book,* ed. Thomas Vennum, Jr., pp. 101–4. Washington: Smithsonian Institution, 1986.

Verrier, Hugh, ed. *The Songs of Wade Hemsworth.* Waterloo, Ontario: Penumbra, 1990.

Voigt, Vilmos. "The Concept of *Today's Folklore* as We See It from Budapest, Hungary, Europe." *Journal of Folklore Research* 21 (1984): 165–75.

von Schmidt, Eric, and Jim Rooney. *Baby, Let Me Follow You Down: The Illustrated Story of the Cambridge Folk Years.* Garden City, N.Y.: Anchor, 1979.

von Sydow, C. W. "On the Spread of Tradition." In *Selected Papers on Folklore,* ed. C. W. von Sydow, pp. 11–43. Copenhagen: Rosenkilde, 1948.

Wain, John. "In the Echo Chamber." Review of *A Spaniard in the Works,* by John Lennon. *The New Republic,* 7 Aug. 1965, pp. 20–22.

Wallace, Anthony F. C. "Revitalization Movements." *American Anthropologist* 58 (1956): 264–81. Reprinted in *Reader in Comparative Religion: An Anthropological Approach,* ed. William A. Lessa and Evon Z. Vogt (3d ed. New York: Harper, 1972).

Warner, Anne. *Traditional American Folksongs from the Anne and Frank Warner Collection.* Syracuse: Syracuse University Press, 1984.

Warner, Frank, Anne Warner, and Frank Proffitt. "Frank Noah Proffitt: A Retrospective." *Appalachian Journal* 1.3 (Autumn 1973): 163–98.

Welding, Pete. "Gambler's Blues: Shakey Jake." *Living Blues* 10 (1972): 10–17.

West, Max. *The Revival of Handicrafts in America.* Washington: U.S. Department of Commerce and Labor, Bureau of Labor (Bulletin 55), 1904.

Whisnant, David. *All That Is Native and Fine: The Politics of Culture in an American Region.* Chapel Hill: University of North Carolina Press, 1983.

——— . "Finding the Way Between the Old and the New: The Mountain Dance and Folk Festival and Bascom Lamar Lunsford's Work as a Citizen." *Appalachian Journal* 7.1/2 (Autumn-Winter 1979–80): 135–54.

——— . "Public Sector Folklore as Intervention." In *The Conservation of Culture,* ed. Burt Feintuch, pp. 233–47. Lexington: University Press of Kentucky, 1988.

——— , ed. *Folk Festival Issues: Report from a Seminar.* Los Angeles: JEMF (Special Series, 12), 1979.

White, John I. *Git Along, Little Dogies: Songs and Songmakers of the American West.* Urbana: University of Illinois Press, 1976.

Whyte, William H. *The Organization Man.* New York: Simon, 1956.

Wilgus, D. K. *Anglo-American Folksong Scholarship since 1898.* New Brunswick, N.J.: Rutgers University Press, 1959.

——— . "Aunt Molly's Big Record." *Kentucky Folklore Record* 7 (1961): 171–75.

——— . "From the Record Review Editor." *Journal of American Folklore* 80 (1967): 204.

——— . "From the Record Review Editor: Revival and Traditional." *Journal of American Folklore* 81 (1968): 173–79.

——— . "A Note on 'Songs from Rappahannock County.' " *Journal of American Folklore* 64 (1951): 320.

Williams, Raymond. *Keywords*. New York: Oxford University Press, 1976.

———. *The Long Revolution*. New York: Columbia University Press, 1961.

Wilson, Joe. "Confessions of a Folklorist." *Old-Time Herald* 2.3 (1990): 25–31, 43.

Wilson, Joe, and Lee Udall. *Folk Festivals*. Knoxville: University of Tennessee Press, 1982.

Wolfe, Charles K. *Tennessee Strings: The Story of Country Music in Tennessee*. Knoxville: University of Tennessee Press, 1977.

Woliver, Robbie. *Bringing It All Back Home: Twenty-Five Years of American Music at Folk City*. New York: Random, 1986.

Woods, Fred. *Folk Revival*. Poole, Dorset, Eng.: Blandford, 1979.

Wright, Patrick. *On Living in an Old Country: The National Past in Contemporary Britain*. London: Verso, 1985.

Zimmerman, Don, and Melvin Power. "The Everyday World as a Phenomenon." In *Understanding Everyday Life*, ed. Jack Douglas, pp. 80–103. Chicago: Aldine, 1970.

Discography

Alan Lomax Presents: Folk Song Festival at Carnegie Hall. United Artists UAL 3050, 1959.
American Banjo Scruggs Style. Folkways FA 2314, 1957.
Anthology of American Folk Music. Folkways FA 2951–2953, 1952.
Armstrong, Jack. *Jack Armstrong, Celebrated Minstrel.* Saydisc SCL 252, 1974.
Baez, Joan. *Joan Baez.* Vanguard VRS 9078, 1960.
Blue Sky Boys. *The Blue Sky Boys in Concert 1964.* Rounder 0236, 1989.
Brubeck, Dave. *Jazz Goes to College.* Columbia CL 662, ca. 1954.
Carawan, Guy. *Guy Carawan Sings, Volume 2.* Folkways FG 3548, 1959.
Child Ballads Traditional in the United States, I & II. Library of Congress L57–58, 1960.
Clawhammer Banjo. County 701, 1966.
Clough, Tom. *Holey Ha'Penny.* Topic 12TS283, 1976.
The Country Blues. Record, Book, and Film Sales RBF 1, 1959.
Cut and Dry Dolly. Topic 12TS278, 1976.
Dyer-Bennet, Richard. *Folksongs: Richard Dyer-Bennet.* Remington RLP 199–34, 1951.
Eanes, Jim. *Jim Eanes and the Shenandoah Valley Boys, The Early Days of Bluegrass, Volume 4.* Rounder 1016, 1978.
Folksay Trio, The. *Folksay: Volume II.* Stinson SLP 6, 1951.
Folkways: A Vision Shared; A Tribute to Woody Guthrie and Leadbelly. CBS 44034, 1988.
Fraley, J. P., and Annadeene. *Wild Rose of the Mountain.* Rounder 0037, 1974.
Fuzzy Mountain String Band. *The Fuzzy Mountain String Band.* Rounder 0010, 1972.
Galax International: Old Time, Mountain & Bluegrass Music by International Visitors to Galax, Va. Heritage HRC 067, 1988.
Green Fields of Illinois. Campus Folksong Club Records CFC 201, 1963.
Greenway, John. *The Songs and Stories of Aunt Molly Jackson.* Folkways FM 5457, n.d.

Here Today. *Here Today.* Rounder 0169, 1983.

Hollow Rock String Band. *Traditional Dance Tunes.* Kanawha 311, 1969.

Hopkins, Sam "Lightnin'." *Early Recordings Vol.* 2. Arhoolie 2010, 1971.

————. *Fast Life Woman.* Verve 8453, 1962.

————. *Lightnin' Hopkins.* Folkways FS 3822, 1959.

Hutton, Joe. *Joe Hutton of Coquetdale.* Mawson and Wareham MWM 1024, 1980.

Kingston Trio, The. *The Kingston Trio: Close-up.* Capitol T 1642, 1961.

————. "Tom Dooley." Capitol 4049, 1958.

Leadbelly and Woody Guthrie: Folkways: The Original Vision. Smithsonian Folkways SF 40001, 1988.

Ledbetter, Huddie. "Bourgeois Blues." Musicraft 227, 1939.

McTell, Willie. *Blind Willie McTell: 1940—The Legendary Library of Congress Session.* Melodean MLP 7327, 1962.

Marin, Cheech, and Tommy Chong. *Cheech and Chong.* Ode SP77010, ca. 1972.

Ohrlin, Glenn. *The Hell-Bound Train.* Campus Folksong Club Records CFC 301, 1964.

Philo Glee and Mandolin Society. *The Philo Glee and Mandolin Society.* Campus Folksong Club Records CFC 101, 1962.

Pigg, Billy. *The Border Minstrel.* Leader LEA 4006, 1971.

Powerhouse for God. University of North Carolina Press, 1982.

Really! The Country Blues. Origin Jazz Library OJL-2, ca. 1961.

Reid, Alan, and Brian McNeill. *Sidetracks.* Topic 12TS 417, 1980.

Rogers, Stan. *Fogarty's Cove.* Fogarty's Cove FCM 1001, 1976.

Seeger, Peggy. *Courting and Complaining Songs: Peggy Seeger.* Signet FL 5401, 1954.

Warner, Frank. *Frank Warner Sings American Folksongs and Ballads.* Elektra EKL-3, 1952.

Watson, Doc. *Doc Watson.* Vanguard 9152, [1964].

Weavers, The, with the Gordon Jenkins Orchestra. "Goodnight, Irene." Decca 27077, 1950.

Contributors

Since 1970 RICHARD BLAUSTEIN has taught folklore, sociology, and an-thropology at East Tennessee State University. He established and was the first director of the Center for Appalachian Studies and Services at that institution. His publications include video and sound recording documentaries of the musical tra-ditions of eastern Tennessee.

The author of the provocative and award-winning *Bluegrass Breakdown*, ROBERT CANTWELL has taught at Kenyon College, Georgetown University, the University of Iowa, and the University of North Carolina at Chapel Hill. As a cultural critic and historian, he has written on a number of topics, including aspects of the folksong revival in America.

The director of the Center for the Humanities in the College of Liberal Arts at the University of New Hampshire, and editor of the *Journal of American Folklore*, BURT FEINTUCH previously taught in the folk studies program at Western Kentucky University in Bowling Green. His publications include *The Conservation of Culture* and *Kentucky Folk Music: An Annotated Bibliography*.

KENNETH S. GOLDSTEIN has been chair of the Department of Folklore and Folklife at the University of Pennsylvania, head of the Department of Folklore at Memorial University of Newfoundland, and president of the American Folklore Society. The author of *A Guide for Field Workers in Folklore*, he has conducted extensive fieldwork in Appalachia, England, Scotland, Australia, and Newfoundland.

The author of *Only A Miner*, a study of recorded coal-mining songs, and former librarian for the Institute of Labor and Industrial Relations at the University of Illinois, ARCHIE GREEN taught at Illinois, Ohio State, and the Universities of Louisville and Texas. The principal moving force behind the creation of the Amer-ican Folklife Center, he has published extensively on aspects of labor lore, hillbilly music, and the role of folklore and folklife in issues of public policy.

PAULINE GREENHILL taught Canadian studies at the University of Waterloo before moving to her current position in women's studies at the University of Winnipeg. Her award-winning book *True Poetry: Traditional and Popular Verse* is a study of community poetry in Canada. Her other publications include *Lots of Stories: Maritime Narratives from the Creighton Collection.*

Since 1976 ALAN JABBOUR has been director of the American Folklife Center at the Library of Congress. He previously served as director of the Folk Arts Program at the National Endowment for the Arts, and head of the Archive of Folk Song at the Library of Congress. He has taught at UCLA, and published extensively on a variety of topics relating to cultural conservation and on instrumental folk music. He is a former president of the American Folklore Society and presently serves as chair of the Fund for Folk Culture.

A filmmaker and prolific author, BRUCE JACKSON is SUNY Distinguished Professor and director of the Center for Studies in American Culture, State University of New York at Buffalo. He served as a member of the Newport Folk Festival Board, president of the American Folklore Society, editor of the *Journal of American Folklore,* and chair of the board of trustees of the American Folklife Center.

Like many ethnomusicologists, ANNE LEDERMAN divides her time between performance and academic work. An accomplished fiddler and singer, she was for a number of years a member of the Toronto-based duo Muddy York and has also worked in bluegrass and klezmer bands. She has published a number of recordings and articles based on her research into Métis fiddling in Manitoba.

A professor of English and music at Kanazawa University in Kanazawa, Japan, TORU MITSUI has written extensively—mainly in Japanese—on traditional English and Scottish ballads, Appalachian music, rock and roll, bluegrass, and other English-language musical forms. He has also translated into Japanese a number of books on American and European popular music. His most recent book-length work is a biography of Jimmie Davis, the Louisiana singer who popularized "You Are My Sunshine," one of the best known English-language songs in Japan.

PETER NARVÁEZ teaches in the Department of Folklore at Memorial University of Newfoundland. The former president of the Association for the Study of Canadian Radio and Television, and the Folklore Studies Association of Canada, he coedited (with Martin Laba) *Media Sense,* a collection of studies in the relations between folklore and popular culture, and more recently edited *The Good People: New Fairylore Essays.*

PHILIP NUSBAUM is folk arts program associate with the Minnesota State Arts Board. Previously he worked at KUNI/KHKE, public radio, in Cedar Falls, Iowa, where he produced programs on folk music and conducted field research. He has published on a variety of topics, including Norwegian ethnic music, polka music, jam sessions, and conversational creativity.

I. SHELDON POSEN is a folklife consultant who has conducted public-sector projects for clients in Canada and the United States, including the Canadian Museum of Civilization and the Library of Congress. A former president of the Folklore Studies Association of Canada, he is the author of *For Singing and Dancing and All Sorts of Fun,* an ethnography of a century-old local ballad still sung in kitchens and dance halls in the small Canadian community from which it emerged.

A professor of folklore at Memorial University of Newfoundland, NEIL V. ROSENBERG was the first archivist of, and later director of, the MUN Folklore and Language Archive. The author of *Bluegrass: A History,* he is the former president of the Folklore Studies Association of Canada and of the Atlantic Canada Institute. He is presently sound recordings review editor for the *Journal of American Folklore.*

ELLEN J. STEKERT began her teaching career at Wayne State University, where she was director of the Wayne State University Folklore Archive. The first Minnesota State Folklorist, she presently teaches at the University of Minnesota. A former president of the American Folklore Society, her publications include *The Urban Experience and Folk Tradition.*

From 1969 to 1971, JEFF TODD TITON was the guitarist in the Lazy Bill Lucas Blues Band, a Minneapolis-based group that played in the 1970 Ann Arbor Blues Festival. His early publications, including the acclaimed *Early Downhome Blues,* focused on African-American music. More recently he has studied southern white religious expression in Appalachia, publishing his work under the title *Powerhouse for God* in the form of a record, a book, and, in collaboration with Tom Rankin and Barry Dornfeld, a film. He leads a string band and teaches ethnomusicology in the Department of Music at Brown University, and is editor of the journal *Ethnomusicology.*

General Index

Index of Song Titles

Following some titles are parentheses containing either a combination of a capital letter and a number, or simply a number. The former refers the reader to the parallel syllabi of G. Malcolm Laws, Jr., *American Balladry from British Broadsides* (Philadelphia: American Folklore Society, 1957) and *Native American Balladry* (Philadelphia: American Folklore Society, 1964). The single number refers to the numbering scheme in Francis J. Child's *English and Scottish Popular Ballads*, North American versions of which are referenced in Tristram Potter Coffin and Roger deV. Renwick, *The British Traditional Ballad in North America* (Austin: University of Texas Press, 1977).

Books in the Series Folklore and Society

Sinful Tunes and Spirituals: Black Folk Music to the Civil War
Dena J. Epstein

Joe Scott, the Woodsman-Songmaker
Edward D. Ives

Jimmie Rodgers: The Life and Times of America's Blue Yodeler
Nolan Porterfield

Early American Music Engraving and Printing: A History of Music Publishing
in America from 1787 to 1825, with Commentary on Earlier and Later Practices
Richard J. Wolfe

Sing a Sad Song: The Life of Hank Williams
Roger M. Williams

Long Steel Rail: The Railroad in American Folksong
Norm Cohen

Resources of American Music History:
A Directory of Source Materials from Colonial Times to World War II
D. W. Krummel, Jean Geil, Doris J. Dyen, and Deane L. Root

Tenement Songs: The Popular Music of the Jewish Immigrants
Mark Slobin

Ozark Folksongs
Vance Randolph; edited and abridged by Norm Cohen

Oscar Sonneck and American Music
Edited by William Lichtenwanger

Bluegrass Breakdown: The Making of the Old Southern Sound
Robert Cantwell

Bluegrass: A History
Neil V. Rosenberg

Music at the White House: A History of the American Spirit
Elise K. Kirk

Red River Blues: The Blues Tradition in the Southeast
Bruce Bastin

Good Friends and Bad Enemies:
Robert Winslow Gordon and the Study of American Folksong
Debora Kodish

Fiddlin' Georgia Crazy: Fiddlin' John Carson,
His Real World, and the World of His Songs
Gene Wiggins

America's Music: From the Pilgrims to the Present
Revised Third Edition
Gilbert Chase

Secular Music in Colonial Annapolis: The Tuesday Club, 1745–56
John Barry Talley

Bibliographical Handbook of American Music
D. W. Krummel

Goin' to Kansas City
Nathan W. Pearson, Jr.

"Susanna," "Jeanie," and "The Old Folks at Home":
The Songs of Stephen C. Foster from His Time to Ours
Second Edition
William W. Austin

Songprints: The Musical Experience of Five Shoshone Women
Judith Vander

"Happy in the Service of the Lord":
Afro-American Gospel Quartets in Memphis
Kip Lornell

Paul Hindemith in the United States
Luther Noss

"My Song Is My Weapon": People's Songs,
American Communism, and the Politics of Culture
Robbie Lieberman

Chosen Voices: The Story of the American Cantorate
Mark Slobin

Theodore Thomas: America's Conductor and Builder of Orchestras, 1835–1905
Ezra Schabas

"The Whorehouse Bells Were Ringing" and Other Songs Cowboys Sing
Guy Logsdon

Crazeology: The Autobiography of a Chicago Jazzman
Bud Freeman, as Told to Robert Wolf

Discoursing Sweet Music: Brass Bands and Community Life in
Turn-of-the-Century Pennsylvania
Kenneth Kreitner

Mormonism and Music: A History
Michael Hicks

Voices of the Jazz Age: Profiles of Eight Vintage Jazzmen
Chip Deffaa

Pickin' on Peachtree: A History of Country Music in Atlanta, Georgia
Wayne W. Daniel

Bitter Music: Collected Journals, Essays, Introductions, and Librettos
Harry Partch; edited by Thomas McGeary

Ethnic Music on Records: A Discography of Ethnic Recordings
Produced in the United States, 1893 to 1942
Richard K. Spottswood

Downhome Blues Lyrics: An Anthology from the Post-World War II Era
Jeff Todd Titon

Ellington: The Early Years
Mark Tucker

Chicago Soul
Robert Pruter

That Half-Barbaric Twang: The Banjo in American Popular Culture
Karen Linn

Hot Man: The Life of Art Hodes
Art Hodes and Chadwick Hansen

The Erotic Muse: American Bawdy Songs
Second Edition
Ed Cray

Barrio Rhythm: Mexican American Music in Los Angeles
Steven Loza

The Creation of Jazz: Music, Race, and Culture in Urban America
Burton W. Peretti

Charles Martin Loeffler: A Life Apart in Music
Ellen Knight

Club Date Musicians: Playing the New York Party Circuit
Bruce A. MacLeod

Opera on the Road: Traveling Opera Troupes in the United States, 1825–60
Katherine K. Preston

The Stonemans: An Appalachian Family and the Music That Shaped Their Lives
Ivan M. Tribe

Transforming Tradition: Folk Music Revivals Examined
Edited by Neil V. Rosenberg